*Educational Research in Action*

# Educational Research in Action

*N. J. Entwistle and J. D. Nisbet*

*University of London Press Ltd*

ISBN 0 340 16356 9 Boards
ISBN 0 340 16357 7 Unibook

University of London Press Ltd
St Paul's House, Warwick Lane, London EC4P 4AH

Printed and bound in England by
Richard Clay (The Chaucer Press), Ltd.,
Bungay, Suffolk

# Contents

# Preface

The theme of this book is 'research in action'. Readings from research reports are used to bring to life many of the points made in our earlier textbook, *Educational Research Methods*. The aim has been to select empirical studies which are intrinsically interesting and which illustrate important research strategies. As far as possible studies which depend on complex statistics for their interpretation have been avoided. By concentrating on real investigations, rather than on the theory of how to do research, it is possible to point out the practical constraints which make educational research so difficult to carry out according to the rule-book. This comparison between the ideal and the possible is a crucial step towards understanding both the strengths and the limitations of this type of empirical research. Our previous text described some of the important techniques required in carrying out research. It is hoped that the extracts in this book will help to show the contribution which research can make to the development of education, without creating unrealistic expectations.

In Part I the emphasis is on general approaches to educational research—drawing the distinction between experiment and survey, indicating where to find research reports and illustrating various methods of sampling. Practical problems which intervene between research design and reported findings are illustrated in a survey and a field experiment, while a further research report brings out the multi-disciplinary approach to an educational problem.

Part II presents a series of research topics in which typical studies are used to indicate the techniques of measurement and to give a résumé of the findings. The areas chosen enable a wide range of studies to be introduced, from large-scale social surveys, such as those concerned with home environment and the school, to small-scale studies of friendship patterns or of curriculum evaluation. While the coverage has been made as wide as possible, important omissions were inevitable. In particular the decision to restrict ourselves mainly to studies using simple statistics has excluded complex experimental designs. As a result the choice perhaps overemphasises the place of survey research in education. It can be argued, nevertheless, that this balance is a realistic reflection of the methodology adopted by research workers who are interested in education itself, rather than in educational psychology.

The final section is again more general in approach. The penultimate chapter provides a lengthy check-list for evaluating, or designing, educational research, as part of a discussion of interpreting and reporting findings. Illustrations are drawn from previous chapters to suggest trends in research design which may influence future studies. The final chapter is also concerned with the future, but in a wider sense. It looks at the role which educational research could play in the development of education, and how this relates to the administrative structure of education and the involvement of teachers in research work.

Although the difficulties in carrying out research become plain in the succeeding chapters, it is still possible for people without much training to carry out small-scale studies under guidance. Such investigations rarely produce definitive findings, but they can have considerable value for the participants. Techniques of measurement, statistical methods and strategies of thinking are all easier to understand through active involvement. It is also important to realise that it is possible to carry out educational research without recourse to complex statistics, and to report the findings in relatively simple language. As the plea for effective communication between researchers and teachers recurs at several points in this book, it seems appropriate to start with an example of a straightforward study carried out by eleven student-teachers without any previous research training in a project which was completed in just three weeks. Chapter 1 is thus intended as an apéritif. It may encourage those who think that research is both dull and difficult to suspend their judgement for at least the next few chapters, where some technical concepts have to be introduced. Once the actual studies are introduced—from Chapter 4 onwards—the methodology can be supplied appropriately spiced with interesting research findings to maintain the appetite thereafter.

# Acknowledgments

The authors and publisher would like to thank the following for permission to reprint copyright material in this book:

Random House Inc., New York, for an excerpt from J. L. Simon, *Basic Research Methods in the Social Sciences* (copyright © 1969 by Random House Inc., and reprinted by permission of the publisher); The National Foundation for Educational Research in England and Wales and individual authors for the article (in part) 'Finding out about educational research', by C. W. J. Higson from *Educational Research*, 11 (specially revised by Dr Higson for the present volume; grateful thanks are due to her for her help), for an excerpt from S. Hilsom and B. S. Cane *The Teacher's Day*, for the article (in part) 'Some problems in evaluating i.t.a.: a second experiment', by J. A. Downing and B. Jones from *Educational Research*, 8, for an excerpt from B. S. Cane and C. Schroeder, *The Teacher and Research*, for two excerpts from J. C. Barker Lunn, *Streaming in the Primary School*, for an excerpt from R. H. Thouless, *A Map of Educational Research*, for the article (in part) 'The future of educational research', by W. D. Wall from *Educational Research*, 10, and for the paper (in part) 'Educational research and the State', by T. Husen from *Educational Research and Policy Making*; The Controller of Her Majesty's Stationery Office for excerpts from *Standards of Reading, 1948–56*, from *Early Leaving*, from *Primary School Survey: a study of the teacher's day*, by J. H. Duthie (two excerpts), from *Children and their Primary Schools* (the Plowden Report: two excerpts), from *Enquiry 1: Young School Leavers*, by R. Morton-Williams and S. French (a Schools Council report), from *Multiple Marking of English Compositions* by J. N. Britton, N. C. Martin and H. Rosen, and from *Trends in Education*, 26 (an article by 'Question Master'); Peter Davies Ltd for two excerpts from J. W. B. Douglas, J. M. Ross and H. R. Simpson, *All Our Future*; the Scottish Council for Research in Education for excerpts from their Publication 43, *Home Environment and the School* by E. D. Fraser; the editor of the *British Journal of Educational Psychology* and the individual authors for articles from volume 41 (P. E. Vernon, 'Effects of administration and scoring on divergent thinking tests' (in part), N. Bolton and P. N. Richards, 'Type of mathematics teaching, mathematical ability and divergent thinking in junior school children', and B. Macdonald and J. Rudduck, 'Curriculum research and development projects: barriers to success'); the editor of the *British Journal of Psychology* and the individual authors for an article from volume 57 (P. Hasan and H. J. Butcher, 'Creativity and intelligence: a partial replication with Scottish children of Getzel's and Jackson's study'); Dr A. E. G. Pilliner for his paper 'Examinations' from *Educational Research in Britain, 1* (University of London Press Ltd); Mrs B. Sloane for a passage from P. B. Ballard, *The New Examiner* (University of London Press Ltd); the editor of the *Audio-Visual Language Journal* and the author for an article from volume 9 (B. Farrington, 'A computer-aided test of aural comprehension'); Routledge and Kegan Paul Ltd and the authors for excerpts from J. Ford, *Social Class and the Comprehensive School*, for a passage from D. H. Hargreaves, *Social Relations in a Secondary School*, and for an article from volume 17 of the *British Journal of Sociology* (C. Lacey, 'Some sociological concomitants of academic streaming'); Penguin Books Ltd for excerpts from D. Barnes *et al.*, *Language, the Learner and the School* (copyright © Douglas Barnes, James Britton, Harold Rosen and the London Association for the Teaching of English, 1969, 1971); Mr E. C. Wragg for his article from *Education for Teaching, 81*, 'Interaction analysis as a feedback system for student teachers'; Schools Council Publications and the 'Science 5–13' Project of that Council for the figure on page 266, from the Project's *Newsletter 2*; the editor of the *Journal of Curriculum Studies* and the authors for an article from the November 1972 issue (J. D. Nisbet and J. Welsh, 'A local evaluation of primary school French'); Dr W. G. A. Rudd for his paper 'Curriculum model building' from *Educational Research in Britain, 2* (University of London Press Ltd); the editor of *Research in Education* and Manchester University Press for a passage from an article in volume 1 (S. Wiseman, 'Curriculum development and curriculum evaluation'); the Society for Research into Higher Education Ltd for an excerpt from the presidential address given to that Society by the Vice-Chancellor of the University of Lancaster at its 1971 annual conference.

Grateful thanks are also due to Miss Kathleen Fern for undertaking the bulk of the typing and preparation of the manuscript, and to Mrs Ellen Crampton for her work in preparing an index at short notice.

# PART ONE
# General Approaches to
# Educational Research

# 1    Research by Students

*Analyses of Children's Essays (1966)*[1]

The project was chosen so that it would be possible for us to reach some definite and, we hoped, interesting conclusions within a three-week period. Initial planning had ensured that our area of investigation was clearly defined and we were given help with the statistical computations. Apart from this, we worked on our own, going through most of the stages involved in a real research project, except the data collection.

The origins of the study were not propitious. Instead of allowing us three weeks' hard-earned freedom prior to graduation, the Aberdeen College of Education sentenced us to three-weeks' hard labour with the University Education Department. All thoughts of mutiny were quelled on our first day, when we were introduced to the task which lay before us.

The Department is engaged in a long-term project on 'Age of Transfer'.[2] One of the educational measures used was an essay from which it was hoped to assess the children's educational and vocational aspirations. Our task was to read a representative sample of these essays and undertake a more detailed analysis than was practicable on the whole age-group of children involved in the main project.

First we had to decide how to obtain our representative sample. This was really predetermined, as a true random sample was impracticable and we wanted to investigate differences between schools. We thus took a stratified sample. We selected schools from the three main housing areas—west-end, estate and

[1] 'Children's essays: an analysis of essay-writing ability and the aspirations and attitudes shown by Aberdeen twelve-year-olds.' Unpublished report prepared in the Department of Education, Aberdeen University, by eleven students of Aberdeen College of Education. (This extract is taken from the actual report as it was written at the end of the project.)
[2] Subsequently published in two reports (Nisbet and Entwistle, 1966, 1969).

east-end. These represented schools with decreasing percentages of middle-class families. Schools were chosen so that there would be eleven schools, one for each marker, and also so that the total number of children in the sample from each housing area would be proportional to the total number in the age-group in these schools. As a result we had 687 essays to read out of a total age group of 3286.

The essay which had been given to these children in their final year of primary school was:

'Imagine you are quite old, at least 40 years old. Look back over your life and write a story about what has happened to you and what you have done during these years.' The following leading questions were added:

How did you enjoy life at school?
When did you leave school?
Did you have special training for a job?
What job did you do?
Did you get married?
What was your husband or wife like?
Where did you live?
What sort of house did you live in?
What did you do in your spare time?

We had two main aims: first to assess the scripts as essays and then to analyse the replies to some of the questions asked. To make these assessments consistent, each of us took one or more assessments and read all of the essays, rating each one of them in turn. Five of our number decided to mark the essays on general impression and one other aspect. This proved to be the hardest job of all as it involved reading the whole essay and making two separate assessments 687 times over.

After some discussion each of the remaining six markers chose to assess one or more replies to the questions posed. The next step was for each marker to decide on a rating scale and to test this with some practice marking, looking for difficulties. The ratings were coded and each marker entered her codings on to a separate school mark sheet. This was done to avoid markers being influenced by previous ratings. The codings were then transferred on to a small white card, one for each child. The top left-hand corner was cut off if the card belonged to a girl. This facilitated later sorting. Each assessment was allocated a particular position on the card and alternate red and blue ink was used as the codings were entered. This again helped when it came to sorting.

The cards were sorted within schools by sex and then sorted on each assessment. The totals in each category were tabulated and from these tables most of us did chi-square tests of significance and percentages with the aid of calculating machines and with advice on the many statistical and computational problems we encountered.

Finally each marker wrote a report on her work, including all the tables of results. These were edited to make the styles more consistent and to eliminate occasional errors and repetition. Shortened reports on three of these assessments form the basis of the following sections.


### ESSAY MARKING

The aim was to give a mark for each essay. This could be done in two ways, either by giving a mark for the general impression of the essay or by giving different marks for various aspects of each essay. It was decided that five markers, A, B, C, D and E, should each give the individual essays a mark for their general impression. The scale originally decided on was a six-point one ranging from 0 to 5. In addition, markers A and B each gave a mark for the mechanical accuracy of the essays (spelling, punctuation and paragraphing). Markers C and D each gave a mark for the essay's originality and content. Marker E gave a mark for vocabulary.

While doing practice marking in order to obtain individually consistent standards, the six-point scale was abandoned in favour of a five-point scale (1–5) which gave a definite mark of 3 for the 'average essay'. When all the essays had been marked the scores were averaged and entered on to the children's cards. The scores for the general impression were averaged and then doubled to give a score out of 10.

Product–moment correlation coefficients between markers were calculated for the general impression marking on 187 essays. The values were found to be between 0·44 and 0·58. The agreement between the two markers using mechanical accuracy as a criterion was indicated by a correlation of 0·45, while a value of 0·51 was found on originality and content.

Comparing mean scores by sex and by housing area on the whole sample produced the expected pattern of results, which is shown in Table 1:1. There was little to choose between children

TABLE 1:1   *Mean scores by housing area and by sex*

|  | West-end | Estate | East-end | Boys | Girls |
|---|---|---|---|---|---|
| Interest | 3·00 | 3·07 | 2·63 | 2·90 | 3·49 |
| Vocabulary | 2·60 | 2·50 | 2·10 | 2·40 | 2·50 |
| Mechanical accuracy | 2·56 | 2·97 | 2·70 | 2·74 | 3·06 |
| General impression | 5·79 | 5·78 | 5·03 | 5·37 | 5·78 |
| (N) | (185) | (300) | (202) | (359) | (328) |

from west-end and estate schools in their essay-writing ability, but these two groups of pupils were distinctly better than those from the east-end schools. While girls in this sample were only slightly better than boys in vocabulary scores, they were markedly superior in interest scores. These results are in line with previous findings on essay-writing abilities.

## DID YOU ENJOY LIFE AT SCHOOL?

Answers to this straightforward question were easy to analyse. The essays were coded into four categories, no mention at all, no clear indication, dislikes school and likes school.

To investigate possible differences between boys and girls and between housing areas, the results of the sorting were tabulated and chi-square tests of significance applied. Both tests were significant. Boys disliked school more than girls (significant at the 0·01 level) and children in west-end schools tended to dislike school more than children in estate and east-end schools, although this did not apply in all schools. Table 1:2 uses percentages to illustrate these differences.

TABLE 1:2   *Percentage replies by housing area and by sex*

| Did you enjoy life at school? | % West-end | % Estate | % East-end | % Boys | % Girls |
|---|---|---|---|---|---|
| Yes | 47·0 | 60·6 | 57·9 | 48·2 | 64·9 |
| No | 11·9 | 7·0 | 8·4 | 10·6 | 6·7 |
| Not sure | 10·8 | 11·7 | 7·4 | 12·8 | 7·3 |
| No reply | 30·3 | 20·7 | 26·3 | 28·4 | 21·1 |
| (N) | (185) | (300) | (202) | (359) | (328) |

While the large number of children in the 'no reply' category makes it difficult to be certain about the results, there were distinct differences between the responses of the remainder. The sex difference between enjoyment of school is not surprising. Teachers in primary schools tend to find boys less amenable than girls at this age.

The difference between areas is surprising. The opposite direction might have been expected, with east-end children disliking school most. Possibly the result obtained is true only of this year-group of primary school children where pressures from middle-class schools increase to ensure a maximum number of places for their pupils in senior secondary (grammar) schools. These pressures are not so apparent where parental expectations are lower.

The findings related to housing areas are not clear-cut as there are significant differences between schools in the same area. School A, which was the most representative west-end school, showed only 9% of children disliking school, although this is still above the average of both estate and east-end schools. School Y, in the east-end, had 22% of children who disliked school, while the average of the other three east-end schools was only 4%.

## WHAT JOB DID YOU DO?

Most children answered this question and it was possible to identify twenty-two different categories, most of which represented a single popular job. During practice marking it was found convenient to group a number of closely connected jobs under one heading. In this way 'secretaries' were included with 'shorthand-typists', and 'builders' with 'joiners' and 'plumbers'. For the analysis shown in Table 1:3 these separate job-categories were

TABLE 1:3  *Percentage choice of job by housing area*

|  | %<br>West-end | %<br>Estate | %<br>East-end |
|---|---|---|---|
| Professional | 44·3 | 26·7 | 22·3 |
| Skilled | 34·1 | 50·0 | 42·1 |
| Unskilled | 20·5 | 22·0 | 33·2 |
| No reply | 1·1 | 1·3 | 2·4 |
| (N) | (185) | (300) | (202) |

merged into three larger categories covering professional, skilled and unskilled occupations.

The above tables show the expected differences between housing areas. Children in the west-end schools show a preference for professional occupations and children in east-end schools prefer unskilled jobs. We also found that girls in our sample were more interested in obtaining professional jobs than were boys.

The social differentiation is also clear from the percentages wanting particular jobs. Teaching is particularly popular amongst girls and especially those at west-end schools. Nursing is also a popular career for girls, again being most popular in the west-end. Many east-end girls anticipate being shop-assistants, nurses, shorthand-typists and hairdressers. Many east-end boys anticipate being joiners, electricians or mechanics, and also serving in the Army, Navy or Air Force. A surprising choice for 2% of the east-end boys is to be an architect. The west-end children showed a greater range in their choices than east-end children. Twenty-five per cent in the west-end chose jobs outside the main categories compared with 15% in the east-end.

Nowadays very few boys want to be engine drivers—boys who are looking for the excitement of speed aim rather to be pilots or astronauts.

### DID YOU GET MARRIED?

The majority of those children who answered in the affirmative had a definite idea of the age at which they expected to marry. It was thus possible to make a survey, not only of whether the children favoured the idea of marriage but also which ages were most popular. Preliminary trials allowed us to decide on appropriate categories for both questions.

Then all the essays were read and these two assessments were made. The chi-square technique was used to test differences between boys and girls and also differences between housing areas. Significant differences were found in all four comparisons. The direction of these differences can be seen from the percentages shown in Tables 1 : 4 and 1 : 5.

TABLE 1 : 4  *Percentage response on marriage by housing area and by sex*

|  | % West-end | % Estate | % East-end | % Boys | % Girls |
|---|---|---|---|---|---|
| Yes | 66·0 | 86·3 | 76·2 | 68·5 | 88·1 |
| No | 17·8 | 4·7 | 13·9 | 14·8 | 6·7 |
| No reply | 16·2 | 9·0 | 9·9 | 16·7 | 5·2 |
| (N) | (185) | (300) | (302) | (359) | (328) |

TABLE 1 : 5  *Age at marriage of those definitely marrying*

| Years | % West-end | % Estate | % East-end | % Boys | % Girls |
|---|---|---|---|---|---|
| 19 or less | 3·1 | 4·0 | 9·7 | 3·1 | 7·5 |
| 20–25 | 58·5 | 75·2 | 72·2 | 62·0 | 78·2 |
| 26 or more | 38·4 | 20·3 | 18·1 | 34·9 | 14·3 |

The chi-square tests in conjunction with the pattern of results shown in these tables showed that more girls than boys had decided they would be married. The girls also expected to marry at an earlier age. The west-end children were less keen to marry than the other children and also expected, if they did marry, to do so at a later age. It is interesting to note that this pattern of expectations, as with job choice, corresponds quite closely to what actually does happen. Children from west-end schools choose professional jobs and extended training, which will (or used to) prevent the possibility of early marriage.

*The students who carried out this research study used a simple research design and the most elementary statistical tests and yet the results make sense. The experience also provided useful insights into research procedures, and provided realistic experience of conducting research. A major difficulty, however, is to design small-scale projects from which interesting findings may be derived in a sufficiently short space of time. One way of solving this* problem is to use projects which concentrate on the design of a method of measurement, such as a short attitude scale or questionnaire; an alternative and possibly better method is to use data which are already available. Where the staff in a department or college of education are themselves actively engaged in research, this latter approach is quite feasible. Part of the work can be 'farmed out', or students may be allowed to use data which have already been analysed. Admittedly this does not give students experience of the practical difficulties in collecting data, such as those discussed later in Chapter 4. But even if the early stages of a project cannot be carried out, the details can be carefully described, so as to ensure full involvement. It is possible to take the students through the stages of defining the problem and reviewing the literature and, by discussion, to generate hypotheses which the data may then be used to test. Thereafter all the problems of coding information, condensing the data into tabular form, analysing and interpreting can be experienced in reality. These technical aspects of research are less difficult to discuss as practical examples than to think about in the abstract. Statistical analysis, in particular, often makes sense only by doing the calculations; the concepts may otherwise seem altogether alien to all but the numerate minority. When a research project reaches the stage where interesting results can only be obtained by statistical computation, it is surprising how easily numerical blockages dissolve.

Data may already be available in colleges or universities, but small-scale research may also be carried out by the teacher in the classroom. The extract in this chapter showed how useful essays can be in providing data. Although they are not sufficiently structured to allow convincing comparisons to be made between pupils, they do provide many interesting insights when analysed systematically. Kathleen Evans (1968) has provided a simple guide to Planning Small-Scale Research in Education which indicates alternative approaches to obtaining data. The problem for the teacher is often knowing where to start or what sort of topic might be worth investigation on a small scale. Although many of the research studies described in this book are large-scale surveys or experiments, some of the topics could be investigated in a single classroom as a case-study or as a piece of 'action research'. Case studies look in depth at individual institutions or at small numbers of individuals. Often the techniques of measurement are identical to those used in larger studies—interviews, questionnaires, psychological tests and so on. The difference is that the results are specific to the group tested. Without careful sampling, as we shall see in Chapter 3, results cannot be generalised. Nevertheless, studies in a single institution can provide ideas which form the starting-point of full-scale surveys.

'Action research' is less concerned with understanding the educational process; its aim is to introduce effective means of dealing with immediate problems. Fox and Lippitt (1964) initiated schemes for helping teachers to develop action research strategies by gathering and analysing data about their own classrooms as a basis for the introduction and evaluation of new or modified procedures. Teachers are often half-way towards doing action research whenever they introduce innovations. All that is required is a more systematic approach towards planning, and careful attempts at evaluation.

The topics mentioned in Chapters 13 and 14 would be particularly suitable for action research, and ideas for small-scale projects can also be found among suggestions made by teachers in Chapter 8, or in ideas reported in many of the other summaries of research in Part II. Additional lines to follow are sure to be found among the many reviews and bibliographies described in the next chapter.

# 2    Reviewing the Situation

*In* Educational Research Methods *we gave a framework of seven stages within which the processes of educational research may be fitted.*

1   *Identifying and precisely defining the problem.*
2   *Reading previous research on relevant topics.*
3   *Deciding on techniques to be used for collecting and analysing information.*
4   *Selecting and defining the sample to be studied.*
5   *Collecting the data.*
6   *Processing, analysing and interpreting the results.*
7   *Writing the report.*

*Most of the projects described later in this book have gone through all of these stages; they are important and time-consuming, but are seldom described fully in research papers. Usually only the briefest indication will be given of the origin of the problem and the review of the literature will present simply the evidence for the hypotheses being tested. As a result this chapter presents readings of a general nature. The first, by J. L. Simon, is relevant to the planning of an investigation, and reviews the relative merits of survey and experiment. Though it is in the setting of economics and social psychology, the points are directly applicable to many aspects of educational research. The second extract, by C. W. J. Higson, provides a useful guide to the formidable task of finding out about previous research, and shows how a proper understanding of library facilities can help this second stage of inquiry.*

*Some initial explanation may be necessary of important terms used in the extract from Simon's book.[1] In the simplest form of experimental design, a change is made in the value of one variable*

---

[1] For a fuller explanation of these and other technical terms refer to one of the following textbooks: Borg (1963), Burroughs (1971), Fox (1969), Nisbet and Entwistle (1970a), Travers (1969) or Van Dalen (1966). Full details will be found under References (page 333 et seq.).

—*the* independent variable—*and the effect of this change on another variable is observed*—*the* dependent variable. *Taking a hypothetical example on the teaching of reading, one might investigate the relationship between attainment in reading and length of time spent in teaching reading. A simple experiment might compare the improvement in reading of two groups of children under different conditions or* treatments. *One group continues to spend, say, one hour a day in being taught to read—this is called the* control group. *The other group—the experimental group—is given more time on reading, say, two hours each day. The two groups thus represent different values of the independent variable—time spent on reading. A pre-test of reading—the dependent variable—is given, the treatment is continued for enough time for any effects to occur, and then there is a post-test of reading. If there is a significant improvement of one group over the other, it may be possible to suggest that this change in performance has been caused by the change in the time spent on reading. But this interpretation would only be justified if the two groups were initially* matched *so as to be comparable on all variables except the independent variable, and there was no subsequent difference in the treatments of the groups, except in the time spent on reading. With care, as Simon explains, experiments do have the great advantage of giving much clearer evidence of cause and effect than do surveys.*

## Basic Research Methods in Social Sciences
(J. L. Simon, 1969)[1]

### ADVANTAGES OF EXPERIMENTS

*Establishing Direction of Causality*

The most important advantage of the experiment is that the relationship that you *actually observe* is clear in its causal direction ... In an experiment it is you, the experimenter, who manipulates the independent variables. If you observe variations in the dependent variable, they must therefore be caused by the variations in the independent variable and not by some other force that is affecting both the independent and dependent variables at the same time. This property of the experiment makes it possible to talk confidently about one aspect of causation.

[1] Slightly edited extract from *Basic Research Methods in the Social Sciences* (New York: Random House), pages 237–44.

## Cost

The absolute cost of a laboratory experiment can often be low compared to that of alternative research methods. For example, an advertiser can pretest the effects of two advertising campaigns in a laboratory situation with a very few people, whereas a field experiment or survey would require actually carrying out advertising campaigns in expensive field tests. For another example, an engineer can make a structural analysis of a building's strength by constructing two-foot models in his laboratory, instead of constructing real buildings experimentally or making exhaustive studies of actual buildings that collapse.

## Convenience

An experiment can be run whenever you like, to suit your convenience. If you are going to create a mock riot experimentally, you can pick your time and place so that you will have observers and equipment ready to observe the results. Real riots happen at unexpected times and unexpected places, which is one reason we know so little about riots.

## Adjustability of Variables and Parameters

Unlike a survey, an experiment permits you to arrange the parameters and vary the variables in whatever fashion you desire, to look for whatever effects interest you. If you are studying the causes of riots, you can vary the temperature in the place where the riot will occur to see whether or not people respond more vigorously when it is hot. In real riots, however, you must take the temperature as it comes. In his research on memory of nonsense syllables, Ebbinghaus could first vary the length of the syllable list, then the number of repetitions, then the time between learning and testing, and then the order of the words. Another investigator can then vary the amount of the reward given for correct memorization and so on, until he has systematically explored all the important possibilities. Only an experiment permits such detailed examination.

An experiment often allows you to investigate extremes of the independent variable that are not found in everyday life. It is only in an experiment that you can observe a man who has been awake for four days straight, who has been sleeping only fifteen minutes every four hours, or who has been subjected first to absolute quiet and then to enormous noise. But Festinger (1953)[1] argues that, in social psychology :

[1] References given within an extract will be found immediately after that extract : other references will be found in a separate section at the end of this book (page 333 et seq.).

'It is extremely difficult to create in the laboratory forces strong enough for results to be measurable. In the most excellently done laboratory experiment, the strength to which different variables can be produced is extremely weak compared to the strength with which these variables exist and operate in real-life situations' (page 141).

This is not only because experiments are difficult to do, but because 'many dangers are present in the execution'. This comment makes sense when one reflects on the sort of phenomena that social psychologists deal with: race riots, conflict, love, and prejudice.

In experimentation you can systematically refine the relationship you are investigating. Perhaps you have been told by an Indian villager that a particular root has wonderful properties for reducing the blood pressure and tranquilizing excited patients. First you can experiment with samples of the root material. If it works, you probably will want to know exactly what it is in the root that has this medicinal effect. Therefore, your next move might be to experiment with the juice from the root. If the juice alone works without the fiber of the root, then next you might try various constituents of the juice. And so on until you have 'isolated' the 'active principle'. Similarly, the researchers in the Hawthorne experiments were able to vary many aspects of the workers' environment, including how much attention the workers got from researchers, and they obtained knowledge of the causes of morale and work output that would have been difficult to learn by survey alone. The key to the Hawthorne research was the ability to try one thing after another, to 'sneak up' on the knowledge they sought.

*Replication*

One occurrence is seldom enough to convince you that what you think happened really happened. For example observers vary from time to time in what they observe. By repeating ('replicating') an experiment, you can obtain an average result; your conclusion is then not based on a single observation that might be unusually high or unusually low. Replication is one of the most useful tools in obtaining valid results, which is why classic experiments are often repeated, sometimes under slightly different circumstances, to ensure that it was not just an idiosyncrasy of the environment that caused the original results. Study of the jury system was long hampered by the one-time nature of trials. Furthermore, the particulars of cases differ greatly. Therefore, it was formerly difficult to investigate how juries react to various types of cases. In the experimental-jury paradigm invented by Strodtbeck, the experimenter repeats the same recorded trial to many juries and thereby obtains a sample of workable size (Simon, 1967).

## Unravelling Multivariable Causation

If two independent variables are closely related in the world outside the laboratory, a survey cannot easily determine which of them causes variation in the dependent variable. Because the laboratory experiment holds some factors constant as it varies others and then vice versa, the experimenter can track down the extent to which each is responsible for change in the dependent variable. (Of course, there are some cases in which it is only the combination or interaction of the two variables that will cause changes in the dependent variable; experimental designs that vary both variables simultaneously will reveal such interaction, however.)

### DISADVANTAGES OF EXPERIMENTS

The neatness of an experiment is very appealing, especially when the investigator is frustrated by the annoying shortcomings of survey data. Stouffer (1950), who, more than any other one man, was responsible for *The American Soldier*, once wrote, 'I would trade a half dozen Army-wide surveys on attitudes toward officers for one good controlled experiment' (page 211). But, if pressed, Stouffer would surely have qualified that statement, for the disadvantages of experiments can also be grave.

## Lack of 'Reality'

The most important disadvantage of the laboratory experiment (but not of the real-life field experiment, of course) is that you can never be sure that the analogy between the experiment and the real world really holds. In other words, there is always some risk involved in generalizing from what happens in the laboratory to what happens in the real world. Smoking causes cancer in laboratory experiments on rats, but is it correct to reason that the same thing happens with humans?

The riskiness of a generalization from a laboratory experiment depends on how well you specify your variables. Obviously it makes more sense to generalize about the effects of smoking from a laboratory experiment in which apes smoke tobacco than from a laboratory experiment in which fish are exposed to the smoke from corn silk. On the other hand, much important theoretical work takes place in experiments with very 'unrealistic' materials, because more realistic materials are too complicated to allow us to get a simple picture of what happens. From studies with unrealistic nonsense syllables, Ebbinghaus learned much about the learning process that he could not have with such complex subject matter as texts on Shakespeare or physics. It is much harder to run a 'clean' experiment with Shakespeare or physics as the materials to be learned, because the subjects' prior knowledge complicates the experiment greatly.

## Unrepresentative Samples

Another danger in drawing conclusions about the universe of interest from the laboratory experiment is that the subjects on whom the experiment is run in the laboratory may be very unlike the people in the real world about whom you wish to draw conclusions. Often it is difficult to persuade a fair sample of the universe to come into the laboratory. Consider these examples: first, economists try to experiment in the laboratory to find out how competing big businesses behave under certain competitive circumstances. But, because it is not possible to lure the presidents of, say, General Motors, Ford, and Chrysler into the laboratory for the experiment, the researchers study the behaviour of students who are playing a business game. Can one generalize from the students' behaviour to that of real executives? Second, a researcher wanted to experiment with the reactions of jurors to a mock trial after they had been given sensational or unsensational newspaper clippings about the trial, to find out the effect of newspaper publicity on the course of justice. But a disproportionate number of the people who agreed to take part in the experiment were from the middle and professional classes. In that study, the unrepresentative sample probably did not affect the direction of outcome (Simon, 1966). In another study, however, the same experimenter found it necessary (and possible) to draw subjects from actual jury pools with the assistance of the courts, which ensured representative samples (Simon, 1967). Third, a market-research firm runs experiments on people invited by postcard to come to free movies. During the movies commercials are tested. But people who come to free movies in the afternoon are not necessarily typical of the people who might be exposed to the same commercials on television—which is what the advertisers are really interested in.

What is important, of course, is that the subjects be representative on the characteristics relevant to the experiment. Pavlov's dogs were not representative of all dogs with respect to size, colour, thickness of coat, and so forth, but there was no reason to think that any of those characteristics would affect the outcome of the type of experiment he was doing. Similarly, Ebbinghaus' sample was not representative with respect to his education, intelligence, or nationality, but these characteristics did not make him a-typical in his memory.

*Expense*

Low cost was listed as one of the possible advantages of the experimental method. But some experiments may be very costly indeed, more costly than other research methods. Some structural testing may require fifty-foot models rather than two-foot models, and fifty-foot models may be expensive to build. Or it may be too expensive to gather together as many subjects as are necessary for the conditions of a real riot. Or giving players real money to obtain the necessary realism may be too expensive for some economics experiments.

*Hazardous Outcomes*

It may be impossible to experiment with some real-world situations. For example, it is too dangerous economically to run controlled experiments on the national economy. And most sex experiments are unethical or objectionable to good taste. Smoking experiments on human beings violate all civilized ethics.

### THE NATURE OF SURVEYS

The term 'survey research' is applied to two very different sorts of investigation. The first aims to learn about relationships between variables, especially causal relationships. Causal-analysis survey research is quite analogous to experimentation, with the single (but overwhelmingly important) difference that the independent variable(s) is not controlled and manipulated by the researcher. Instead the researcher seeks out groups of people that have already been exposed to different levels of the independent variable. For example, instead of subjecting randomly selected groups of people to different amounts of cigarette smoke, the researcher finds people who have smoked various numbers of cigarettes. Or a researcher who wants to study the effect of family income on juvenile delinquency does not choose various groups of families to receive various incomes; rather, he finds and assesses the amount of delinquency in families with different incomes.

The steps in pursuing causal-analysis survey research are much the same as those set forth for an experiment. Therefore, we shall not pursue the matter further in this chapter, except to summarize the advantages and disadvantages of the survey method for causal analysis.

*Advantages of the Survey Method for Relationship Research*

First, with a survey you can get closer to the real hypothetical variable than with a laboratory experiment. You can actually inspect the variables in their real-world setting; for instance, you can examine real cases of lung cancer and real movements of the economy and its constituents without having to abstract from the real variables to a mocked-up laboratory situation. This is the pre-eminent advantage of a survey over an experiment in those cases in which you want to investigate relationships but in which real-world experiments are impossible.

Second, a survey is often quite cheap, especially if you can use already existing records and data. If data exist for the prices and amounts of onions sold each month for several years, using them to explore the relationship between price and quantity is obviously cheaper than setting up a laboratory situation in which women are given quantities of money and opportunities to purchase onions and other foods at varying onion prices.

Third, huge masses of data are often already available or can be culled from existing records—voter-registration lists, for example. This is a major statistical advantage, because the large samples provide high internal reliability. Such huge samples are seldom available in experimentation.

*Disadvantages of the Survey Method for Relationship Research*

The major disadvantages described here apply only to causal and noncausal relationship research and not to census-type research.

First, the crucial disadvantage of the survey method in causal analysis is the lack of manipulation of the independent variable. Because there is no 'controlled' variation in the independent variable, it is always possible that the correlation between the independent and dependent variables is not 'causal'. But it is a mistake to say that survey results never show causation. Whether or not the results of a survey are causal depends upon many things. One short example here : changes in state liquor taxes are accompanied by changes in the prices of liquor. The effects of these changes in price upon liquor consumption can be studied. The changes in consumption may reasonably be said to be caused by the changes in price because there is no likely connection between consumption and the moment when the legislators decide to raise the tax; the states act in much the same way that an experimenter would if he were randomly selecting when to raise taxes. There is no other likely relationship between the tax rise (and the price change) and the change in consumption, and therefore it is reasonable to say that the price change causes the change in liquor consumption.

To repeat the main point, a survey lacks the almost clinching proof of actually trying out the relationship by varying the independent variable to see whether or not it is indeed followed by changes in the dependent variable.

A second disadvantage of the survey is that one cannot progressively investigate one aspect after another of the independent variable to get closer to the 'real' cause. One cannot first try out the cigarette, then the cigarette paper and the tobacco separately, and so forth until the ingredient that really causes cancer is isolated.

Third, statistical devices are not always able to separate the effects of several independent variables when there is multivariable causation, especially when two independent variables are themselves highly associated. For example, the same people tend to have high incomes and high education; therefore, it is very difficult to tell from survey results whether, say, it is education or income that causes the purchase of books and 'high class' magazines.

My final comment on the choice of survey or experiment for causal analysis is old stuff to you by now. Several methods are better than one. If you can seek the knowledge you want with both a survey and an experiment and if the results jibe reasonably well, you have a much stronger basis for belief in your results than if your conclusions were based on just one of the techniques.

REFERENCES

FESTINGER, L. (1953) 'Laboratory experiments.' In FESTINGER, L., and KATZ, D. (eds.) *Research Methods in the Behavioral Sciences.* New York: Holt, Rinehart and Winston.
SIMON, R. (1966) 'Murder, juries and the press.' *Transaction,* 3, 40–2.
SIMON, R. (1967) *The Jury and the Plea of Insanity.* Boston: Little Brown.
STOUFFER, B. (1950) 'Afterthoughts of a contributor.' In MERTON, R. K., and LAZARSFELD, P. F. *Continuities in Social Research.* New York: Free Press.

## *Finding out about Educational Research*
## (C. W. J. Higson, 1968)[1]

### LIBRARIES

Britain's libraries are not organized in a hierarchical system, and it is therefore all the more necessary to be aware of the wide

---

[1] The original article (*Educational Research, 11,* pages 33–7) has been shortened and more recent references have been incorporated into the text. Dr Higson's assistance in checking the alterations is gratefully acknowledged.

range of library facilities that are available to any inquirer. At the local level, where inquiries should begin, there is the municipal or county library, with its own stock of books and periodicals backed up by the Regional Inter-Library Loans Service. For teachers and others engaged in educational work, there is also the library of an Institute or School of Education. A network of these libraries, working in close co-operation, covers England and Wales, and, apart from the one in London, they all provide a service for the ordinary teacher. Almost all lend books, both directly and by post, to teachers and others engaged in education in their areas, and they will supply bibliographical information. Their addresses can be found in either the *Education authorities directory and annual* or the *Education committees year book*, which most public reference libraries stock. In the same town as the Institute of Education there will also be a University Library, which may be available for reference to people who are not members of the University, and may even lend books to teachers engaged in special studies, possibly on payment of a small subscription. Teachers in some areas will have at their disposal a library maintained by the local authority, sometimes sited in a teachers' centre. There may also be local College of Education libraries, and these have in the past few years built up much larger stocks and acquired more staff, so that many of them can now cope with readers outside their own student-body. There may also be a Technical College Library where books can be consulted by arrangement with the Librarian.

At the national level there are the copyright libraries, such as the British Museum, the Bodleian, and the National Library of Wales, which are reference libraries only. There is also the National Lending Library for Science and Technology, at Boston Spa, Yorkshire, which lends especially periodicals, and has now enlarged its scope to cover the social sciences, including education. Publications in the NLL are available to anybody through a photocopy service, and to organizations through a postal loans service.

Libraries may be supplemented by specialist information bureaux, such as the one maintained by the National Foundation for Educational Research at The Mere, Upton Park, Slough, the National Centre for Programmed Learning at the University of Birmingham, or the Youth Service Information Centre at Leicester.

An inquirer should, as has already been said, begin with local libraries, which can often provide much more information than is generally realized. National libraries and specialist libraries in London get so many requests for information which could have been obtained locally that the patience of their staff wears thin.

If the local library does not itself stock a book or periodical wanted, the librarian may be able to borrow it, or to obtain photocopies of articles required, through the inter-library loan system. Most public and university libraries belong to the regional inter-library loans schemes and to the National Central Library, and the Institutes and Schools of Education have their own inter-lending system, with a union catalogue maintained by the University of Birmingham School of Education. Again, the attempt to borrow should always be made through the local library, as libraries prefer to lend to other libraries rather than to unknown individuals.

No matter what library you use, it will pay you to get to know it thoroughly. This does not take long, and may save a lot of time in the end. To use a library efficiently one should understand the arrangement of its catalogue, and find out, for example, how the publications of governments and of societies are treated, and how works on specific subjects may be located. It is well to know, also, the principles by which the books are arranged on the shelves, and to know what kinds of books are not on the open shelves, but kept in the reserve store, and what materials other than books, such as files of pamphlets, microfilms, test materials, and periodicals the library possesses. Many libraries issue printed or duplicated guides explaining such points, and if they do not the staff are usually happy to give the explanations. The library may produce bibliographical guides of its own, such as lists of books added to stock, lists of books in special subject fields, or select lists of recent periodical articles. Some libraries, such as the central public library in a large town, may have union catalogues which include the stock of branch libraries. There may also be available printed or duplicated union lists of books, covering wider areas.

The first rule for assistants in Reference Libraries is 'Find out what the inquirer really wants', and here you can help by formulating your request as precisely as possible. Many inquirers are reluctant to ask for a specific subject, but prefer to make a general inquiry, probably thinking, often wrongly, that nothing has been written on their specific subject. For instance, a teacher wanting material on the influence of class size might ask for books on school organization, not realizing that monographs and articles exist dealing specifically with class size. On the other hand, more general books should not be ignored.

REVIEWS OF RESEARCH

Having got to know your libraries and formulated the exact subject of your search, how do you set about finding out what has been written on this subject (apart from asking the librarian)? The quickest way to approach a subject is often via an encyclopaedia, and a good general survey of educational research is to be found in the *Encyclopedia of educational research*, issued by the American Educational Research Association. New editions are published at ten-yearly intervals, and it reached its fourth edition in 1969. As subject coverage varies slightly in the different editions, earlier editions may still be useful. The encyclopaedia contains critical articles on almost every aspect of education, with summaries of past research, and useful bibliographies. It is supplemented by the *Review of educational research*, issued by the same association, 1931 to date. Until 1970 the review treated research areas separately in 3-year cycles, but the organisation of this publication has since been changed, giving in each issue reports on research in various fields of education. The review relies on research from 'well known journals and readily available books', but this is understood as referring to the USA. Both the encyclopedia and the review have a strong American bias, though the review has an occasional issue on research outside the USA.

More detailed information on research in specific fields, together with relevant abstracts or bibliographies, is provided by a number of handbooks and literature surveys, such as the three volumes in *Educational Research in Britain*, edited by H. J. Butcher (and H. B. Pont, vols. 2 and 3), London, 1968, 1970, 1973 (in the press); *Handbook of research on teaching*, edited by N. L. Gage, Chicago, 1963; *Review of child development research*, vols. 1–2, edited by M. L. and L. W. Hoffman, New York, 1964–6; or *The emotional and social adjustment of physically handicapped children. Abstracts, with a critical review of the literature published between 1928 and 1962*, by M. L. Kellmer Pringle, 1964, and its companion volume on blind children.

Since such handbooks and surveys summarize and comment on the research, they are usually more selective than the pure subject bibliography. The humanities in general are well provided with special subject bibliographies, and education is no exception to this. It is usually possible to track down a bibliography on most educational topics. The chief guide to current bibliographies in general is the *Bibliographic index*, New York, 1938 to date, which includes bibliographies relating to education. It is published semi-annually, with bound annual and larger permanent cumulations, and lists the bibliographies under subjects. Examples of useful bibliographies relevant to research in education are:

BLAUG, M. (1970) *Economics of education: a selected annotated bibliography* 2nd edition. London: University of London, Institute of Education.

GOSDEN, P. H. J. H. (1967) *Educational administration in England and Wales: a bibliographical guide.* Leeds: Leeds University Press.

NOSTRAND, H. L. *et al.* (1965) *Research on language teaching: an annotated international bibliography 1945–1964.* 2nd revised edition. Seattle: Washington University Press.

PETERS, A. J. (1967) *A guide to the study of British further education: published sources on the contemporary system.* Slough: National Foundation for Educational Research.

POWELL, J. P. (1966, 1971) *Universities and university education: a select bibliography.* 2 vols. Slough: National Foundation for Educational Research.

RICHMOND, W. K. (1972) *The literature of education: a critical bibliography, 1945–1970.* London: Methuen.

## JOURNALS AND OTHER PUBLICATIONS

Much recent research appears for the first time in the publications of research associations and in research journals. In England, the National Foundation for Educational Research issues a series of occasional publications, research reports, a journal, and a newsletter, and has recently begun a series of paperback books and pamphlets intended for the classroom teacher, and summarizing in a very readable form the results of research. The Scottish Council for Research in Education, the Society for Research in Higher Education, the Australian Council for Educational Research, the National Society for the Study of Education (USA) are further examples of associations which have all issued valuable series of publications. Among organizations concerned rather with development than research are the Nuffield Foundation and the Schools Council, both of which issue publications of interest to the teacher. Surveys of the various projects of these bodies are to be found in their annual reports. The Social Science Research Council, which is an organizing and co-ordinating body, issues a newsletter.

Among research journals the most useful to the ordinary teacher in Britain is probably *Educational research*, 1958 to date, issued by the National Foundation for Educational Research (N.F.E.R.). Other journals publishing original research in education are, for example, *British journal of educational psychology*, 1931 to date; *British journal of educational studies*, 1952 to date, dealing especially with the philosophical and historical aspects of education; *British journal of educational technology*, 1970 to date; *Durham research review*, 1950 to date; *Educational review*, 1947 to date; *Educational and psychological*

B

*measurement*, USA, 1940 to date; *Harvard educational review*, USA, 1930 to date; *Higher education*, 1972 to date; *Journal of curriculum studies*, 1968 to date; *Journal of educational research*, USA, 1920 to date; *Journal of experimental education*, USA, 1932 to date; *Journal of research in science teaching*, USA, 1963 to date; *Ontario journal of educational research*, 1958 to date; *Research in education*, 1969 to date; *Research in physical education*, 1966 to date; *Scottish educational studies*, 1967 to date; *Scientia paedagogica experimentalis*, Belgium, 1964 to date; *Trends in education*, 1961 to date.

To trace incomplete references, and to provide information on periodical articles in general, various indexes have been compiled. The oldest of the current indexes to educational literature is *Education index*, published by the H. W. Wilson Company, New York, 1929 to date. At present it indexes about 200 educational periodicals, proceedings, yearbooks, bulletins and monographic series published in the USA, Canada and Great Britain, but the great majority are from the USA. A recently established index is linked to the ERIC retrieval system (Education Resources Information Center) which has a world-wide coverage, although it is based in the USA. Its *Current index to journals in education*, 1969 to date, together with its literature searches by computer, provide one of the most sophisticated indexes currently available. For British periodicals there is *British education index*, 1954 to date. This appears three times a year, with two-yearly cumulations; in 1971 it indexed some 88 periodicals and this number is expected to increase substantially. The cumulations also include articles on educational topics published in general periodicals.

Abstracting journals give information about periodical articles, and sometimes about current books, and it is often possible to tell from them whether reference to the original article is worth while. There is not yet adequate coverage in abstracts of educational periodicals, nor is there co-ordination between the various issuing bodies. Technical education is covered in Britain by the publication *Technical education abstracts*, 1961 to date, dealing with periodicals and pamphlet material, and arranged in a classified sequence, with alphabetical author, title and subject indexes. Other British abstracting journals are *Sociology of education abstracts*, 1965 to date; *Language-teaching abstracts*, 1968 to date, compiled by the English-teaching Information Centre of the British Council and the Centre for Information on Language Teaching, and preceded by *English-teaching abstracts*, 1961–67. Occasional abstracts also occur regularly in the periodicals *New Education* and *Programmed learning and educational technology*. In the related field of psychology there are two old-established American abstracting journals. *Child development abstracts and bibliography*, 1927 to date, includes in separate sequences abstracts of periodicals and reviews of books. *Psychological abstracts*, 1927 to date, covers books, dissertations and periodical articles, and includes much of interest for education.

Another form of serial publication that often contains research articles is the year book, such as the *World year book of education*, 1965 to date, with its predecessor *Year book of education*, 1932–1940 and 1948–1964. *Paedogogica europaea*, 1965 to date, also appears yearly. *Mental measurements yearbook*, despite its name not an annual, has appeared at intervals since 1938, with the seventh issue, edited by O. K. Buros, published at Highland Park, New Jersey, in 1972. It contains reviews and descriptions of test materials. A companion volume, also edited by Buros, *Tests in print*, Highland Park, New Jersey, 1961, gives details of tests available at the time of publication.


THESES

So far we have been mainly concerned with published materials (books and periodicals), but unpublished materials in the shape of theses for higher degrees often contain the latest findings of research. Modern British university theses can be traced through the Aslib *Index to theses accepted for higher degrees in Great Britain and Ireland*, 1950/51 to date. This is arranged in classified order of subjects treated, with an author index. Some individual universities also issue lists of their own degree theses. For the USA there is *Dissertation abstracts*, Ann Arbor, 1952 to date, and its predecessor *Microfilm abstracts*, 1938–1951, which as the name implies give much more detail than the Aslib index.

For British theses in educational fields, accepted 1918 to 1957, the best guide is A. M. Blackwell's *List of researches in education and educational psychology, presented for higher degrees in the universities of the United Kingdom, Northern Ireland and the Irish Republic*, 1918–48 and 1949–51, issued by the National Foundation for Educational Research in two volumes, 1950–53, with supplements 1–3 covering the years 1952–57. It is arranged in classified order, with author and subject indexes. To supplement this from 1958 the Scottish Council for Research in Education has issued *A list of researches in education and educational psychology presented for degrees in Scottish universities from 1958 to 1961*, and further lists for later years are included in their annual reports.

Surveys of research in special fields of education can be found in various publications, such as *Religious education: a series of abstracts of unpublished theses in religious education*, by J. W. Daines, Nottingham, 1963–4, 2 vols.; *Research into higher education abstracts*, issued by the Society for Research into Higher Education, 1966 to date; *Survey of British research into audio-visual aids* (covering published and unpublished material), 1965 with supplements; *A summary of research in the English language arts*, 1960/61 to date, issued by the National Council of Teachers of English (USA); *Research list* (work completed and in progress) of the Comprehensive Schools Committee, 1967; and *Some recent British research on the social determinants of education: an annotated bibliography*, by A. Griffiths, Leeds, 1971.

British university theses are not normally lent for home reading, since they exist only in two or three copies. A library can usually obtain them on loan for consultation in the library only, and some can be obtained on microfilm. European theses are frequently printed in small runs, and copies can sometimes be obtained by approved institutions.

United States theses included in *Dissertation abstracts* can be supplied in microfilm or Xerox form. Since unpublished material is not copyright, a declaration that use will not be made of it without acknowledgement is often required of the reader. American report material (not commercially published) is abstracted and indexed by the Educational Resources Information Center (ERIC) of the US Office of Education, in *Research in education*, 1967 to date, monthly.

REGISTERS OF RESEARCH

Research in progress can be traced through various publications, none of which gives complete coverage. The Warren Spring Laboratory's *Register of research in the human sciences*, 1959/61, 1960/63 and 1962/65, has been succeeded by *Scientific research in British universities and colleges, vol. 3: Social sciences*, 1966/67 to date, issued by the Department of Education and Science and the British Council. The Social Science Research Council also issues its own list of research supported by it, 1967 to date. For education there is *Current researches in education and educational psychology*, issued by the National Foundation for Educational Research; the 1970 issue covered research commenced or completed in the academic year 1968–69. The Society for Research into Higher Education maintains a *Register of research into higher education*, and the journal *Scottish educational studies* includes reports on work in progress in Scotland. For Australia there are the Commonwealth Office of Education's bulletin, *Educational research being undertaken in Australia*, annually 1950 to date, and *Educational writing and research in Australia*, 1960–1965, by C. Sanders, Perth, 1966. For

France the *Courrier de la recherche pedagogique* lists researches in progress about once a year, and for the USA one can consult various official publications, such as *Research relating to children*, issued by the US Children's Bureau.

### SOURCES OF STATISTICS

The collection of statistics may be considered a form of research, and the principal sources for educational statistics in England and Wales are the publications of the Department of Education and Science and its predecessors. At present the Department's statistics are published separately from the annual report, and have grown steadily in size since 1961, when two parts and a supplement were all that was needed. The Scottish Education Department also now issues a separate publication, *Scottish educational statistics*, 1966, continuing. Statistics relating to universities were to be found in the University Grants Committee's annual *Returns from universities and university colleges in receipt of Exchequer grant* up until 1965; they now appear as Volume 6 of the D.E.S. *Statistics of Education*. Local authority statistics are to be found in *Education statistics* issued annually by the Institute of Municipal Treasurers and Accountants. Unesco's *Statistical yearbook*, 1963, continuing, and its *World survey of education*, 4 vols., 1955–66, provide international statistics. An additional source for English statistics is to be found in many of the official reports on education, e.g. *Early leaving* (Gurney-Dixon report), 1954; *15 to 18* (Crowther report), 1959–60; *Higher education* (Robbins report), 1963–4; *Half our future* (Newsom report), 1963; and *Children and their primary schools* (Plowden report), 1967.

Government publications in general often contain much useful information on educational progress, and the whole of the second volume of the Plowden report is devoted to research and surveys. H.M. Stationery Office produces daily, monthly and annual lists of its publications, while separate sectional lists are available for the publications of the Department of Education and Science and the Scottish Education Department.

Obviously no teacher, or prospective researcher, is going to need to consult all the books mentioned in this article, but the time taken in searching for information may be much shortened if one realizes what tools for the purpose are available.

*This chapter has been concerned with the early stages in planning and carrying out a research project. One important decision will be the choice of research design, and the reading by Simon brought out some important differences between experiments and explanatory surveys. All the planning will be dependent on finding out what research has previously been done, and Higson's article shows the wide range of sources which are available. The planning stages will not be complete until appropriate measurement instruments have been chosen and the sample selected. Problems in choosing variables are discussed in many of the succeeding chapters, particularly in Chapters 4 and 6, and in the extract by Fraser which comes in Chapter 7.*

*While the problems of measurement can be dealt with more effectively within the context of the illustrative studies, the techniques of sampling are more easily understood when the examples are drawn together within a framework.*

# 3    Selecting the Sample

In educational research the 'opportunity sample' is all too frequently used. It may be a school where some interesting experiment is being tried, or a group of volunteers, or the research worker's own students. For a pilot study, or for trying out an idea, this procedure is acceptable. But results from samples of this kind cannot be generalised to all schools or to all students. Volunteers may well be quite atypical of other people. Indeed the very attitudes which lead them to volunteer almost guarantee the formation of a non-representative group. Similarly, results based on research in a single institution must be treated with caution. Differences between schools and between teachers may affect the observed relationships in unknown ways and hence replications in other schools would be necessary before such results could be accepted. The drawbacks in using casual samples explain the emphasis on sampling to be found in professional surveys. If general conclusions are to be drawn, we must be persuaded that the sample does truly reflect the major characteristics of the population it represents.

Descriptions of samples inevitably contain technical terms, some of which must be introduced here. More detailed explanations may be found in a monograph by Butcher (1966) The first stage in sampling is to define the population—for example, all fifteen-year-old boys in local authority schools in Derbyshire. The results of the study cannot be generalised beyond this population. The sampling unit describes what is being sampled. It may be initially schools and subsequently pupils in schools. The sampling frame refers to the list of all the units from which the sample may be drawn. The sampling ratio or fraction indicates the proportion of the population included in the sample, say 1:100.

The simplest method of obtaining a sample is the random sample, which is obtained by selecting at random, either out of a hat or from a table of random numbers. Essentially, every member of the population has an equal and non-zero probability of appearing in the sample. A more convenient method of *selection is* systematic sampling *in which names are selected from a list according to the sampling ratio, choosing, say, every hundredth name. In obtaining national samples more complex procedures may be necessary.* Multi-stage *sampling and* stratified *sampling are commonly found. In multi-stage sampling progressively smaller sampling units are used sequentially. For example, geographical areas may be sampled first, followed by local authorities, followed by schools, followed by children. In each of these stages the sampling may be random from the full sampling frame, or it may be stratified. For example, in choosing schools it may be important to obtain numbers of infant, primary and secondary schools in the exact proportion which occur in the population. A strict random sample would not necessarily achieve this outcome. But if these 'strata' of types of schools can be decided in advance and the random sampling carried out within each type separately, it is possible to control the numbers of each type of school contained in the final sample. Besides the convenience of this method, there is an additional advantage. It is sometimes useful to apply differing sampling ratios to each stratum, so as to boost the numbers in groups which would otherwise be poorly represented (see the extract from Douglas, page 35).*

*Some of these more complex sampling procedures are illustrated in the extracts which follow. The ideal sample, from a statistical point of view, is the simple random sample. But the method is really impracticable in large-scale studies; imagine trying to list the names of all fifteen-year-old boys in the whole country! As a result most national surveys nowadays use some form of multi-stage or stratified sampling. This is standard practice now in large-scale surveys, but it is also a sensible policy even for smaller inquiries, in which a well-designed sampling strategy may extend the application of the findings without adding to the labour or cost of investigation.*

*In Britain, pioneer work in developing sampling techniques appropriate to educational surveys was done by Gilbert Peaker in the Ministry of Education in the early 1950s. One of the first problems for which the techniques were developed was the assessment of standards of reading ability, the subject of national surveys in 1948, 1952, 1956 and subsequently. The same test was applied on each occasion to samples of eleven-year-old and fifteen-year-old pupils. In the following extract from the report on these studies the method of sampling is described, and the procedures in 1952 and 1956 are contrasted with the crude method adopted in 1948. In 1948, samples were drawn from fourteen local education authorities, and the following extract starts with a criticism of the procedure used on that occasion.*

## Standards of Reading
(Ministry of Education, 1957)[1]

Although the samples used in 1948 were not strictly random they were a great improvement, for their purpose, on the pre-war samples. A strictly random sample is one chosen by lot. The selection may be made by successive stages—for example the selection of local education authorities at the first stage, of schools within the areas of selected authorities at the second, and of pupils within selected schools at the third—but at each stage the selection must be made by drawing lots, or by some ana-logous process, if the sample is to be random, and it is only to samples that are random in this sense that probability calcula-tions about the limits of sampling error strictly apply. With a random process of selection the most probable sample is a fair, or representative, sample, and the probability of any specified departures from fairness can be calculated from the internal evidence of the sample itself. The 1948 samples were chosen not by lot but by judgment; the disadvantage of the use of judgment samples is that although, with good judgment, they will be fair, yet no evidence can be obtained from the samples themselves that they are so.

The samples taken for the 1948 test consisted of 3,419 child-ren of fifteen (i.e. aged between 14·9 and 15·3) in schools in the areas of ten local education authorities, and 2,802 children aged eleven in the areas of four local education authorities. Although the samples were chosen by judgment and not by lot, the evid-ence of the later samples (of 1952 and 1956), which were strictly random, is to some extent applicable to them, and leads to the conclusion that the risk of serious unfairness is slight, particu-larly in the senior sample. The difference between the two samples chosen in 1948 arises from the fact that the senior sample included ten local education authority areas, and the junior sample only four. To ensure fairness a sample must in-clude an adequate number of primary sampling units (local edu-cation authority areas in this case), and the later surveys showed that for this purpose an adequate number means ten or more. In the pre-war samples there were only two or three units, and even in the 1948 junior sample there were only four. With so few units in a sample, the margin of uncertainty is wide, and it

---

[1] Extracted in full from *Standards of Reading, 1948–1956* (H.M.S.O.), Appendix II, 25–8. The results of these and more recent studies may be found in summary form in *Children and their Primary Schools* (the Plowden Report) (1967), Volume 2, pages 260–6.

is chiefly for this reason that the evidence for the post-war gains is much more cogent than that for the war-time losses.

For the 1952 and 1956 surveys an attempt was made to improve the sampling design. A three-stage sampling process was devised, in which the first stage consisted of the selection of local education authority areas and the second of the selection of schools from within selected local education authority areas, the selection being random in each case. Within selected schools all children in a three month age range centred on 11·0 or 15·0 were taken (except in the smaller schools, for which the sampling fraction for the selection of schools was reduced and the age range correspondingly widened). Before the selections were made local education authority areas were stratified into county boroughs, urban parts of administrative counties, and rural parts of administrative counties, schools were stratified by type, and various other devices were employed to ensure that the standard errors of sampling should be as small as possible for the size of the samples.

These samples were, in fact, quite small. In 1952 the samples consisted of pupils from the areas of 15 local education authorities. In 1956 the senior sample consisted of 1,741 pupils from 108 secondary and 31 all-age schools in the areas of 7 county boroughs, the urban parts of 10 administrative counties, and the rural parts of 6 administrative counties; and the junior sample of 1,374 children from the same 31 all-age schools and 107 primary schools drawn from the same areas.

A few modifications were made in the sampling design of 1956 in the light of the experience of 1952. In each there were three stages of sampling, namely the selection of areas, the selection of schools within selected areas, and the selection of pupils within selected schools. The chance of an area being selected was made proportional to its size, which was defined as the number of children in grant-aided schools according to the latest available information at the time when the draw was made.

An alternative way of describing the design used in 1956 is to say that it was tantamount to dividing the whole country into a thousand primary sampling units, each containing about the same number of children and each lying entirely within one local education authority area, each administrative county being reckoned as two areas—its urban parts, and its rural part. A county borough containing 2 per cent of the school population of England would contain twenty of these primary sampling units, and this is all that needs to be known until the first stage of the draw has been made.

The three lists of areas—county boroughs, urban parts of counties, and rural parts of counties—were written down in geographical order and the number of primary sampling units entered against each one. A running total was then made for each list, and the sample was drawn by taking a random start and a sampling interval of fifty p.s.u. (primary sampling units) for each list. This, as will be seen, produced a sample of twenty p.s.u. Only three of these p.s.u. were rural, since the rural parts of counties contain only 15 per cent of the school population. Three is not enough, so the process was repeated for the rural list, to give three more p.s.u., or six in all, in the rural part of the country.

Until a p.s.u. has been drawn its existence may be merely notional; if it is drawn it becomes necessary to embody it. To construct the twenty p.s.u. contained in the county borough mentioned above the schools of various types in the county borough can in principle be dealt out into twenty lots, so that each lot contains its due proportion of each type. These lots then constitute the p.s.u. for the borough; they are interpenetrating samples of the borough's schools. In practice it is only necessary to construct one of them. For the rural areas the p.s.u., having been doubled in number, were halved in size to compensate for this.

It will be seen that the process so far described would produce a 2 per cent sample of the schools in the country. This is about the right size for secondary schools, but needlessly large for the smaller and more numerous primary schools, so half the primary schools drawn could be discarded (again in principle; it was not necessary actually to draw the discarded half). A further economy in the number of visits needed was made by again halving the number of primary schools taken in the rural areas and, in compensation, doubling the proportion of pupils taken from each of these very small schools.

*Though the description is detailed and at times complex, it clearly demonstrates the precision necessary in sophisticated sampling. A key point is made at the end of the first paragraph: it is important not only to obtain a representative sample, but also to draw it by a procedure which allows an estimate of the degree of error involved in the sampling.*

*Another example from this period is to be found in the report on* Early Leaving. *The grammar school sample on which this survey was based numbered 8690, and the description of the sampling procedure includes estimates of the range of accuracy of the results.*

*Early Leaving*
(Ministry of Education, 1954)[1]

The sample was a stratified random sample drawn from the whole population of grammar schools in England. The sampling unit was the school. Schools were drawn with constant probability and a uniform sampling fraction of one in ten. The schools were stratified before selection by (1) Type (boys, girls, mixed); (2) Status (maintained or direct grant); (3) Region (the ten Ministry of Education divisions). A further stratification by size seemed inadvisable for so small a sample; consequently the standard error for size (three per cent) is much larger than the other errors ...

The sampling was single-stage. Within selected schools all pupils in the age-group were included.

There were 120 schools in the sample, and replies were received from all but six ...

Standard errors were calculated for some of the major variables; their size accorded with expectation. For the larger strata (the three kinds of maintained school) they were of the order of one per cent; for the smaller strata (direct grant schools) they were correspondingly larger ...

*An illustration of the value of precise sampling is given in* Rising Standards in Scottish Primary Schools, *the report of two surveys carried out by the Scottish Council for Research in Education (1968). Standards of performance in English and Arithmetic of ten-year-old children in 1953 were compared with the performance in the same tests of ten-year-old children in 1963. In 1953, the tests were given to all the ten-year-olds in Scotland, numbering about 76,000. In 1963, a one-in-fifteen sample of schools was drawn, stratified by size of school and different types of area (to ensure that all sizes and all areas were adequately represented, since the results were subsequently analysed separately by size and area). Thus it was possible in 1963 to obtain comparable results (within a small range of error) by testing only 5,209 children of the 82,000 pupils in the age-group in Scotland that year, and only 175 of some 2,700 schools were involved.*

*Even a relatively simple stratification may be of value in distributing the research effort appropriately. The National Survey of Health and Development, which led to the reports,* The Home and the School *(1964) and* All Our Future *(1968), provides*

[1] Edited extract from *Early Leaving* (H.M.S.O.), Appendix III, page 95.

*an example. Douglas describes the sample which formed the basis of a twenty-year follow-up study from birth to maturity.*

### *All Our Future*     (J. W. B. Douglas, J. M. Ross and H. R. Simpson, 1968)[1]

The 5,362 young people in this sample were selected from all those born in Great Britain in the first week of March 1946. Illegitimate and twin births were excluded, and, from the remaining legitimate single births, all middle class and all agricultural workers' children were taken, but only 1 in 4 of the other manual workers' children. The sample is therefore overloaded with those from middle class families.

This has the advantage for the Survey that appreciably more have gone on to higher education (approximately one and a half times) than would be expected from a random sample of the same size. A minor disadvantage is that, when giving descriptions that are intended to refer to the whole population, it is necessary to adjust for this sampling. To do so, all that is necessary is to give a weight of 1 to the middle class and agricultural workers' families and a weight of 4 to the remainder. The resulting rates or 'population estimates' for grammar school admissions, age of leaving school, 'O' level results, etc., lie close to known national figures, and there is every reason to believe that, when adjusted in this way, the observations made during this Survey give a true picture of the educational experience of the national age group of pupils which this sample is intended to represent.

*There is no single correct procedure for sampling. The method chosen depends on the purpose of the inquiry, on the type of analyses to be made, and on certain restrictions—time, staff, facilities—which have to be accepted as external constraints. Two brief examples illustrate differing approaches to sampling in parallel projects. These are taken from The Teacher's Day and Primary School Survey. Both were concerned with observation of the work of teachers, but the two projects differed in their aims and the differences are reflected in the sampling procedures.*

[1] Extracted in full from *All Our Future* (Peter Davies), page 8.

### The Teacher's Day
### (S. Hilsum and B. S. Cane, 1971)[1]

DESCRIPTION OF THE SAMPLING

#### a.   The Selection of the Schools

The sample was drawn from all schools in Surrey containing children of junior age. To ensure that all parts of the country were represented, the sample was stratified by the seven administrative areas into which Surrey is divided. The sample was also stratified by size of school—the size of a school being the number of junior children (7- to 11-year-olds) it contained. Four size groups were chosen so that the number of schools falling into each group was approximately equal.

The design required 54 schools to be selected, but to allow for schools which might be unable to participate or would not be suitable for some reason, a replacement sample was drawn at the same time as the main sample. Random numbers were used to select the sample—about one-third of the junior schools in Surrey. This sample was randomly divided into three groups, one for each term.

The change of design for the Autumn term, requiring more schools than originally planned, meant that a sample of further schools had to be drawn for this term.

#### b.   The Selection of the Teachers

The design required that two teachers were to be selected from each school, one inexperienced and the other experienced. Before each term began, the schools for that term were approached and asked to supply a list of junior teachers with details of their experience. For the Spring term it was found that the median experience lay between three and four years. 'Inexperienced' was therefore defined as 0–3 years and 'experienced' as 4 or more years.

Within each school one of each type of teacher was randomly selected; teachers unable to participate were replaced by another in the same experience group. In some schools it was not possible to find teachers with suitable experience and these schools were replaced by others. It should therefore be appreciated that to some extent the very small schools may be underrepresented in the final sample.

[1] Extracted from The Teacher's Day (N.F.E.R.), page 273.

## Primary School Survey
### (J. H. Duthie, 1970)[1]

The main purpose of the study is two-fold: to produce evidence upon which can be based systematic suggestions for the employ-ment of auxiliaries in Scottish primary schools; and to make an estimate of the ratio of auxiliaries to teachers which could be justified on the basis of our observations. To perform these tasks adequately we required first of all to carry out our observations in a sample of primary schools which was representative of all primary schools in Scotland; and secondly to design our investi-gations in such a way, and so to select techniques of statistical analysis that we could measure where real differences among schools lie. These two issues—sampling and statistical analysis— are related. We deal with the sampling issue first.

Our preliminary observations and discussions had suggested that the important distinguishing characteristics for schools and classes in respect of the incidence of non-teaching activities are:

    a.   size of school, and

    b.   yearly stage of class.

The simplest way of choosing a sample taking into account these characteristics is a two-stage one involving some form of random selection:

    a.   of particular schools;

    b.   of classes within these schools.

In other words, we first of all selected schools at random and having made the selection of schools, selected at random classes within these schools. (Other possible stratification variables were considered. None of these however met the twin requirements of feasibility and relevance. E.g., it would have been useful for us to have stratified our sample according to sociological criteria such as urban—suburban—rural. On enquiry, however, we found that the lack of such information about the 2,610 primary schools in Scotland made such a course of action impracticable.)

Details of the two-stage sampling method which we adopted are given below.

#### (A) STAGE ONE: SELECTION OF SCHOOLS

It was not enough to select schools at random. Given the limita-tions imposed on the sample size by availability of manpower and time, we ran the risk that random selection might omit, or

[1] Extracted from *Primary School Survey: a Study of the Teacher's Day* (H.M.S.O. Edinburgh), pages 23–6, omitting paragraph (d).

at least under-represent, particular sizes of school. To avoid this danger we grouped or stratified the schools by size, and ensured that each of these groups was adequately represented in the final sample. (The technique employed is described below.)

Preliminary observations had suggested that the differences in incidence of non-teaching activities among adjacent school sizes are greater in the smaller schools, e.g., the differences between, say, one- and two-class schools appeared to be greater than the differences between fifteen- and sixteen-class schools. We therefore decided to represent school sizes singly at the lower end of the range and to employ increasingly large groups towards the higher end of the range. The actual stratification employed is as follows:

1 class; 2 classes; 3–4 classes; 5–6 classes; 7–9 classes; 10–13 classes; 14+ classes.

### (B) STAGE TWO: SELECTION OF CLASSES

Our preliminary observations indicated differences in the incidence of non-teaching activities in the different yearly stages and for reasons similar to those put forward for stratifying schools by size we stratified by yearly stages according to the grouping P.1 and P.2 ('Infants'); P.3 and P.4 ('Juniors'); and P.5 P.6 and P.7 ('Seniors').

For reasons to do with the analytical techniques employed it was necessary to observe four classes in each school where this was possible. (In smaller schools we visited all classes.) Again, two of these classes had to be from one of our strata and two from another. Thus in one school, we visited two infants classes and two junior, in another, two infants and two senior, and in another, two junior and two senior.

As in the case of selection of schools, selection of classes within strata was also at random where there were more than two classes in a department. Selection of the strata to be used in a particular school was also made at random and allowed for equal representation of each of the strata over the sample as a whole.

### (C) THE SIZE OF THE SAMPLE

In determining the size of our sample, we had to consider our resources in terms of manpower and time. One condition of our entering classrooms to observe teacher activities was that the non-teacher member of the Team had to be accompanied by a teacher-member. Because of this it was necessary to divide the Team into two pairs, each pair containing a teacher member.

Given the need for the development of observation categories and the need to provide adequate time for the analysis of the data and the writing of the Report, it was necessary to restrict the period of the main experiment to six months.

The final restriction was the period of time for which it was necessary to observe any one class. Clearly the short answer is: 'the longer, the better'. Experience suggested that one complete day was perhaps the best compromise, provided that we had met the teacher beforehand to reassure her as to our purposes. We felt it necessary to observe a complete day, rather than part of a day, because the day is one of the basic educational units, i.e., in our observations, teachers' requirements for auxiliary help varied more within the day than from one day to the next. (Variations from day to day could be picked up in the analysis since the schedule of school visits ensures that each school day is represented equally often.)

The approximate number of classes which we could observe was thus dictated by three factors; the number of pairs of observers available (two); the amount of time available (six months); and the length of time to be spent in each class (one day). Bringing these three factors together and allowing time for travel and for analysis of the data, it was possible for the Team to observe, in the course of the main study, approximately one-hundred-and-twenty classes.

### (D)  PROCEDURE FOR SELECTING THE SAMPLE

We have described how the sample was a two-stage one in which we first of all selected schools and then classes within these schools. In order to select schools in their appropriate groupings, we first of all numbered all the schools in the population consecutively, as they appeared in the information sheets provided by the Scottish Education Department. We then entered a table of random numbers and selected schools from the population at random until each of the strata given above was complete. Thus if the random number first drawn was, say 574 and school number 574 was in the two-class grouping, that school was selected and the number of schools available for selection in the two-class category reduced (from four, the number required for the sample) to three. When all schools in a particular category had been selected (e.g., seven in the case of the one-class category), any random number which subsequently fell within that particular grouping was ignored.

Four substitutes were also selected for each of the strata in case any schools opted out for any reason. However, we are glad to be able to report that all schools approached co-operated and that these substitutes proved to be unnecessary.

The next step was to select classes within the schools. Since precise information was not available on a national scale concerning the yearly stage of the classes in the schools selected, we wrote to the Directors of Education concerned once the schools were known. We asked Directors in making their returns to exclude those classes which were not being taken by certificated teachers. (In practice this course of action created none of the sampling problems which we had anticipated—e.g., that we would not have a sufficient number of classes in the required strata.)

*To conclude, a model example of careful sampling is described in Volume 2 of the Plowden Report. This is the National Survey among Parents of Primary School Children, which was conducted for the Plowden Committee by the Government Social Survey. Those who have followed the descriptions in the earlier extracts in this chapter will find the technical detail in this part of the Plowden Report quite straightforward.*

## Children and their Primary Schools
### (Department of Education and Science, 1967)[1]

### THE SAMPLE DESIGN

The enquiry was conducted amongst the parents of a sample of children of certain age-groups in maintained primary schools in England.

The sample design was a stratified random one in two stages with maintained primary schools in England as the primary sampling units. At the second stage, a sample of children in the specified age-groups was selected such that the overall probability of selection of each child was uniform.

In designing the sampling frame the maintained primary schools were divided into four main size strata :
  i.   schools with 25 or less pupils
  ii.  schools with 26 to 50 pupils
  iii. schools with 51 to 200 pupils and
  iv.  schools with 201 and more pupils.

As the population of the first stratum, i.e. schools with 25 or less pupils being under 0.5 per cent of the total primary schools

---

[1] Edited extracts from *Children and their Primary Schools*, Volume 2, (H.M.S.O.), Appendix 3, Annex 1, pages 147–50.

population it was decided to exclude this stratum from the frame. Within the remaining three size strata, schools were broken down into the four types:

a.  infants only
b.  junior with infants
c.  junior without infants
d.  all-age.

An estimate of the population of each of the 12 cells was obtained by taking the mid-point of each of the size-bands as given in Table II of *Statistics of Education, 1963*, multiplying these by the number of schools in each of the size groups and adding together to form the strata given by type and size of school. A sample of approximately 3,500 was distributed between the cells in proportion to the estimated populations.

From the junior with infants and all-age schools, the sample was to consist of children in three age-bands defined as 'top infants', 'bottom juniors' and 'top juniors.' From the 'junior only' schools only two age-bands could be selected and the third—'top infants'—was to be selected from the 'infants only' schools feeding the selected 'junior only' schools. From selected schools in the largest size stratum it was decided that 12 children per age-group would be selected; from schools in the 51–200 size group eight children per age-group would be selected and in the smallest size stratum four children would be selected from each size stratum.

Then within each of the cells, other than 'infants only', from which the primary units, schools, were to be selected, the schools were arranged by local education authority and in size order and the requisite number selected with probability proportionate to their size. One hundred and seven schools were selected in this manner. The total number of schools in the sample were increased to 173 by taking the 'infants only' schools from which the selected 'juniors only' schools recruited their intake.

At the second stage a systematic sample of children was selected for each of the three age-groups, 4, 8 or 12 children being selected from each dependent upon the size-stratum into which the school fell. Before selecting the sample of children's names all those comprising the survey population were arranged within each age-group:

i.   by class
ii.  by stream or group, where the school adopts this procedure and
iii. by sex within.

The age-groups taken were those defined as :—

1  Top juniors—in general those born between 1/9/1952 and 31/8/1953 (both dates inclusive).

2   Bottom juniors—in general those born between 1/9/1955 and 31/8/1956 (both dates inclusive).
3   Top infants—in general those born between 1/9/1956 and 31/8/1957 (both dates inclusive).

The design produced a set sample of 3,349 children in 173 schools distributed by age-group as follows:

| 1 | Top juniors | 1,104 |
|---|-------------|-------|
| 2 | Bottom juniors | 1,086 |
| 3 | Top infants | 1,159 |

From this selected sample children living in institutions or who had parents teaching in the sampled school were withdrawn. When more than one child in a family had been selected one child was picked at random as the subject of the interview. For one or other of these reasons 112 names (i.e. three per cent of the total) were deleted from the original sample, leaving an interview sample of 3,237.

The extent to which the sample was representative of the population of primary school children in respect of type of school attended and Department of Education Division is shown below. The sex distribution was the same in the sample as in the total population of children. The population figures are taken from *Statistics of Education Part 1 1964*, and refer to the position in January, 1964. The sample was drawn in April/May, 1964.

| Type of school attended | Sample % | All primary children % |
|-------------------------|----------|------------------------|
| Juniors with infants | 41 | 42 |
| Juniors only | 38 | 33 |
| Infants only | 21 | 23 |
| All-age | 0 | 2 |

| Department of Education Division | Sample % | All primary children % |
|----------------------------------|----------|------------------------|
| Northern | 8 | 9 |
| Yorks., E. and W. Riding | 13 | 10 |
| North Western | 16 | 16 |
| North Midlands | 8 | 9 |
| Midlands | 8 | 12 |
| Eastern | 12 | 12 |
| Metropolitan | 8 | 10 |
| South Eastern | 11 | 9 |
| Southern | 9 | 6 |
| South Western | 6 | 8 |

Total   (3,092)

# 4 Practical Constraints in Conducting a Survey on Students

*One dilemma for students or teachers who read about educational research is the gap between theory and practice. The textbooks on research methods often recommend elaborate and sophisticated experimental designs, while research journals present a succession of explanatory or descriptive surveys. Even the rules of sampling are broken. Why does this happen? The cynical observer might be led to believe that the people who write methodology textbooks have actually never done research projects themselves. Certainly the main reason for the gap between theory and practice seems to be the enormous difficulty in doing real educational research. Technical problems of measurement abound, but there are also unexpected practical difficulties which may prevent the proposed design from being carried out in its original form. But research workers seldom describe in their reports the problems they have encountered in collecting data, or the way in which their research design has been affected by chance events. Partly, this is just a convention in reporting, as readers are interested mainly in the findings; partly, it is a form of self-defence, for nobody likes to draw attention to possible weaknesses in his own data. Consequently, it is difficult to find examples to illustrate practical problems which arise in conducting a survey or an experiment in educational research. The reader is thus left with the uncomfortable feeling that the research report and the conventional textbook on design are products of an unreal world. Fortunately, some writers have been prepared to admit to the intrusion of the unexpected. In the evaluation of the initial teaching alphabet (i.t.a.), the initial misgivings among parents, teachers and education authorities had a seriously limiting influence on the design of the first experiment. Downing's article, in which he discusses the problems he faced in evaluating the effectiveness of teaching reading by i.t.a., appears in the next chapter. In Chapter 7, the extract from Fraser's book,* Home Environment and the School, *describes some of the unexpected complications in conducting an interview sur-*

vey. Failing to find a similarly revealing but more general article about surveys has left us with only personal experience on which to draw.

## THE ACADEMIC PERFORMANCE OF STUDENTS

Practical problems will be found in research at any age level, but the constraints are particularly severe beyond age sixteen. Research in schools is unlikely to be actively resisted by most administrators or headteachers, so long as the research has been carefully planned, avoids delicate areas, and is not too demanding of time or staff involvement. Agreement from the headteacher more or less guarantees the research worker a captive population, who will acquiesce, at least outwardly, to his requests. The same situation does not apply in higher education and the difficulties faced in a recent study on students serve to illustrate the impact of hard reality on what seemed at first to be a straightforward research design.

The starting-point of this project was a memorandum from the trustees of the Joseph Rowntree Memorial Trust. In essence the problem was the future structure of higher education in Britain and, in particular, the extent to which present methods of selection for universities are efficient and fair. Specific questions followed from this general statement. Are students accepted for courses which are best fitted to them? Are they admitted to the most appropriate form of higher education? By narrowing these problems down and interpreting them from a psychological viewpoint, a research design emerged. It was decided to investigate the characteristics of students with comparable entry qualifications who were successful in different areas of study and different types of institution.

A review of the literature indicated which 'characteristics' were likely to be relevant to academic success. It was decided that the most important variables would be previous academic attainment, academic aptitude, motivation, study habits, methods and attitudes, examinaion technique, self-concept, personality, details of previous education, father's occupation and parental education. In addition, because of the emphasis on contrasting areas of study, it was decided to identify patterns of relevant interests. The next problem was to obtain valid and reliable measures of these dimensions. Many of the background details could clearly be collected by questionnaire, but there were no British scales of motivation, study methods or examination technique. Such scales would have to be specially constructed. A later chapter will show that the development and validation of an attitude scale is a considerable undertaking. Measures of self-

*concept are relatively easy to obtain—although there may be doubts about their validity. Eysenck's Personality Inventory provides scores on two important dimensions, extraversion and neuroticism, while a project supported by the Committee of Vice-Chancellors and Principals has been developing a test of academic aptitude which measures numerical and verbal abilities.*

*Even at this planning stage of the project practical constraints had to be considered. Just how long would students submit to intensive psychological testing? Previous experience indicated that a single session lasting some two and a half hours was as much as could be expected. On this basis our list of tests was already rather long and yet we still wanted to add a measure of 'interests'. The limitation of time forced us towards short, simple scales and we chose two—the Allport, Vernon and Lindzey Study of Values and Eysenck's* Social Attitudes Questionnaire.

*The next task, after choosing the methods of measurement, was to secure the co-operation of a wide range of institutions of higher education. Limited resources prevented any possibility of a truly national sample, but it was feasible to look for universities and colleges in the north of England and the Midlands, which would be representative of institutions elsewhere. It was important to include all types of institution, old universities, civic and new universities, local authority colleges of education and denominational colleges, and polytechnics. An approach was made to thirty-three institutions giving details of the research design and of the information which would be required. In particular it was important to make clear to institutions precisely the amount of additional work the project would involve. It was also necessary to avoid sensitive areas, such as 'failure rates'. Two paragraphs from the outline sent to institutions illustrate this approach.*

*'Early in the Spring term the students would be asked to spend an afternoon completing aptitude booklets and filling in the inventory and questionnaire. It is hoped that the institution would be able to provide a suitable room for this purpose. Research officers working on the project would supervise the invigilation. The institution could be reimbursed from the research grant for any expense involved in providing the necessary facilities.*

*At the end of the first year departments would be asked to rate each student's first-year academic performance. Our sample would contain only a small proportion of an individual department's students. At the beginning of the second and third years, institutions would be asked to provide information about students who had left the university or college. Institutions would also be asked to provide details of the*

final qualifications obtained by the students. All this information from institutions and departments would be collected
on lists especially designed to reduce the time spent on completing them and would be strictly confidential.'

We had anticipated no more than a 50 per cent rate of co-
operation. The initial responses were, in fact, more favourable
than we had anticipated: twenty-five institutions expressed their
willingness to be involved, but some replies contained restrictions. Two institutions insisted on choosing the sample for us,
and several expressed reservations about our method of selecting
students on the basis of A-level qualifications. A more general
concern was felt about the possibility that we might 'pester'
students by repeated requests for information. This constraint
restricted us to a single postal contact with each student in which
we requested co-operation. Our attempt at systematic random
sampling could be taken no further. If there was to be any survey,
it would have to be on the terms laid down—a sample contaminated by self-selection, with all the attendant weaknesses
already mentioned in the preceding chapter.

In such a situation there is at least one way out. If the effect
of self-selection can be determined, appropriate care can be
taken in interpreting the findings. At one institution it was possible to contact a proportion of the students who did not co-
operate. As anticipated those not responding did differ to some
extent from the sample. They had lower levels of motivation and
entry qualifications. In other words our sample was rather homogeneous—restricted in range—on these two important variables.
However it seemed unlikely that this distortion would cause any
serious mistakes in the analyses. If anything, it would cause us to
under-estimate the strengths of relationships between variables,
but the pattern of results would be almost unaffected.

The first letter to students at registration sought to persuade
them to volunteer for test sessions which would take place in the
following term. It was quite a different problem to persuade these
students to honour their pledge by turning up in the right place
at the right time. We had managed to arrange rooms in each
institution, but, although examination conditions had been
stipulated, we were never sure until we arrived how these
requirements had been interpreted. The rule book states that
conditions for testing should be identical from session to session.
The variations in facilities from institution to institution prevented this ideal from being realised. By the time we had coped
with one hundred students in a tiered lecture hall, or invigilated
an even larger group in an assembly hall, the idea of standardised
conditions of testing was already wearing rather thin. In practice,

however, the situations were effectively controlled by providing our own invigilators on each occasion.

Another problem which caused much discussion prior to our first session was how students would react when they discovered exactly what they were expected to do. Would they walk out straight away? We also felt that two and a half hours non-stop was too fierce. Coffee was thus provided wherever possible, but would this present a ready-made opportunity for an early exit to those who were still there? In fact, our fears proved groundless and we were pleasantly surprised that not only did the vast majority of the students complete all the tests, but many of them were sufficiently interested in their ordeal to stay behind afterwards asking questions about the project. The typical student of our survey was unrecognisable in the stereotypes being developed by the communications media.

'Collecting data' is a stage normally dismissed in the textbooks in a couple of paragraphs, but it should already be clear that it can involve a considerable exercise in logistics. To make sure that students would remember the test sessions, we arranged to send postcards by first-class mail three days beforehand. A postal strike nearly wrecked this organization for one institution. At the session itself the whole battery of tests was presented to each student in an envelope. In this way no completed tests were mislaid or left unidentified. The envelopes were handed in at the end of the session and it might have been thought that all problems in data collection had by then been solved. Again the unexpected intervened. One car carrying the entire set of scripts from an institution in the north-east became stuck in a snowdrift on the Pennines and there it stayed overnight. Fortunately both occupants and scripts survived the ordeal, but those data were hard-won.

Data processing comes next. Again there are considerable organisational problems in marking some 13,000 scripts, making random checks on the accuracy of marking, and transferring scores to punched cards. As several groups of people were involved in these procedures a flow-diagram was used to decide the 'critical path'. In which order should the tasks be tackled so as to complete this phase of the project in a minimum time? The figure shows a simplified version of the flow diagram, which proved particularly useful in plotting the progress of the various chores.

Computers make statistics easy—in theory. But computers demand complete accuracy in everything they process and infallibility is not a human characteristic. As a result, there is generally a prolonged argument between man and machine, before the welcome print-out of statistical tables finally appears. Then all that remains is to sort out the mass of tables into a form which can be reported.

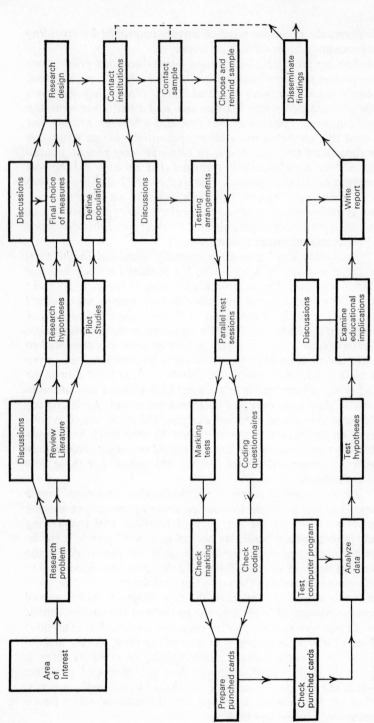

*Flow diagram of follow-up study on students*

*Naturally many of the snags have had to be omitted from this brief summary. The collection of first-year and final results from institutions created another series of problems, as did the follow-up questionnaire sent out to students. But enough has been said about each stage in this survey to indicate the nature of some of the practical problems which interfere with the implementation of an initial research design.*

*As this survey on students has yet to be completed, only an indication of the results can be given. The extract below, from a preliminary unpublished report, provides an indication of the initial results.*

### Educational Objectives and
### Academic Performance in Higher Education
### (N. J. Entwistle, K. A. Percy and J. B. Nisbet, 1971)[1]

RESULTS FROM PRELIMINARY ANALYSIS

Just over half our sample was used to provide a preliminary indication of the potential value of our results. This smaller group (from 3 universities, 4 colleges of education and all 5 polytechnics) consisted of 898 university students (492 men, 406 women), 562 students in colleges of education (161 men, 401 women) and 190 students in polytechnics or colleges of technology (140 men, 50 women).

As expected, there were differences in entry qualifications and in educational and social backgrounds between students in the different sectors. The universities cream off sixth-formers with the highest grades in the Advanced Level examinations of the G.C.E. We found, in our sample, that about 69 per cent of the university students had grades equivalent to three C's (the scale is A–E) or better. Comparable figures for colleges of education and the polytechnics were 7 per cent and 5 per cent. There would appear to be little overlap in the abilities of the students attending universities and those in colleges. Using the scores from the Test of Academic Aptitude, this ability gap was confirmed, though its size appears to have been over-emphasised by the A-level grades. Dividing the scores into five categories we found 44 per cent of university students in the top two groups and only 4 per cent in the bottom category. The polytechnics contained 21 per cent of

[1] Extracted from pages 7–14 of an unpublished report prepared by the Department of Educational Research, University of Lancaster. The first two of the final analyses from this survey on students are expected to be published by Routledge and Kegan Paul in 1973 under the title *The Academic Performance of University Students: Two Research Studies.*

their students with above average scores and 15 per cent in the lowest category. Comparable figures for colleges of education were 11 per cent and 24 per cent. The large number of college of education students with very low aptitude scores is partly attributable to a greater degree of self-selection in the samples from the other sectors, but this by no means fully explains the difference.

Turning to previous educational experience, a majority of students in all three sectors had been to grammar schools. At university nearly a quarter of the intake had attended either independent schools or the highly selective 'direct-grant' grammar schools. At the other end of the secondary school spectrum—the so-called secondary modern schools—1 per cent of the university students had attended these schools, compared with 19 per cent of those in polytechnics.

Social class differences were also apparent. 61 per cent of university students, 56 per cent of college of education students, and 45 per cent of polytechnic students, had fathers in professional or managerial occupations; equivalent percentages in manual jobs were 27, 33 and 45. A chi-square analysis of the detailed breakdown of social class by type of institution showed that these differences were statistically significant ($p < 0.01$). Similar results were obtained from an analysis against father's education.

The final difference among the background details related to residence. Exactly half the polytechnic sample lived at home, compared with about 5 per cent of the other students. In our sample of university and college of education students the majority were living in college or in halls of residence. The exact figures, however, are not informative, as our sample cannot be considered representative in this respect.

*Study Habits*

We asked students to indicate the proportion of time they had spent in the previous term on various types of studying. We also obtained details of the number of hours spent at lectures, seminars or tutorials, and practicals and of the length of time spent on independent studying in the week immediately preceding the test session. During the test session we also provided an opportunity for free comment in the open-ended questionnaire. Certain rather acrimonious remarks from students in the polytechnics alerted us to expect the differences which emerged in the subsequent statistical analyses.

At university students have, on average, 14 contact hours during the week; in colleges of education, 19 hours; and in the polytechnics, 22 hours. The significance of these differences—both statistical and educational—appears to be unmistakable.

The opposite trend is found, not surprisingly, in the time spent in studying; the comparable numbers of hours being 23 in universities and 17 in both types of colleges. The interpretation of these findings is, however, not as clear-cut as might at first appear. Within the universities there are equally wide divisions in the balance between formal sessions and independent work in the different areas of study. In social studies the timetable includes on average some 10 hours formal contact; in languages and social science there is the equivalent of one extra lecture. Pure and applied scientists, on the other hand, are expected to attend for some 19 hours a week. It appears, therefore, that a large part of the difference between universities and polytechnics can be explained by the different types of courses being offered.

A similar effect is noticeable with the type of work students in the different areas of study had done in the previous term. Arts and social science students, in both polytechnics and universities, had spent most of their time in reading recommended books, background reading, making notes from books, preparing for tutorials, and in preparing for and writing essays. This last activity took up a 'large' or 'extremely large' proportion of the time of 81 per cent of the students taking social studies at university. Pure and applied scientists presented a totally different pattern of studying in their response to this question. These students had spent most of their time in working on set problems, writing up practicals and, to a lesser extent, in reading recommended books or in background reading. 65 per cent of applied scientists indicated that they had spent a 'large' or 'extremely large' proportion of their time in writing up practicals. This was by far the most heavily endorsed activity. In fact, among these applied scientists at university, 22 per cent admitted that they had spent no time at all reading recommended books in the preceding term.

The pattern of study habits reflected in this analysis suggests that arts students and scientists have quite different experiences of higher education. It looks also as if the educational objectives of staff in the different disciplines must be in striking contrast to each other, or perhaps the difference lies in the ways the students have perceived these aims and translated them into patterns of studying. Certainly the term 'reading' for a degree appears to be a misnomer, when applied to the typical engineer at university. Also the complaints we heard from polytechnic students, that they were overtaught and were required to present too much formal work, appear to be justified in comparison with other institutions. But again it must be remembered that these complaints come predominantly from those in applied science departments.

*Personality, values and attitudes*

Previous work, particularly in the United States, shows that students in different institutions tend to have different profiles of personality and attitudes. Some of these differences presumably reflect selection by the college or university; some may be the result of choice by the student in terms of the institution's public image; but a residue, at least, must represent changes caused by the interaction between the students and their academic social environment. Using a test of academic aptitude with separate numerical and verbal scores, Eysenck's scales of extraversion, neuroticism, tendermindedness and radicalism, the Allport–Vernon dimensions from the *Study of Values* and a self-rating on 'ambition', we were able to construct profiles of mean scores to draw attention to possible differences between students in the different sectors of higher education. We found, as in the previous section, that many of the variations in profile between institutions reflected differences in the courses offered. We therefore performed additional analyses by area of study.

The large intellectual differences between universities and colleges have already been mentioned. On the non-intellectual variables the differences, after controlling for inter-disciplinary variations, were rather small. The most consistent difference was in personality. Students in the colleges were more extraverted than university students. But as we also found a correlation of $-0.18$ between extraversion and A-level grades, at least part of this difference may be explained as an incidental effect of selection procedures. Apart from this, we found that college of education students had consistently higher social values and lower political values than university students. Students in the polytechnics were found to have high scores on neuroticism, high economic values and low religious values compared with students in the other sectors. But again part of this difference reflects subject area variations, and the most interesting results from this part of the study come from comparisons of the profiles of university students studying different disciplines, after controlling for possible sex differences in personality and attitude.

The differences in profiles between students taking contrasting courses of study are sufficiently large even to be taken as an illustration of C. P. Snow's ideas on the 'two cultures' as found in *The Two Cultures and the Scientific Revolution*.

> 'Literary intellectuals (are) at one pole—at the other scientists ... Between the two (there is) a gulf of mutual incomprehension ... They have a curious distorted image of each other. Their attitudes are so different that even on the level of emotion, they can't find much common ground.'

In terms of the variables included in this survey, the comparison between linguists and pure scientists fits Snow's experience curiously well. Students in language departments tend to have very high verbal ability and similarly high aesthetic values. In social attitudes they are radical and in personality, predominantly emotionally unstable. Linguists also tend to have below average scores on political, economic and theoretical values. The scientists are opposite in all these respects. They have, not surprisingly, high numerical ability, but they also have low aesthetic values combined with high political, economic and social values. Scientists are emotionally stable and in social attitudes are conservative. With mean scores in opposite directions in nine out of thirteen possible variables, it would not be surprising if there were difficulties in communication between students representing the 'two cultures'.

Although there are basic similarities between the different groups of arts students and between scientists taking different types of subject, there are still differences. Students taking social studies have high political and religious values; they are also tenderminded and see themselves as lacking in ambition. Social science students again have high political values linked to very high scores in radicalism. But they are tough minded and have low religious values.

Applied scientists contrast with pure scientists in that they tend to be neurotic, not stable, their social attitudes are even more conservative, their scores on economic values are higher and they see themselves as being more ambitious. Mathematicians are much less neurotic, but are particularly introverted and have extremely high theoretical values. Some of the smaller differences could certainly be chance characteristics of this particular sample, but the large differences between arts and science students are highly significant.

Nevertheless it must be recognised that statistical significance does not imply *total* dissimilarity between students in contrasting areas of study. The differences are between groups of students and there is still considerable overlap between the scores of arts students and scientists as individuals. There is simply a tendency for the groups as a whole to show characteristic differences.

*Characteristics of successful students*

In any prediction study the choice of the criterion is crucial. Academic performance is a peculiarly difficult criterion to measure effectively. At school level teachers' estimates of scholastic attainment have proved, after careful scaling, to be useful and valid measures. In higher education, specialization and the diversity of courses offered make problematical the comparisons between institutions, or even between students in the same institution. Degree or certificate classification will provide our final criterion. Considerable efforts are put into ensuring, within the limits of current procedures, that these assessments are fair and accurate. For the purposes of a follow-up study, however, this criterion provides only limited information with its broad divisions. Where percentage marks are provided for assessment made at the end of the first year, the criterion of academic performance can be more informative, but cross-institutional comparisons may be misleading. Certainly, the academic standards between universities and some of the colleges cannot be expected to be comparable. Analyses of academic performance can only be done separately by type of institution.

Another problem which has to be faced involves the different usages of percentage scales by the different disciplines in similar institutions. Mathematicians use the full range of marks, whereas social scientists may restrict themselves to marks 10–15 per cent either side of the mean. Using unscaled marks as a criterion can thus lead to undesirable artefacts caused by differing standard deviations. For the preliminary analysis first-year marks, where these were fully available, were scaled to produce the same spread across the different areas of study. It was not possible, however, to eliminate fully these variations in the use of marks. Beyond this technical difficulty, there is the more serious problem of interpretation. Attainment in the different disciplines is assessed by staff who are looking, presumably, for evidence of rather different sets of abilities and qualities of mind. We should not be surprised, therefore to find quite different characteristics related to student success in the various areas of study, as well as differences across the three sectors of higher education. Our first concern, however, was with variables which predicted academic performance consistently for all students. Previous research had indicated the type of variables to include in the analysis. Previous scholastic attainment, academic aptitude, motivation, study attitudes and introversion have all been shown to correlate with academic performance; all these measures were included in this study. Students were also asked to rate themselves on being 'hardworking—compared with the average university student', using a seven-point scale. The correlations of these variables, together with others previously mentioned, with the criterion are shown in Table 4:1. The relationships are not close, being affected by both homogeneity and unreliability, but the consistency in the results is heartening. There seem to be few major differences between the sectors of higher education in the characteristics of successful students. It seems possible that there may be differences in the relationships between the personality dimensions and the criterion, but these may again be attributed to area of study differences.

TABLE 4:1  *Correlations with the criteria of academic performance*

|  | Universities | | Colleges of Education | | Polytechnics | |
|---|---|---|---|---|---|---|
|  | Men | Women | Men | Women | Men | Women |
| Variables (N) | (492) | (406) | (161) | (401) | (140) | (50) |
| A-level grades | 0·29 | 0·34 | 0·32 | 0·39 | * | * |
| Academic aptitude | 0·08 | 0·19 | −0·15 | 0·19 | −0·04 | 0·08 |
| Motivation | 0·22 | 0·15 | 0·19 | 0·26 | 0·22 | 0·26 |
| Study methods | 0·22 | 0·14 | 0·29 | 0·19 | 0·32 | 0·31 |
| Exam-technique | 0·18 | 0·15 | 0·18 | 0·20 | 0·20 | 0·07 |
| Self-hardworking | 0·30 | 0·29 | 0·26 | 0·11 | 0·24 | 0·18 |
| Hours studying | 0·21 | 0·16 | 0·15 | 0·21 | 0·18 | 0·30 |
| Extraversion | −0·13 | −0·10 | −0·21 | −0·12 | −0·02 | 0·06 |
| Neuroticism | −0·01 | −0·08 | −0·16 | −0·14 | −0·07 | −0·41 |

* Correlations misleading due to a substantial number of O.N.C. entrants.

The differences in profiles discussed in the previous section led us to analyse separately by area of study, using the same group of variables as before. Our hypothesis was that students who did particularly well would show, in an exaggerated form, the general profile of scores obtained by students in that discipline. The opposite would be anticipated for students who did badly. If this were true, we should expect the correlations to follow the same pattern of values as shown by the standardized mean scores in the earlier analysis. On the whole our hypothesis was substantiated; there were certainly large differences in the relationships between the predictor variables and the criterion for arts and science students. Also the shapes of the profiles of correlations are substantially similar to the profiles of mean scores mentioned earlier.

Successful linguists, on the whole, have higher verbal aptitude than those who do badly. They are, like all the students with high attainment, more introverted, but they also have rather high scores on the neuroticism scale. High social and religious values are balanced by low political, economic and theoretical values. Successful linguists are not as ambitious as those who do less well, but this is the only discipline in which there is a negative correlation between academic performance and the self-rating on ambition.

The outstanding characteristic of students who obtain high criterion scores in social studies departments is their emotional stability, which is in striking contrast to the high neuroticism scores of the successful linguists. Among social science students there is only one correlation with the criterion of any note; high attainment is apparently related to low religious values.

Among scientists numerical aptitude is related to achievement, as might be expected. High theoretical values and low aesthetic values are consistently linked with success. The curious

C

difference in mean scores on neuroticism is even more striking in the best students. Successful pure scientists are noticeably stable, while for applied scientists there is apparently an advantage in being neurotic. The possibility of there being distinct differences in the relationship between neuroticism and academic performance may explain some of the contradictions in findings reported in previous research.

The problem of identifying measures which will enable us to predict future academic performance, not just in general but in a particular discipline, has subtle intricacies. We have shown that, after a term, students in the various areas of study have contrasting patterns of values and attitudes. Presumably the processes of selection and of choice, first at school and then on entry to university, will have created many of these differences before the courses begin—though additional evidence will be required to justify this assumption. If so, these groups of students will already be homogeneous on the very variables which are also the most useful for prediction purposes. Can we wonder that the resulting correlations are still low?

*This example of a survey was chosen specifically to draw attention to practical constraints. It is thus atypical of survey reports in general. The extracts in Chapters 7, 8 and 9 provide much better illustrations of surveys in action. The Social Survey for the Plowden Report, the National Survey by Douglas and the Schools Council Enquiry 1 about young school leavers are probably the best-known examples of this approach to educational research.*

# 5 Practical Constraints in Arranging a Field Experiment on i.t.a.

In conducting a survey the research worker is concerned with measuring relationships without imposing external control over the situation. Nevertheless institutions may object to even the limited intrusions created by such research. In an experiment, as Simon explained in the extract in Chapter 2, the research worker is generally attempting to control the situation itself in some way. It is not difficult to see why experimental designs in education are uncommon. Attempts at persuading headteachers to change their school organisation or curriculum are unlikely to meet with much success. If experiments are to be done, either they must be done by the teachers themselves within the school, or there must be an exceptional case made out by the research worker; i.t.a. proved to be one such exceptional case.

Sir James Pitman's ideas for teaching reading through the use of a modified alphabet, which avoided mis-matches between sound and syllable, had a mixed reception from teachers, ranging from enthusiastic support to incredulous hostility. Many teachers who tried the alphabet found that it worked to their satisfaction, but some parents, and also local authorities and other teachers, were alarmed at its introduction. What was needed was an objective evaluation of its merits compared with the use of traditional orthography (t.o.). Much of the early research was conducted in London by John Downing at the Reading Research Unit. But although this was an objective evaluation, the initial results, which were favourable to i.t.a., were met with suspicion from some other research workers. In particular Vera Southgate criticised the interpretations put on to the results by Downing. The following article presents both answers to Southgate's criticisms and a description of the problems in arranging a field experiment. The article is reproduced in full except for the detailed results, school by school, which have been omitted.

*Some problems in evaluating i.t.a.: a second experiment*    (J. A. Downing and B. Jones, 1966)[1]

INTRODUCTION

'Almost invariably in a scientific investigation, when one sets out to confirm or confute some plausible theory, the result is seldom the plain straightforward "Yes" or "No" that cross-examining counsel loves to demand. Usually it appears that there are elements of truth in both the opposing views: and more often than not the most rewarding results are the discoveries made by the way. Fresh problems, quite unforeseen, nearly always emerge: new facts, quite unsuspected, are vividly brought to light.'

Thus Burt (1962) wrote about the Initial Teaching Alphabet (i.t.a.) experiment when it began in 1961. Now, four years later, we at the Reading Research Unit are in the thick of the 'new problems' which Burt predicted, and our first really detailed report on the original experiment is in the final stages of preparation.

Meanwhile a number of controversial articles have been written on the i.t.a. research, some favouring i.t.a., others against the new writing-system devised by Sir James Pitman (1961). Interim reports from the Reading Research Unit urged caution until more definitive reports could be published, and we have supported others who have suggested that, pending these reports, educators should defer final judgement on i.t.a.'s effectiveness in our schools. Sometimes, however, writers who have suggested that teachers should be cautious have themselves displayed a lack of caution. This paper attempts to clear up misconceptions which may have been created by Southgate's (1965) recent article. It also includes a report of a second experiment with i.t.a. which we began in 1963, in an attempt to extend control over certain incidental variables including some of those to which Southgate referred.

PROBLEMS OF EVALUATING i.t.a.

The title and purport of Southgate's article suggested that educators should be 'Approaching i.t.a. Results with Caution'— a view we endorse and have expressed repeatedly in our earlier

[1] The original article was published in *Educational Research* 8, 100–14.

publications on the i.t.a. research. We agree with Gans (1964) that:

'The i.t.a. approach is at its beginning. As yet there are not enough results from the experimentation going on to warrant the extravagant claims that are being made for it. Only broad and longitudinal evaluation which yields reliable conclusions can determine its permanent place in the teaching of reading.'

This 'broad and longitudinal evaluation' is being conducted by the Reading Research Unit, and the first definitive report of the large-scale experiment begun in September 1961 is currently being prepared for publication.

In 1968 it is planned to publish a similar report on the attainments of the same children after transfer from i.t.a. to traditional orthography (t.o.). Until these reports are available no conclusions can be regarded as based on adequate empirical research findings. Even then there will undoubtedly be many unanswered questions.

As Southgate very properly points out, 'sober appraisal of what the results of this project may mean' is very difficult when a detailed account of the experimental design and the actual procedure followed by the experimenters has not yet been published. Such an account of the design and method of the main i.t.a. experiment (not only what was attempted but what actually happened) will form a part of the report to be published in 1966. It is probably the absence of such a full report which has led Southgate to make several incomplete comments on the design and execution of our experiment.

Before discussing these, however, we should examine the unusual conceptual framework used by Southgate in her discussion of the various motivating forces which she believes may have influenced the results of the main experiment begun with i.t.a. in 1961. As well as the 'Hawthorne Effect' Southgate suggests that we should consider other possible sources of bias in reading experiments—including the 'Reading Drive', the effects of visitors to the experimental classes, and publicity for i.t.a.

Southgate's concept of a 'reading drive' is somewhat idiosyncratic: 'the main factor (accounting for results in the experimental classes) is the effects of what might be termed a 'drive' in the teaching of reading ... A reading drive is an extremely potent force.' A 'reading drive' is described in Southgate's article as follows:

'A reading drive is basically a new surge of inspiration through the teaching of a subject. It ferments in the teacher and bubbles over on to the children who are thrust forward on its

waves of enthusiasm. The drive is accompanied by an increase in interest, motivation and application which is inevitably followed by an improvement in attainments. A reading drive can stem from one ingredient or from a combination of many ingredients. These may include a new teacher
or head teacher, a new scheme or method, new books, new
apparatus, a new library, testing, recording, regrouping or
cross classification of children, lectures and discussion groups
for teachers.'

This is a popular use of 'drive' and differs from the use of the
word in its strictly technical psychological sense—e.g. a hunger
drive.

Even if this concept of reading drive were refined to permit its
consideration as a possible 'intervening variable' in reading research, a great deal of empirical work would need to be done to
determine the relative potency of the various ingredients listed
by Southgate. But instead of using a vague umbrella term it
would perhaps be more useful to differentiate the various motivational factors present in such teaching situations.

In her discussion of reading drive Southgate comments on
certain aspects of our original i.t.a. experiment. These comments
may prejudice rather than aid judgement since they are based
upon an inaccurate picture of what was actually done in the
course of our experiment. For example, Southgate claims that
'The provision of equipment differs for experimental and control
classes', and suggests that this difference entirely favoured the
experimental group: 'The experimental classes have been supplied with complete new *Janet and John* schemes, including
supplementary apparatus, all printed in i.t.a. They have also
received stocks of new books for the book corners.'

The truth about the provision of books and other materials
to experimental and control classes in our main experiment is
more complex than this. The 'Field Experiment' approach which
has been followed in our first main experiment requires the
maintenance of everyday-life conditions as far as is possible
within the limits imposed by the need for control of variables.
In order to keep close to the real-life classroom situation of
Britain it was decided to use the *Janet and John* series—the most
popular series of basic readers in this country. The experimental
classes had their *Janet and John* books printed in i.t.a. while the
control classes continued to use *Janet and John* books in traditional orthography (t.o.). In addition to the basic readers the
various items of teaching apparatus published with this series
were also produced in i.t.a. for the experimental classes.

In British infants' schools much emphasis is placed on the
importance of the Book Corner or classroom library, and it was

recognised from the outset that, if the experimental conditions were to be representative of the normal approach in this respect, it would be necessary to produce many books in i.t.a. for the Book Corner. It must be realized that the matching of the conditions in respect of materials fell short of the ideal in our *initial* experiment. The children in the i.t.a. classes were at a *dis-* advantage in respect of the shortage of supply of i.t.a. materials, and there were delays in supplying the schools with properly produced i.t.a. books for the library corner. To make good this shortage the Reading Research Unit duplicated sheets of i.t.a. text which the teachers pasted over the original t.o. printed pages.

The effect of this 'pasting-in' of i.t.a. pages into books which were often already fatigued can be imagined. On the other hand, the i.t.a. *Janet and John* books were new and fresh in the experimental classes, whereas in only some of the control classes were the t.o. *Janet and John* books new and fresh. Thus many control schools continued working with used copies of the t.o. *Janet and John* books. It is possible, to some extent at least, that these differences have balanced out. The i.t.a. classes had new and fresh basic readers but suffered from a restricted choice of Book Corner materials, many of which were of the improvized 'paste-in' variety. The t.o. classes often had 'tired' copies of the basal readers but had a much wider selection of materials for the Book Corner.

In accordance with our aim to make a 'Field Experiment' approach, we considered other aspects of the child's environment in respect of books. In order not to disturb normal conditions in the experimental group it was decided not to attempt to isolate children learning i.t.a. from their normal t.o. environment. If the teacher in the infants' classroom normally used reference books which could not be produced in i.t.a because of the cost, these remained in the classroom in their normal t.o. edition. Also, of course, children in the i.t.a. classes continued to meet t.o. at home and in the streets. From the point of view of the early learning stages the i.t.a. children were thus at a disadvantage because they did not have their classroom experiences reinforced to the same extent by experiences with printed English outside school. To offset this in some degree, i.t.a. materials were made available outside school for the experimental group in two ways. Public libraries in the locality kept a stock of i.t.a. books and headteachers arranged for parents to buy i.t.a. books for their children's birthdays and for Christmas.

Essentially, then, the difference between the experimental group and the control group was not one of a pure contrast between the former using i.t.a. materials and the latter using t.o. materials. Actually the situation was that the experimental group had experience of both i.t.a. and t.o. while the control group's experience was limited to t.o.

Probably the experimental group's experience of both i.t.a. and t.o. may have had an important effect on these children's ability to transfer from i.t.a. to t.o. at the later stage, but in judging the results of the earlier phase when the experimental group was using the i.t.a. basic series and being tested on i.t.a. tests, it must be taken into account that in the first two years of our initial experiment the i.t.a. children seem likely to have been at a disadvantage in terms of frequency of exposure to the letter and word forms they were learning. By the third year (1963), when over a hundred experimental i.t.a. schools had entered the research, the i.t.a. book situation had improved. Now, in 1965, a much greater variety of books is available in i.t.a. and it would be possible to provide a more adequate i.t.a. book environment for an experimental group (see, for example, the National Book League's list of i.t.a. books). However, in evaluating our main i.t.a. experiment it must be remembered that supplies of i.t.a books in 1961 and 1962 were very limited and improvization of the kind described above was necessary. Certainly it is misleading to suggest that the i.t.a. classes had a definite advantage in respect of the quality or quantity of books available.

A second issue raised in Southgate's article is the degree of success achieved in our unusual attempt to control the Hawthorne Effect in our main experiment. She states that: 'The experimental group of teachers attend regular monthly meetings to consider problems and discuss progress', but 'Few refresher courses have been provided for teachers in control schools nor have "regular meetings" been usual.'

Since i.t.a. was a highly novel approach, some features of which were a source of considerable misgiving to teachers and parents as well as the experimenters in 1961, we felt bound to keep a close watch on developments to safeguard the interests of the children. We tried, therefore, to hold meetings of the teachers of the i.t.a. experimental classes as often as possible at first in order to bring out in discussion any difficulties which they were experiencing. These difficulties turned out to be chiefly concerned with such matters as delays in supplying i.t.a. materials. These meetings of the experimental group teachers were conducted by a member of the Reading Research Unit and were generally held after school at a local centre. In 1961–62 when there were teething troubles in the administration of the experiment, the experimental group teachers had the opportunity of attending seven such meetings. In 1962–63, when the majority of schools in our research began the first year of their experimentation, the initial problems had been cleared up. It was, therefore, not necessary to meet so frequently and only three meetings were held.

Since then not more than two meetings each year have been provided.

In the design of this initial experiment it was recognized that while these meetings would be essential for the teachers using i.t.a., at the same time they might increase the Hawthorne Effect in this group although, of course, the importance of the Hawthorne Effect has yet to be demonstrated in educational research. Therefore, it was proposed that meetings of the control school teachers should also be held in an attempt to induce a similar increase in Hawthorne Effect (if any) in this group. It seems probable that these meetings of control group teachers have not been wholly matched in quality with those of the teachers using i.t.a. The purpose was obviously different. We tried, however, to show our concern for the teaching of reading in the control schools where t.o. was being used as usual. Each year a training college lecturer seconded to the Unit was given responsibility to meet this need to show special interest in the teachers in the control schools. Sometimes an outside speaker well-known as an expert in infants' school teaching methods was engaged to give an address followed by discussion. Sometimes the seconded training college lecturer conducted the meeting alone. For example, one series of control group meetings included an exhibition of the latest t.o. books and teaching apparatus for reading at the infants' school level, a lecture from the seconded training college lecturer and a discussion of children's books by the control group teachers.

These control group meetings were sometimes held in the afternoon, and in some cases lasted longer than the experimental group meetings. It seems inappropriate to attempt to compare these meetings of the two groups in terms of hours and minutes, but for the record we note that control meetings were held by the seconded training college lecturer on average twice each year, although these arrangements have not been uniformly successful. It seems fair, however, to suggest that although the experimental group leaders met rather more frequently, a reasonable demonstration of our interest in the work of the teachers in the control group was in fact provided.

After our main experiment had begun in 1961 we recognized that it would not be possible to control all of the many important factors in the experimental situation. We became concerned about two of the possible motivating influences noted by Southgate, i.e. visitors and publicity. Southgate comments that 'If equality of visitors and publicity was actually aimed at for experimental and control schools, it is doubtful whether this was achieved.' With this we agree, but it cannot be assumed that the presence of visitors is a tonic for teachers and children which automatically produces improvement in reading, because it could equally be a source of distraction and interference in the learning situation.

Large-scale experiments conducted in the normal social setting involve many complex problems of design, analysis and interpretation. These problems arise from the complexity of the educational situation in which there are many factors which are either known to affect attainment or which are believed to do so. Before giving a report on our second experiment we should first consider the incidental variables in research in i.t.a. By 'incidental variables' we mean all those factors which may affect reading attainment, other than the one being studied. We may distinguish between those incidental variables which are a normal part of the educational situation and those which are associated with the experiment.

The first group includes, for instance, intelligence and home background of the pupils, teacher ability, methods of teaching and class size. The second group of incidental variables includes all those which arise from the experiment itself or from incidental circumstances surrounding the experiment and which may produce motivational effects not normally a part of the educational situation. Such 'extrinsic' motivational effects would not persist when the experiment and its surrounding circumstances cease to operate, and so are not a normal part of the educational situation.

The Hawthorne Effect, to which reference has already been made, falls within this second group. 'Hawthorne Effect' may be defined as an improvement in performance consequent upon participation in an experiment and independent of any other factors. It is presumed to be mediated by motivational changes. In our research in i.t.a., experimental and control groups both participate in the experiment, and insofar as both have been treated in the same way, there is no reason to suppose that there are any differential Hawthorne Effects.

However, it is possible that other extrinsic motivational effects have been produced in the i.t.a. experiment. The launching of the i.t.a. research required the simultaneous introduction of a new writing-system, and this innovation aroused considerable interest in the press, on television and in educational circles. These two factors, newness and public interest, *could* have had an effect on the performance of the experimental children, operating through changes in their own level of motivation or, more likely, through that of their teachers and/or families. There may also have been 'compensating' effects on the control group.

Except perhaps under laboratory conditions, extrinsic effects arising from newness and public interest are virtually outside the control of the educational researcher. It has been suggested that these factors could be controlled by adding a second experimental group using a second new medium or method, but it is doubtful if another new method would be equal to i.t.a. either in terms of perceived newness or the amount of public interest aroused. Probably the only way in which further information could be obtained on this point would be to study results obtained over time—not the usual kind of longitudinal study of pupils but a longitudinal study of groups of children entering the experiment in successive years, it being plausible to assume that initial enthusiasm which it is claimed is aroused by newness and public interest is likely to diminish to vanishing point over the years.

In our original and main experiment begun in 1961 it is important to recognize that we have not had a free hand. We have always been dependent on teachers volunteering to join the experimental and control groups. At the beginning of the first experiment in 1961, the numbers of volunteers were small and as we were unable to use random sampling procedures, we attempted to establish experimental and control groups which were matched on certain school variables, which could be measured easily, i.e. size, urban/rural location, type of organization, pupil/teacher ratio, minimum age on entry, socio-economic level of the catchment area, and facilities of the school building.

We also attempted to match the two groups on certain pupil variables; age, sex, social class (as defined by father's occupation), Raven's Matrices score, Crichton Vocabulary score. All of the pupils were new entrants and they comprised the entire intake of a particular term or particular year depending on the size of the school. Experimental pupils began to learn to read with i.t.a., and control pupils with t.o. As we have indicated earlier in this paper, we tried to give equal attention to teachers and pupils in both groups, visiting schools of both types and holding research meetings for teachers in both groups, although our attempts were not entirely successful.

In brief, we were able to control or measure many of the variables which are a normal part of the educational situation. Others, including teacher variables and the less easily measured school variables, were not taken fully into account. Due to constraints beyond our control, we were unable to make any systematic assessment of teachers' attitudes or to deal very effectively with changes of attitude arising from certain extrinsic variables.

## AIMS AND DESIGNS OF THE SECOND
## EXPERIMENT WITH i.t.a.

Our concern about the differences in the experiences of experimental and control groups and the lack of control over the
teacher variable led us to launch a second i.t.a. experiment in
September 1963. This second i.t.a. experiment controlled some of
these incidental variables more rigorously than the earlier study
had done. According to the design of this second i.t.a. experiment
each participating school was to contain one experimental and
one control running in parallel. On admittance, pupils were to be
allocated randomly to these two classes, holding sex and age
distributions constant. The two class teachers thus involved were
to share their time between the classes in such a way that each
teacher spent half of her time with each class. One of the
teachers was to take the main responsibility for teaching reading
to both classes, to one class with i.t.a., and to the other with t.o.,
using the same methods and giving the same amount of time to
the teaching of reading with both classes. Both groups used the
same series of basic readers. The experimental classes used *Janet
and John* in i.t.a. while the control classes used *Janet and John* in
t.o. The second teacher would, of course, have to do some reading
work incidental to number and other activities but the reading
teacher was to deal with activities directly specific towards the
development of reading and writing skills. Both teachers were to
keep the work done with one class parallel, in broad terms, with
that done with the other class. This division of labour required
that the teachers should change classes frequently, daily intervals
being the largest that could be tolerated.

The advantage of this design is that most of the variables
normally associated with reading attainment are controlled.
School and pupil variables, in particular, are controlled
effectively. Some important teacher variables, such as ability to
teach reading and more general aspects of teaching ability
dependent upon personality factors, are also controlled. Interactions between teacher and social group (class) are not controlled, nor are variables which are necessarily related to the
writing-system. It may be that some teachers do best with i.t.a.
while others get better results with t.o., or that a given teacher
finds one class of children easier to teach than another. Neither
of these possibilities is taken into account in the design. However,
it seems unlikely that either of these effects would be as large as
the general factor of ability to teach reading. In other words, a
good teacher is likely to do well with either i.t.a. or t.o., though
she may do relatively better with one than the other. It seems
possible the teachers who have used i.t.a., after having been
trained to do so, may show a general improvement in their per-

formance as teachers of reading even when using t.o. However, the design of our second experiment ensures against a bias arising in this way also.

On the basis of this plan sixteen headteachers agreed, presumably after consultation with their teachers, to take part in the experiment and to allow all of their 1963/64 entrants to participate. Over the whole school year this yielded a sample of 548 experimental and 554 control pupils, excluding those who left before the end of the first term.

In practice there have been some deviations from the original plan as far as the teacher variable is concerned. From the beginning we doubted that we should be able to find teachers who would adopt a procedure which flew in the face of current infant school practice. Once we had recruited sufficient voluteers it soon became clear that it would be difficult to maintain control of the teacher variable as rigorously as had been intended.

Preliminary discussions with headteachers confirmed our own opinion that it would be necessary to delay the 50/50 pattern of sharing teachers until the pupils had settled in school. The decision as to when the 50/50 pattern should be put into operation had to be left to headteachers. In some cases this happened within a few days of the beginning of term, but at the other extreme two schools took six weeks to implement the 50/50 plan completely.

In addition, other circumstances and events such as shortage of staff, absence of research teachers and festivities have led to the suspension of the 50/50 pattern for varying periods of time. Many of the teachers have expressed a dislike of moving from one class to another and it is probably this rather than any other reason which has led to lapses in some of the schools ... (But only in two schools did the ratio deteriorate to less than a 40/60 balance of time between the classes.) ... The rest of this report refers only to the remaining thirteen schools.

Another point which was conceded in some schools was that for administrative purposes each teacher should be associated with only one class. In practice this has meant that a particular teacher always spends the first period of the day (usually about fifteen minutes) with one class and never with the other. During this period she takes registration and deals with other business. This procedure has been adopted by four of the thirteen schools.

It seems possible that departures from the 50/50 pattern as it was envisaged in the original design may have favoured the experimental group children using i.t.a. In schools where an imbalance existed it was always the reading teacher who spent most time with the experimental class, and in those cases where one teacher became associated with one class for administrative purposes it was always the reading teacher who became so associated with the experimental class.

Turning now to other variables which the design was intended to control, no significant differences between the total experimental and control groups have been found on any of the following pupil variables: age, sex, social class (as defined by father's occupation), intelligence, vocabulary, measured as in the earlier project. Indeed, the distributions of control and experimental groups on all of these variables were very similar, as one would have expected.

Each teacher had been asked to use the same methods of teaching and to give the same amount of time to the teaching of reading in both her experimental i.t.a. class and in her control class. They were frequently reminded of the necessity of complying with this request. Five out of twelve teachers said that they did phonic work earlier with the i.t.a. class than with the t.o. class, but this was not seen as a change of method, because it was said to be response to the children's interest and development. As such, it was regarded as an essential part of the method used with both classes.

Care was taken to accommodate parallel experimental and control classes in rooms with comparable facilities and to avoid similar class libraries. However, in three schools a shortage of i.t.a. books was experienced during the first half term. Although public libraries stocked i.t.a. books and parents were able to buy them, in general they were less readily available outside school than t.o. books were. Thus with regard to the supply of materials the t.o. classes appear to have had an advantage.

It had been suggested to us that the results might be contaminated if the control children were exposed to i.t.a. accidentally as might happen when experimental and control classes are situated in the same school. Consequently headteachers were asked to allow control children to enter experimental classrooms as little as possible. According to the teachers this has only happened very occasionally.

Steps were taken to reduce the differential operation of possible sources of motivation. When it was necessary to hold meetings for parents of experimental pupils to explain i.t.a. to them, parallel meetings were held for the parents of control pupils. Headteachers were requested to close the doors to visitors as far as possible and to make sure that those who could not be avoided were made to visit control as well as experimental classes. It is recognized that this does not guarantee that equal interests, approval, etc., was shown by visitors in both cases, any more than our meetings for parents ensure comparable attitudes on their part.

Outside agencies cannot be expected to be much concerned

with the problems of educational research and their interest has generally been focussed on i.t.a. and the activities of the experimental classes. This is true of articles in the national and local press. We were, however, able to a large extent to prevent publicity for the schools actually participating in this second experiment. But incidents which we did not anticipate have been brought to our attention. For instance, at the end of the first year headteachers received without our knowledge or consent, a mailed questionnaire concerning their opinions about i.t.a., which was heavily biased towards answers favourable to i.t.a.

As far as extrinsic motivational effects operating through the teachers are concerned, this second experiment, as compared with the earlier main experiment of 1961, presents a rather different context in which such effects might be felt. Whereas in the first project the experimental and control teachers were usually working in different schools, generally not coming into contact with one another, in the second project the role of experimental teacher and that of control teacher are combined in one person.

While this arrangement effectively controls the factor of teacher ability there are other possible consequences which need to be considered. When the same teacher takes both the experimental i.t.a. class and the control t.o. class, she is able to make immediate comparisons of the progress of the two classes she is teaching. If i.t.a. does permit an easier beginning, a 'spiritual' motivational effect may occur. Quicker progress in the i.t.a. class may produce positive attitudes in the teacher which enhance her work with i.t.a. Furthermore, she may become pessimistic about t.o., with a possible negative influence on her work in the control class.

Some evidence on this question is available from the questionnaires completed by the teachers at the end of the first year. Nine out of twelve reading teachers said, *in retrospect* that, at the beginning of the experiment, they were of the opinion that i.t.a. would be better than t.o. Two thought t.o. would be better and one said she had formed no opinion. 'Better' was taken to mean that the children would learn to read in t.o. more easily. Seven out of twelve teachers said that they had preferred teaching with i.t.a. One had preferred teaching with t.o. and four had no preference. Both of these items indicate that the majority of the teachers were biased in favour of the experimental i.t.a. group, by the end of the first year, if not earlier.

Ten out of the twelve teachers said that quite apart from their preference for the writing-system, they preferred teaching the experimental i.t.a. *class*. In other words, this preference is for a particular group of children rather than for a particular writing-system. Two teachers had no preference. The bias which appears to exist here is probably related to the special association which grew up between reading teachers and experimental i.t.a. classes which was described earlier. Nine of the teachers said that apart from the writing-system preferences, they found the experimental class easier to work with. Two had no preferences and one found the control class easier.

In an effort to counteract such expected preferences, teachers were reminded often of the need to give the two classes equal treatment and they may have succeeded in keeping their preferences covert. In considering this problem one should also take into account the possibility that any increase in motivation engendered by the i.t.a. teaching situation might spill over to the other in t.o. This seems to be true also of any improvement in teaching technique due, for example, to improved knowledge of the structure of English through experience with i.t.a.

The testing programme of this second experiment was the same as that used in the original main project. All of the testing was done by testers employed for that purpose. Testers were trained to give all tests, other than the Schonell Graded Word Reading Test for which they received mailed instructions only. The same tester tested both i.t.a. and t.o. groups within one school and the testing schedule was balanced to control time factors.

The chief object of the Reading Research Unit's experiments with i.t.a is to determine whether t.o. is an important cause of difficulty for children in the initial stages of learning to read. For this purpose i.t.a. is the representative for simplified writing and spelling systems which may be contrasted with the complex and irregular t.o. writing system. To test the hypothesis that t.o. is a cause of difficulty in beginning reading it is necessary to compare i.t.a. attainments with t.o. attainments. Therefore the pupils in the experimental group are tested in reading the i.t.a. which they are learning, and their results are compared with those obtained from testing in t.o. the control group pupils who are learning to read with t.o. This applied to the first three tests given (Schonell Graded Word Reading Test, given twice, and the Neale Analysis of Reading Ability, Form C).

After this *both* groups are tested in t.o. Although the chief concern in all our research on i.t.a. is the comparison of i.t.a. attainments of children learning to read with i.t.a. with t.o. attainments of children learning with t.o., we have also to investigate the practical problem of transfer from i.t.a. to t.o. when children have begun with i.t.a. The Neale tests in Form A represent a measure of the effectiveness of transfer from i.t.a. to t.o. in the experimental group. However, this measure is clearly premature because one month before the test was given only 17% of the experimental i.t.a. group had been transferred by their teachers to t.o. reading materials, but *the whole* of the i.t.a. group was tested *in t.o.* This study had not yet progressed far enough to provide useful data on this second question.

## RESULTS OF THE SECOND EXPERIMENT

(The detailed results presented in the original article led to the following conclusion.)

The chief trends which appear in the results of the second experiment are similar to those in the original experiment. Pupils beginning with i.t.a. make more rapid progress and achieve superior word-recognition, speed and comprehension scores in reading i.t.a. than do pupils learning and reading with t.o. However, the results obtained in this second study are by no means identical with previously analysed results from the original i.t.a. experiment which began in 1961. We have found that, in general, the differences between the experimental and control groups of the second experiment are smaller than those between the experimental and control groups of the original experiment. The scores of the experimental group of the second experiment tend to be lower than the scores of the experimental group of the original experiment. Preliminary analysis suggested that the same is true, though to a smaller extent, of the comparison between the two control groups. Nevertheless, although there are differences between the two experiments, and firmer conclusions must await a more detailed comparison of the results from them, this second i.t.a. experiment provides further, although still incomplete, evidence to support our previous tentative findings that t.o. represents a serious initial handicap to teachers and pupils engaged in the business of developing the basic skills of reading and writing in English-speaking countries.

## REFERENCES

BURT, C. (1962) Preface to DOWNING, J. *To be or not too bee.* London: Cassell.

DOWNING, J. A. (1964) *The i.t.a. Reading Experiment.* London: Evans Bros.

DOWNING, J. A. (1965) 'Current misconceptions about i.t.a.' *Elementary English*, May 1965, 492–501.

GANS, R. (1964) 'The initial teaching alphabet.' *Grade Teacher*, October 1964, 35 and 118.

NATIONAL BOOK LEAGUE (1965) *i.t.a. Books for the Teacher and the Child.* London: National Book League.

NEALE, M. (1963) *Neale Analysis of Reading Ability.* London: Macmillan.

O'DONNELL, M., and MUNRO, R. (1949) *Janet and John*. Welwyn: Nisbet.

PITMAN, I. J. (196) 'Learning to read: an experiment.' *Journal of Royal Society of Arts, 109,* 149–80.

SCHONELL, F. (1949) *Psychology and Teaching of Reading*. Edinburgh: Oliver & Boyd.

SOUTHGATE, V. (1965) Approaching i.t.a. results with caution.' *Educational Research, 7, 2.*

### ADDITIONAL REFERENCES

DOWNING, J. A. (1967) *The i.t.a. Symposium*. Slough: National Foundation for Educational Research.

WARBURTON, F. W., and SOUTHGATE, V. (1969) *i.t.a.: an Independent Evaluation*. London: Murray/Chambers.

*The evaluation of i.t.a. provides a particularly valuable example of a field experiment. But as can be seen from the methodological problems encountered by Downing, the realistic setting of field experiments carried out on a large scale makes the advantages of the experimental procedure less telling. In particular the research by Downing does not illustrate Simon's comments about the way in which an experimenter can control different variables in succession. Although it is difficult to alter classroom settings so as to control variables, it is possible to adopt a successive choice of variables in analysis and so approximate to an experimental design. In general, however, the practical difficulties in organising effective experimental situations have deterred research workers from making full use of this approach, and the majority of studies in research journals rely on the use of exploratory surveys with a consequent loss of information about causation.*

# 6 A Multi-Disciplinary Approach: Transfer to Secondary Education

*The previous two chapters have drawn attention to the many practical problems which may prevent a research design from being fully implemented. But how are the various steps in a research project decided in the first place? Chapter 2 discussed the initial steps of choosing between survey and experiment and reviewing previous empirical studies. In educational research the starting point is often a problem which arises either from practical difficulties in the classroom or from a wider educational setting. Whatever particular research design is chosen a systematic approach is crucial; every facet of the problem must be considered. In the same way as a detective in popular fiction builds up his case, piecing together the evidence, deciding where to look for clues or who to question, so the research worker has to examine his problem and decide what information to collect. One strand of evidence will convince no one. A network of interconnecting threads must be built up into a solution. All too often problems in education have been tackled with the help of just one of the contributory academic disciplines, such as history, philosophy, sociology or psychology. Increasingly it has become necessary to use multi-disciplinary inquiries; a single discipline provides only a blinkered view.*

*To show what is meant by a multi-disciplinary approach, an extract has been chosen for this chapter which reviews recent research on the transition from primary to secondary education. At what age should children transfer from primary to secondary school? In Scotland pupils transfer a year later than in England: is there any advantage or disadvantage in delaying the transition? Does the 'middle school' provide an appropriate solution? In primary schools, each class usually has its own teacher, but in secondary schools, there are specialist teachers for each subject: is the changeover in methods and organisation too abrupt? All these questions are inter-related, and at first sight they seem too complex to be answered by research. But as the extract in this chapter shows, a variety of approaches to the problem can bring the relevant evidence together; and though research may not provide a simple answer, it identifies and clarifies the issues on which judgement must be made.*

*The review of research which follows does not attempt to distinguish and identify the different styles of approach to the problem. These different styles are more sharply differentiated in the two reports of the five-year research project which is referred to in the reading. A brief outline of this project may help to high-light the successive stages of inquiry.*

*The starting point of the investigation was the difference in age of transfer between England and Scotland. How, and why, had this difference come about? Are the original reasons still valid, or is the current situation sufficiently different to warrant a change? These questions required a historical style of research. The decision to choose 11 plus as the age of transfer in England could be traced to the Hadow Report of 1926; the decision in Scotland was affected by quite different considerations; and neither set of reasons appears to carry much weight in present circumstances.*

*The case presented in the Hadow Report linked the age of transfer to secondary education with the age of onset of puberty. A review of more recent physiological evidence, together with a survey investigation into a possible link between physiological and intellectual development, showed that this argument was unsound. A more promising line of inquiry was the study of intellectual development, and this introduced the psychological aspect of the inquiry. An examination of American growth studies, in which groups of children had been studied throughout the whole period of childhood and adolescence, provided evidence of the continuity of mental development. Piagetian studies, which had identified stages in children's thinking, were also examined.*

*The final approach in this initial review of the problem was a comparative survey, although this is not mentioned in the extract later in this chapter. Wide varieties in the age of transfer were found in foreign countries. In Russia there was no transfer at all; children stayed at the same school until moving on into work or into vocational training. Elsewhere it was possible to point to systems with transfer at ages between 10 and 13. Indeed in several countries it had already been decided that there would be a transitional period during which primary approaches to teaching were gradually dropped and secondary education began.*

*Against this background of information, a follow-up study of a year-group of Scottish children was designed. Over a period of four years, two in the primary school and two in the secondary school, the progress of these children was recorded by tests and teachers' assessments, and relevant information about their home background and attitudes was also gathered. Here, too, a variety* of approaches was used: a survey of the opinions of headteachers in primary and secondary schools; a detailed statistical analysis of the performance records of the children over the four-year period; and an open-ended exploration of the children's own reports on their experiences during and after transfer.

A useful first step in a research project is to ask detailed questions of people who are familiar with the problem. Both primary and secondary headteachers were asked whether or not they thought the sharp break between primary and secondary school caused problems. The answers were rather contradictory; it appeared that transfer was too sudden for some children, but not for others. This is where research comes into its own. Precise questions can be formulated to which quantified answers can be sought. How many children are affected and what type of children suffer most under the existing arrangements? The research findings are again to be found in the reading which follows.

The final step was a field experiment. This attempt to find out what actually happened when transfer conditions changed was not part of the original research design. It was fortuitous, but nevertheless just what was required to complete the evidence. Had we approached the local authority and asked to conduct an experiment of this kind, there would have been no chance at all of acceptance. Changing the whole transfer procedure for even a single school would have been unthinkable—at least at our behest: and rightly so. Such a decision rests firmly with the school itself, its headteacher and governors, and the local authority. As it happened one headteacher decided to change his transfer procedure, partly as a result of our research activity. His school had been involved in a pilot study in which we tried out an essay concerned with pupils' experiences on entering secondary school. The headteacher read these essays and found them disturbing. Not only did he change his procedure, but he asked us to evaluate the effect. Serendipity—capitalising on a chance event—has always played a large part in scientific progress. In this study it provided an ideal conclusion.

The reading which follows describes the Aberdeen project in more detail. It is intended to bring out the two main aspects of research methodology which have been mentioned in this introduction. In education a multi-disciplinary attack on a problem is often crucial, but even using this approach there may still be no straightforward answer to the question posed. Again, within a single discipline it is usually best to approach a problem on a variety of fronts. It is always more convincing to be able to argue from different types of evidence, particularly if these seem to be converging on a single conclusion.

*Transfer from Primary to Secondary Education*
(J. D. Nisbet and N. J. Entwistle, 1970)[1]

### HISTORICAL ANALYSIS AND REVIEW OF THE LITERATURE

The historical analysis traced the origin of the 11+ as the age of transfer to a distinction between primary and secondary education made in the Hadow Report on *The Education of the Adolescent* (Board of Education, 1926). There, primary education was stated to be the 'education of childhood'; secondary education was seen to be the 'education of adolescence'. This clear but simplified distinction has been as misleading as it has been influential in linking transfer to onset of puberty. A famous paragraph in the introduction to the report states the argument.

'There is a tide which begins to rise in the veins of youth at the age of eleven or twelve. It is called by the name of adolescence. If that tide can be taken at the flood, and a new voyage begun in the strength and along the flow of its current, we think that it will "move on to fortune". We therefore propose that all children should be transferred at the age of eleven or twelve...'

Since 1926 much of the thinking about the transfer to secondary education has accepted two of the assumptions contained in that paragraph. First that adolescence begins at the age 11 plus and secondly that it occurs at the same age for all children. Tanner's evidence (1961, 1962) destroyed both assumptions. His data on onset of menarche drawn from the records kept in various countries suggest than in 1926 girls in Britain were likely to have reached adolescence, on average, at about the age of $14\frac{1}{2}$ —not at 11 plus. Since then there has been a secular trend towards earlier puberty, but even so 11 plus would still not be the average age. Beyond this, Tanner's evidence shows that the range of individual differences is far too great to allow us to fix any generally applicable age of transfer on this basis. Further discussion on this topic can be found in the Plowden Report (Department of Education and Science, 1967).

Sexual maturity is clearly not the most important criterion for determining an age of transfer. Secondary education emphasises the systematic treatment of topics, perhaps implying that a new stage of mental development has been reached. The secondary school approach to the curriculum certainly seems to

[1] Adapted from a chapter in Butcher, H. J., and Pont, H. B., *Educational Research in Britain, Volume 2* (University of London Press).

assume that some fundamental change in the thinking processes of pupils occurs at present around the age of eleven or twelve. Again previous research findings can be used to test this assumption.

First, is there a discontinuity in mental development at this time? The growth studies in the United States which included individual tests or group tests of intelligence found no such discontinuity. On the contrary, the curves of mental development drawn from the data collected in these investigations indicated continuous growth from the ages of six to eighteen (Bayley, 1949; Dearborn and Rothney, 1941; Ebert and Simmons, 1943; Freeman and Flory, 1937; Shuttleworth, 1939). Bloom (1964) reanalysed Bayley's data and showed that correlations between intelligence at the time of testing and intelligence measured at maturity increase smoothly with age before reaching a maximum value in early adolescence. British follow-up studies provide partial confirmation of this finding (Entwistle, 1967; France, 1964).

An alternative approach to the problem of discontinuity is connected with the emergence of special abilities. Early factor analysis of batteries of intellectual tests showed certain special abilities. There was some evidence that a crystallization of special abilities from the general factor 'g' occurred during early adolescence, but Vernon (1950) concludes that changes in the factor structure of abilities cannot be dissociated from the educational experiences provided for children. The results of factor analysis in this instance may only serve to remind us of the different approaches to teaching used by primary schools and secondary schools. Analyses of data from surveys must inevitably reflect the influences already present; experimental studies provide more fruitful possibilities and lead to the second part of this problem.

Even if there is no evidence of a discontinuity in over-all mental development around the age of twelve, there may still be qualitative changes in children's thought processes at this time. Piaget's work, viewed in a simple-minded way, suggests such a possibility. At eleven there is supposed to be a change from 'concrete operations' to 'formal operations' (Butcher, 1968). British replications of Piaget's work confirm, in general, children's development through definite stages (Lunzer, 1961; Wallace, 1965), but there is considerable doubt about the age ranges attached to these stages (Berlyne, 1957). Peel (1959) suggests that the emergence of formal operations depends more upon the child's mental age than his chronological age. There even seems to be doubt whether children of average intelligence ever completely reach this stage of formal operations (Hebron, 1966). This rather pessimistic view can be countered by Bruner's emphasis

(1960, 1966) on the importance of teaching method in influencing conceptual development. It also seems that the stage of formal operations may be reached at different ages in different subjects, depending possibly on both the method of teaching and the complexity of the concepts being taught.

The psychological evidence thus suggests no justification for sudden changes in teaching method at age eleven or at any other age. Quite the reverse appears to be true. There would seem to be a need to emphasize continuity of educational treatment. In practice children face considerable changes in teaching methods as they move from primary to secondary schools.

### THE FOLLOW-UP STUDY

Blyth (1965) has presented a clear picture of some of the adjustments eleven-year-olds have to make when they enter the secondary schools. From being the senior members of a small school, they become the most junior members of a much larger, mainly adolescent, community. Physically the secondary school is usually much larger and can be awe-inspiring. The teaching methods tend to be subject-centred and the first-years face the change-over from a class teacher to several subject specialists. Blyth has also commented graphically on the present tendency by both teachers and administrators to concentrate their interest on either the primary or the secondary sector of education. Until recently there has been little interest in whether primary and secondary education should be made to match.

'It is deplorable that so little opportunity is normally encouraged for teachers in primary and secondary schools to understand and appreciate each other's work ... All too often, primary and secondary teachers live in mutual suspicion rather than mutual respect ... Rites of passage in pre-literate societies are, after all, carried out before the faces of the elders of the tribe, rather than in a gap between two groups of elders facing in opposite directions' (pages 144-5).

The differences between primary and secondary schools and this lack of communication between teachers in the two types of school might well cause problems for children at transfer. But do children actually report difficulties in adjusting to the new environment of secondary school?

The follow-up study in Aberdeen (Nisbet and Entwistle, 1966, 1969) attempted to answer this question by using several different approaches. The main analysis was based on data obtained from a five-year follow-up of 3,000 children—the complete year group in both education authority and independent schools. Besides using a large number of psychological tests, the children were also asked to write essays describing their experiences at transfer. But the first step was to ask headteachers to comment on the arrangements for transfer. The replies showed a wide range in opinion, between the extremes quoted below.

'The sharp division between primary and secondary which exists at present imposes a severe strain on some pupils— probably more than we realize—and provides for not a few a traumatic experience from which they hardly recover.'

'I found that, while the sudden switch upset one or two, the vast majority, irrespective of ability, liked it. It was a stimulant. Youngsters who came up with rather unflattering reports about their attitude to work ... became revitalized' (Nisbet and Entwistle, 1966, page 81).

The views of the first of these two headteachers suggests that sudden changes at transfer will affect some children. But what proportion of the children are affected? An analysis of the essays written by the children helped to answer this question. Murdoch (1966) analysed a sample of 552 essays in which the children had described their experiences in secondary school compared with their primary school. The essays provided only a subjective and retrospective impression of the children's reactions to transfer, but it was possible to estimate that as many as 57 per cent of the boys and 64 per cent of the girls had experienced identifiable problems in adjustment. After six weeks or more in secondary school 80 per cent of the sample preferred their present school to primary school, suggesting that the 'trauma' is not severe for a large majority of children.

The difference in headteachers' opinion of transfer also highlights another problem. Which particular children suffer under the present system? The follow-up study provided some answers. Correlations between various test scores and attainment in secondary school are shown in Table 6:1. With certain variables, such as socio-economic rating and parental encouragement, there is a clear increase in the strength of the relationship with school attainment between primary and secondary school.

A factor analysis of the full correlational matrix yielded three factors: an intellectual factor (v:ed) and two non-intellectual factors. One of the non-intellectual factors distinguished between attainment in the secondary school and earlier attainment. The non-intellectual variables which showed high loadings on this factor, included 'academic motivation', 'parental encouragement', 'socio-economic rating' and 'ambition'. After

TABLE 6:1   *Correlation with attainment*

Boys (N = 1,293)

| Test | School | Primary | | Secondary | |
|------|--------|---------|---|-----------|---|
| | Age | 11 | 12 | 13 | 14 |
| Academic motivation | 13 | 0·386 | 0·412 | 0·502 | 0·480 |
| Neuroticism | 13 | −0·133 | −0·126 | −0·148 | −0·150 |
| Attitude to work | 12 | 0·677 | 0·703 | 0·696 | 0·696 |
| Parental encouragement | 12 | 0·571 | 0·577 | 0·603 | 0·612 |
| Social maturity | 12 | 0·443 | 0·444 | 0·417 | 0·405 |
| Ambition | 12 | 0·438 | 0·459 | 0·460 | 0·451 |
| Socio-economic rating | 10 | 0·287 | 0·285 | 0·308 | 0·323 |

Girls (N = 1,245)

| Test | School | Primary | | Secondary | |
|------|--------|---------|---|-----------|---|
| | Age | 11 | 12 | 13 | 14 |
| Academic motivation | 13 | 0·352 | 0·361 | 0·418 | 0·428 |
| Neuroticism | 13 | −0·139 | −0·171 | −0·196 | −0·198 |
| Attitude to work | 12 | 0·711 | 0·707 | 0·700 | 0·704 |
| Parental encouragement | 12 | 0·573 | 0·573 | 0·586 | 0·588 |
| Social maturity | 12 | 0·503 | 0·504 | 0·498 | 0·493 |
| Ambition | 12 | 0·407 | 0·413 | 0·402 | 0·418 |
| Socio-economic rating | 10 | 0·288 | 0·276 | 0·310 | 0·325 |

similar analyses of related data on social background it was possible to paint an impressionistic pen-picture of a child who might be expected to deteriorate in attainment after entering the secondary school.

'Transfer, under existing conditions, may adversely affect the attainment of the working-class child, especially one in the younger half of the age group, whose poorly educated parents fail to give him the right sort of encouragement and cannot appreciate the need for a quiet place to study. The lack of ambition and poor attitude to work in the primary school will be paralleled by low academic motivation after transfer. Also associated with decreasing school achievement will be lower social maturity and a higher level of neuroticism' (Nisbet and Entwistle, 1969, page 84).

In essays written by the children their reactions to transfer are often made painfully clear.

On the day that I was to start secondary school I awoke early. I was a little worried but ... I told myself that I would just have to like it, as I had to stay ...

Before the bell rang my chum and I went around the playground without anything to do ... hoping someone would ask us to join in, in a game, but no-one did ... I now know what is like to be youngest in a school—my brother now expects me to call him 'Sir' . . . It's like being a little fish in a big pond, whereas you were a big fish in your primary school . . .

I was quite scared, it was not what I had expected, it was huge compared to the last school I attended and it was awful old looking . . . My primary school had one corridor and one flight of stairs and this has so many corridors and flights of stairs I didn't know whether I was coming or going . . . As I walked into the classroom I suddenly took fright. I really felt lost. My heart was nearly tearing my ribs apart and I wished that I could run from the fear inside me . . .

Primary schooling had been a very sheltered life with the teacher you knew so well and could understand children's feelings about school life . . . A teacher for every subject was puzzling because you had to remember their name and the subject they taught you . . . Sometimes I wish I was back at primary school, but life must go on . . .

When I got home, everybody asked how you got on at school. You couldn't say 'It was horrible', so you had to say 'Yes, I like it' (Nisbet and Entwistle, 1969, pages 85–7).

### CHANGES IN THE TRANSFER OF PROCEDURE

The follow-up study provided evidence from a variety of sources that some children react adversely to sudden changes at transfer. But what would happen to children's attitudes, if attempts were made to smooth the transition? While the follow-up study in Aberdeen was in progress one headteacher who had been associated with the project decided to change the transfer procedure and the first-year teaching in his school. Children from the feeding primary schools came to the secondary school during the term prior to transfer. Teachers showed the children round the school and invited them to attend school functions, such as sports day and open day, during the summer term. The first-year classes were also unstreamed and project work was introduced into blocked periods giving pupils the same teacher for a considerable proportion of the week. It was possible to compare essays about transfer written by sixty children who entered this school in 1965 under the traditional system, with a matched group coming into the modified system two years later. Philip (1968) found that children in the 1967 intake had significantly more favourable attitudes towards secondary school than had children who had experienced the previous arrangements (see Table 6:2). The improvement in attitudes was most marked among children from the lower social classes.

TABLE 6:2   *Differences in level of adjustment to secondary school for different intakes*

|        | Level of adjustment | | | | | | |
|--------|------|------|------|-----|------|------|------|
| Intake | Good | Fair | Poor | N   | G %  | F %  | P %  |
| 1967   | 53   | 4    | 3    | 60  | 88·3 | 6·7  | 5·0  |
| 1965   | 40   | 15   | 5    | 60  | 66·7 | 25·0 | 8·3  |

$$\chi^2 = 6·88 \qquad p < 0·01$$

This finding links up with the evidence discussed in the previous section which showed that children from working-class families tended to deteriorate in their school attainment immediately after transfer. It was not possible to assess separately the effectiveness of the various changes introduced into the transfer procedures at this school, but the children's comments gave the impression that the introduction of group project work was a powerful influence in improving their attitudes.

Other experiments have been carried out in various parts of the country which have aimed at modifying both the transfer procedure and the teaching methods in the first years of secondary school. It would be interesting to know if there have been similar attempts to measure the effectiveness of these changes.

REFERENCES

BAYLEY, N. (1949) 'Consistency and variability in the growth of intelligence from birth to eighteen years.' *J. genet. Psychol.*, 75, 165–96.

BERLYNE, D. E. (1957) 'Recent development in Piaget's work.' *Br. J. educ. Psychol.*, 27, 1–12.

BLOOM, B. S. (1964) *Stability and Change in Human Characteristics.* New York : Wiley.

BLYTH, W. A. L. (1965) *English Primary Education.* 2 vols. London : Routledge and Kegan Paul.

BOARD OF EDUCATION (1926) *The Education of the Adolescent.* Report of the Consultative Committee (The Hadow Report). London : H.M. Stationery Office.

BRUNER, J. S. (1960) *The Process of Education.* Cambridge, Mass : Harvard University Press.

BRUNER, J. S. (1966) *Towards a Theory of Instruction.* Cambridge, Mass : Harvard University Press.

BUTCHER, H. J. (1968) *Human Intelligence.* London : Methuen.

DEARBORN, W. F., and ROTHNEY, J. (1941) *Predicting the Child's Development.* Cambridge, Mass : Sci-Art Publishers.

DEPARTMENT OF EDUCATION AND SCIENCE (1967) *Children and their Primary Schools* (The Plowden Report). 2 vols. London : H.M. Stationery Office.

EBERT, E., and SIMMONS, K. (1943) 'The Brush Foundation study of child growth and development.' *Monographs of Soc. for Res. Child Dev.*, 8, no. 2.

ENTWISTLE, N. J. (1967) *The Transition to Secondary Education*. Unpublished Ph.D thesis, University of Aberdeen.

FRANCE, N. (1964) 'The use of group tests of ability and attainment: a follow-up study from primary to secondary school.' *Br. J. educ. Psychol.*, 34, 19–33.

FREEMAN, F. N., and FLORY, C. D. (1937) 'Growth of intellectual ability as measured by repeated tests.' *Monographs of Soc. for Res. Child. Dev.*, 2, no. 2.

HEBRON, M. E. (1966) *Motivated Learning*. London: Methuen.

LUNZER, E. A. (1961) *Recent Studies in Britain Based on the Work of Jean Piaget*. Slough: National Foundation for Educational Research.

MURDOCH, W. F. (1966) *The Effect of Transfer on the Level of Children's Adjustment to School*. Unpublished M.Ed. thesis, University of Aberdeen.

NISBET, J. D., and ENTWISTLE, N. J. (1966) *The Age of Transfer to Secondary Education*. Scottish Council for Research in Education. Publication 53. London: University of London Press.

NISBET, J. D., and ENTWISTLE, N. J. (1969) *The Transition to Secondary Education*. Scottish Council for Research in Education. Publication 59. London: University of London Press.

PEEL, E. A. (1959) 'Children's perception and thinking.' *Br. J. educ. Psychol.*, 29, 95–101.

PHILIP, L. (1968) *The Effect of Changes in the Traditional Transfer Procedure on Children's Adjustment to Secondary School*. Unpublished M.Ed. thesis, University of Aberdeen.

SHUTTLEWORTH, F. D. (1939) 'The physical and mental growth of boys and girls age 6 to 19 in relation to age at maximum growth.' *Monographs of Soc. Res. Child Dev.*, 4, no. 3.

TANNER, J. M. (1961) *Education and Physical Growth*. London: University of London Press.

TANNER, J. M. (1962) *Growth at Adolescence*. 2nd edition. Oxford: Blackwell.

VERNON, P. E. (1950) *The Structure of Human Abilities*. London: Methuen.

WALLACE, J. G. (1965) *Concept Growth and the Education of the Child*. Slough: National Foundation for Educational Research.

# PART TWO
## Summaries of Typical Research Studies

# 7 Home Environment and the School

There are not many areas in educational research where a direct link can be established between research findings and government policy. But influence of research on both sides of the Atlantic into home environment and scholastic attainment has been considerable. Certainly, large outlays of public money and significant policy changes have followed the publicity given to these research reports. Project 'Head Start' in the USA and the establishment of educational priority areas in Britain may be seen as the practical outcome of many years of research effort. In research on the influence of home environment, one of the methods commonly used is the interview. The procedures for designing interview schedules and questionnaires have been described in Educational Research Methods; the present aim is to show these techniques being applied to a particular research area. The emphasis here, and in succeeding chapters, is partly on the method of measurement and partly on the results which have been obtained in typical studies.

Three major surveys have been chosen to illustrate different approaches to this research area. The first was carried out by E. D. Fraser in Aberdeen. This work was one of the first British studies to probe beneath the global variable of 'father's occupation' and to isolate important underlying cultural and attitudinal dimensions. The reading which is taken from Fraser's book Home Environment and the School is particularly useful for the way in which the underlying rationale of the research design is explained and practical difficulties are openly discussed.

The second study presents part of the cross-sectional survey conducted to provide empirical evidence for the Plowden Committee. In this investigation detailed descriptions of parental circumstances were collected by interview and put together as scales of attitudes and 'circumstances'. The analysis of these variables attempted to look in a statistically sophisticated manner at the values and attitudes underlying social class differences.

The final extract presents some of the findings from the sur-
D

*vey conducted by J. W. B. Douglas and his colleagues, which has already been mentioned in Chapter 3. The main strength of this study was the long time-span of this follow-up study. The sample was identified soon after the children had been born; in the book from which the extract is taken,* All Our Future, *results relate to school attainment at ages 15 and 16; and contact has been maintained as the children in the sample have moved into higher education or employment. Taken together the three studies present a persuasive demonstration of the influence of home environment on school attainment.*

## Home Environment and the School
(E. D. Fraser, 1969)[1]

### GENERAL PLAN

The general aim of the investigation was to discover whether any relationship exists, beyond that which can be attributed to intelligence, between factors in the home environment of the child and his progress in school. A secondary aim was to ascertain, if such a relationship were found, which factors in the home environment contributed most to it.

The plan of the research was, in essence, quite straightforward : to choose a sample of children who were representative of a wider population (in this case Aberdeen school children) and to obtain for each child :

    *a.*   intelligence test results,
    *b.*   information on his home environment,
    *c.*   a measure of his school progress;

then, by appropriate statistical treatment of the data to discover whether environmental factors were related to school progress in greater degree than one might expect as a result of the common factor of intelligence ...

Six schools were eventually found which provided a sample of 470 children, whose average IQ was almost exactly the same as the average of the total age-group, who covered the same range of IQ, and whose social status rating was also closely comparable with that of the whole age-group ... The sample was somewhat depleted ..., but on a final group of 408 children, information was available on three main counts, intelligence test results, home environment and school progress, and this group proved

[1] Edited extracts from *Home Environment and the School* (Scottish Council for Research in Education Publication 43) (University of London Press), pages 20, 23, 29–35 and 41–72.

to be no less representative of the whole age-group than the original sample of 470.

(Intelligence test scores were obtained as part of the normal selection procedure when the children were aged twelve years and school progress was assessed in the following year from examination marks carefully scaled to allow comparisons between schools.)

### ASSESSMENT OF HOME ENVIRONMENT

One important problem was how to obtain the required information on home background. There were three possible ways of doing this : one was to ask the children to provide it : the second was to send a questionnaire to the parents; and the third was by means of a personal visit to the homes. From every point of view (except the time involved) a visit to the home was desirable.

Questions put to the children would have had to be severely restricted, information provided by them was likely to be unreliable, and only a very superficial assessment of the home would have been possible by this method.

The questionnaire method was likely to prove just as unsatisfactory. Inevitably there would have been considerable wastage—questionnaires not returned, returned incomplete, or inaccurately completed—and the analysis of data would have been extremely untidy. Further, both the wastage and the unreliability were likely to be unequally distributed throughout the sample; a few parents proved later to be on or below the illiteracy borderline and would have been incapable of reading the questions, far less able to answer them in writing.[1] Some correction for this differential wastage would have been necessary, and the original sample would have been much reduced.

Lastly, there were some questions which could be asked and some information which could be gleaned in an interview that would have been impossible to obtain through a questionnaire. In particular, assessment of the emotional atmosphere of the home required a careful and tactful approach; in an interview it is possible to lead up gradually to questions of family relationships, parental harmony and the like, and to gauge the most propitious time for broaching the subject; a bald question in a questionnaire is quite a different matter and would either have aroused antagonism or have had to be omitted.

[1] One mother when asked in the interview how many children she had replied, 'About five'. The lack of certainty implied by her answer led to a detailed probe and she finally gave the names of ten with information about their schooling and employment. A further check on this information proved the latter estimate to be the correct one.

The visit to the home was therefore decided upon, and the approval of the Director of Education was sought, since the addresses of the children were to be provided by the schools. This approval was granted.

## CHOICE OF INTERVIEW QUESTIONS

The main principle governing the choice of questions to be asked in the interview was that the information obtained should be factual, objective and as free from interviewer bias and prejudice as possible. Since the interviews were all to be conducted by one person, the question of variation between interviewers did not arise; but it would be surprising if, in the course of over 400 home visits conducted at all times of the day and evening and in all weathers, no variations occurred in the mood and temper of the one interviewer. If subjective impression had been allowed too much weight in assessing the home environment, this factor might have reduced considerably the reliability of the assessment. Moreover, the usual 'halo effect' would have tended to increase the correlations between the separate items on the interview form. Space was accordingly left at the end of the form for the interviewer to note general opinions and impressions of the home atmosphere. These data were later coded separately. During the interview, the information provided by the parents and by direct observation was recorded on the interview schedule in the raw form in which it was given, and coding of the data was not begun until all the home visits were completed. The data obtained can be classified under four main headings.

a. *Cultural.*    Information in this category concerns such factors as the educational level of the parents, the books in the home, the reading habits of the parents, and their leisure interests.

b. *Material and Economic.*    Into this category fall data on income of parents and of siblings, and general living conditions as measured by the number of rooms in the home in relation to the number of persons sharing them.

c. *Motivational.*    In this category the relevant items are those concerned with the parents' attitudes towards the child's educational progress and future employment, and the encouragement the parents give him in his schoolwork.

d. *Emotional.*    In this category the relevant information comprises the degree of harmony in the home, the emotional security of the child, and the interest taken by the parents in the child's general welfare.

Considerable overlap inevitably occurs between these main divisions, but some attempt was made to sample specifically all four types of environment.

The order in which the items appear on the interview form was determined by the course which the interview was expected to follow, so that recording of the information should be as unobtrusive as possible and not interrupted by continual turning over of the form. Frequently when the parent (who was usually the mother) had clearly forgotten that she was being 'interviewed' and was relating with considerable frankness her family and marital problems, the recording of the information was delayed until immediately after the interview in order not to 'break the spell'.

The amount of information asked for was limited by the time factor. It was decided that, on average, the interview should require not more than 30 minutes to complete, in order not to weary the parents and to keep within reasonable limits the time to be spent on the home visits. Many interviews were over in 20 minutes, but a considerable number extended far beyond the 30-minute limit, though not always at the wish of the interviewer; only one or two of all the parents interviewed became restive before the end of the interview.

Three points of procedure were decided before the home visits began. One was that if the parents showed themselves reluctant to reveal their income, no further questions should be asked about it. The second was that the approach to the delicate question of parental harmony should be indirect and as tactful as possible. Occasionally in the case of divorced or separated parents the information emerged naturally out of questions about the number of persons living in the home or about family income. Sometimes the mother or father volunteered information on family problems and discussed them openly, frequently at length. Usually, however, when the mother was being asked, for example, about the future of the child, a question such as 'Does your husband agree with you on this?' or 'What job does *he* want the boy to have?' elicited some information on the relationship between the parents. Information obtained in this way was, however, always relegated to the 'Impression' section.

The last decision was that information obtained about the home other than in the course of the interview should not be used. In some schools head teachers kept dossiers for the children containing information about the family background which might have had a bearing on the child's school progress. Not all teachers did this, and it was felt that the use of such dossiers would introduce a serious uncontrolled variable. The children for whom this information was available were those who had, because of poor progress, or misdemeanour or for some such reason, attracted the attention of the head teacher. They were likely to be a selected group as far as school attainment was concerned and the use of additional information on them, obtained over a period of months or years, might have biassed the results. These dossiers were therefore not consulted, nor were records of the Children's Welfare Department, the Juvenile Court, or other similar bodies.

### THE HOME VISITS

The time taken to visit the homes of all the children in the sample was far in excess of what had been estimated. At first it was thought that an average of seven or eight visits a day might be possible but it soon became clear that the completion of eight interviews a day was to be regarded as a rare event and the probability of its being repeated extremely low.

There were several reasons for the very slow rate of progress. The times of day when it was politic to visit homes unannounced were limited; 9.15 a.m. was regarded as the earliest hour, since the chances of a favourable reception were not likely to be high while children were still being hurried off to school. Mealtimes were also avoided; the time of the midday meal ranged from noon until 1.30 p.m. or later, and the children did not go back to school until 2 p.m.; the evening meal often began at 5.30, so that the effective time available for interviews during the day was restricted to about three hours in the morning and three in the afternoon. The allowance of some time for locating the homes and for moving from one to another reduced even further the effective interview time.

Visits were made in the evening only as a last resort, if both parents were at work during the day, or if repeated visits in morning or afternoon had proved fruitless; the difficulties of locating homes were increased by darkness; and other hazards, such as unlighted tenement stairs with an occasional step missing, had to be faced.

Much more important as a cause of delay, however, was the number of wasted visits. Over and over again the home was located and visited only to be found empty—the mother was out shopping or visiting friends—and another attempt had to be made. Frequently five, six or more attempts were necessary before contact was finally made. Most frustrating of all were the attempts to locate families who had recently changed their addresses. The investigation took place at a time when new housing areas were mushrooming all around the city (and when, incidentally, no adequate bus service had been organised to serve them). Many of the families concerned had moved from the centre of the city to one or other of these housing areas, and locating them was no simple matter. A housing area in its very early days appears to have no shape or pattern; it is a collection of identical houses dropped in groups here and there in the middle of a sea of mud and clay; streets do not exist or, if they do, have no name; a house has a number, but the series to which it belongs is obscure; and neighbours do not know one another, for they have just congregated from all parts of the city. Experience showed that the best solution was to arrange the time of one's arrival in the district to coincide with that of the postman, and to make use of his superior local knowledge. Occasionally, even he was at a loss.

Each change of address meant therefore a wasted journey to the old address, a visit to the Education Office to discover the new one (since the child had moved to a new school) and a fresh attempt to find the new address. To avoid disturbing the Education Office staff too frequently, the usual procedure was to wait until several new addresses were required; in one or two cases the family had in the interval moved back from the new housing area to the city, and a fresh start had to be made.

As the home visiting progressed, the law of diminishing returns began to operate; the remaining homes became more and more scattered over the city, and, when only twenty or thirty were left, whole days went by without a single contact.

Once contact was made, however, it was found that the vast majority of parents were extremely co-operative and ready to answer most of the questions asked. In only eight cases, out of the 435 where the parent was seen, was an interview refused. Very often it seemed that the mother, instead of resenting interruption of her work or intrusion into her family affairs, was only too glad to break off from washing or polishing, to talk for half an hour (or longer) about herself and her family. All but a very few were willing to provide the information asked for, and many were only too willing to volunteer a great deal of quite irrelevant information; the difficulty then lay not in extracting the necessary data but in stopping the flow of confidences and in making a not too abrupt departure.

One surprising feature of the interviews was the lack of curiosity shown by the majority of parents about the purpose of the visit. No doubt in these days of market-research and opinion surveys the public is highly survey-conscious and sophisticated in these matters. Nevertheless, it seemed odd that a complete stranger should be admitted into the home, should ask for and obtain information about the private life of the family, without generally being asked to say why the information was wanted and without being required to produce credentials of any kind.

The variety of home background covered by the sample was

enormous, ranging from the wealthy, cultured home where the child was given every facility for reading, for study, and for developing hobbies and outside interests, to the home where mere existence was the immediate problem. The physical conditions in which some families lived were unbelievably sordid. One mother with two illegitimate children, a boy of thirteen and a girl of three, lived in a tiny room at the top of a stairway which, even in broad daylight, was pitch dark; the door into the room could not be shut, having no knob or lock, but was hooked by a piece of string to a nail in the doorpost; the floor, which sagged alarmingly in places, was covered with sacks; and one wall, completely innocent of plaster, ran with damp and rain. The mother and girl slept in an unsavoury-looking bed in one corner of the room, and the boy in a truckle-bed on the floor in the other. Washing facilities appeared not to exist, at least in that room, yet the boy (whose IQ was 118) seemed surprisingly clean, with face shining and hair well combed. The same could not be said of his mother.

Some of the worst home environments were to be found in what had once been a Government-owned block of buildings, but was now used to house families who had difficulty in obtaining other accommodation, chiefly because they rarely paid any rent. Here were congregated men and women who were frequently in trouble with the police; breaches of the peace and drunken brawls were common events, and the living conditions, apart from the moral atmosphere, far from satisfactory. One family to one room was the general rule, and although the room was fairly large, to quote Burt, 'decency was difficult, delicacy impossible'.[1] Conditions as extreme as these were nevertheless relatively rare, and although overcrowding was a common occurrence it was seldom accompanied by such squalor.

Coding of the information obtained during the home visits was begun when all the visits had been completed, and all the coding was done before the school progress of the children in the sample was assessed.

MEASURES OF HOME ENVIRONMENT

(Eleven measures of different aspects of the home environment were obtained within the four broad categories mentioned earlier. One variable from each category is used to illustrate the way in which data from interviews can be transformed into scores prior to statistical analysis. For details on the other variables, which are merely listed here, see the original text, pages 40–70.)

[1] C. Burt (1945) *The Young Delinquent* (4th Edition) London: University of London Press, page 88.

## a. Cultural

### 1 Parents' Education

An assessment was made in this section of the educational attainments of and educational level reached by the parents. Education was interpreted in a broad sense so that attendance at or participation in any course of instruction, after fourteen, the age at which the majority of parents had left school, was given some credit.

Points were awarded arbitrarily on the basis of (a) the duration of the course, (b) any qualifications resulting from it, and (c) the academic standard required by the course.

Thus, for example, for each year which was spent in school beyond the age of fourteen, 3 points were given for what was called at the time intermediate (now junior secondary) education, and 5 for senior secondary. An additional bonus of 2 points for a Day School Certificate, and 5 for a Higher Leaving Certificate were given. A university training added a further 5 for each year spent there, with an extra 5 for an Honours degree.

Attendance at adult evening classes of a non-academic kind, e.g. dressmaking, cookery, etc., was credited with 1 point for each session, and attendance at commercial and technical subjects with 2 points per session. Other courses falling somewhere between these two extremes were given points on an intermediate scale.

### 2 Reading Habits of Parents and Children ...

## b. Material

### 3 Income

What was required here was some assessment of the financial position of the family as distinct from the socio-economic status reflected by the father's occupation. The assessment was rendered difficult by several factors. In the first place, some parents were reluctant to reveal their income, and some others stated a figure which was not even faintly plausible. In other cases, where the mother was interviewed, it occasionally happened that she was genuinely unable to say how much her husband earned, since she knew only how much she was allowed for housekeeping each week. The assessment was further complicated by those families where elder children were working and contributing to the family income. In some households (particularly as regards the younger members) the children handed over their whole wage and were given pocketmoney; their clothes and other expenses were paid for by the parents: in others, the children themselves were responsible for these expenses and gave their parents a certain amount each week for board and lodging.

It was generally possible, however, to make a fairly accurate assessment of the total income coming into the home; since the occupations of both father and siblings were known, it was usually possible to discover the appropriate wage, and it was in only a few instances, when, for example, the father ran his own business, that an estimate was very difficult or impossible to make. The total income (from all sources, including family allowances stated or estimated) was divided by the number of persons benefiting from it, children under ten counting as half-persons. Seventeen households, where no assessment was possible, had to be omitted.

4   Occupation of Father ...

5   Family Size ...

6   Living Space ...

c.  *Motivational*

7   Parents' Attitudes to the Education and Future Employment
    of the Child
For this factor, a rating was made on a six-point scale, which took into account parents' attitudes to the value of education in general and to the education of their own children, their attitudes to further education or vocational training, their attitudes to blind-alley occupations and similar factors. Because of the very wide range of ability of the children concerned some account had to be taken of this circumstance in the assessment of the parents' attitudes. What would for a boy of IQ 85 be a very favourable parental attitude would obviously not be so for a boy of IQ 130; and what would be a reasonable attitude on the part of parents of a boy or girl of good ability would be a totally unrealistic one in the parents of a less able child.

The attitudes of parents were, therefore, assessed on the six-point scale, with the ability of the child in mind, in such a manner that a wish to send a bright child to the university and to see him launched in a profession was given the same rating as a willingness, on the part of the parents of a less able child, to forfeit initially high wages in a blind-alley job for the long-term advantages of a skilled occupation. At the other end of the scale, the attitude expressed in such words as: 'I don't care what he does as long as he earns some money to help out at home', was rated very low. The attitudes to education and to occupation were found to be so closely related that it was not thought necessary to assess them separately.

8    Parental Encouragement ...

*d.    Emotional*

9    Abnormal Home Background
The usual definition of a normal home has been accepted here: that is, the child is the legitimate son or daughter living with both parents in a home apparently free from acutely disturbing conditions. In the category of children with abnormal home background, the following have therefore been included:
  *a.*    illegitimate children
  *b.*    adopted children
  *c.*    children whose parents were either divorced or separated
  *d.*    children with one or both parents dead.

In addition, children have been included in this category when there was strong evidence of friction and discord between their parents, when one or both parents were chronic invalids, and when the father was absent from home for very long periods.

Finally, a few cases were included which are not readily classifiable, but would by most people be accepted as abnormal, e.g. one child of deaf and dumb parents, one child whose father was psychotic, one child of a nomadic family, one child with a delinquent sibling, and two children living in conditions of poverty so extreme that they were set clearly apart from the normal range.

10    General Impression of the Home Background ...

11    Mother out at Work ...


ANALYSIS OF RESULTS

(Correlational analyses were used to establish the relationships between the indices of home environment and school progress on the one hand, and intelligence test scores on the other. Results for three of the variables mentioned above are shown below. A different method of analysis was used with the measure of abnormal home background.

|  | School progress | Intelligence score |
|---|---|---|
| 1. Parents' education | 0·490 | 0·423 |
| 3. Income | 0·444 | 0·350 |
| 7. Parents' attitudes | 0·391 | 0·297 |

These values show that measures of home environment are consistently related more closely with attainment than with intelligence.)

It now remains to consider the various items of home background, not in isolation but together, in order to determine how great is this increased relationship with school progress, and which of the items contributes most to it. To do this, multiple correlation technique is necessary, which takes into account not only the correlation of each home item with intelligence and with school progress, but also the correlation of each home item with every other.

The results of this multiple correlation show that, when all the home items are taken together, they give the following correlations:

Home environment and intelligence test score: $r = 0.687$

Home environment and school progress : $r = 0.752$

The difference between these two figures is highly significant statistically.

Of the ten items which go to make up this composite assessment of home environment, three stand out as being mainly responsible for the higher correlation with school progress. These are, in order of importance, abnormal home background, income, and parents' attitudes to the education and future occupation of the child ...

These three items, assessed in the way we have described, appear to be the most important features of the home environment, in so far as its effect on the child's school progress is concerned. There would appear to be a common thread linking them together; a normal home background, emotional stability, freedom from tension and from economic insecurity, and consistent encouragement from parents are necessary for a child if his schoolwork is to reach the level allowed by his intelligence.

*The National Survey for the Plowden Committee also investigated the aspects of home environment which are most closely related to attainment. The pupils in this Survey, however, were primary school pupils. The method of sampling has been referred to in Chapter 3. The main study was cross-sectional, with several measures taken at one point in time, although a follow-up of the subsequent progress of these pupils has recently been published (Peaker, 1971). Again, the main instrument was an elaborate interview schedule from which a large number of indices of environmental influences were obtained. School attainment was measured by a test of reading comprehension—a criterion which has been criticised as being insubstantial for the subsequent analysis (see Chapter 15).*

*In Volume 2 of the Report, Children and their Primary Schools, a simple account of the relationship between the various home influences and school attainment is given in Appendix 13. The main question, however, is: which of these influences is the most important?*

*The interview schedule produced responses to eighty different items. These were put into fourteen major groupings, using factor analysis. This procedure indicates how the responses can be grouped meaningfully so as to produce a smaller number of more general variables or factors.*

> *'It was desirable to group together questions which tended to be answered in the same way, or in statistical terms were correlated. (For example, parents who said that it was very easy to see the teachers whenever they wanted also tended to say that the teachers seemed pleased when parents went along to see them. Other parents tended to disagree with both statements.) To find which questions in the interview tended to be answered similarly a statistical analysis (factor analysis) was carried out on 80 items of the interview data' (page 145).*

*In addition, some sixty school variables were obtained from H.M.I.'s ratings and reports. With all these measures it was possible to piece together some of the most likely environmental influences on attainment.*

*Readers with the stomach for strong statistics can be recommended to read G. F. Peaker's elegant description of step-wise multiple regression analysis, from which the following extracts are taken. In essence, this complex approach has been designed to isolate from a large number of variables a much smaller number which, taken together, 'explain' school attainment as effectively as possible. The analysis picks out relevant variables, not simply in terms of their correlation with the criterion, but also allowing for their inter-relationship with all the other measures.*

## The Regression Analyses of the National Survey
## (G. F. Peaker, 1967)[1]

The variables were grouped into three broad categories of 'classes' to simplify the task of reporting the analysis:

(1) parental attitudes, (2) home circumstances, (3) schooling. The estimate for the first class shows the effect on the child's progress of hopeful and encouraging interest on the part of the parents. The second class shows the effect of the parents' material circumstances, and of their own education. The third class shows the effect of the variation of various school circumstances. Before the inquiry it was plain that parental encouragement and support could take the child some way. What the inquiry has shown is that 'some way' can reasonably be interpreted as 'a long way',

[1] Edited extracts from *Children and Their Primary Schools, Volume 2* (H.M.S.O.), Appendix 4, pages 180–9.

and that the variation in parental encouragement and support has much greater effect than either the variation in home circumstances or the variation in schools.

Qualitatively the results are in no way surprising. Common sense and common observation lead us to expect that a child's school achievement will be determined, to some extent, by the attitudes of his parents, and that these attitudes in turn will partly depend upon their material circumstances. It was indeed this common-sense expectation that guided the planning of the inquiry. What could not be foreseen, until the inquiry was complete, was the quantitative aspect. We could foresee that parental attitudes, parental circumstances, and schooling would each make a contribution. What we could not foresee, and what the inquiry has shown, is the relative size of these contributions. The fact that attitudes play so large a part is hopeful, since it is at least possible that attitudes may be open to persuasion.

In the first part of our inquiry we have used multiple regression with the children's achievement in school as the criterion, and parental attitudes, parental circumstances, and school variables as the predictors. But we can also use it with parental attitudes as the criteria and parental circumstances as the predictors. In this way we can test the firmness of the link between attitudes and material circumstances. Without falling into the error of assuming that correlations are sufficient, as well as necessary, evidence of causal relations we can, at any rate, make an assumption, or set up a model, and work out its consequences. For example, we can assume that causal lines run from parental circumstances to parental attitudes, and thence to the children's achievement, in the way shown in the diagram below (Figure 7 : 1).

(The numbers on the lines shown in the diagram show the percentage of the variance of one variable attributable to the other. By looking at these values it is thus possible to pick out those variables which are explaining most of the variation in attainment. For example, almost 29 per cent of attainment can be explained in terms of aspiration for the child, which in turn can be explained to a considerable extent by the two variables of parental education in the left-hand column. Nevertheless throughout the analysis a substantial amount of variance is unexplained (the arrow marked 'R' for residual). The apparently slight influence of schooling (6 per cent) is curious at first sight, but there is an explanation.)

The reason why the school variables play so small a part is not, of course, that schooling is unimportant. It is that the variation between schools is much less than the variation between parental attitudes. If the least co-operative parents rose to the level of the most co-operative the effect would be much larger

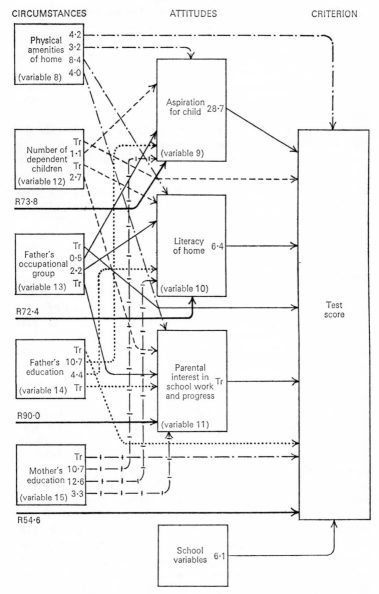

CIRCUMSTANCES       ATTITUDES       CRITERION

Physical amenities of home (variable 8) 4·2 3·2 8·4 4·0

Number of dependent children (variable 12) Tr 1·1 Tr 2·7

R73·8

Father's occupational group (variable 13) Tr 0·5 2·2 Tr

R72·4

Father's education (variable 14) Tr 10·7 4·4 Tr

R90·0

Mother's education (variable 15) Tr 10·7 12·6 3·3

R54·6

Aspiration for child (variable 9) 28·7

Literacy of home (variable 10) 6·4

Parental interest in school work and progress (variable 11) Tr

Test score

School variables 6·1

FIGURE 7:1   *A path diagram*

than if the worst schools rose to the level of the best or the least prosperous parents to the level of the most prosperous, because the effect of the range in co-operation is much greater than the effect of the range in parental prosperity or that of the range in schooling.

*(The following extracts illustrate some of the complexities of analysis in this area of research, and conclude with a summary of the findings.)*

This part of the inquiry shows how much could be gained if less co-operative parents became more co-operative. It throws no light on the extent to which this could be brought about by persuasion. On this point we have two kinds of evidence. In the first place we can use regression again to test the firmness of the link between the parents' attitudes and their circumstances. It is reasonable to regard the attitudes as being partly determined by the other circumstances, and if we take the attitudes as criteria and the other circumstances as predictors we can get some light on the interpretation of 'partly'. We find that up to a quarter of the variation in attitudes can be put down to the variation in circumstances. This leaves three-quarters or more to be accounted for in other ways. It is reasonable to suppose that among these other ways persuasion, from a great variety of sources, must play a large part, and it is therefore reasonable to hope that attempts to change attitudes by persuasion might have some success. On the other hand such direct evidence as we have on this point is not very encouraging. It falls under three heads. In the first place several of our variables (e.g. Is there a parent/teacher association? How many meetings with parents are held?) were intended to measure aspects of persuasion already in use. But these variables often failed to reach significance in the regression analyses. Secondly, a special group of schools where the relations between parents and teachers were thought to be particularly good was selected by H.M. Inspectorate. But although the evidence subsequently collected from these schools vindicated the judgements that led to their selection there was little difference between the average achievement of the children in this group and those in the representative sample. Thus the special group merely confirmed the result from the sample (which was, of course, not yet known when the special group inquiry was planned). In the third place rather more encouraging results were obtained from the experimental attempt to influence parental attitudes that was carried out in one school with the co-operation of the Institute of Community Studies. In this case a small but recognisable improvement in the children's achievement was obtained. The first two results are less encouraging than might have been hoped, though perhaps not surprising when we remember the vast sums spent by the advertising industry in attempts to change attitudes about relatively trivial matters. On the other hand the modest success of the experiment is encouraging, and suggests that we should remember the principle, though not the particular instance, of Mr Pickwick's views on brandy and water as a prophylactic—that where it failed it was because the sufferer had fallen into the vulgar error of not taking enough of it. On the evidence we may be confident that there is ample scope for persuasion, while recognising that to find the right kind and amount of persuasion will be a matter of difficult and delicate experiment, needing ingenuity and above all tact.

The new results extend, but are not incompatible with, those derived from the surveys reported in *Early Leaving, Fifteen to Eighteen* and *Half our Future*. Those surveys dealt with parental variations of the second kind. The new survey brings in the first kind (parental attitudes) as well. The effect of bringing in the attitude variables is two-fold. In the first place much more of the variation in the children's achievement is accounted for. Secondly, part of the variation that would be attributable to home circumstances, if attitudes were ignored, is transferred to the account of attitudes when these are brought in. This is analogous to the relations between the statures of fathers, mothers, and children. Tall fathers tend to have tall sons partly because they tend to marry tall wives. The simple correlations are 0·5 between parents and children and 0·3 between spouses. If fathers alone are considered they account for 25 per cent of the variations in sons. But when mothers are brought into the picture the total accounted for rises from 25 per cent to 38 per cent, but the father's contribution is reduced from 25 per cent to 19 per cent, because in the earlier assessment he was, so to speak, borrowing from the mother. In this way bringing in the parental attitudes increases the total amount of variation accounted for while reducing somewhat the amount attributed to the other kind of variable before the attitudes were brought in.

### SUMMARY

Two questions may be asked at the end of any inquiry. They are:
  *a.*   Are the conclusions compatible with earlier evidence?
  *b.*   If so, have we learnt anything that we did not know at the outset?
Here there is no difficulty about the first question. The starting point of the inquiry was the previous evidence that both the attitudes and the home circumstances of parents had a good deal to do with the progress of their offspring in school. What the previous evidence did not indicate was the relative importance of the two sides, and the relation between them. Were attitudes

more important than circumstances, or vice versa? And how far were attitudes conditioned by circumstances? Do parental circumstances operate directly on children's school progress, or do they operate indirectly by conditioning attitudes, or do they operate partly in one way and partly in the other? It is on these questions that our inquiry has thrown some new light.

The conclusions suggested are that :

1  The specific contributions made by the variation in parental attitudes are greater than those made by the variation in home circumstances, while the latter in turn are greater than those made by the variations between schools and teachers that we have taken into account.

2  Only about a quarter of the variation in parental attitudes is conditioned by the variation in circumstances. The remainder must be conditioned to a large extent by communication and persuasion, so that it is reasonable to hope that an attempt to improve the co-operation of parents and teachers by persuasion might attain some success.

3  Although parental attitudes are largely independent of home circumstances they are conditioned by them to some extent. For this reason, and also because parental circumstances operate directly, as well as through parental attitudes, on children's progress it is reasonable to hope that the latter will improve as circumstances improve.

*The large national sample used by Douglas in his longitudinal study of the influence of social variables on attainment has been described in Chapter 3. An account of the methods used is readily accessible in paperback publications—*The Home and the School *and* All Our Future—*and thus the emphasis here is placed on the findings. As this was a longitudinal study in which the same children were tested at different ages there is rather more possibility of establishing causal relationships than in other cross-sectional studies. The wide range of variables measured is shown in the first extract, followed immediately by a summary of the main findings and of their educational implications.*

## *All Our Future*    (J. W. B. Douglas, J. M. Ross and H. R. Simpson, 1968)[1]

### AGES AT WHICH INFORMATION WAS COLLECTED

Interview with mother—eight weeks, two, four, six, seven, eight, nine, eleven, fifteen years.

Medical examination—six, seven, eleven, fifteen years.

School teacher reports—seven, ten, thirteen, fifteen, sixteen years.

Tests—eight, eleven, fifteen years.

Questionnaire completed by Survey member—thirteen, fifteen years.

Running absence records—six and a half to ten and a half years.

Headteachers' forms—eleven, fifteen years.

### INFLUENCE OF HOME AND SCHOOL

The additional information gathered during the secondary school years, reiterates and underlines the importance of the home in shaping educational attitudes and attainment. This book provides many indications that the influences are greatest at two periods; first during the pre-school years, and second at the end of the compulsory school period when many pupils leave, including a number of very able boys and girls.

The importance of the home influences in the pre-school years was obscured in *The Home and the School* by the fact that there appeared to be an increasing social class gap in test performance, between the ages of eight and eleven. This was interpreted as indicating the growing influence of the environment on the measured ability and attainment of primary school children, an interpretation that, with the additional information available, must now be modified. The divergence of the intelligence test results seem to be a temporary artifact of the stresses of secondary selection rather than the result of real changes in the ability of the boys and girls. The gap between the social classes in non-verbal test scores is no greater at fifteen than at eight, and while there is a slightly greater gap between them in attainment at fifteen, this is largely owing to the high scores made by the upper middle class boys and girls. It seems then that once the pupils are grouped by their family background, the main

[1] Extracted from *All Our Future* (Peter Davies), Appendix 2 followed by Chapter 24, complete with the exception of one paragraph.

characteristics of their test performance are determined by the age of eight and possibly earlier, though how much earlier we do not know.

We attribute many of the major differences in performance to environmental influences acting in the pre-school years. Many factors appear to have exerted their main influence on measured ability by the time children leave the infant schools. For example the low attainment of pupils in the manual working classes, or in large families where there are many brothers and sisters near to them in age, or who have many signs or symptoms of disturbed behaviour, is present at eight and changes little in the subsequent seven years. And the same holds for the superior attainment of elder boys in two-child families and of both boys and girls with median birth intervals of 2–4 years.

That pupils are influenced during their years at school by their home circumstances is also clear from this study. These influences undoubtedly shape attitudes to school and learning; they are more apparent in leaving age, in the results of the General Certificate of Education examinations and in the wish to enter higher education, than they are in the test score results. This stems in part from the parents' choice of school. Some parents are able and anxious to pick out the better schools and, particularly in the middle class, are more prepared and better able to move to areas where good schools are known to be available. Parental attitudes may also perhaps explain some of the relative deterioration of girls in the tests given at fifteen, although much depends on the type of school they attend; in co-educational schools for example the girls have at fifteen a similar level of achievement to the boys.

In the primary schools, deficiencies of interest and ambition on the part of the parents are, to some extent, offset by good teaching. The influence of the primary schools extends also to the secondary schools and affects later development and progress. For example the persisting influence of streaming in the primary schools is illustrated by the secondary school histories of children who, as reported in *The Home and the School*, had been placed in one or other stream of two-stream schools, allocation being based on estimates of ability made before eight. In the later years at primary school, the pupils in the top stream improved in measured ability, whereas those in the bottom deteriorated. They conformed much more closely than would have been expected to early estimates based on relatively crude measurements of ability. The lower stream pupils who, with one exception, went to secondary modern schools, did not show any further fall in measured ability and attainment compared with those who had been in the upper stream. Indeed the manual working class boys who had been in the bottom stream improved their test performance between eleven and fifteen years, particularly in reading and mathematics. At each level of ability at fifteen however the pupils who had been in the lower stream when they were in their primary schools, left earlier than those from the top. There is conflicting evidence here; on the one hand the depression of test performance for those in the lower stream does not persist at fifteen, on the other hand they leave the secondary modern schools early. How far is this to be explained by the expectations of academic failure that were fostered in the primary schools?

There is evidence that the social background of the primary schools has a persisting influence on secondary school performance. Some primary schools recruit their pupils mainly from families of clerks and other middle class workers, including those in the professions, while others recruit them predominantly from the manual working class. Between the ages of eight and eleven, pupils in those primary schools which enrolled their pupils predominantly from the manual working class fell behind the rest in their test performance and at each level of ability were less likely to be allocated to grammar schools. These same pupils are likely to leave early and so seldom sit the General Certificate examinations. At secondary modern schools, they are only two-thirds as likely to stay to the end of the 1961/2 session as are those of similar measured ability coming from primary schools with a largely non-manual intake. If they go to grammar schools, they are also at a similar disadvantage. The influence of the primary school is particularly strong for the manual working class child; if he has been to a primary school that is predominantly middle class, he is more likely to succeed at secondary school, than if he had been to a primary school recruiting its pupils mainly from the manual working class.

These observations suggest that children acquire, early in their years at school, attitudes to learning that are related to later success or failure. The primary school influence is most clearly seen among the secondary modern pupils, perhaps because they have a less positive attitude towards education than those at grammar school and so are less able to alter the expectations and habitual attitudes that were acquired at a younger age.

Social inequalities in selection to the secondary schools are most apparent for those at the borderline level of ability—the boys and girls of high ability having similar chances of securing grammar school places, whatever their home circumstances. It was to be expected that nearly all the pupils of high ability, some of whom have struggled against considerable difficulties to reach grammar schools, would be supported by the academic traditions of their schools and stay on at least to enter the sixth form. This is not so and it is disturbing to find that so many leave early and fail to sit the General Certificate examinations.

In order to summarize the extent to which educational progress is influenced by the home and the school we have related the length of school life of the lower manual working class pupils of borderline ability and above to a large number of factors in their homes and schools. The lower manual working class was chosen as showing the greatest waste of talent, and the borderline and high ability pupils were chosen as comprising the majority of those in this social class who would be likely to benefit from sixth form work and who, if they came from middle class homes, would mostly do so. We felt that, with the available educational criteria, it was more realistic to study waste among those of high ability than failure to provide opportunities for those of lower ability. At a later stage, when success can be judged in a wider setting, we hope to extend this comparison to those of average ability and below.

The lower manual working class groups of both high and borderline ability show on the whole the expected relationships between the length of school life and the various factors we have discussed throughout this book. Those who were picked out by their teachers as being nervous or aggressive are more likely than the rest to leave early, so also are those who were reported at fifteen to have one or more symptoms of disturbed behaviour, to be inattentive, troublesome, or often away in either their primary or secondary schools, or to be delinquent or truant. Pupils aiming at professional as opposed to other employment after leaving school are more likely to stay on, especially in the group of borderline ability.

By definition all the parents of these lower manual working class boys and girls had left school themselves before reaching the age of 15, but the pupils whose parents had attempted to obtain some further education after entering employment are nearly twice as likely to stay on as the rest. This applies equally to the fathers' and the mothers' education. Poor health of either parent is related to early leaving in the high ability group, and in both groups those whose mothers have high neuroticism scores on the Maudsley Personality Inventory are more likely to leave early. A high level of parental interest, high employment ambitions for the child and a good record of visits to the school on the part of the father are all associated with longer school life.

Clear evidence of the importance of the primary school is found for those of high ability. In this group the average age of leaving school is later for those who were at primary school in urban areas, with good amenities, with good past records of 11 + success or with a predominantly middle class intake of pupils. None of these primary school characteristics was however related to the length of school life in the borderline group; this is unexpected for in *The Home and the School* it was shown that the relationship between the primary schools' past record of 11 + successes and the pupils' chance of reaching grammar school was particularly high for pupils at this level of ability.

At the secondary schools the position is complicated by the need to split the sample into selective and secondary modern school pupils. The 157 lower manual working class boys and girls of high or borderline ability attending selective schools are not sufficiently differentiated in respect of the size, amenities, or staffing of their schools, to make a detailed study profitable.

There are much larger differences in the characteristics of the schools attended by the 176 secondary modern school pupils, and these we now relate to age of leaving. Early leaving is more frequent in secondary modern schools that have less than 600 pupils, are built on poor or noisy sites, have a majority of children of unskilled manual workers, have a poor past record of retaining pupils beyond the statutory leaving age, have few graduates on the staff and have a high ratio of pupils to teachers.

We now turn from a general description of the individual factors influencing the age of leaving secondary modern schools to an assessment of the relative importance of the school and the home on the length of school life of these lower manual working class pupils. Owing to the many factors involved, it was necessary to construct two simple scales, one assessing parental attitudes and the other assessing the characteristics of the secondary modern schools. These are more inclusive than our previous measures of 'parental interest' and 'school type'.

We have grouped the parents of these able lower manual working class boys and girls according to the following criteria.

a. One point was given if either the father or the mother or both had sought further education after leaving school;

b. One point was given if the father had visited the school to discuss his child's progress on more than two occasions and/or the parents were assessed by the teachers as taking a high level of interest in their children's work;

c. One point was given if the mothers wished their children to follow a full-time educational course on leaving school and/or to enter a profession.

The lowest score on this scale is 0, showing the least parental involvement, the highest is 3; in practice however so few scored 3 that we grouped them with those who scored 2. Combining the high ability and borderline pupils 33 per cent of the parents of those at secondary modern schools scored 0, 51 per cent scored 1 and 15 per cent were in the highest group, that is to say scored 2 or 3.

The secondary modern schools were also grouped into three in the following way, their scores running from 0 to 2.

a. One point was given for either good school amenities or more than 600 pupils, or both of these;

b. One point was given for 20 per cent or more graduate staff or for a pupil/teacher ratio of less than 19, or both of these.

Twenty-eight per cent of the lower manual working class pupils under consideration were at secondary modern schools in which there were deficiencies of both staffing and amenities (i.e. a score of 0), 39 per cent were in schools scoring intermediately and 33 per cent were in schools both with good amenities and a satisfactory staff.

By relating the two scales—parents' attitudes and school characteristics—9 groups of boys and 9 groups of girls in secondary modern schools are obtained.

There is a clear relationship between the parental and school scores, the favourably assessed parents are also the most likely to send their children to the favourably assessed schools. Of the boys and girls whose parents scored 0 on the attitude scale, 34 per cent were at the least satisfactory secondary modern schools, whereas of those whose parents scored the highest, only 22 per cent were at these schools. One cannot say of course how much of this difference represents choice on the part of the parents and how much the impact of the schools, both primary and secondary, on the attitudes of the parents and on their expectations.

In order to remove the overlapping effects of sex, parental interest and school characteristics on the proportions of pupils staying to the end of the 1961/2 session, we have used an analysis of variance method involving the fitting of constants. The results of this analysis (see figure 7.2) show that there are no significant differences between the proportions of boys and girls staying to the end of the 1961/2 session, 32 per cent of the boys and 33 per cent of the girls. There is however a sharp rise in the proportion of pupils staying on as the parental score increases—for example of those with parents who have a score of 0, 23 per cent stayed on, of those with a score of 1, 35 per cent and of those with a score of 2 or 3, 50 per cent. There is also a similar gradient when we look at the school scales, though here it is only the schools with a score of 0 who differ from the rest; in these schools only 15 per cent stay on to the end of the 1961/2 session, this compares with 40 per cent of the pupils in schools with a score of 1 and 42 per cent in schools with a score of 2. It is only when schools are adversely assessed on both criteria that the leaving pattern is affected.

The Plowden Committee suggested that priority areas should be established in which additional money should be earmarked to raise the standards of the local primary schools—both buildings and teaching. It seems that there is also a need for similar priority areas at the secondary stage. Twenty-eight per cent of these lower manual working class pupils of relatively high ability were in secondary modern schools that lacked amenities and had serious staffing problems and the evidence is that these pupils left the earliest, even if the level of their parents' interest was high. For example if their parents' interest and aspirations were

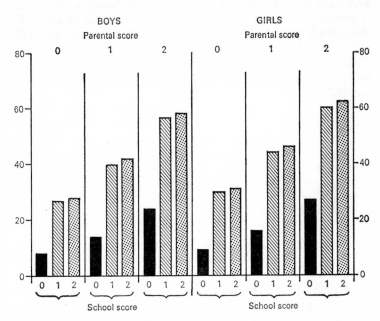

FIGURE 7:2    *The percentages staying at least to the end of 1961/2 session related to parental attitudes and school characteristics—lower manual working class pupils of borderline ability and above, at secondary modern schools*

high only 25 per cent of these boys and girls stayed to the end of the 1961/2 session in the worst schools, compared with 60 per cent in the best. Among those with the least favourably assessed parents 9 per cent and 30 per cent stayed on in the poor and well equipped schools respectively. It seems that high parental interest alone is insufficient to counter the deficiences of the schools. The following quotation from the Plowden Report is as relevant to the secondary as to the primary schools: 'It should not be assumed that even the ablest children can surmount every handicap, they may suffer as much as any from adverse conditions.'

The conclusions of this study are that, in the selective secondary system which existed between 1957 and 1962, social inequalities in educational opportunity could have been greatly reduced by raising the standards of many of the existing schools, by increasing the provision of grammar, direct grant and technical schools and by removing local inequalities in the provision of selective places—these inequalities are largely historic and bear little relation to the ability of the pupils living in each area. A general improvement in the staffing and amenities of many of the schools and the elimination of local discrepancies are, and will be, no less necessary in the comprehensive system of secondary education which is now evolving: it requires and will require an equally great investment and direction of both capital and staff.

# 8 Teachers' Opinions and Attitudes

In many areas of educational research, it is important to take systematic soundings of teachers' opinions and attitudes. For example, in Chapter 6, the research on the transition to secondary education began in this way. In choosing a procedure for sampling opinion, one must take account of the way in which the results are to be used. Thus, if the purpose is exploratory, unstructured or semi-structured interviews with teachers make it less likely that free expressions of opinion will be inhibited. A structured questionnaire or interview schedule may not allow for perceptive comments, and classification or coding of responses necessarily means losing some of the rich diversity of attitudes. On the other hand it is almost impossible to obtain precise estimates of the strength or the range of opinions without the use of a structured instrument. For this purpose comparable responses must be obtained from all the people questioned.

In the previous chapter Fraser commented on the advantages of the interview procedure in assessing home environment. The advantages there were clear-cut: the opportunity to visit the home was important and many of the respondents might have misunderstood nuances of language if a questionnaire had been used instead. In other studies the impersonal and possibly anonymous nature of the replies to a questionnaire has advantages. It increases the likelihood of straight, even blunt, answers. Social conventions operate strongly in a face-to-face situation and may prevent the person from expressing what he feels to be socially or professionally unacceptable views.

Problems in questionnaire surveys hinge around the difficulty of obtaining a satisfactory response rate. It is also crucial to make the questions clear and unambiguous, as explanations cannot be given. But careful planning can minimise these difficulties, and the questionnaire survey is particularly appropriate where the respondents are well able to understand the subtleties of the written word and have technical knowledge or expertise. Teachers thus make ideal targets for inquiries of this type and, as *a result, a problem has arisen in some areas over the frequency of questionnaire surveys, particularly when students have been encouraged to collect such data in their projects. The first extract comes from a study which was concerned, among other things, with the extent to which teachers were being overburdened with requests to fill in research questionnaires.*

*This N.F.E.R. survey was also designed to discover teachers' views on educational research itself. Are teachers hostile to research? To what extent do research findings actually reach the teacher? How many teachers are interested in being involved in research projects? What sort of research is considered to be of practical value? A questionnaire survey, supplemented by interviews, produced answers to these questions derived from a representative group of teachers. For the benefit of those readers who have not been asked to fill in a research questionnaire, this first extract illustrates the way in which the questions are presented. These questions form only a small part of a much longer questionnaire.*

## The Teacher and Research
### (B. S. Cane and C. Schroeder, 1970)[1]

### THE TEACHER AND EDUCATIONAL RESEARCH

What research in education would *teachers* like to see done?

This question is of ever greater importance to the educational research bodies now that research funds have increased to their present level. Clearly, only practising teachers can supply the answer—hence this questionnaire which the N.F.E.R. now invites you to complete.

The questionnaire also attempts to assess the extent of the 'communication gap' known to exist between research workers and practising teachers.

The N.F.E.R. is an *independent* organization supported by many educational bodies including teachers' professional associations, local education authorities and universities.

The project, 'The Teacher and Educational Research' of which this questionnaire is the main part, is sponsored jointly by the N.F.E.R., the Schools Council and the Department of Education and Science. *Your answers could have a direct influence on the course of future research and development in education,* and on the means by which it is communicated to teachers. Thank you for agreeing to help.

[1] Edited extracts from *The Teacher and Research* (N.F.E.R.), pages 28–32, 58–61, 68–72, 78, 81, 82.

## I. AREAS FOR DEVELOPMENT AND/OR RESEARCH—SUGGESTED PRIORITIES

In recent years teachers have suggested many areas in education that might be the subject of research or development work. In this questionnaire these areas have been arranged under the following headings:

| | |
|---|---|
| Teaching methods | Assessment and examination |
| Curriculum | Psychological/sociological research |
| Grouping children | Teachers and training. |

In one section of this questionnaire we ask which of these general subdivisions of education should, in your view, have the highest priority in the planning of research and development work.

First, however, we would like you to look at the areas under each heading and say in which areas you think it is most important for research and development work to be carried out. Please note that the given areas do not themselves constitute descriptions of research or development projects. They simply outline various fields in education within which it may or may not be important to conduct such projects.

In this questionnaire no rigorous distinction is made between those activities commonly called 'development' and those called 'research'. The distinction can be important in some contexts, and space has been left for you to indicate which activity you have in mind where you feel it is necessary to do so.

*Important* PLEASE CONSIDER THE EDUCATIONAL AREAS THAT FOLLOW IN RELATION TO YOUR OWN SCHOOL WORK.

We are *not* asking you to speak for teachers as a whole.

### I. TEACHING METHODS

Please indicate what priority you think should be given, in the planning of research and development projects, to the areas below by circling *one* number against each. Where an area is not relevant to your school work circle 'O'.

Please consider each area in relation to the others *on this page* only. When you circle '2' against an area, write in a specific *topic* for research or development within that area if you have one in mind.

| | Not rel. | Low priority | High priority | Office use |
|---|---|---|---|---|
| A Methods of teaching in classes having a wide ability range | 0 | 1 | 2 | 19 20 |
| B Methods of using modern teaching aids | 0 | 1 | 2 | 21 22 |
| C Methods of teaching backward or gifted children, early or late developers, or other exceptional children | 0 | 1 | 2 | 23 24 |

D Methods of compensating for the adverse factors in a child's home or social background

| | | | | |
|---|---|---|---|---|
| | 0 | 1 | 2 | 25 |
| | | | | 26 |

E Please write in any high priority topic on TEACHING METHODS which you have in mind, and which does *not* come within any of the areas above. If none, leave blank.                                    27

..............................................................

..............................................................

Please circle the *one* letter below corresponding to the area which you think should have the *highest* priority in the planning of research or development projects. Note inclusion of categories E and NONE.

| A | B | C | D | E | NONE | |
|---|---|---|---|---|---|---|
| (1) | (2) | (3) | (4) | (5) | (6)—numbers for office use only | 28 |

## II. THE COMMUNICATION GAP

The purpose of the questions that follow is to give some idea of the nature and extent of the 'communication gap' known to exist between researchers and practising teachers.

Office use

In answering, by all means look at those publications with which you are *already* familiar to a greater or lesser extent, but please, only in order to refresh your mind on the details asked for.

### SOURCES OF RESEARCH AND DEVELOPMENT WORK— PUBLICATIONS

How frequently—never, seldom, irregularly or regularly—do you read articles in the following publications? Please circle the appropriate number against each title.

| | Never | Seldom | Irreg. | Regu-larly | |
|---|---|---|---|---|---|
| British Journal of Educational Psychology | 0 | 2 | 2 | 3 | 28 |
| Educational Research (N.F.E.R.) | 0 | 1 | 2 | 3 | 29 |
| Educational Research News (N.F.E.R.) | 0 | 1 | 2 | 3 | 30 |
| Trends in Education (D.E.S.) | 0 | 1 | 2 | 3 | 31 |
| The Teacher (N.U.T.) | 0 | 1 | 2 | 3 | 32 |
| New Schoolmaster (N.A.S.) | 0 | 1 | 2 | 3 | 33 |
| Times Educational Supplement | 0 | 1 | 2 | 3 | 34 |
| Teacher's World | 0 | 1 | 2 | 3 | 35 |
| Education | 0 | 1 | 2 | 3 | 36 |
| New Education | 0 | 1 | 2 | 3 | 37 |
| New Society | 0 | 1 | 2 | 3 | 38 |
| Forum | 0 | 1 | 2 | 3 | 39 |
| Where? | 0 | 1 | 2 | 3 | 40 |
| Publication of a 'subject' association | | 1 | 2 | 3 | 41 |

### INVOLVEMENT IN EDUCATIONAL RESEARCH— OTHER THAN CURRICULUM DEVELOPMENT

Have you ever been involved in an educational research project (other than curriculum development and other than the present survey?) Please circle the number against the statement which is most applicable.

| | |
|---|---|
| No, and I have never been asked to take part | 0 |
| No, I have been asked to take part, but declined to do so | 1 |
| | 43 |
| Yes, but I thought that on the whole the project was unsatisfactory | 2 |
| Yes, and I thought that on the whole the project was worthwhile | 3 |

## THE PROJECT

The project aimed to establish those areas and topics of research that teachers regarded as immediate priorities. Additionally, the purpose was to explore teachers' attitudes to educational research: what did they know of it, to what extent had they participated in it, what did they think its function ought to be and what value did they attach to it?

The field work was carried out in 1968. One thousand and sixty staff in 119 primary schools and 35 secondary schools completed questionnaires; 915 were assistants, and 145 Heads. Four different areas were covered—two in the North, two in the South; the East Riding of Yorkshire, the city of York, the county of West Sussex and the city of St Albans. Except for St Albans, where project resources were limited, the response rates were very good, averaging 80 to 90 per cent. In addition, there were 63 interviews with Heads and 102 with assistants, all selected from the questionnaire respondents.

## THE RESULTS

### Priorities

Results were calculated separately for Heads and assistants, primary and secondary schools and the four localities involved. The most significant findings were those where teachers of one type showed the same preference in all four, or at least three of the four, localities. Of the six general areas listed 'Teachers and Training' was the major overall choice for top priority. Within the areas (that is, among more detailed specific options) the favoured topics were as follows:

All groups of teachers picked out the question of streaming and non-streaming as one of their highest priorities. A majority of primary assistants also favoured research into the diagnosis of children's particular difficulties; and primary heads gave preference to methods of teaching wide ability-range classes.

A majority of secondary assistants preferred the topic of in-service training to others under the 'Teachers and Training' heading, and gave highest priority under a different heading to research into making syllabus content more relevant to modern life. Secondary heads asserted the need for research into the content of initial training courses and also gave as one of their other highest priorities the problem of compensating for the adverse factors in a child's home or social background.

(Teachers had been invited to add their own suggestions for research which should be undertaken.) There was only a small proportion of respondents who preferred their own added topic to any on the list—on average about five per cent—but this minority deserves special attention as it probably includes some of those who had thought most deeply about the subject. Some of the added suggestions could have been included under one of the listed headings, others contained valuable ideas not anticipated by the compilers of the questionnaire. Even where the suggestions, however, were not in any way original, they help to fill out our picture of those problems about which teachers felt most strongly in connection with research.

## Teaching Methods

Many of the suggestions under this heading by primary staff overlapped with the third area (grouping children) in that they related to problems of organizing children for teaching. Other subjects put forward for evaluation were: compensating the younger child in an age group; team teaching; specific teaching aids such as reading laboratories; open plan schools; school journeys; different approaches for boys and girls, and the slow learner or ESN child for whom there is no special provision. Some teachers turned the question round and demanded research on learning rather than teaching.

Team teaching was a frequently suggested topic among secondary staff. Another was the teaching of children whose learning was mainly visual, who had particular manual dexterity or who were unusually imaginative. The development and evaluation of teaching aids of all kinds was often mentioned.

## Curriculum

Religious Education was frequently written in here by primary staff: they were interested in approaches geared to the needs of modern society and acceptable to teachers, parents and children alike. Wider aspects of the curriculum were also thought to need investigation: the overall development of the syllabus from infant to secondary levels; co-ordination of the work of small rural with large urban schools; the question of whether subject timetables should be abolished, and subject specialism among teachers in primary schools, especially in view of the introduction of many new subjects.

In relation to this area, secondary staff were concerned with the organization of the educational system. They hoped that curriculum research would take account of school leavers' groups, links with further education, the integration of subjects, general studies in the sixth form, pupils not taking public examinations and so forth.

## Grouping Children.

Research on 'family grouping' was written in frequently by primary staff: how could it be made successful in large schools, was it suitable for older age groups, and did vertical groupings have decisive advantages over age-grouping? Did the success of the grouping employed depend on the individual class teacher's ability or on the children? Some teachers suggested research on integrating physically handicapped children into normal schools, others on groupings for exceptional children—those with special difficulties in reading or number, and those with outstanding intelligence or creativity. Should children of outstanding ability be sent to regional centres? How did you get the best out of lazy but highly gifted children in non-streamed classes? Several teachers suggested research on children by personality type, sociability, friendship patterns, or temperament. Finally, further research was called for on ages of entry to school and ages of transfer.

Secondary staff favoured research on problems of secondary school organization such as house and year systems, middle schools and sixth form colleges. They wanted evidence on the optimum organizational structure in schools of various sizes.

## Assessment and Examinations

Some primary staff suggested the development of national assessment records available at every school a child attends. Linked with this was the interest shown in selection procedures in different LEAs. Other teachers raised the sophisticated question of allowances (for time, age, etc.) in standardized tests. Some teachers called for ways of assessing potential ability in late developers and under-achievers, while others were concerned with the assessment of personality and emotional development—conscientiousness, loyalty, leadership, love, depth of feeling, altruism, perception, idealism and aesthetic sensitivity.

Secondary staff suggested research into a minimum attainment test for early school leavers, accumulated records of children's work for comparison with end-of-course assessments, and the establishment of national systems of objective testing.

## Psychological/Sociological Research

This heading produced the largest number and widest range of additional topics. Teachers of infants stressed the importance of research into the causes and effects of maladjustment, emotional insecurity at school and school refusal. What were the effects on young children of membership of a class of 40? How did they adjust to other children? What was the effect of a disturbed five-year-old on his fellows in a reception class? Infant teachers asked for studies designed to improve understanding and co-operation between schools and welfare workers, and to develop the organization of local (as against county) centres for psychological and sociological advice to teachers and parents.

Infant teachers also emphasized the early identification of

E

potential delinquency, and assessment of the value of nursery schooling. What were the factors that encouraged a child to extend and develop his learning at an early age? What were the long-term effects on a child's school progress of insecurity, maladjustment and disturbance in the pre-school and infant years?

An outstanding request by both infant and junior teachers was for research into the interaction of the personalities of child and teacher. This was thought to have significance for children's motivation, for example in learning to read. The teacher's speech patterns, and their limitation of the child's response, were included in these requests. Many wanted this research to probe the triangular relationship of parent, teacher and child.

Primary staff had a particular interest in the relations between character, temperament, ability and attainment. What were the connections between intellectual and emotional maturity? Could the school help with emotional growth and moral development, and if so, through which activities? How could the school encourage integrity, and responsibility for others' welfare?

A number of primary staff were also interested in research on the phenomenon of 'fallow periods' that many children were observed to experience. Were these periods necessary to development, and what should be the reaction of teachers? How might teachers expect this phenomenon to vary with IQ, age and subjects? What were the periods of time for which you could expect children of different abilities or ages to concentrate? What caused some children to withdraw from involvement in the class and their work? What was the explanation for differences in the speed of development of boys and girls, and in their abilities in mathematics?

Primary and secondary staff alike wanted research on the immediate and long-term effects of different kinds of discipline exercised by teachers. What were the outcomes in terms of motivation, concentration, attainment, social attitudes and so forth? Quite a number of secondary staff developed the theme of the teacher–pupil relationship, and wanted to know about the attitudes that structured or were structured by, this relationship.

Like their primary colleagues, a number of secondary staff wanted research on the effects of 'visual bombardment' in modern living, and the decrease in the use of words. There was a concern for the influence of mass media on teenagers, and a need for ways in which the schools might act as a compensatory or complementary influence.

## Awareness of Research

More than half the assistant teachers in the schools sampled were completely unfamiliar with the works of eleven out of fourteen prominent educational researchers listed in the questionnaire; but a majority of assistant teachers claimed knowledge of the research of at least two of the three remaining names.

Among the bodies sponsoring research or development in education, the Nuffield Foundation was the most familiar. Examples of its work had come to the notice of over 85 per cent of primary and 60 to 70 per cent of secondary assistants. The Department of Education and Science was the next best known body, while about half the primary assistants also mentioned the work of Local Education Authorities, and over half of secondary assistants mentioned associations devoted to individual subjects. The Schools Council and National Foundation for Educational Research were reasonably well known to heads and less so by assistants (30 to 50 per cent of assistants knew of their publications).

When it came to reading habits, over 80 per cent of assistants said that they read *The Times Educational Supplement* at least occasionally; most primary heads and assistants read *The Teacher* and *Teachers World*, and 70 to 80 per cent of secondary staff read the publications of subject associations. Approximately 70 to 90 per cent of all assistant teachers never saw specifically research publications such as *Educational Research*, or the *British Journal of Educational Psychology*; however, Heads claimed a greater acquaintance with such journals, and in one area 85 per cent of primary heads saw *Educational Research* (the NFER journal) as it was circulated to them by the LEA.

Teachers felt that reading research was a small part of their professional life but they nevertheless attached importance to it. Some of those interviewed said that these writings were often incomprehensible, too long, phrased in tactless language, biased in their presentation or of limited applicability. While some were enthusiastic about research publications that spoke directly to the classroom teacher, many complained of inadequate reporting in the more popular journals. They believed that research findings ought to be disseminated through some system of regular comprehensive summaries.

*Involvement*

More than 75 per cent of the assistant teachers sampled had never taken part in educational research, and 60 per cent had never taken part in curriculum development. The percentages for involvement were greater for heads of schools, particularly in the case of curriculum development projects. Among the assistant teachers interviewed, very few had ever been asked to fill in a research questionnaire. On the whole, the heads had filled in many more, but the distribution was very uneven. The majority of teachers who had taken part in projects of some kind had found them worthwhile.

*Opinions*

Both on the questionnaire and in the interviews, most teachers regarded research as a necessary professional activity, and some went out of their way to stress that they recognized its value even if they had reservations about how it was done. A frequent comment was that involvement in research helped teachers to reconsider the aims of their work.

A large number of constructive suggestions were made. There was a widespread feeling that the objectives of innovations should be more clearly defined before teachers were asked to take up new curricula and methods, and that more stress should be placed on the evaluation of innovations under ordinary working conditions. Many teachers spoke of possible pitfalls in research method. They considered that objectivity should be rigorously safeguarded and adequate account taken of the many imponderables in school life. They hoped to be consulted fully when research was being planned, and doubted that research workers sufficiently recognized subtle differences in local conditions or the uniqueness of each teacher–class relationship. They wanted research to become less remote than they felt it to be at present, and made suggestions as to how this could be achieved. Many heads and teachers were seriously concerned that important research findings had been ignored, and were likely to be ignored in the future, by those who had authority to take decisions and develop policy in the educational world. The implementation of findings was seen as a vital corollary of the research itself.

This abundance of criticism and suggestions should not be regarded as evidence of massive discontent. Some of the criticisms were reasonable and showed great insight, others might be regarded by researchers as presumptuous. At any rate, great interest was manifest on all sides. While teachers' recall of specific researches and publications showed that this kind of concentrated reading is still a fringe activity, the widespread desire to be involved in and receive the benefits of future research is a rewarding indication of the growing impact of this pursuit on the profession which it serves.

*The second extract in this chapter comes from another N.F.E.R. enquiry. The Department of Education and Science sponsored a long-term study on the effects of streaming in primary schools. In a wide-ranging report Barker Lunn presented detailed information on aspects ranging from the characteristics of the teachers, through attainments in streamed and non-streamed schools, to children's attitudes and interests. In this chapter the emphasis is on teachers' attitudes to streaming. The pilot study used a free-ranging interview to establish the range of opinions likely to be encountered as a basis for the subsequent questionnaire survey. The special interest of this study was the way in which it explored the influence of teachers' attitudes to streaming on their pupils' attainments.*

## Streaming in the Primary School
## (J. C. Barker Lunn, 1970)[1]

### THE AIM OF THE EXPLORATORY RESEARCH

Since little was known about the nature of streamed or non-streamed schools, it was decided to carry out exploratory research in the form of semi-structured interviews with teachers.

These interviews made available data about prevailing teaching techniques, and the values and aims of teachers in streamed and non-streamed schools. They also provided a general picture of teacher attitudes and made available statements for use in developing attitude scales.

### METHOD AND SAMPLE

A total of 31 interviews were carried out during October 1963 in twelve schools situated in Essex, Buckinghamshire, Berkshire and London.

Each teacher was interviewed in private for about one hour and was encouraged to talk about many aspects of the junior school. The interviewer adopted a permissive and non-critical role but at the same time developed opportunely each theme which was related to any area he had been briefed to investigate. An interview schedule had been prepared beforehand and was used as a rough guide. Each interview was taped and later transcribed.

### REPORT ON THE EXPLORATORY INTERVIEWS

The 31 interviews were divided among three interviewers. Based on a verbatim record of the interviews, an individual report was written by each interviewer. The results which follow are a condensation of the three individual reports. For convenience they are discussed in three sections:

[1] Edited extracts from *Streaming in the Primary School* (N.F.E.R.), pages 14, 15, 26, 52, 56, 69–73 and 281–91.

I.   Attitudes to streaming
II.  Methods of teaching
III. Discipline

## I. Attitudes to Streaming

ATTITUDES TOWARDS STREAMING

Most of the teachers in streamed schools interviewed supported streaming; most in non-streamed schools were against streaming. A number of teachers in both types of school were critical of the organization used by the head. In some schools the head had imposed an organization apparently without explaining his reasons to the staff; as one teacher said: 'The head had some reason for introducing non-streaming but I don't know what it was.'

The teachers who supported streaming evaluated it in quite different terms from those who did not support it. The attitudes of these two groups will be discussed separately (and are summarized below).

*Attitudes of teachers in favour of streaming:*

   *a.*   Streaming ensures that brighter children make maximum progress;
   *b.*   Streaming 'removes' the dull child;
   *c.*   Streaming ensures that backward children receive special education;
   *d.*   Streaming makes teaching more efficient and easier for the teacher.

*Attitudes of teachers in favour of non-streaming:*

   *a.*   Non-streaming gives each child a fair chance;
   *b.*   Non-streaming leads to better adjustment;
   *c.*   Non-streaming results in happier staff.

*Criticisms of non-streaming*

A number of teachers in non-streamed schools had criticisms of non-streaming:

   *a.*   Bright children are neglected or mis-used;
   *b.*   With non-streaming, backward children continue to feel inferior;
   *c.*   Non-streaming is only possible with small classes.

## II. Methods of Teaching

### FORMAL VERSUS INFORMAL APPROACH TO TEACHING

Two extreme views concerning the function of the primary school could be distinguished. One emphazised learning and the acquisition of knowledge; the other emphazised the child, interesting him and developing his potentials.

The attitudes of the two types of teacher to various aspects of teaching are examined below.

### a. Teachers Using Formal Methods

Teachers using formal methods tended to be in streamed schools. They believed that formal methods were more efficient: 'The old fashioned method of blackboard and chalk is still the best.' They had little enthusiasm for more practical methods; for example, the use of concrete methods in arithmetic was considered by some not only a waste of time, but a possible hindrance to the child's development to think abstractly. 'When I teach area, I teach length times breadth equals area, and then the children have to apply the formula—none of this nonsense of racing round measuring up the school yard!' Another teacher said: 'I don't think there's any point in messing around with toys and glue when the important thing is to know tables and be able to manipulate figures.'

On the other hand, many felt that formal teaching methods were the most effective for preparing children for the eleven-plus selection test: 'I believe in formal methods, especially if the eleven-plus test is going to continue.'

### b. Teachers Using Informal Methods

Teachers using informal teaching methods tended to be in non-streamed schools. These teachers stressed the importance of children discovering things for themselves. 'When a child says, "Cor, look 'ere!", then I feel that somebody has learnt something there.' Formal abstract methods were considered unsuitable: 'Children may be able to learn abstract ideas, but they cannot apply them when they come up against a difficult problem.' 'Getting sums right is not as important as knowing what they are doing and why.' They felt that making children interested in school was a major aim, particularly with children from poorer homes where there was little interest in education. 'The formal approach has killed interest in mathematics, though basically juniors are very interested.'

Informal teaching methods emphasized individual discovery,

practical experience, and gradual comprehension of the principles involved. In arithmetic this involved measuring, shopping,
sharing and the use of apparatus (Colour Factor, Dienes, etc.). In
English the emphasis was on creativity and keeping the child's
interest rather than on correct spelling, punctuation and class-
prepared compositions.

### III. Discipline

There appeared to be two main aspects of the subject of discipline. The first, emphasized by 'authoritarian' teachers,[1] was an
insistence that children should show a respect for adults and
authority and that rules and regulations were to obeyed. Quiet
classroom atmosphere, good deportment, clean and tidy appearance and good manners were important to these teachers. The
second aspect was much more emphasized by the 'democratic'
teachers[2] and concerned the effect of one child's behaviour upon
another or society in general.

Teachers of the first type would make remarks such as : 'I do
demand clean hands and faces', or 'I would like to see in the
junior school much more emphasis on self-control—sitting properly in class, not biting nails, sucking fingers, fidgeting.' 'Control
of one's body is a most important thing; once you have personal
control, you can listen.' The ideal child was perceived as 'responsive, very polite, gets on with his work and does exactly as you
ask him'.

Fewer rules were laid down in the 'democratic' approach and
the basis of these was that they were made for the protection of
society, and by keeping to the rules, the child showed consideration for those about him and protected himself from harm.

Teachers of the second type might agree with one head who
said : 'Don't expect good manners from my children because you
won't get them.' She believed her children were spontaneous,
individualistic and natural and would keep these qualities if not
subjected to rules about things which, as far as she was concerned, were relatively unimportant.

### PUNISHMENT

The more 'authoritarian' teachers were prepared to use physical
punishment in order to make children conform to school rules.

[1] Teachers holding 'authoritarian' views also tended to be 'knowledge-
centred'.
[2] Teachers holding 'democratic' views also tended to be 'child-centred'.

They felt that smacking children was an effective and justifiable punishment:

'I'm quite prepared to smack bottoms and legs for disobeying rules.'

'A good slap in the right place at the right time does an awful lot of good.'

'If the child goes over the line it's punished—all this soppy talk about hurting its ego with a good smacked bottom is a lot of nonsense.'

'I've been in this business long enough to know that a slap on a child's leg is far more effective than talking to him like a Dutch uncle.'

Other teachers completely ruled out physical punishment: 'It is completely unnecessary.' 'If I can't deal with a child by talking to him about what he's done, then I feel there is something wrong.'

The interviews and visits to schools suggested that streamed and non-streamed schools were not only different in organization but that the teaching staff held contrasting attitudes and used contrasting teaching methods. It also became clear that these differences might possibly outweigh the effects of streaming or non-streaming *per se*. A good deal of attention was therefore given to the construction of questionnaires to assess the methods of teaching and attitudes of the teacher.

From the material recorded at the interviews with teachers, three questionnaires were devised. The first was concerned with biographical information such as sex, age, and teaching experience. The second was concerned with information about the methods of teaching used and the way in which children were organized for learning. The purpose of the third questionnaire was to obtain the opinions of teachers on such matters as streaming, and eleven-plus selection. (Details of the methodology and sampling are omitted here.) From the results of the questionnaire survey, it was possible to identify what were called Type 1 and Type 2 teachers. The former favoured non-streaming and informal methods, while the latter preferred to use streaming and formal teaching (see Table 8:1). (These descriptions agreed well with the more impressionistic results obtained from the interviews.)

Fifty-two per cent of teachers in non-streamed schools were classified Type 1 and conformed to the pattern of the non-streamed school; the other 48 per cent were indentified as Type 2. Eighty-three per cent of teachers in streamed schools were Type 2 and the remaining 17 per cent were Type 1.

Where schools have changed to non-streaming, some are non-streamed in name only, for their staff have retained their former streaming views, classroom practices and teaching methods. The greater conformity among streamed school teachers in their attitudes and beliefs would be expected, since the organizational policy of the schools is the conventional one. The changeover to non-streaming is fairly new and at the time of the research, this form of organization was a comparative rarity. Since of all junior schools in the country which were large enough to do so, 65 per cent streamed (3 or 4 year groups) and only six per cent did not stream (any year group), it seems reasonable to suppose that most

TABLE 8:1   *Attitudes and classroom practices of Type* 1 *and Type* 2 *teachers*

| Type 1 | Type 2 |
| --- | --- |
| Believed in non-streaming | Believed in streaming |
| No streaming by seating | Some streaming by seating |
| More favourable attitude to slow child | Less interested in slow child |
| 'Permissive' | 'Non-permissive' |
| Tolerant of noise and talking in the classroom | Less tolerant of noise and talking in the classroom |
| Less favourable attitude to physical punishment | Favourable attitude to physical punishment |
| Made less use of 'traditional' lessons | Frequent use of 'traditional' lessons |
| Frequent use of 'progressive' lessons | Made less use of 'progressive' lessons |
| Tests at least once a month | Tests at least once a month |
| Formal sums about once a week | Formal sums every 2–3 days |

junior school teachers were in favour of streaming and that relatively few were firmly committed to non-streaming. Since attitudes for or against streaming seem to form part of a whole syndrome of views, practices and beliefs, the opinions of Type 2 teachers on teaching methods and other educational matters seem to represent the majority viewpoint. This makes it difficult for schools attempting to practise non-streaming. And it is clear that a mere change in organization, such as the abandonment of streaming, unaccompanied by a serious attempt to change teachers' attitudes, beliefs and methods of teaching, is unlikely to make much difference; in fact it is likely to result in a change from streaming between classes to streaming within classes.

## ATTAINMENTS IN STREAMED AND NON-STREAMED SCHOOLS

### a. Conventional Attainment

An examination was made of the progress of approximately 5,500 pupils in English, reading, mechanical and problem arithmetic, number concept, verbal and non-verbal reasoning during their junior school course. The results were analysed by three social class and three ability levels. Comparisons made between the achievement gains of pupils of comparable ability in 36 streamed and 36 non-streamed schools revealed no pattern favouring either type of school. Comparable pupils, whether bright or above average, average, or below average made similar progress in the two types of school. An additional analysis by teacher-type revealed no difference in terms of the progress made by their pupils; but any effect may well have been blurred by pupils changing from one teacher-type to another in consecutive years.

## b. 'Creative' Writing

The children wrote two essays each year, choosing in each case from a list of topics which aimed at providing a stimulus for an interesting and imaginative story. The titles offered were deliberately unconventional in the ideas they presented, the aim being to lure the children away from producing a formal 'stereotyped' composition. Again it was hypothesized that in the more progressive type of school, teachers practising such methods would devote greater attention to the free expression of ideas, and would thus produce better results than teachers in schools where the more formal structure type of essay received greater emphasis.

It was further hoped to discover whether the contrasting types of school experience differed in their effect on the 'creative' performance of pupils of different ability levels; for instance, whether the effect of streaming was such that the curriculum considered appropriate for children in lower streams did not include the encouragement of free writing essays and expression. At the other end of the ability range the most able children might also be given less opportunity to develop their creative writing abilities in schools where formal academic attainment was given priority.

Since type of teacher seemed likely to be of importance in this, as in other areas of the streaming inquiry, it was decided to take this factor into account, as well as the organizational differences between schools. Again, children in streamed schools were not subdivided by type of teacher, as the great majority of teachers in these schools were Type 2, holding similar attitudes and employing similar methods. Children in non-streamed schools, however, were divided into two groups: (1) those whose fourth year teachers were Type 1, tending to be 'progressive' in their teaching methods and with typical non-streamed attitudes, and (2) children whose fourth year teachers were Type 2 and who were less in favour of 'progressive' lessons and, in terms of attitude and personality, more characteristic of the type of teacher found to predominate in streamed schools.

(The results are shown in Tables 8:2 and 8:3 where the percentages of children in these three types of classes scoring in either the top or bottom 20 per cent on the essays are reported.)

Type 1 teachers, therefore, were not only associated with the greatest number of high scorers, but also with the smallest pro-

TABLE 8:2    *Percentage scoring in the top 20 per cent on the Free Writing Essays*

|  | Social Class | Non-streamed Type 1 | Non-streamed Type 2 | Streamed |
|---|---|---|---|---|
| Boys | 1, 2, 3 | 21% | 18% | 21% |
| Boys | 4, 5 | 14% | 4% | 12% |
| Girls | 1, 2, 3 | 35% | 31% | 27% |
| Girls | 4, 5 | 20% | 16% | 21% |

TABLE 8:3    *Percentage scoring in the bottom 20 per cent on the Free Writing Essays*

|  | Social Class | Non-streamed Type 1 | Non-streamed Type 2 | Streamed |
|---|---|---|---|---|
| Boys | 1, 2, 3 | 19% | 21% | 28% |
| Boys | 4, 5 | 37% | 46% | 31% |
| Girls | 1, 2, 3 | 8% | 10% | 8% |
| Girls | 4, 5 | 18% | 15% | 25% |

portion of children whose scores fell in the bottom 20 per cent on the test. Type 2 teachers, on the other hand, seem to be the least successful in developing the divergent thinking of their pupils. A possible explanation is that this type of teacher is something of a 'misfit' in non-streamed schools. His allegiance to the aims of formal academic attainment often means that he practises, with a full ability range, methods suitable only in the context of a streamed class, no doubt increasing the difficulty of the perceived teaching task. This type of teacher is likely to have less time, if not inclination, than colleagues in streamed schools to create a classroom atmosphere in which learning can proceed in a self-initiated, unchannelled way.

(In conclusion), if one is to judge the streaming–non-streaming issue solely on the basis of academic performance, the findings of this study lend small support to either side. The decision to stream or non-stream must rest upon factors other than formal attainments.

# 9    Children's Attitudes, Motivation and Personality

*The previous chapter described how teachers' views and attitudes were sampled by questionnaire and interview. More often attitudes are measured by one of the many forms of inventory or attitude scale. Inventories are also used to measure psychological areas closely related to attitudes, such as motivation and personality.*

*The extracts in this chapter start where the last one finished, with Barker Lunn's study on streaming. Besides looking at teachers' opinions and pupil achievement, she also examined children's attitudes in streamed and unstreamed schools. To do this she had first to develop an appropriate set of attitude scales.*

### Attitudes of Pupils
### (J. C. Barker Lunn, 1970)[1]

The effects of type of school organization on pupils' attitudes towards school has often been put forward as a crucial factor in the debate for or against streaming. The atmosphere in which the pupil finds himself seems to differ considerably between streamed and non-streamed schools, particularly for children of different ability levels. So one might expect to find that children in the two types of school display different attitudes to school and to teachers.

#### EXPLORATORY RESEARCH AND CONSTRUCTION OF SCALES

Since only a small amount of research has been done in this country on pupils' attitudes, exploratory work in the form of

[1] Edited extracts from *Streaming in the Primary School* (N.F.E.R.),—pages 113–17, 130, 132–3, 146–7, 150–1.

discussions and interviews with children was carried out. The aim was to determine what attitudes children actually held and how these feelings were expressed.

Briefly, the exploratory research indicated marked differences between streamed and non-streamed situations; it also confirmed the importance of the teacher, whose behaviour and attitudes appeared to determine the social and emotional climate of the classroom. The findings suggested that the type of teacher affected the pupil's behaviour and attitudes, particularly those concerning his relationship with the teacher, his motivation or desire to learn, his degree of anxiety in the classroom and his self-image.

(As previous attitude scales were unsuitable it was necessary to develop new inventories.) It was considered important that children's actual language should be used in constructing scales; consequently a major principle was to obtain items from statements made by children in the group discussions. Each scale was made up of a number of items selected after factor analysis and scalogram analysis.[1] Ten attitude scales were successfully constructed. These were: (a) academic self-image; (b) anxiety; (c) social adjustment; (d) relationship with teacher; (e) importance of doing well; (f) attitude to school; (g) interest in school work; (h) conforming versus non-conforming; (i) attitude to class; (j) other image of class. (Scales (a)–(d) relate to personality and social relations, while scales (e)–(j) deal with attitudes.)

## WHAT DO THE SCALES MEAN?

The 'relationship with teacher' scale emphasized the teacher's degree of concern for the child, as perceived by the child, rather than the child's liking for the teacher. Some of the items were: 'Teacher thinks I'm a trouble-maker', 'Teacher is interested in me', 'Teacher is nice to me.'

The 'academic self-image' scale reflected self-image in terms of school work. For example: 'I'm useless at school work', 'I'm very good at sums', 'My teacher thinks I'm clever.'

The 'anxiety' scale reflected anxieties, fears or worries in the classroom. For example: 'I would feel afraid if I got my work wrong', 'Children who can't do their school work feel ashamed', 'I'm scared to ask my teacher for help.'

The 'social adjustment' scale was concerned with the child's ability to get on well with his classmates. It included such items as 'I have no one to play with at playtime', 'I think the other children in my class like me.'

The scale used to measure 'importance of doing well at school'

[1] For an explanation of scalogram analysis see, for example, Oppenheim (1966).

stressed achievement orientation, for example: 'I work and try very hard in school', 'Doing well at school is most important to me.'

The 'attitude to school' scale was concerned with general rather than specific aspects of school. It included statements such as: 'School is fun', 'I would leave school tomorrow if I could.'

The 'interest in school work' scale was concerned both with school work in general and with particular lessons. An example of the former is: 'I enjoy most school work', and of the latter, 'We spend too much time doing arithmetic.'

The 'conforming versus non-conforming' scale covered the range of these two opposing types of behaviour. For example, the scale included items such as: 'I dislike children who are noisy in class', 'I like people who get me into mischief', 'When the teacher goes out of the room I play about.'

Items in the 'attitude to class' scale referred to the favourableness or otherwise of being a member of a particular class. For example: 'I'd rather be in my class than the others for my age' and 'I hate being in the class I'm in now.'

The 'other image of class' scale was concerned with the way a pupil felt other classes in the school viewed his class. For example: 'Other classes make fun of my class', 'Other children think we are nice in my class', 'Other classes think they are better than us.'

*(Full details of the sampling procedure will be found in the original text. The essential details are as follows. The attitude scales were given on two occasions, with an interval of one year. The analyses thus report changes in scores on these tests for children in streamed classes and in unstreamed classes with 'progressive' (Type 1) and 'traditional' (Type 2) teachers.)*

### DISCUSSION OF PUPILS' PERSONALITY ASSESSMENTS

The results indicated that neither school organization nor type of teacher made much difference to the personal and social adjustment of children of above average ability. Children of average ability, on the other hand, developed a better teacher–pupil relationship and academic self-image in non-streamed schools with a Type 1 teacher. Boys of below average ability had a more favourable teacher–pupil relationship in non-streamed schools with Type 1 teachers, but more of them had a good self-image in streamed schools. The findings were not conclusive for girls of below average ability.

One of the most interesting findings was that showing the influence of teacher-type in non-streamed schools—particularly in the development of the teacher–pupil relationship, academic self-image and, to a lesser extent, degree of anxiety in the classroom. In the attitude areas discussed so far, pupils taught by Type 1 teachers improved significantly in their score (see Table 9 : 1).

**TABLE 9:1**   *Summary of results concerning personality development*

| Attitude Scale | | Non-streamed Type 1 | Non-streamed Type 2 | Streamed |
|---|---|---|---|---|
| Relationship with teacher | Overall | +** | + | − |
| Academic self-image | Overall | +** | − | +* |
| Anxiety | Overall | +** | + | + |
| Social adjustment | Overall | +*** | +*** | +*** |

| Attitude Scale | | Non-streamed Type 1 | Non-streamed Type 2 | Streamed |
|---|---|---|---|---|
| Relationship with teacher | Above average | +** | + | +* |
| | Average and below average | + | − | −* |
| Academic self-image | Above average | +* | + | + |
| | Average and below average | + | − | + |
| Anxiety | Above average | + | + | + |
| | Average and below average | +* | + | + |
| Social adjustment | Above average | +*** | + | +** |
| | Average and below average | +*** | +*** | +** |

+   = obtained higher score
−   = obtained lower score
*   = attitude change significant at 5% level
**  = attitude change significant at 1% level
*** = attitude change significant at 0·1% level

These results are not surprising when one considers the different values held by the two teacher-types. Type 1 teachers were sympathetic towards the non-streamed philosophy and their approach tended to be more child-centred, their concern being for the all-round development of each pupil. Type 2 teachers, on the other hand, were opposed to non-streaming; they were more concerned with and interested in the bright child and emphasized academic success. These contrasting attitudes were reflected in the feelings of the two teacher-types about children of different abilities. Both expressed similar atttudes to pupils of above average ability and girls of average ability. But Type 2 teachers, in contrast to Type 1, had less sympathy for boys of average and boys and girls of below average ability, finding them less pleasurable to have in their class.

## DISCUSSION OF SCHOOL ATTITUDES

Just as the personality scales had shown little difference between children of above average ability in the different circumstances, a similar pattern was found here; wherever they were, these pupils tended to have favourable attitudes.

Children of average and below average ability, on the other hand, became more motivated to do well in school and were more satisfied with their class and its 'other image' in non-streamed schools.

Children of all ability levels became more non-conforming in the fourth year; differences between school and teacher-type were not conclusive.

The school's organization seemed to play a more important part in the development of the children's attitudes to their class, their 'other image' of class and their motivation to do well in school, than in the development of their personal and social attitudes. In these three attitude areas, the non-streamed setting appeared a better environment for children of average and below average ability.

The table below, which summarizes the change in attitude

TABLE 9:2   *Summary of attitude change results*

| Attitude Scale | | Non-streamed Type 1 | Non-streamed Type 2 | Streamed |
|---|---|---|---|---|
| Importance of doing well | Overall | +** | + | + |
| Attitude to school | Overall | + | + | + |
| Interest in school work | Overall | ‡ | − | − |
| Conforming versus non-conforming | Overall | − | − | −*** |
| Attitude to class | Overall | +*** | + | + |
| Other image of class | Overall | + | + | − |

| Attitude Scale | | Non-streamed Type 1 | Non-streamed Type 2 | Streamed |
|---|---|---|---|---|
| Importance of doing well | Above average | + | + | + |
| | Average and below average | +** | + | − |
| Attitude to school | Above average | + | + | + |
| | Average and below average | + | + | − |
| Interest in school work | Above average | + | + | + |
| | Average and below average | − | − | − |
| Conforming versus non-conforming | Above average | − | + | −*** |
| | Average and below average | −* | − | −*** |
| Attitude to class | Above average | + | − | + |
| | Average and below average | +*** | + | − |
| Other image of class | Above average | + | + | − |
| | Average and below average | + | + | −* |

+ = obtained higher score
− = obtained lower score
* = attitude change significant at 5% level
** = attitude change significant at 1% level
*** = attitude change significant at 0·1% level
‡ = equal numbers obtaining a lower and higher score

results, shows that the tendency in streamed schools was for those of above average ability to improve and those of average and below average ability to deteriorate in their attitude scores. No such negative trends were observed among pupils of average and below average ability in non-streamed schools.

*Another important study of children's attitudes focused on an older age-group. The Schools Council's Enquiry 1 concerned young school leavers. The data were collected from interview schedules, but through factor analysis it was possible to condense groups of statements about school into coherent scales.*

## Schools Council Enquiry 1—Young School Leavers (R. Morton-Williams and S. French, 1968)[1]

### THE PURPOSE OF THE ENQUIRY

The introduction to and opening paragraphs of the Newsom Report set in relief the importance of the relationship created by the attitudes of parents, pupils and teachers towards secondary education. The first lines of this Report pose basic questions.

> 'Boredom with everything school stands for, or enthusiasm? Conflict between school and home, or mutual support? Tongue-tied inadequacy, or social competence? What is the true picture of the educational situation of hundreds of thousands of young people to-day?'

Questions concerning effective communication and good relationships between parents, pupils and teachers call for urgent consideration. The purpose of the enquiry, whose findings are given in the following pages, was to provide some evidence about current attitudes, at home and at school, which would focus and sharpen discussion on all the work schools do for their pupils. The enquiry's background was outlined in the Schools Council's Working Paper No. 2 :

> 'The intended raising of the school leaving age to 16 marks a further stage along the road, mapped out in the Education Act of 1944, leading to secondary education for all. This decision is a bold act of faith. It means retaining in school for a fifth year of secondary education some 60% more of the age group than now stay on voluntarily. The majority of

[1] Edited extracts from *Schools Council Enquiry 1* (H.M.S.O.), pages iii–iv, 2, 211–12, 218–20 and 372.

those affected will have an aptitude for scholastic work which is average or below average. Some will come from homes which attach small value to extended schooling. For many vocational motivation will be weak; it will be difficult to engage their interest and sense of relevance. Some will actively resent having to stay longer in school.'

The success or failure of raising the school leaving age will hinge on the success of the attempt to engage pupils more closely throughout their new five-year course. Put at its lowest, the raising of the age could mean little more than the extension of a struggle between pupils who feel that school has little to offer to them and teachers who feel that they meet little other than boredom and resistance. Schools are, by contrast, likely to be most successful with those pupils who are supported by their parents and whose interest, motivation and sense of relevance are captured by the work they do. The attempt to achieve this can better be undertaken if the schools have more information about the attitudes of those involved. It was for this reason that the Secretary of State for Education and Science commissioned on behalf of the Schools Council an enquiry by the Government Social Survey into the interests and motives of pupils between the ages of 13–16 and their views of the adequacy of their preparation for adult life and work; the teachers' knowledge of what is relevant to their pupils; and the parents' view of their own and the schools' role in the education of their children.

### THE METHOD OF ENQUIRY

The survey was carried out by means of individual interviews using structured questionnaires. Besides the interviews, assessments of the youngsters were made by teachers and information about the schools was collected from the heads and from Department of Education and Science records.

*(A two-stage sampling procedure produced a sample of 149 maintained schools in England and Wales. Within these schools random samples were drawn to give totals of 4,825 13–16-year-old pupils and ex-pupils, although the actual numbers varied somewhat from analysis to analysis through incomplete data.)*

The factor analysis thus indicated that the 18 attitude items fell into six groups. The first group appeared to show how interesting a youngster found school life as a whole. At one extreme came young people who thought that there were lots of interesting things going on in school, that teachers took a great deal of interest in them and helped them a lot and that most of what they were taught at school was very useful to them. They also liked school very much and on most days looked forward to going. They disagreed with the statements that school was the same day after day, week after week, and that teachers forgot

Table 9:3  Items included in the factor analysis and their factor loadings

| Variables | Factor loadings (decimal points omitted) | | | | | |
|---|---|---|---|---|---|---|
| | 1 | 2 | 3 | 4 | 5 | 6 |
| 1. Percentage of subjects taken which are useful | −06 | 86 | −01 | 04 | −06 | 00 |
| 2. Percentage of subjects taken which are interesting | −18 | 81 | −02 | 12 | −07 | −02 |
| 3. Whether would have liked longer school day (yes) | −08 | −15 | 04 | −59 | −13 | −15 |
| 4. Liking for school (liked very much) | 50 | −06 | 08 | −54 | 13 | 05 |
| 5. Most days looked forward to going to school | 49 | 00 | 04 | −46 | −10 | 03 |
| 6. You get fed up with teachers telling you what you can and can't do (disagrees) | 12 | −11 | 05 | −10 | 62 | −16 |
| 7. School is the same day after day, week after week (disagrees) | 42 | 02 | −01 | −26 | 26 | 06 |
| 8. Teachers take a good deal of interest in you and help you a lot | 67 | −05 | 12 | 08 | 12 | −03 |
| 9. You were delighted when you had an excuse to stay away from school (disagrees) | 29 | −07 | 15 | −45 | 21 | 06 |
| 10. There were lots of interesting things going on in school | 67 | −05 | −01 | −11 | 11 | −02 |
| 11. Teachers forget you are growing up and always treat you like kids (disagrees) | 31 | −02 | 11 | 00 | 63 | −14 |
| 12. Most of your friends come from near home rather than school (disagrees) | −12 | −01 | −02 | −08 | 56 | 20 |
| 13. Most of what they teach you at school is very useful to you | 62 | −17 | −01 | −01 | −08 | −05 |
| 14. Whether any advantages in staying at school if not taking exams (yes) | −03 | −03 | −12 | −34 | 15 | −47 |
| 15. Whether work better or worse than school (better at work) | −05 | −02 | −01 | 56 | −19 | −05 |
| 16. How hard a worker at school (very hard worker) | 05 | −05 | 71 | −11 | 15 | 05 |
| 17. Whether shy or withdrawn (no) | −05 | −04 | −07 | −13 | 03 | 82 |
| 18. Whether aggressive (no) | 04 | 02 | 79 | −01 | −05 | −06 |
| Percentage of the variance accounted for | 12·3 | 8·2 | 6·7 | 9·1 | 7·6 | 5·7 |

Total amount of variance accounted for by these factors = 50%

(Factor loadings may be interpreted as the equivalent of correlations between the factors and each item. The meaning of each factor can be inferred from the group of items which show high loadings on that factor. The high values have been put in boxes in the above table.)

they were growing up and treated them like kids. They were not pleased when they had an excuse to stay away from school. At the other extreme came youngsters with entirely opposite views, who disagreed that school was interesting, that teachers took a great deal of interest in them and helped them a lot or that most of what they were taught at school was very useful. They disliked school, did not look forward to going and were delighted when they had an excuse to stay away. They thought school was the same day after day, week after week and that teachers forgot they were growing up and treated them like kids. In later discussions this group in items is referred to as describing the attitude dimension of 'Interest of school'.

The second group indicated pupils' 'Attitudes to the subject curriculum' and the most important items here were the percentages of school subjects found useful and interesting. The third showed pupils' attitudes to school as seen by teachers, the major items being teachers' assessments of whether the pupil was aggressive in attitude or behaviour and how hard he or she worked in school. This is referred to as 'Acceptability of school behaviour'. A fourth set of items appeared to indicate youngsters' 'Identification with school', a positive identification being shown by those who would have liked a longer school day, who thought that being at work was or would be worse than being at school, who liked school very much, looked forward to going to school, were not delighted when they had an excuse to stay away, considered that there were advantages in staying on at school for people who were not taking examinations and did not think that school was always the same. A fifth group of items assessed pupils' 'Attitudes to school discipline'. Here the unfavourable attitude is easiest to describe. It was shown by those who thought that teachers forgot they were growing up and always treated them like children, who resented teachers telling them what they could and could not do, who said that most of their friends came from near home rather than school, that school was the same day after day, week after week, who were delighted when they had an excuse to stay away from school and thought that being at work was or would be better than being at school. The sixth group of items appeared to identify those youngsters who lacked confidence and wanted to avoid having to face new situations. The main items here were that the teacher assessed the pupil as shy and withdrawn; the pupil considered that there were advantages in staying on at school for those not taking examinations and said that most of his or her friends came from near home rather than near school. This is referred to as 'Timidity'.

*(Similar factor analyses also produced scales of 'School Objectives' and 'Values, Interests and Home Backgrounds'. These three major dimensions and their sub-scales were then used to compare the attitudes of pupils who stayed on at school with those who had left. The results are summarized in the figure on page 140.)*

The diagram shows the average scores for the two sub-groups, 15 year old leavers and those staying on at school, on each of the six attitude dimensions, the five school objective dimensions and

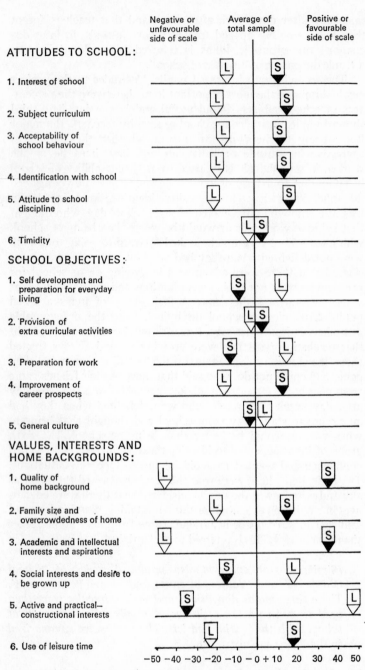

L = Youngsters leaving school at 15     S = Youngsters staying on at school

Comparison of average scores of 15 year old leavers and stayers on dimensions of attitudes to school; school objectives; values, interests and home backgrounds.

the six for values, interests and home backgrounds. Again on each dimension the average for the whole sample of youngsters is zero. It can be seen that 15 year old leavers differed most of all from those staying on at school in the quality of their home backgrounds which were much less favourable for leavers; in being very much less inclined to have any intellectual or academic interests; and in being much more generally of an active than a sedentary bent and more interested in practical-constructional activities than were stayers. They also showed differences from those staying on at school on a number of other dimensions, although to a lesser degree. They tended to come from larger families and more overcrowded homes. On the whole they occupied their leisure time less satisfactorily than did the stayers and more easily became bored or gave their parents cause for anxiety. They were more inclined than stayers to resent school discipline, they were less identified with and interested in school life, they considered their subject curricula less useful and interesting and their behaviour in school was more likely to be considered unsatisfactory by their teachers. Even more than those staying on they wanted their education to be concerned with preparing them for their working life but they were less anxious than stayers that it should be concentrated on improving their career prospects. They more generally wished the school to help them to develop as people and to make the most of themselves and they wanted to learn things which would be useful in everyday life.

Enquiry 1 thus emphasized the difficult task facing teachers following the raising of the school-leaving age. The Schools Council has been active in encouraging the development of more interesting courses for the extra year in an attempt to change the unfavourable attitudes of some young school leavers. The study illustrates only one of several ways of measuring attitudes. But whichever method is used, it is still important to obtain detailed evidence of reliability and validity. Any measurement instrument should give very similar results on repeated application to the same person (reliability); it should also measure the dimension it is expected to measure (validity). The following research article illustrates the rather lengthy process required to demonstrate the utility of an attitude scale. The items in this 'academic motivation' scale seem to have much in common with what Barker Lunn has called an attitude, and termed 'importance of doing well at school'. The distinction between 'attitude' and 'motivation' perhaps needs clarifying.

## Academic Motivation and School Attainment
### (N. J. Entwistle, 1968)[1]

#### I. INTRODUCTION

Academic motivation is a concept which has been introduced to explain some of the differences in the school attainment of children with similar measured abilities. Differences between children in their determination to succeed in their academic studies are familiar to teachers, but assessment of these differences has proved difficult. Various attempts have been made to relate this 'academic motivation' to the more general personality trait of 'achievement motivation.' Most of the work on this 'n-ach' variable has been done in America by McClelland (1953) and Atkinson and Feather (1966), using a thematic apperception test. The results obtained when this measure has been used to predict academic achievement in school have been largely contradictory (Lavin, 1965). A more specific measure of 'academic motivation' appears to be necessary.

The most promising attempts at measuring this specific motivation have also been made in America. Schlesser and Finger (1962) devised a self-rating scale, the Personal Values Inventory, which indentified attitudes and personality traits related to behaviour in school and college. In a factor analysis of the sub-scores from this inventory Finger and Schlesser (1965) showed that a factor of 'academic motivation' was clearly related to grades in high school. This factor appeared to cover 'aspiration', 'attitudes to school' and 'study habits'. In Britain Astington (1960) used a simple unrefined scale and more recently Buxton (1966) reported the early stages of the development of two scales of 'academic achievement motivation'. In Aberdeen an 'academic motivation' scale was devised as part of a follow-up study into the age of transfer to secondary school (Nisbet and Entwistle, 1969).

#### II. DEVELOPMENT OF ABERDEEN ACADEMIC MOTIVATION INVENTORY

Following on the work of Finger and Schlesser and other similar scales derived from existing personality tests (Austrin, 1965; Taylor and Farquhar, 1966), thirty-six items were produced which appeared to cover, in the British setting, the dimensions

[1] Edited version of an article whch appeared in *British Journal of Educational Psychology, 38*, 181–8.

contributing to academic motivation. The Personal Values Inventory had used both direct and indirect items to measure the children's attitudes. The indirect items asked the child to report what his teachers, parents or peer group thought of his behaviour. A similar approach was used in the pilot Aberdeen inventory.

An item analysis was used to refine this scale, based on the responses of 150 first-year children from a Scottish comprehensive school. Three teachers were asked to put each child into one of five defined categories of motivation. Items were rejected if they failed to discriminate between groups with high or low teachers' ratings. In this way the number of items was reduced to twenty-four. Apparently indirect items such as 'Do your parents think you should work harder-' were not meaningful to Scottish 12-year-olds. The majority of such items were eliminated by this analysis. It was also found that certain items had to be modified to make the question less extreme or to avoid an indirect measurement of intelligence. The pattern of responses by the children rated highly by their teachers was used as the basis of the revised scoring scheme. (The final scale contained items such as)[1]

Is it important to you to do well at school?
Does your mind often wander off the subject during lessons?
Do you enjoy most lessons?
When you are given a difficult problem, do you enjoy trying to find the answer?
Do you generally find lessons rather dull?
Do you dread being given a test on your homework?
Do your friends think that you never take work seriously?
Would you like to leave school as soon as possible?

The revised version of this inventory was cross-validated in another comprehensive school by comparing teachers' ratings with pupils' scores on the inventory. The mean academic motivation scores for the various groups shown in Table 9:4 show

TABLE 9:4  *Mean scores on the Academic Motivation Inventory of pupils in high or low streams rated by their teachers as having either high or low motivation*

| | Rating on academic motivation | | | | Significance of difference between high and low groups | |
| Streams | High | N | Low | N | t | p |
| --- | --- | --- | --- | --- | --- | --- |
| ABC | 20·73 | 41 | 18·76 | 67 | 4·17 | <0·001 |
| DE | 17·50 | 12 | 14·68 | 38 | 2·24 | <0·05 |

significant differences between children rated high and those rated low by their teachers. But there were also significant differences in mean academic motivation score between high and

[1] The full scale is given in the original article.

low streams, suggesting that pupils with high academic motivation scores also tended to be more intelligent.

This cross-validation indicated that the scale had some concurrent validity, though the evidence was not conclusive. It was realised that the criterion of validity used was open to criticism as the pupils had only been in secondary school for a term, and thus further evidence of concurrent validity was sought.

Test-retest reliability was investigated with a group of 88 children who were retested after an interval of $2\frac{1}{2}$ months. A reliability coefficient of $+0 \cdot 81$ was obtained with this sample. Correction for homogeneity raised this value to $+0 \cdot 83$.

### III. CORRELATIONAL ANALYSIS

As part of the follow-up study being conducted in Aberdeen, the academic motivation inventory was given to a complete age-group of children towards the end of their first year in secondary school. The analysis was limited to those children for whom complete data had been obtained on tests given between the ages of 11 and 13. This sample was about 80 per cent of the age-group and was shown to be representative of the age-group as a whole.

School attainment was measured using teachers' estimates averaged over five subjects, scaled against Moray House Advanced Verbal Reasoning Test 12 by the method described by Yates and Pidgeon (1957, page 88). The previous tests given to this age-group were: NFER Non-verbal Test 1 at age 11; Moray House Verbal Reasoning Test 72 at age 12; and primary teachers' estimates of attainment scaled on Moray House attainment tests at age 12. The correlations of these tests with the inventory are shown in Table 9:5. Allowing for the decrease in correlation as

TABLE 9:5 *Product-moment correlation coefficients between academic motivation inventory and various intellectual measures by sexes*

| Variable | Age | Boys (N = 1385) | Girls (N = 1322) |
|---|---|---|---|
| Teachers' estimate of attainment | 13 | 0·501 | 0·412 |
| Verbal reasoning | 13 | 0·385 | 0·339 |
| Teachers' estimate of attainment | 12 | 0·412 | 0·360 |
| Verbal reasoning | 12 | 0·369 | 0·326 |
| Non-verbal reasoning | 11 | 0·301 | 0·283 |

time interval increases, it is clear that the inventory correlates more highly with attainment than with reasoning ability. This result suggests that the inventory is measuring a non-intellectual trait independently related to school attainment, and gives a much more satisfactory indication of concurrent validity.

### IV. ANALYSIS OF 'IMPROVING' AND 'DETERIORATING' PUPILS

Much of the previous research on 'over-achievers' and 'under-achievers' has been affected by statistical regression to the mean (Thorndike, 1963). If children are identified whose attainment scores are higher or lower than their reasoning test scores, it is inevitable that the 'over-achievers' will contain a majority of less intelligent children. These children with low reasoning test scores have more room for improvement than children with much higher scores. The differences in intelligence between such groups of over- and under-achievers prevent any valid conclusions being drawn about the improved correlates of performance.

In the present analysis of changes in attainment, regression effects were controlled by sorting into 'improvers' and 'deteriorators' at different levels of ability.

*(The groups were subsequently recombined and a highly significant difference in scores on the academic motivation inventory was found between 'improvers' and 'deteriorators' in both senior secondary (grammar) and junior secondary schools.)*

The possible social origins of 'achievement motivation' have recently been discussed by Swift (1966). It was thus anticipated that the scale of academic motivation might be an indirect measure of social class. The analysis was thus repeated within social class. For this purpose three bands of father's occupation were formed on the basis of Fraser's (1959) previous findings in Aberdeen. These bands were: (*a*) social classes I and II on the

TABLE 9:6    *Differences in the mean scores on the Academic Motivation Inventory of 'improvers' and 'deteriorators' within social class*

| Social class | Type of secondary school | Improving group | | Deteriorating group | | Significance of difference | |
|---|---|---|---|---|---|---|---|
| | | Mean | (N) | Mean | (N) | t | p |
| High | Senior | 19·43 | 82 | 17·33 | 41 | 2·83 | <0·01 |
| (I, II) | Junior | 17·41 | 22 | 15·68 | 34 | 1·46 | NS |
| Intermediate | Senior | 19·88 | 74 | 17·43 | 83 | 4·88 | <0·001 |
| (III a, b) | Junior | 17·81 | 98 | 15·73 | 101 | 3·54 | <0·001 |
| Low | Senior | 18·35 | 40 | 17·23 | 66 | 1·77 | NS |
| (IIIc, IV, V) | Junior | 17·38 | 80 | 14·91 | 153 | 4·28 | <0·001 |

Registrar General's Scale; (*b*) social class III (non-manual and highest skilled manual) and (*c*) social classes III (remaining occupations), IV and V. The mean scores of 'improving' and 'deteriorating' groups on the academic motivation inventory, within social class, are shown in Table 9:6. These results show that the academic motivation scores distinguish between 'improvers' and 'deteriorators' within each social class, although the

differences are not significant in every group. Certainly academic
motivation scores are related to social class, but not to any great
extent. This dimension describes marked differences in children's
behaviour within the social classes and these differences are
related to changes in school attainment.


## V. DISCUSSION OF RESULTS

The implications of the present findings seem to be that social
class is not closely related to 'academic motivation' as measured
by the Aberdeen Inventory. The theory of the origins of this
motivation has not been developed far enough to give satisfactory
explanations. Certainly a child's achievement motivation is likely
to reflect parental attitudes and patterns of child rearing (Rosen
and d'Andrade, 1959). But the Plowden Social Survey (1967) has
shown that there are wide differences in 'parental aspiration'
within social classes, and that this measure shows a much greater
independent relationship with primary school attainment in
reading than does the variable of 'father's occupation'. Swift
(1967) has stressed that 'social class' is too broad a measure to
describe the different home environments experienced by children. The significant differences in academic motivation within
social class found in the present investigation reinforce this conclusion. But this may not be a complete explanation. We cannot
assume that all children react in the same way to similar environments. Eysenck (1957) has suggested that inherited differences in
'conditionability' may affect children's reactions to their environment. The attitudes and behaviour making up 'academic
motivation' presumably represent the result of interactions
between the child's environment and his basic temperament,
rather than simply more specific environmental variables within
social class. It seems likely that any attempt to formulate a
satisfactory theory of 'academic motivation' must take account
of both temperamental traits and environmental variables.

The present study, however, was not an attempt to construct
such a theory: its aim was to measure academic motivation by a
self-rating inventory. The design of such an inventory demands
caution. The questions must be meaningful to the child and must
also avoid any undesirable mental set. Most indirect items were
found to be unsuitable for Scottish children and the other
questions were chosen to avoid any implied value judgments on
the behaviour being reported. The results obtained from the
correlational analysis and from the analysis of 'improvers' and
'deteriorators' show that this scale is measuring a behaviour trait,
other than intelligence, which is related to school attainment.
The content of this inventory covers attitudes to school, aspira-

tions, work habits and the determination to do well in school work. It seems reasonable then to assume that this scale has been effective in measuring 'academic motivation'.

REFERENCES

ASTINGTON, E. (1960) 'Personality assessments and academic performance in a boys' grammar school.' *Brit. J. Educ. Psychol.,* 30, 225–36.

ATKINSON, J. W., and FEATHER, N. T. (1966) *A Theory of Achievement Motivation.* New York : Wiley.

AUSTRIN, H. R. (1965) 'Cross-validation of an attitude scale for the indentification of high and low academic achievers.' *J. Educ. Res.,* 58, 9, 426–8.

BUXTON, C. E. (1966) 'Evaluations of forced-choice and Likert-type tests of motivation to academic achievement.' *Brit. J. Educ. Psychol.,* 36, 192–201.

EYSENCK, H. J. (1957) *The Dynamics of Anxiety and Hysteria.* London : Routledge and Kegan Paul.

FINGER, J. A., and SCHLESSER, G. E. (1965) 'Non-intellective predictors of academic success in school and college.' *School Rev.,* 73, 14–29.

FRASER, E. (1959) *Home Environment and the School.* Scottish Council for Research in Education Publication 43. London : University of London Press.

LAVIN, D. E. (1965) *The Prediction of Academic Success.* New York : Russell Sage Foundation.

MCCLELLAND, D. C. (1953) *The Achievement Motive.* New York : Appleton-Century-Crofts.

NISBET, J. D., and ENTWISTLE, N. J. (1969) *The Transition to Secondary Education.* Scottish Council for Research in Education Publication 59. London : University of London Press.

PLOWDEN SOCIAL SURVEY (1967) in *Children and their Primary Schools* (Volume 2). London : H.M.S.O.

ROSEN, B. C., and D'ANDRADE, R. (1959) 'The psycho-social origins of achievement motivation.' *Sociometry,* 22, 185–218.

SCHLESSER, G. E., and FINGER, J. A. (1962) *Personal Values Inventory.* Hamilton, New York : Colgate Univ. Press.

SWIFT, D. F. (1966) 'Social class and achievement motivation.' *Educ. Res.,* 8, 83–95.

SWIFT, D. F. (1967) 'Family environment and 11 + success : some basic predictors.' *Brit. J. Educ. Psychol.,* 37, 10–21.

TAYLOR, R. G., and FARQUHAR, W. W. (1966) 'The validity and reliability of the human trait inventory designed to measure under- and over-achievement.' *J. Educ. Res.,* 59, 227–30.

THORNDIKE, R. L. (1963) *The Concepts of Over- and Under-*

*achievement*. New York : Teachers' College, Columbia University.

YATES, A., and PIDGEON, D. A. (1957) *Admission to Grammar Schools*. London : Newnes and N.F.E.R.

*The extracts in this chapter have shown how attitude scales can be developed by summing the scores on a series of questions. Ideally these scales should be carefully refined by factor analysis so as to cover a single attitude dimension. Normally this process is carried out well in advance of the investigation in order to leave time for validation, but it is possible, as in Enquiry 1, to form the scales retrospectively. The dangers in this approach are that some dimensions may be represented by one or two questions and that no independent evidence of validity is collected prior to using such 'scales'.*

*Barker Lunn was able to develop scales of both personality and attitudes using similar questions in a single inventory. This is not surprising. The main differences between personality and attitudes are that personality traits are considered to be less likely than attitudes to change over time and that attitude dimensions are specific—attitudes towards something or somebody. Evidence collected in the studies reported in this chapter shows the importance of knowing about children's attitudes and motivation. Increasingly educational objectives are being formulated in ways which emphasise non-cognitive aspects of attainment.*

*In Chapter 8 teachers called for further research into personality. In fact there has already been some research into the relationship between personality and attainment, and this has recently been summarised (Eysenck and Cookson, 1969; Entwistle, 1972). Examples of such studies are not included here, as several articles have recently been made widely available in Personality Growth and Learning (Cashdan and Whitehead, 1971). To complete this chapter, however, a short extract from one of the recent reviews of research in this area follows.*

## Personality and Academic Attainment
### (N. J. Entwistle, 1972)[1]

Personality has been defined by Allport (1963) as 'the dynamic organisation within the individual of those psychophysical systems that determine hischaracteristic behaviour and thought'

[1] Adapted from an article in *British Journal of Educational Psychology*, 42, 137–51, a fuller version of which appears in Butcher, H. J., and Pont, H. B. (1973) *Educational Research in Britain, Volume 3* (University of London Press).

(page 28). If this definition is accepted it appears inevitable that personality will be an important determinant of classroom behaviour and ultimate scholastic success. The measurement of personality is, however, far from simple and the initial lack of success in isolating personality correlates of school attainment to a large extent can be attributed to this difficulty. The advent of pencil and paper group tests which have been carefully developed and validated has stimulated renewed interest in this research area. As a result there is now a sufficiently large literature for certain trends to emerge. Most of the British studies have used the personality inventories developed by either Eysenck or Cattell. This review thus concentrates on these factorial approaches to the measurement of personality.

Eysenck and Cattell have used different methods of identifying the factors which can be used to describe human personality. The resulting structures appear dissimilar at first sight. Papers by Burt (1965) and Adcock (1965) and a recent book (Eysenck and Eysenck, 1969a) have compared and contrasted the two approaches. Basically Eysenck had strong theoretical grounds for hypothesising two important, yet distinct, dimensions underlying human behaviour. Factor analysis designed to produce unrelated factors, allowed Eysenck to choose items for his inventory which measured the traits of extraversion and neuroticism (emotional instability).

An understanding of the terms extraversion and neuroticism, as used by Eysenck, demands a study of the items included in the various inventories (Maudsley or Eysenck in both junior and adult versions). Neuroticism is characterised by unnecessary worrying, by feelings of restlessness, by moodiness and by general nervousness. The stable person shows behaviour which is generally controlled; he tends to be reliable, even-tempered and calm. The typical extravert is 'sociable, likes parties, has many friends, needs to have people to talk to, and does not like studying by himself. He craves excitement, takes chances, often sticks his neck out, acts on the spur of the moment, and is generally an impulsive individual ... The typical introvert, on the other hand, is a quiet retiring sort of person, introspective, fond of books rather than people; he is reserved and distant except with intimate friends. He tends to plan ahead, "looks before he leaps", and distrusts the impulse of the moment' (Eysenck, 1965, pages 59–60). Scores on these two dimensions are expected to be normally distributed with the majority of people being neither extraverted nor introverted, neurotic nor stable. For certain analyses, however, it is useful to identify individuals with above or below average scores on each trait and to describe four personality 'types'—stable extraverts, stable introverts, unstable extraverts and unstable introverts.

Cattell (1965) prefers to use an alternative method of factor analysis which produces inter-related factors. Out of a vast range of items, he has isolated up to 17 primary source traits which are given an alphabetic notation (e.g. A, G, N, Q,). Because the factors are inter-related it is possible to simplify Cattell's structure by repeated factor analyses which extract higher order factors. Warburton (1968) provided a lucid summary of the pattern of higher-order factors. The five second-order factors are reduced by successive analyses down to two fourth-order factors, as shown below :

| Second-order | Third-order | Fourth-order |
|---|---|---|
| Stability ⎱<br>Conservatism ⎰ | Adaptation ⎫ | Integration |
| Extraversion ⎱<br>Toughmindedness ⎰ | Thrust ⎭ | |
| Conscientiousness ⎱<br>or Morality ⎰ | Morality | Morality |

It is interesting to note that the two most important second-order factors are extraversion and stability, which are similar to Eysenck's major dimensions. Another two factors carry labels identical to what Eysenck sees as social attitudes (Eysenck, 1951). Eysenck has also moved away from the simple two-factor structure both by adding a psychoticism dimension (Eysenck and Eysenck, 1969b) and by subdividing extraversion into sociability and impulsivity (Eysenck and Eysenck, 1963). There are thus elements in common in these two descriptions of personality.

## RELATIONSHIPS WITH ACADEMIC ATTAINMENT

One large-scale study on school children was conducted by Eysenck and Cookson (1969). In the introduction to their report they review previous research in the area and conclude that extraverts tend to be better at schoolwork in late primary and early secondary school. Stability (low neuroticism) is also associated with high attainment at this age level. The authors also comment on the likelihood of an age effect. By the time pupils enter higher education there has been an apparent reversal in the relationships with attainment. Neurotic introverts seem to make the most successful students. More recent research on students has, however, altered the picture. Introversion is consistently related to good degree results, but the effect of neuroticism is far from clear. It seems to be dependent on area of study (Entwistle, 1972), and this is but one of the complications which has been encountered in this area of research.

Repeatedly, throughout the review of the literature, the possible effect of intervening variables has been implicit in research reports. An intervening variable is one which affects the size or the direction of the relationship between the two main dimensions under consideration. It is already clear that sex and age have been acting in this way. Further analysis of the data obtained from the follow-up in Aberdeen secondary pupils (see Chapter 6) by Entwistle and Welsh (1969) suggested that there might also be different relationships among bright children compared with those found for pupils of below average ability. Dividing their sample into top and bottom thirds in terms of ability level, they found that introversion was linked to high achievement for bright boys, whereas extraversion was the more favourable trait in the low ability group. The results for girls were similar, but less marked.

There are other intervening variables which may affect the relationships between personality and attainment. A number of studies, such as the one by Cattell and Butcher (1968), have observed differing relationships among urban children and rural children, but these may be a reflection of differences in classroom organisation, in average class size or in methods of teaching. The range of approaches in primary schools, between formal and informal methods, suggests that different personality types would be successful in contrasting educational climates. These possibilities are being investigated at present. In addition, it seems probable that there will be an interaction between the teacher's personality and the performance of children of differing personality types. There are formidable obstacles to research of this kind, but it may be crucial to overcome them. It may be only in this way that the observed relationships between personality and attainment will be fully explained.

Finally, it may be salutary to look for practical, rather than theoretical, importance in the research findings. It still requires considerable faith and imagination to see where these results may lead. The lack of generality in relationships and the probable link between teaching methods and personality correlates of success both reinforce the growing realisation of the importance of variety in the presentation of material to be learned. Even at the same intellectual level no one teaching method or way of organising learning experiences will be ideal for all pupils or for all students. Ultimately, it may be possible to allow the 'consumers' to choose the method of instruction, at least in the later stages of education. Formal, systematic presentation may still be preferred by some; unstructured freedom may suit others. An understanding of personality differences may help to anticipate such preferences. Research into the relationships between personality and academic attainment, with an emphasis on changes

F

with age, may provide guidance as to the appropriate provision of alternative methods of presentation at different educational stages.

## REFERENCES

ADCOCK, C. L. (1965) 'A comparison of the concepts of Cattell and Eysenck.' *Br. J. educ. Psychol.*, *35*, 90–8.

ALLPORT, G. W. (1963) *Pattern and Growth in Personality*. New York: Holt, Rinehart and Winston.

BURT, C. (1965) 'Factorial studies of personality and their bearing on the work of the teacher.' *Br. J. educ. Psychol.*, *35*, 368–77.

CATTELL, R. B. (1965) *The Scientific Analysis of Personality*. Harmondsworth: Penguin Books.

CATTELL, R. B., and BUTCHER, H. J. (1968) *The Prediction of Achievement and Creativity*. New York: Bobbs-Merrill.

ENTWISTLE, N. J. (1972) 'Students and their academic performance in different types of institution.' In BUTCHER, H. J., and RUDD, E. *Contemporary Problems in Higher Education*. London: McGraw-Hill.

ENTWISTLE, N. J., and WELSH, J. (1969) 'Correlates of school attainment at different ability levels.' *Br. J. educ. Psychol.*, *39*, 57–63.

EYSENCK, H. J. (1951) 'Social attitudes questionnaire and scoring key.' *Br. J. Psychol.*, *42*, 114–22.

EYSENCK, H. J. (1965) *Fact and Fiction in Psychology*. Harmondsworth: Penguin Books.

EYSENCK, H. J., and COOKSON, D. (1969) 'Personality in primary school children: 1—Ability and achievement.' *Br. J. educ. Psychol.*, *39*, 109–22.

EYSENCK, S. B. G., and EYSENCK, H. J. (1963) 'On the dual nature of extraversion.' *Br. J. soc. clin. Psychol.*, *2*, 46–55.

EYSENCK, H. J., and EYSENCK, S. B. G. (1969a) *Personality Structure and Measurement*. London: Routledge and Kegan Paul.

EYSENCK, H. J., and EYSENCK, S. B. G. (1969b) ' "Psychoticism" in children: a new personality variable.' *Res. in Educ.*, *1*, 21–37.

WARBURTON, F. W. (1968). 'The assessment of personality traits.' In MORRIS, J. F., and LUNZER, E. A. *Development in Learning, Volume 3—Contexts of Education*. London: Staples.

# 10 Convergent and Divergent Thinking

*A succession of studies has demonstrated that 'intelligence' tests correlate closely with school attainment and a book of readings on human intelligence has recently been published (Butcher and Lomax, 1972). But conventional measures of intelligence have tended to concentrate on the assessment of logical reasoning: the well-known Moray House Intelligence tests, used in the past in many areas of Britain for 11 plus selection, have now been re-named Verbal Reasoning Tests. To each item in such tests, there is a single answer; the child's thought processes are expected to* converge *on that answer by logical reasoning. But can a definition of intelligence include only this type of thinking? What about the productive use of imagination? Dissatisfaction with a narrow definition of intellectual abilities stimulated research into creativity and divergent thinking. Part of a chapter from R. H. Thouless's* Map of Educational Research *provides the background to research on creativity and leads to three examples of recent studies which have looked at various aspects of divergent thinking as contrasted with convergent abilities.*

### Creativity
### (R. H. Thouless, 1969)[1]

Research on creativity has been active for some years, particularly in the USA. The educationalist may regard this research as challenging the bias in conventional education towards training pupils to produce the 'right' answers, with relative neglect of the type of intellectual activity which explores new possibilities and looks for original answers to intellectual questions.

It is not only teaching practice that tends to favour the right answer and to discourage novelty of response; this bias is also to be found in educational testing. The measurement of intelligence

[1] Extracted from *Map of Educational Research* (N.F.E.R.), pages 271–6.

by the use of intelligence tests is, for example, to a considerable extent, an assessment of how successful the candidate is in giving the right answer to a problem in which one answer is right and all other answers are wrong. A simple example of such a problem is the item in Terman's test of intelligence in which the child is asked: 'Snow is white; coal is ...?' The required answer here is 'black' and any other answer is treated as wrong. Such problems may be called 'single-answer' problems. They have the obvious advantage that their results are easy to assess.

There has been for some time a suspicion among some educationalists that although an IQ obtained by means of such items is a useful prognosticator of academic success, there may also be another range of intellectual abilities important in many tasks of everyday life and for the higher levels of academic achievement. Dr Hudson (1964), for example, has asked the question whether, with present methods of assessment, including intelligence testing, a selecting board could have reasonably offered a research grant to either Einstein or Darwin. He suggests that the answer is that they could not, and he may well be right. Both of these men had high intelligence, but they had somewhat erratic habits of work and showed no marked early interest in their subjects, yet they had some quality that made them brilliantly successful discoverers in their own fields. It does not follow that this additional quality can be either exactly specified or measured.

The additional quality may provisionally be given some such name as 'creativity', and the psychologist may hope to devise tests for measuring it. If he succeeds, it may be possible in the future to make a different kind of assessment of a budding Einstein or Darwin that would make a selecting board unhesitatingly accept these two men as promising research students. Both the specification of creativity and the devising of ways of measuring it are problems on which research is now active; they are not yet fully solved.

Research on creativity was to a great extent started by interest in the question of what the inventor or successful research worker needs more than the mere ability to give the right answer to a single answer question. It is not, however, only the inventor or research worker who needs to be able to think along unaccustomed lines and to produce new solutions to problems, and the practical educational problem of creativity is not that of making all children into inventors or research workers. The idea that has guided much educational research into this topic is that the more creative individual is the more fully developed and better adjusted personality, and that an educational system which discourages or thwarts the creative aspects of ability in children may be stunting and deforming their personality development. The ordinary child, too, must be encouraged to produce new solutions to problems that have more than one answer.

Examples of creative activities are writing an essay or painting a picture. At any point of development of these tasks there is not only one sentence or one patch of paint that is the right one for the next step; there are an indefinitely large number of alternatives to choose from, some of which are better than others. The successful completion of such a task depends on the performer being aware of a wide range of choices, and also having the ability to make from that range a wise selection for the purpose in hand.

Such tasks are now commonly called 'creative tasks' and the postulated capacity to perform creative tasks is referred to as 'creative ability'. The term 'creative' is used with a considerable amount of imprecision to denote a range of abilities which may be important in invention or in composition, and which may also be of value in effective social life. The term has not always been used by different writers to cover the same range of abilities, although always it has had the general implication that it refers to the kinds of ability that are used in breaking across the bounds of habitual responses. It would probably not be profitable to try to give the term 'creativity' a more precise meaning than it has in the literature of research into the subject. It seems to be used as a name for a variety of abilities for which it remains a useful class name, as vague and as useful, for example, as the word 'game'. This range may combine a number of different abilities which it may be possible separately to define with precision.

It is not necessary to assume that there is a unitary 'creative ability' or that there is a sharp distinction between creative and non-creative tasks. Rather we seem to have the situation that there is a continuum between highly non-creative tasks such as that of conventionally giving the colour name of coal as 'black' and highly creative tasks such as that of writing a poem on the blackness of coal, with every gradation between these extremes. The degree to which a task is creative or non-creative may also vary with the individual. The task, for example, of replying to the question : 'What is twice two?' may be non-creative for the adult but by no means non-creative to the child in Piaget's 'concrete operational' stage of development who achieves with difficulty insight into what is implied by the statement, 'Twice two is four'.

The idea that the more striking achievements of men of outstanding ability imply something more than the ability to give the 'right' answers to difficult questions is by no means a new one. When Galton (1883) made his pioneer studies into the characteristics of men of genius he pointed out that these were distinguished by originality and not merely by the 'logical' correctness of their ideas. This originality he referred to as the 'fluency and freedom of their associations' which is one element in what is now called 'creativity'. This aspect of mental ability was also explored in an early research by Hargreaves (1927) into the 'faculty of imagination'. The research interest in such questions was, however, quiescent for some years, partly no doubt because they did not fit easily into the thought patterns of a behaviourist psychology. For various reasons, however, particularly perhaps the need for education to develop and encourage the more original kinds of thinking in its pupils, there has been an awakening interest in creativity as a problem for psychological research and for those concerned with education.

This new interest has developed in America, particularly during the last fifteen years. In 1950, Guilford, in his Presidential address to the American Psychological Association, emphasized the necessity for psychologists to interest themselves in the problem of creativity (Guilford, 1950). This suggestion by Guilford has led to a great deal of research in the USA, some of which is of considerable educational importance, particularly the researches of Torrance (1963). Some of the educational implications of the work of Guilford and Torrance have been explored in this country by Vernon (1964), by Hudson (1962) and Goldman (1964).

One of the first research problems in connection with the subject of creativity is in what sense such a category can be said to be a real one. In other words : is there any specifically creative ability as distinct from the 'general' intellectual ability which is measured by existing tests? Guilford (1958) has put forward a model of the structure of intellect as a three-dimensional figure containing 120 cells each of which represents a different kind of intellectual ability. This model is derived by a verbal process of distinguishing four types of content, six types of product, and five types of operation, giving by their product 120 nameable abilities. This model is considered to be justified by a process of multiple factor analysis of batteries of tests to confirm that a given cell has a content. This method of verification does not, however, alter the fact that the model has been derived by a rather doubtful verbal intuitive process. The basic assumption underlying the derivation of the model is that what can be named as an ability is a separate ability. The model remains a product of the language chosen to describe abilities, and subsequent attempts at validation by multiple factor analysis can prove only that this is a useful model and not that it possesses any validity superior to that of any other verbal system of classification of abilities.

The model may, however, be a useful tool of thought, and its justification may lie, not in its supposed verification by multiple factor analysis, but in its usefulness in drawing attention to previously neglected areas of ability. Guilford (1962) points out, for example, that some of the abilities named in his system do not fall within the range of what is measured by the ordinary intelligence test, but fall rather within the field of 'creativity'. In particular, he distinguishes between the kind of operation that he calls 'convergent production' in which there is one acceptable answer, and 'divergent production' leading to a variety of answers. As examples of these, he gives the item: 'What is the opposite of good?' which leads to the one answer 'Bad', and the item: 'What words mean almost the opposite of good?', to which a variety of answers might be acceptable, such as *poor*, *sinful* and *terrible*. Guilford does not equate divergent thinking with creativity, but suggests that in the category of divergent production 'there are many abilities that are somewhat crucial to creative thinking, imagination and invention'.

The traits which Guilford regards as belonging to the category of creativity are: fluency of thinking, flexibility of thinking, originality, re-definition and elaboration. The measuring devices for creativity that he has designed or adapted are based on these traits. His tests require the testees, for example, to suggest improvements in a toy or other industrial product, to produce words containing a specific letter or combination of letters, to produce in a limited time as many synonyms as possible for a common word, to produce phrases or sentences, to name objects with certain properties (e.g. objects that are hard, white and edible) or to give various uses for a common object. Scoring is by considering the number of responses that are clever or unusual, or that call for remote associations.

A good account of the tests that have been devised to measure creative abilities is to be found in an article by Goldman (1964) in *Educational Research*. The first tests were devised by Guilford and were used for students in higher education. These have already been briefly described. A more elaborate test scale (the Minnesota scale) was devised by Torrance (1962a), who was guided by the Guilford model of intellect. He began by adapting some of Guilford's materials to make them suitable for young children. New tests were also introduced and the number of test items was increased. Guilford, for example, had asked his subjects to think of as many unusual uses for a brick as they could; Torrance used the same question but substituted tin cans. Torrance's test scale includes non-verbal tests such as the completion of incomplete figures, verbal tests such as that of asking how a toy dog or toy monkey could be changed in such a way that boys and girls would have more fun in playing with it, and imaginative tasks, such as that of writing a story chosen from among several topics, all of which deal with deviant behaviour of some person or animal such as: 'The dog that doesn't bark' or 'The flying monkey', and so on. The tests are not yet in their final form, and research is being carried on to find out what combinations of tests are suitable for different age groups. Fairly high reliabilities are claimed for the tests.

There remains the question of the validity of these tests, that is, of whether they succeed in measuring anything we should be inclined to call 'creativity'. It has been pointed out truly by Vernon (1964) that we cannot regard a test as valid merely because it looks as if it involves creativity, but only for the reason that the test is actually found to differentiate between individuals known on other grounds to be creative or non-creative.

On the problem of whether creativity is an aspect of ability distinct from intelligence, the situation is by no means satisfactory. The evidence generally quoted for this view is the research reported by Getzels and Jackson (1962). These investigators tested 449 children in grades 6–12 for creativity and for intelligence. The tests for measuring creativity included word associations, a task of suggesting as many uses as possible for various things, finding hidden shapes in geometrical figures, the completion of fables, and questions in which the child had to make up as many arithmetical problems as possible from a story in which a number of numerical facts were given. Omitting those children who had scored highly both on the tests of intelligence and on those of creativity, Getzels and Jackson made a comparison between the 28 individuals who had scored in the top 20 per cent on intelligence tests but not in the top 20 per cent in creativity, and the 24 individuals who had scored in the top 20 per cent in creativity tests but not in the intelligence tests.

They found that school achievement scores for the 28 children of high intelligence were 55·0 while those for the group of high creativity were 56·3. Both figures were significantly different from the average of 49·9 for the total sample of 449 children, but these two figures do not appear to be significantly different from each other. The indication is that the children of high creativity were not any worse in school performance than those of high intelligence, although the mean IQ of this group was somewhat below that of the total sample (which is presumably a result of omitting the group of children who showed both high creativity and high IQ). The evidence is, of course, insufficient for concluding that the high creativity group did better at school than the high intelligence group.

This evidence cannot be accepted on its face value as evidence for independence of creativity and IQ. The sample was untypical since it was drawn from a private university school with unusually high average intelligence which would tend to obscure any correlation between intelligence and creativity that might have been found in a more heterogeneous sample. The statistical procedure of excluding those children who have both high IQ and high creativity, and comparing the remaining sample of high IQ with the high creativity sample, is a somewhat crude one. The only figures from which a reasonably sure conclusion can be drawn are those showing that school achievement of the highly creative sample is no less than that of the IQ sample, although this finding is rendered somewhat less certain by the smallness of these samples. If, however, it is confirmed by other researches using larger groups this will indicate that creativity can be a genuine factor in determining school achievement.

From the finding that there are 28 pupils of high IQ who are not highly creative and 24 who are highly creative without high IQ, no conclusion whatever can be drawn. This would be positive evidence for some independence of creativity and IQ if, and only if, both IQ and creativity were measured without error. The result could follow either from independence of IQ and creativity or from errors of measurement in tests used, and one cannot, from the figures given, discover whether the differences between the groups are larger than can be attributed to error of measurement in the tests. Getzels and Jackson's finding on 'the relatively low relationship between IQ metric and measures of creativity at least at the IQ level of our subjects' is not supported by the figures given; it remains a hypothesis which may or may not be proved by other research.

More adequate analysis of the Getzels and Jackson figures does, in fact, indicate that they do not provide evidence of the independence of creativity and intelligence. The authors give a table of intercorrelations between all the tests used (both of creativity and intelligence) which makes it possible for other investigators to calculate the extent to which their hypothesis of relative independence between creativity and intelligence is supported. This has been done by Marsh (1964), who has applied the method of mutiple factor analysis to these intercorrelations. He finds that they indicate that the factor producing most of the variance is one that is common to the tests of creativity and to the tests of intelligence.

Although the Getzels and Jackson data by no means prove that there is a creative ability to some extent independent of intelligence, there is other evidence that points in this direction.

*(The situation is, however, still not clear, as Hasan and Butcher point out in their report of an attempt to replicate the findings of Getzels and Jackson.)*

REFERENCES

GALTON, F. (1883) *Inquiries into Human Faculty and its Development.* London : Macmillan.

GETZELS, J. W., and JACKSON, P. W. (1962) *Creativity and Intelligence.* New York : Wiley.

GOLDMAN, R. J. (1964) 'The Minnesota tests of creative thinking.' *Educ. Res.*, 7, 3–14.

GUILFORD, J. P. (1950) 'Creativity.' *Amer. Psychologist*, 444–54.

GUILFORD, J. P. (1958) 'A system of psychomotor abilities.' *Amer. J. Psychol.*, 53, 164–74.

GUILFORD, J. P. (1962) 'Parameters and categories of talent.' In Chapter 5 of *The Year Book of Education*. London : Evans Bros.

HARGREAVES, H. L. (1927) 'The faculty of imagination.' *Brit. J. Psychol. (Monograph Supplements)*, 10. Cambridge : Cambridge University Press.

HUDSON, L. (1962) 'Intelligence, divergence and potential originality.' *Nature*, 196, 601–2.

HUDSON, L. (1964) 'Academic sheep and research goats.' *New Society*, October 1964, 9–13.

MARSH, R. W. (1964) 'A statistical reanalysis of Getzels' and Jackson's data.' *Brit. J. educ. Psychol.*, 34, 91–3.

TORRANCE, E. P. (1963) *Education and Creative Potential*. Minneapolis : University of Minnesota Press.

VERNON, P. E. (1964) 'Creativity and intelligence.' *Educ. Res.*, 6, 163–9.

## Creativity and Intelligence
(P. Hasan and H. J. Butcher, 1966)[1]

Torrance (1962) repeated much of Getzels' and Jackson's work in several relatively non-selective schools with varying results. In about half of these replications the results were doubtful or negative, but Getzels' and Jackson's findings were supported in some cases. Yamamoto (1965) has also summarized more recent positive evidence. Edwards and Tyler (1965), on the other hand, working with a sample in a non-selective American junior high school, found almost entirely negative results and concluded that Getzels' and Jackson's findings about the relation of creativity, intelligence and achievement were not widely general-

[1] Extracted from an article, 'Creativity and intelligence : a partial replication with Scottish children of Getzels' and Jackson's study', which appeared in *British Journal of Psychology*, 57, 129–35.

izable. No repetitions of these experiments in Britain appear to have been reported.

The aim of the present investigation was therefore to throw some light on the generality of Getzels' and Jackson's findings, particularly those about relations between creativity, intelligence and attainment. Some slight modifications were made in the tests used in the methods of reporting results. The main difference, however, was in the attempt to apply their methods to a group of children unselected for ability.

METHOD

*Plan for the investigation*

The investigation was a partial replication of Getzels' and Jackson's work with a number of modifications.

 1   It was limited to considering relations between performance on (*a*) a test of verbal reasoning or 'intelligence'; (*b*) tests of divergent thinking or 'creativity'; (*c*) English and arithmetic attainment tests; and (*d*) teachers' ratings on desirability as a pupil. Personality factors and family background could not be investigated.

 2   Additional tests of creativity besides those used by Getzels and Jackson were included. One of their five tests had to be omitted.

 3   In addition to forming contrasting groups of children with high verbal-reasoning quotient (VRQ) and with high scores on tests of creativity respectively, a group which was high on *both* VRQ *and* creativity has also been included.

 4   The Scottish sample of pupils differed from Getzels' and Jackson's by being (*a*) more homogeneous in age and (*b*) more typical in level of ability of the general population of schoolchildren.

*Tests and other measures used.*

Testing was carried out at a Scottish local authority comprehensive school, with 175 pupils (100 boys, 75 girls) in their second year of secondary education. The following procedures were used.

Verbal-reasoning quotients were each child's mean score on two verbal reasoning tests administered by the local education authority for the purpose of secondary-school placement.

Arithmetic and English quotients (AQ and EQ) were obtained from Moray House English and Arithmetic attainment tests given during the course of the experiment.

Teachers' ratings on 'desirability as a pupil' were obtained by asking teachers to rate all subjects on a five-point scale with values of 15, 12, 9, 6, 3 for each category.

The creativity score was the aggregate of scores obtained from ten tests of creativity. (i) Word-Association (Getzels and Jackson, 1962). (ii) Uses of Things (Getzels and Jackson, 1962). (iii) Completing Fables (Getzels and Jackson, 1962). (iv) Make up Problems: modified from Getzels and Jackson (1962). (v) Word-Fluency (from Thurstone's P.M.A. battery). (v) Expressional Fluency: based on Guilford's (1956) model. (vii) Remote Associations Test (2): derived from Mednick's (1962) model, but with two instead of three words in each item. (viii) Remote Associations Test (3): as above, but with three words in each item. (ix) Drawing: subjects were given various geometrical and other shapes (triangle, tear-drop, oval, etc.) drawn on paper; they were required to make as many objects as possible by joining these shapes on tracing paper. (x) Circles (Torrance, 1962).

## Methods of analysis

Scores were treated in two main ways in order to make the results comparable with those of Getzels and Jackson. Intercorrelations were computed for the whole sample (a) among the creativity tests, (b) between creativity and VRQ, (c) between creativity and attainment and (d) between VRQ and attainment. Two contrasting experimental groups were selected in exactly the same way as by Getzels and Jackson; in addition, a third experimental group was formed of those children who scored high both in creativity and intelligence. Scores of the three experimental groups on all four kinds of variable were compared.

### RESULTS

## Relations between creativity and intelligence

The intercorrelation of the ten 'creativity' measures, the correlations of each with the aggregate 'creativity' score derived from them, and the correlations of all eleven 'creativity' variables with the Moray House Verbal Reasoning score are shown in Table 10:1. Every creativity measure correlates positively and significantly with VRQ and these correlations are generally rather higher than the intercorrelations between the measures of creativity. Indeed, the correlations of individual tests of creativity with VRQ are in most cases not very much lower than their correlations with the creativity aggregate, although the latter are part–whole correlations.

It is not possible to make a complete comparison between Table 10:1 and the results of Getzels and Jackson, first because not all the measures of creativity were the same in both studies,

**TABLE 10:1** *Intercorrelations of the ten tests of creativity, creativity aggregate and VRQ*

Boys and girls, N = 175. Coefficients in italics do not differ significantly from zero ($P > 0.05$).

| | 1 | 2 | 3 | 4 | 5 | 6 | 7 | 8 | 9 | 10 | 11 | 12 |
|---|---|---|---|---|---|---|---|---|---|---|---|---|
| 1 VRQ | — | 0·741 | 0·518 | 0·682 | 0·438 | 0·213 | 0·185 | 0·345 | 0·544 | 0·260 | 0·240 | 0·743 |
| 2 Word association | — | — | 0·481 | 0·632 | 0·453 | 0·178 | 0·188 | 0·318 | 0·492 | 0·302 | 0·347 | 0·774 |
| 3 Uses | — | — | — | 0·512 | 0·381 | *0·145* | *0·062* | 0·281 | 0·403 | 0·187 | 0·413 | 0·643 |
| 4 Fables | — | — | — | — | 0·416 | *0·131* | 0·163 | 0·358 | 0·448 | *0·164* | 0·253 | 0·708 |
| 5 Problems | — | — | — | — | — | *0·101* | 0·182 | 0·186 | 0·301 | 0·209 | *0·070* | 0·627 |
| 6 Word fluency | — | — | — | — | — | — | 0·188 | *0·027* | *0·134* | *0·017* | *0·041* | 0·236 |
| 7 Expressional fluency | — | — | — | — | — | — | — | *0·005* | 0·153 | *0·077* | 0·255 | 0·409 |
| 8 Remote associates (2) | — | — | — | — | — | — | — | — | 0·583 | 0·241 | *0·072* | 0·530 |
| 9 Remote associates (3) | — | — | — | — | — | — | — | — | — | 0·170 | 0·269 | 0·682 |
| 10 Drawing | — | — | — | — | — | — | — | — | — | — | *0·124* | 0·399 |
| 11 Circles | — | — | — | — | — | — | — | — | — | — | — | 0·461 |
| 12 Creativity aggregate | — | — | — | — | — | — | — | — | — | — | — | — |

and secondly because almost all Getzels' and Jackson's correlations are reported for boys and girls separately and not for the entire group. But three of the tests of creativity were the same in both studies, and the results for them were also analysed for boys and girls separately (cf. Table 10.2).

TABLE 10:2   *Correlations of three tests of creativity with intelligence (VRQ)*

The coefficients in brackets are the corresponding correlations with intelligence from Getzels & Jackson (1962)

| N... | Boys 100 | | Girls 75 | |
|---|---|---|---|---|
| Word association | 0·772 | (0·378) | 0·598 | (0·371) |
| Uses | 0·551 | (0·186) | 0·317 | (0·147) |
| Fables | 0·726 | (0·131) | 0·468 | (0·115) |

The general impression from Table 10:1 of much more overlap between creativity and intelligence than was found by Getzels and Jackson is confirmed by the direct comparisons. It might be thought that the much higher correlations were a purely statistical effect due to the relatively unselected nature of the Scottish sample, but this is not so. Although the Scottish sample is more typical of the general run of children in level of ability, the actual spread of ability is less than in the American sample.

*Relations of creativity and intelligence to attainment*

This question was examined in two ways. First, correlations were calculated for the entire Scottish sample (cf. Table 10:3), and secondly, the attainment scores of contrasting groups were compared, as in the American study (cf. Table 10:4).

TABLE 10:3   *Correlations of creativity and intelligence (VRQ) with measures of attainment*

Boys and girls, N = 175.

| | Attainment | |
|---|---|---|
| | Arithmetic | English |
| Creativity aggregate | 0·615 | 0·758 |
| VRQ | 0·734 | 0·845 |

Table 10:4 shows that the 'high creativity' group obtained significantly lower scores on both measures of attainment than did the 'high intelligence' group. The children in the 'high creativity *and* high intelligence' group scored highest of all in English, and their average was not significantly lower than that of the 'high intelligence' group in arithmetic. Table 10:4 also confirms the high degree of overlap between 'creativity' and 'intelligence' in the Scottish sample implied by Table 10:1. As can be seen, it was not possible to form a 'high creativity' group which had the highest scores on the aggregate of the creativity

tests and which, at the same time, excluded children with the highest VRQ.

TABLE 10:4  *Mean scores and standard deviations of the whole sample and of the three experimental groups on VRQ, AQ, EQ and Creativity Aggregate*

|  | Whole sample (N = 175) | | High creativity group (N = 17) | | High VRQ group (N = 17) | | Group high on both creativity and VRQ (N = 24) | |
|---|---|---|---|---|---|---|---|---|
|  | Mean | S.D. | Mean | S.D. | Mean | S.D. | Mean | S.D. |
| VRQ | 102 | 12 | 106 | 5 | 115* | 7 | 117* | 5 |
| Arithmetic | 108 | 13 | 113† | 13 | 123‡ | 8 | 119†† | 14 |
| English | 102 | 14 | 108 | 7 | 114 | 8 | 119 | 12 |
| Creativity aggregate | 140 | 40 | 188 | 16 | 152 | 13 | 190 | 18 |

*, †, ‡ Mean scores marked with the same sign *do not* differ significantly ($P > 0.05$). Since the sample includes the experimental groups, $t$-tests were applied only to differences between experimental groups.

*Teachers' ratings of 'creative' and 'intelligent' children on desirability as pupils*

The mean ratings for both the 'high VRQ' and the 'high on creativity *and* VRQ' groups are significantly more favourable than the mean for the 'high creativity' group (cf. Table 10:5). Getzels' and Jackson's findings of relatively low approval for 'creative' children thus receives some confirmation. Two points, however, need to be borne in mind. It would seem not to be the

TABLE 10:5  *Mean scores and standard deviations of teachers' ratings of 'desirability as a pupil' for the whole sample and for the three experimental groups*

|  |  | Whole sample (N = 175) | High creativity group (N = 17) | High VRQ (N = 17) group | Group high on both creativity (N = 24) and VRQ |
|---|---|---|---|---|---|
| Desirability as a pupil | Mean | 10·5 | 10·5 | 12·3 | 12·6 |
|  | S.D. | 2·9 | 2·6 | 2·7 | 2·8 |

higher 'creativity' as such, but to be the lower intelligence that affected the teachers' ratings, since the group high on both (and highest on 'creativity', cf. Table 10:4) received the highest ratings of all. Secondly, Getzels and Jackson contrasted the relative lack of approval received by the 'creative' children with their un-expectedly high attainment, suggesting that it was therefore particularly undeserved. No such conclusion can be drawn from our results.

## DISCUSSION AND CONCLUSIONS

The results presented must strongly suggest that some of Getzels' and Jackson's findings are not generally applicable. Some further evidence and a more detailed account of the experiment described here can be found in Hasan (1965). In some atypical groups of children it may be as easily possible to distinguish 'creative' from 'intelligent' children as has been claimed, but it appears that in a relatively unselected group measures of convergent and of divergent thinking very largely overlap, to such an extent indeed as to lend support to Burt's (1962) remark that the latter would 'form very satisfactory additions to any ordinary battery for testing the general factor of intelligence'. Nor is this merely, as Hudson (1965) calls it, 'a rather academic point'. High hopes have been raised that it might be possible to distinguish by means of open-ended tests of divergent thinking a set of able children whose abilities have hitherto been concealed or minimized by the use of conventional tests. Our results seem to indicate that this will not easily be possible in an unselected group of children by means of the open-ended tests at present available.

The two main points on which our results differ from those of Getzels and Jackson are first the degree of overlap just referred to, and secondly our failure to find that children who score high on tests of divergent thinking (in spite of relatively low conventional IQ's) are thereby likely to show up better than would otherwise have been expected on tests of attainment. Admittedly our criteria of attainment were narrow, standardized and therefore perhaps particularly likely to correlate highly with tests of intelligence or verbal reasoning. But the criteria of achievement used by Getzels and Jackson were also standardized tests, and the large difference in results is unlikely to be ascribable entirely to this cause.

One possible explanation of the discrepancy is the 'threshold' theory (Mackinnon, 1962), according to which 'above a certain required minimum level of  intelligence, which varies from field to field and in some cases may be surprisingly low, being more intelligent does not guarantee a corresponding increase in creativeness'. Barron (1963) has suggested a threshold of about IQ 120, above which intelligence ceases to be so relevant to many forms of achievement. If this theory is valid, Getzels' and Jackson's findings might have received more support if their study had been repeated with another group of particularly able children.

Cultural differences between Chicago and Edinburgh may be relevant, but the varying success of the attempts to establish Getzels' and Jackson's claims in other American studies suggests that it cannot be the whole explanation. A more specific hypothesis about differences between kinds of school, which may interact with national differences, has recently been put forward by Torrance (personal communication) as possibly accounting for the discrepant results; he plausibly suggests, and claims some support for this view from his own experiments, that the success of predominantly divergent thinkers is directly related to the degree of freedom and permissiveness and the lack of authoritarian discipline within a school.

These two theories, one of a threshold effect, and the other of an effect of school atmosphere on divergent thinking and 'creativity', need to be tested.

## REFERENCES

BARRON, F. (1963) *Creativity and Psychological Health*. Princeton, N. J.: Van Nostrand.

BURT, C. (1962) Critical notice of *Creativity and Intelligence* by Getzels and Jackson. *Brit. J. educ. Psychol.*, 32, 292–8.

EDWARDS, M. P., and TYLER, L. E. (1965) 'Intelligence, creativity and achievement in a non-selective public junior high school.' *J. educ. Psychol*, 56, 96–9.

GETZELS, J. W., and JACKSON, P. W. (1962) *Creativity and Intelligence*. New York: Wiley.

GUILFORD, J. P. (1956) 'The structure of intellect.' *Psychol. Bull*, 53, 267–93.

HASAN, P. (1965) *Creativity and Intelligence*. Unpublished B.Ed. thesis, University of Edinburgh Library.

HUDSON, L. (1965) 'Intelligence: convergent and divergent.' *Penguin Science Survey 1965: B*. Harmondsworth: Penguin Books.

MACKINNON, D. W. (1962) 'The nature and nurture of creative talent.' *Amer. Psychologist, 17*, 484–95.

MEDNICK, S. A. (1962) 'The associative basis of the creative process.' *Psychol. Rev., 69*, 220–32.

TORRANCE, E. P. (1962) *Guiding Creative Talent*. Englewood Cliffs, N. J.: Prentice-Hall.

YAMAMOTO, K. (1965) 'Multiple achievement battery and repeated measurements: a postscript to three studies on creative thinking.' *Psychol. Rep., 16*, 367–75.

*The educational theme running through Hasan's and Butcher's research report relates to the possibility of there being groups of highly 'creative' children, who obtain rather low scores on intelligence tests and conventional tests of attainment. From the subsequent careers of some children, dubbed as failures in school, there must be some abilities either which develop only after adolescence or which are not utilised in the traditional school curriculum. Much of the interest in tests of divergent thinking depends on their capability in identifying this latter group of children. Getzels and Jackson made out a strong case for the existence of a significant number of such children. The results of Hasan and Butcher, using a sample which contained the full ability range, imply that this group of children may be quite small.*

*Nevertheless the problem is important. If there are additional abilities which should be considered in formulating curricula, we should find out more about them. At present one of the snags in conducting this type of research is the dubious validity of some of the tests. First, to what extent is 'divergent thinking' related to 'creative production'? The narrow scope of tests of divergent thinking, compared with the multiplicity of ways in which imagination may be utilised, makes the link between tests and performance extremely tenuous. Another weakness of the test lies in the method of scoring. Do you include, for example, all 'uses of objects', including repetitions of ideas and physically impossible uses? Scores will clearly be affected by such decisions, and yet there is no general agreement on marking protocols. Finally there are questions of timing and conditions. Are these tests to be given under strict examination arrangements? It is reasonable to expect 'creativity' to be produced to order under stressful situations? Wallach and Kogan (1965) certainly thought this to be unreasonable.*

*In the next extract P. E. Vernon reviews the research on this problem, showing how the conditions may crucially affect the results obtained. He also summarises the results of a study of his own on Canadian adolescents.*

### Effects of Administration and Scoring on Divergent Thinking Tests      (P. E. Vernon, 1971)[1]

#### SUMMARY OF LITERATURE

Most investigators in the area of divergent thinking, or so-called 'creativity', from Guilford (1950), Getzels and Jackson (1962), and Torrance (1962) onwards, have applied their tests in much the same manner as ordinary convergent tests. That is, they give them in group form, with time limits, and with instructions to produce as many different and unusual or original responses as possible. However, Wallach and Kogan (1965) pointed out that

[1] Extracted from an article which appeared in the *British Journal of Educational Psychology*, 41, 245–57.

this evaluative set might be unfavourable to free production of creative ideas and, therefore, laid great stress in their own study on instilling a game-like rather than a test-like atmosphere. All their testing was done individually by friendly observers who were known to the children, but who were not identified with the school, nor with formal testing. The word test was not mentioned; children aged 10–11 years were invited to play various games, and oral responses were recorded without time pressure. Wallach and Kogan clearly imply that the high intercorrelations of their 10 divergent thinking measures, and the low correlations with convergent intelligence and achievement measures, were due at least partly to these relaxed, informal conditions. However, another possible reason is that their tests were more homogeneous and reliable than those used, e.g., by Getzels and Jackson; and as they did not apply their tests to a control group we do not know whether the same results might not have been obtained with more formal, test-like administration.

*Attempted Replication of the Wallach–Kogan Procedures*

Kogan and Morgan (1969) recognised these weaknesses in experimental design, and suggested that 'situational differences' (i.e., type of administration) interact with motivational differences (such as anxiety or defensiveness), and may affect different kinds of divergent tests differently. This was borne out by their study of 104 5th grade boys and girls, who were given Wallach's Patterns and Uses as group tests, half of them under test-like and evaluative conditions, half under more game-like conditions. In the latter group the experimenter was introduced as coming from a toy company, who would give them games to play like Scrabble. Thus, the individual administration of Wallach and Kogan was lacking, and although there was no time pressure in the game-like group, time limits were, in fact, imposed. Self-report tests for assessing anxiety and defensiveness were also included. The results, in fact, showed smaller rather than greater total responses and unique responses in the game-like group, though the latter did give more hostile and aggressive responses to the Uses test, perhaps because the children are reported as behaving more 'boisterously' than the test-like group. Moreover, the correlations between the divergent and convergent test scores were mostly insignificant or negative, so that there was no clear confirmation that game *versus* test-like conditions affect the degree of separation of the two abilities. A great many significant interactions between administrative conditions, sex, and personality, are claimed by the authors; but it is difficult to take very seriously *ad hoc* explanations of differences which occurred between such small subgroups.

Much more convincing substantiation of Wallach and

Kogan's views was obtained by Nicholls (1972) in a study not yet published. 114 5th grade pupils were given four of Wallach's tests individually under very similar game-like conditions, and subsequently took parallel forms of these tests under test-like conditions. A control group of 115 took the second, test-like, battery only. Some of the main results are shown in Table 10 : 6.

TABLE 10:6  *Results from Nicholls' comparison of divergent thinking tests given under different conditions*

|  | Group I | | Group II |
|---|---|---|---|
|  | Game-like | Test-like | Test-like |
| Mean F score (no. of responses) | 23·8 | 19·2 | 16·0 |
| Mean U score (unusualness) | 4·4 | 2·2 | 1·5 |
| Mean reliability of F scores | 0·87 | 0·76 | 0·65 |
| Mean text inter-correlations | 0·70 | 0·66 | 0·50 |
| Mean divergent–convergent correlations | 0·69 | 0·26 | 0·24 |

The mean F and U scores per test are higher under the game-like conditions,[1] and the mean split-half reliability of the F scores is higher. The DT (Divergent Thinking) inter-test correlations are higher, but their correlations with convergent Lorge–Thorndike IQs are lower than under test-like conditions. Nicholls believes that his findings demonstrate the dependence of DT test performance on the motivations aroused by the conditions of administration; and he implies that different testers or procedures will always tend to get different results because such motivations cannot readily be standardised. He concludes that divergent thinking is affective as well as cognitive, hence it is too simple to think merely in terms of a contrast between individual-oral-game-like and group-written-test-like procedures.

Boersma and O'Bryan (1968) also carried out a controlled comparison which tends to confirm Wallach and Kogan, although their game-like condition involved group testing and (unobtrusive) timing. Two of Torrance's DT tests and the Lorge–Thorndike verbal and non-verbal intelligence tests were given to two groups of 23 4th grade boys. The control group took all of these under test-like conditions. But the experimental group, after completing the Lorge–Thorndike, were given a morning off school in the university gymnasium and swimming pool, under a new tester who slipped in the DT tests under the guise of games. The inter-correlation of the two DT tests was almost identical in experimentals and controls, but the mean correlation between DT and intelligence was reduced from 0·425 in the controls to 0·046 in the experimentals. The authors ask pertinently whether this correlation might have risen again had it been possible to apply the intelligence tests under equally relaxed conditions.

[1] This difference was partly due to a few children who went on excessively long under the untimed game-like conditions. Omitting these, most of the differences were still in the same direction.

Williams and Fleming (1969) did give both the Peabody Vocabulary (convergent) and three Wallach tests under both play and test-like conditions to 36 4-year-olds. There was a rise in fluency scores under play conditions, and a small but non-significant increase in correlation between DT and vocabulary scores when both were evaluative or both play-like. However, the authors concluded that differences between the two abilities are more important than differences in 'set' or administration. An obvious weakness in their design is that as each child experienced both conditions (in varying orders), there might be contamination or influence of one condition on the other. The authors also note a point which recurred in the writer's research, below, namely that in the permissive atmosphere, the children were apt to indulge in too many irrelevant activities.

Ward, Kogan and Pankove (1970) devised an ingenious technique for studying motivational effects. 191 5th grade children were given two pairs of Wallach tests on two occasions, both individually. On the second occasion, one subgroup received a one cent reward for each response immediately, another subgroup were rewarded at the end of the session, and the remaining third were unrewarded. The fluency scores were clearly affected by the reward, averaging 56·4, 52·5 and 45·8 in the three groups. But when Session II results were plotted against Session I, the regression lines were almost parallel, whereas if subjects reacted differently under different motivational conditions, one would expect differences in correlations between the two sessions.

Wallach and Wing (1969) gave much the same battery as in Wallach's 1965 study to some 500 college student volunteers. These were done in written form, i.e., not as individual tests, but in the students' own time and without time limits. Much the same high correlations among divergent measures and low correlations with convergent tests were found as in the earlier study of children. But again there was no comparison with other procedures. Cropley and Maslany (1969) likewise gave Wallach tests to college students as a group, in a university lecture room. However, the students were volunteers and the atmosphere was unusually relaxed. They could move about, help themselves to coffee, and take as long as they liked (some went on working for six hours). They could engage in conversation but Cropley believes that they seldom suggested answers to one another, since they wanted to keep their bright ideas to themselves. The correlations of divergent with convergent (PMA) tests were lower than those obtained when junior high school pupils took the DT tests under test-like conditions (Cropley, 1966), though Cropley points out that the two types of ability are still oblique rather than independent; and he thinks that low correlations occur chiefly when the subjects form a homogeneous, selected group.

Ferris, Feldhusen and van Mondfrans (1971) managed to arrange four different conditions with four groups of students (at 5th, 8th and 11th grade). But they judged the efficacy of the procedures from the correlations of DT results with academic achievement. These conditions were : (1) Previous familiarisation with the kind of tests to be used; (2) Taking the tests home for four days to answer at leisure; (3) An approximation to permissive, game-like conditions; (4) Standard instructions and time limits. Results varied for different school subjects, but on the whole the game-like method produced the least valid, and the second method the best predictions, possibly because the latter most closely resembled ordinary homework.

## Effects of Variations in Instructions

Apparently quite simple modifications can markedly affect the number and type of responses. Manske and Davis (1968) raised the number of 'original' or of 'practical' responses to the Uses test significantly by telling different groups of college students to 'try to be original' or 'try to be practical'. (The Uses test involves writing as many alternative uses as possible for a common object or objects.) However, these two effects tended to vary inversely, and 'try to be original *and* try to be practical' was no more effective than neutral instructions. The instruction to 'feel free to use your wildest imagination' provided much the greatest total responses, but the poorest quality. The authors point out that if responsiveness is so easily manipulated, it is likely that DT scores will also be affected by each subject's auto-instructions, i.e., by his particular interpretation of the object of the test.

Parnes and Meadow (1959) showed that students produced significantly more 'good' uses (i.e., unusual and valuable ideas) under 'brain-storming' instructions. They were told to list all ideas without judging them in any way, and to forget about quality. But under normal instructions they were merely told to give all the good ideas they could think up. The authors deny that increase in quantity of ideas with brain-storming is accompanied by decline in quality. They also found that students who had attended a course in creative thinking produced twice as many good ideas as a matched group of untrained controls.

However, Gerlach et al. (1964) criticise this claim to have increased creative-problem-solving capacity, and suggest that alterations in the instructions, i.e., in the type of cues given to the subjects, would produce equally large increases. They gave the Uses test to six groups of 20 students under different instructions ranging from 'Poor ideas will be penalised' to 'The more imaginative and creative the ideas the higher the score.' The total responses increased significantly under the latter condition

(P=0·05), and the number of good responses more than doubled (P=0·01).

Dentler and Mackler (1964) gave the Tin Can Uses to four groups of 60 students with instructions aimed to induce different attitudes: (1) Psychologically reassuring, tester friendly and knows they will do well; (2) Routine impersonal; (3) Indifferent, devaluing the tests; (4) Emphasising competitive nature of the test and inducing insecurity. Instruction (1) led to three times as many original responses as instruction (4) (P=0·001). Certain smaller differences were attributable to sex, and to scores on an anxiety scale. However, a competitive climate as such does not necessarily reduce production, since other studies (Raina, 1968; Ward et al., 1970) have shown that giving monetary rewards increases DT scores.

Hudson (1968) quotes striking effects of different 'contexts' on the production and originality of responses to the Uses test, though he seldom quotes precise figures. With ordinary, unstructured directions, 7 per cent of bright secondary schoolboys gave 25 or more uses for three objects in 10 minutes. But when 10 responses to each object were asked for, and several examples were provided, 65 per cent of boys produced the same number in the same time. Also, many more responses were unusual, witty, ingenious or macabre. Increases were again produced by telling the subjects to write the responses that might be given (a) by a conscientious, pedantic, computer engineer; (b) by an uninhibited artist who enjoys shocking people. Relatively convergent students did better with (a), divergent ones with (b). Hudson concludes that role-playing releases inhibitions and allows much more uninhibited responses even in cautious convergent boys. However, he claims quite high correlations between scores obtained under these varying instructions. A third experiment appears to spoil his case, or at least to show that the issue is not a simple one. He admits that on one occasion he obtained more and better responses when he himself happened to be angry and treated a class of boys more aggressively than would be normal for a tester who was trying to establish good rapport.

It is unfortunate that almost all the studies surveyed in this section were based on versions of the Uses test only, presumably because it is easy to devise parallel forms, and to explain to one's subjects. However, Christensen, Guilford and Wilson (1957) showed that, while the rate of production of responses to most DT tests tends to tail off with working time, yet more uncommon, remote or inventive responses tend to come later in the test-period. (This supports Wallach and Kogan's preference for untimed conditions.) This finding did not apply to the Plot Titles test, and here Christensen et al. showed that the instruction to write 'interesting, catchy and novel' titles to a series of stories produced many more clever responses than did the instruction to write 'appropriate' titles.

One other study along these lines by Datta (1963) was concerned to show that, not merely productivity, but predictive validity can be influenced by instructions. Fifteen research scientists were asked to make Lowenfeld Mosaic designs, and to give as many written answers as possible to two verbal problems. Sixteen others were told in addition to be 'as creative as possible ... giving ideas that are unusual and worthwhile'. The scores of the latter, but not of the former, group gave a substantial correlation with careful ratings by their supervisor of the creativeness of their work.

## Summary

We have tried to survey all the relevant published work. But the list could have been much extended by including studies of situational effects, or effects of tester or instructions, on responses to projective techniques such as Rorschach. These techniques, like DT tests, are based on the production of uninhibited associations, and there is considerable evidence that both quantity and quality of response are affected by the warmth or coldness of the tester's manner (cf. Lord, 1950), or by the subject's interpretation of the object of the test (Henry and Rotter, 1956).

Several of the investigations cited above lead to conflicting conclusions. But in all of those where adequate controls or comparison samples were tested, there is evidence that the conditions of testing, the wording of instructions, and the subjects' understanding of what is required, affect their responses in some way. Whether it is mainly motivation, or cognitive 'set', that is chiefly affected does not seem to matter greatly. What is important is to arrive at optimal conditions for the production of original responses, which can be applied without excessive costs (such as individual testing), and which are yet sufficiently standardised to be replicable by any investigator without undue variations. The writer's aim was to explore further the effects of different group-testing procedures on the reliability and validity of divergent thinking scores.

### A STUDY OF CANADIAN ADOLESCENTS

(Vernon goes on to report a study of his own in which a large battery of tests and inventories, including seven group tests of divergent thinking, was applied to 400 Canadian boys and girls in Grade 8 classes—about age 14. The classes were divided into two groups of matched ability. The first group was given the divergent thinking tests under ordinary test conditions, the second under more relaxed and informal, and relatively untimed, conditions.)

Analysis of the results showed that:

*a.*  Scores based on grading unusual responses are more consistent and give higher correlations with other variables than frequency scores or per cent of unusual responses;

*b.*  larger numbers of high scores are obtained under relaxed conditions;

*c.*  the factorial structure of 'formal' and 'relaxed' scores are generally similar;

*d.*  correlations of relaxed scores with other variables, including intelligence measures, are generally higher, and particularly with variables relating to creativity.

### IMPLICATIONS

Our major finding is, then, that divergent test scores obtained under relaxed conditions have generally richer psychological meaning than those obtained under more formal, test-like conditions. Particularly, they correlate better with creative variables, teachers' ratings and creative interests. At least in this age group there are no significant differences between the correlations of relaxed and formal scores with convergent tests, i.e., there is no greater factorial separation of 'creativity' from 'intelligence', as Wallach and Kogan and others have found. However, it should be remembered that the contrast between the two conditions was probably less marked than in earlier researches where the relaxed conditions involved either individual, untimed testing or a completely game-like atmosphere.

It is hardly possible to achieve the latter in ordinary school or college usage of the tests. However, the present results, and previous research, suggest that the instructions should emphasise that these are not tests in the usual sense; there are no right answers, but as many unusual, imaginative, original, unconventional and novel responses as possible are desired. Ample examples of the sort of responses can be given. Competition and eventual evaluation need not be denied, though the emphasis should be on competing with one self to produce something different. On the whole it does not seem desirable to suggest completely 'wild' ideas regardless of their relevance or aptness. In other words the situation should be structured so as to define the task clearly; rather than leaving it to the subject to interpret. It should also be made clear that the subjects are expected to concentrate on the task, not to converse with neighbours so that everybody has a good chance to think up bright ideas without distraction. Free discussion with the tester should be permitted.

Probably it is useful if the tester is not a teacher, nor indentified with the school. He or she can be friendly, relaxed and encouraging, and yet show that reasonable control is expected. Although this may make it difficult to arrive at stable test norms, it is preferable to offer the subjects as much time as they like on all the tests, perhaps ensuring that they have other things, e.g., reading, to which they can return when they finish the divergent tests.

REFERENCES

BOERSMA, F. J., and O'BRYAN, K. (1968) 'An investigation of the relationship between creativity and intelligence under two conditions of testing.' *J. Personality, 36,* 341–8.

CHRISTENSEN, P. R., GUILFORD, J. P., and WILSON, R. C. (1957) 'Relations of creative responses to working time and instructions.' *J. Exp. Psychol., 53,* 82–8.

CROPLEY, A. J. (1966) 'Creativity and intelligence.' *Br. J. educ. Psychol., 36,* 259–66.

CROPLEY, A. J., and MASLANY, G. W. (1969) 'Reliability and factorial validity of the Wallach–Kogan creativity tests.' *Br. J. Psychol., 60,* 395–8.

DATTA, L. (1963) 'Test instructions and identification of creative scientific talent.' *Psychol. Rep., 13,* 495–500.

DENTLER, R. A., and MACKLER, B. (1964) 'Originality : some social and personal determinants.' *Behavl. Sci., 9,* 1–7.

FERRIS, P. R., FELDHUSEN, J. F., and VAN MONDFRANS, A. P. (1971) 'The relationship between academic grades and creativity test scores derived from four different methods of testing.' *J. exper. Educ., 40,* 35–40.

GERLACH, V. S., SCHUTZ, R. E., BAKER, R. L., and MAZER, G. E. (1964) 'Effects of variations in test directions on originality test responses.' *J. educ Psychol., 55,* 79–83.

GETZELS, J. W., and JACKSON, P. W. (1962) *Creativity and Intelligence.* New York : John Wiley.

GUILFORD, J. P. (1950) 'Creativity.' *Am. Psychol., 5,* 444–54.

HENRY, E. M., and ROTTER, J. B. (1956) 'Situational influences on Rorschach responses.' *J. consult. Psychol., 20,* 457–62.

HUDSON, L. (1968) *Frames of Mind.* London : Methuen.

KOGAN, N., and MORGAN, F. T. (1969) 'Task and motivational influences on the assessment of creative and intellective ability in children.' *Genet. Psychol. Monogr., 80,* 91–127.

LORD, E. (1950) 'Experimentally induced variations in Rorschach performance.' *Psychol. Monogr., 64,* No. 316.

MANSKE, M. E., and DAVIS, G. A. (1968) Effects of simple in-

structional biases upon performance in the Unusual Uses test.'
*J. gen. Psychol., 79*, 25–33.

NICHOLLS, J. G. (1972) 'Some effects of testing procedure on divergent thinking.' *Child Dev.* In press.

PARNES, S. J., and MEADOW, A. (1959) 'Effect of "brainstorming" instructions on creative problem solving by trained and untrained subjects.' *J. educ. Psychol., 50*, 171–6.

RAINA, M. K. (1968) 'A study into the effect of competition on creativity.' *Gifted Child Quart., 12*, 217–20.

TORRANCE, E. P. (1962) *Guiding Creative Talent.* Englewood Cliffs, N. J.: Prentice-Hall.

WALLACH, M. A., and KOGAN, N. (1965) *Modes of Thinking in Young Children.* New York: Holt, Rinehart and Winston.

WALLACH, M. A., and WING, C. W. (1969) *The Talented Student: A Validation of the Creativity-Intelligence Distinction.* New York: Holt, Rinehart and Winston.

WARD, W. C., KOGAN, N., and PANKOVE, E. (1970) 'Motivation and capacity in children's creativity.' Princeton, N. J.: *ETS Bull.* RB-70-39.

WILLIAMS, T. M., and FLEMING, J. W. (1969) 'Methodological study of the relationship between associational fluency and intelligence.' *Develpmt. Psychol., 1*, 155–62.

*If, as appears from Vernon's careful study, the conditions of administration affect scores on tests of divergent thinking, this finding suggests that classroom climate and method of instruction may also have an effect on 'creative' attainment. The implications which follow such a relationship between teaching method and 'creativity' are far-reaching. In a situation in which 'creative writing' and 'modern maths' are finding a place in many curricula, it seems appropriate that there should be a parallel interest among research workers in the measurement of divergent thinking. In fact the evaluation of innovatory curricula will demand the production of equally novel tests—a problem which underlies some of the discussions of curriculum evaluation in Chapter 14.*

*The final article in this chapter is a small-scale study which looked into this important area, the relationship between teaching method, divergent thinking and, in this instance, mathematical ability.*

## Type of Mathematics Teaching, Mathematical Ability and Divergent Thinking in Junior School Children     (P. N. Richards and N. Bolton, 1971)[1]

### INTRODUCTION

In recent years there has been a growing application of discovery methods of teaching mathematics. In USA the Madison Project (Davis, 1964), for example, has put the emphasis on creative informal exploration by children, and in Britain the Nuffield Foundation has sponsored a Primary School Mathematics Project with the emphasis on learning by discovery. This course is designed to foster in children 'a critical, logical, but also creative turn of mind' (Nuffield Foundation, 1964). However, the evidence for this hypothesis is, at best, inconclusive. Several studies (e.g., Wallen and Travers, 1963; Haddon and Lytton, 1968) have demonstrated that activity methods conducted in formal settings encourage independent and divergent thinking modes, but validation studies of the effects of discovery methods in mathematics teaching on cognitive performance have produced contradictory findings (e.g., Brownell, 1964; Biggs, 1967). These latter studies did not, however, include tests of divergent thinking, whereas the former have not been specifically concerned with new approaches in mathematics teaching. The present study combines these two approaches and is an attempt to clarify some of the relationships involved in the issue of discovery methods in mathematics and convergent and divergent cognitive performance. The study is divisible into two complementary parts, a factor analysis of the test intercorrelations; and an exploratory study in which these tests were administered to matched samples of children in three junior schools which differed chiefly in their approaches to mathematics teaching.

### DESIGN

*Tests*

The tests were selected to measure a wide range of abilities. Thus, as well as the measures of convergent and divergent thinking, we aimed to select mathematics tests which would range from convergent to divergent poles. A test of attitudes to school subjects, including mathematics, was also given to assess the relationship of this variable to teaching method and cognitive style.

[1] This article has been reproduced in full and originally appeared in the *British Journal of Educational Psychology*, 41, 32–7.

*Intelligence Tests*

The 1968 versions of the Moray House Verbal Reasoning Tests 81 and 82 had been given to the subjects shortly before the testing and the results were made available to the writers.

*Divergent thinking tests*

(i) The Circles Test from the Minnesota Tests of Creative Thinking (Torrance, 1965), in which subjects have to sketch in 10 minutes as many objects as possible which contain a circle as their main part. (ii) A Uses for Things Test (Guilford, 1967), in which subjects have to write down as many different uses as they can think of for each of three stimulus objects. Both the Circle Test and the Uses for Things Test are scored for fluency, flexibility and originality of response. (iii) A Consequences Test (Torrance, 1965), in which subjects think of as many possible results of two unusual events. (iv) Pattern Meanings (Wallach and Kogan, 1966), which require as many meanings as possible to three abstract figures. Both Consequences and Pattern Meanings are scored for fluency and originality. (v) A Make-Up Problems Test (Getzels and Jackson, 1962), which requires subjects to invent mathematical problems from information presented in a prose paragraph containing several numerical statements. This test is scored by determining the number of arithmetical operations present in the subject's answers.

*Tests of mathematical ability*

(i) The NFER Concept Test, Part A. This test was used by Biggs (1967) but only the first part was used here, since Biggs found the second part unsuccessful in differentiating between the various groups in his study. (ii) Series completion (Lunzer, 1965), involving the completion of a series of numbers in different ways. (iii) A Gap-Filling Test adapted from Bartlett's (1958) studies on problem-solving. (iv) Easy Problems Test. This consisted of some of Wertheimer's (1961) mathematical problems, each of which involves the subject understanding the structure of the problem to find an 'easy' solution, rather than the application of rote learning. (v) NFER Arithmetic Progress Test C1. This test contains two sections which are termed 'mechanical' and 'problem' respectively. In addition, a total ability score is computed for performance on both parts of the test. (vi) NFER Intermediate Mathematics Test I, a new test designed for use in the fourth year of junior school. It is designed to test understanding of mathematical concepts and involves almost no mechanical computation.

*Attitudes to school subjects*

The battery also included a simple scale, devised by Sharples (1969) to measure attitudes to five school activities—reading, mathematics, writing stories, art and physical education.

*Selection of subjects and procedure*

265 children in their final year at three junior schools in the north-east of England were selected for the study. As Table 10:7 shows, the schools are comparable for intelligence and social

TABLE 10:7   *Age, IQ and social class in the three schools*

| School | A | B | C | All |
|---|---|---|---|---|
| No. of pupils | 102 | 71 | 92 | 265 |
| Mean age (s.d. in parenthesis) | 11y. 2·8m. (3·3) | 11y. 2·6m. (3·6) | 11y. 2·2m. (3·0) | 11y. 2·5m. (3·3) |
| Mean IQ (s.d. in parenthesis) | 103·8 (13·5) | 102·5 (14·3) | 105·0 (12·1) | 103·9 (13·3) |
| Percentage distribution of social class: | | | | |
| Registrar-General's      I/II | 12 | 17 | 16 | 15 |
| Classification      III | 65 | 64 | 53 | 61 |
| IV/V | 23 | 19 | 31 | 24 |

class, *t* tests indicating no significant differences in these variables. The time allocated in each school to mathematics is exactly the same, one hour per day. Thus, the schools differ principally in the manner in which they teach mathematics. In School A a conscious attempt is made to 'keep a balance' between traditional and new methods, in School B the mathematics teaching is largely traditional and oriented to the whole class, whereas School C, as a school in one of the Nuffield pilot areas, is enthusiastically committed to a discovery approach.

The tests were assembled into a booklet and administered as group tests to each set of subjects in three sessions.

RESULTS

Table 10:8 presents the results of a Varimax analysis of the test results. Factor 1 may be identified as a factor of general ability, with intelligence, mathematical ability and several of the divergent thinking tests loading highly. Factor 2 may be identified as a factor of divergent thinking with the Uses for Things and the Pattern Meanings Test providing the highest loadings.

It is evident from this analysis that performance on tests of intelligence, mathematical ability and divergent thinking, at least for the range of ability studied here, is largely determined by a common factor which can be identified as general ability. The test battery aimed to sample both convergent and divergent aspects of mathematical ability. That the tests of divergent thinking emerge as a second factor, with only a few of the tests of mathematical ability having slight positive loadings implies that the most important determinant of the performance in mathematics is general ability and that divergent thinking plays

TABLE 10:8 *Varimax analysis of the whole data (31 variables, 265 cases)*

| | I | II | III | IV | V | VI |
|---|---|---|---|---|---|---|
| 1 Moray House VR81 | 85 | | | | −23 | |
| 2 Moray House VR82 | 86 | 20 | | | −21 | |
| 3 NFER Inter. Maths (raw score) | 92 | | | | | |
| 4 (standard score) | 91 | | | | | |
| 5 NFER Arith. Progress C1 (mech.) | 81 | 29 | | | (17) | |
| 6 (problem) | 87 | 25 | | | (15) | |
| 7 (standard score) | 88 | 27 | | | (18) | |
| 8 Arithmetic Concept A (raw score) | 84 | | | | | |
| 9 (standard score) | 84 | | | | | |
| 10 (mensuration concept) | 76 | | | | | |
| 11 Series Completion | 81 | 20 | | | | |
| 12 Filling Spaces | 74 | | | | | |
| 13 Easy Problems | 74 | | | | −25 | |
| 14 Circles (fluency) | | 37 | | | −79 | |
| 15 (flexibility) | | 37 | | | −83 | |
| 16 (originality) | | 21 | | | −82 | |
| 17 Uses (fluency) | 28 | 82 | | | −27 | |
| 18 (flexibility) | 37 | 81 | | | −25 | |
| 19 (originality) | 34 | 76 | | | | |
| 20 Consequences (fluency) | 33 | 53 | | | −47 | |
| 21 (originality) | 23 | 36 | 20 | | −52 | 26 |
| 22 Pattern (fluency) | | 81 | | | −21 | |
| 23 Meanings (originality) | 20 | 81 | | | −23 | |
| 24 Make-up Problems | 57 | 35 | | 23 | −26 | |
| 25 Attitudes (reading) | 24 | | | 62 | | |
| 26 (mathematics) | | | | | | 83 |
| 27 (writing stories) | | | | 73 | −25 | |
| 28 (art) | −20 | | −71 | | | |
| 29 (p.e.) | | | −69 | | | −34 |
| 30 (summed score) | | | −73 | 51 | | 42 |
| 31 Sex | | | | −44 | | |
| Percentage of Total Variance | 32·7 | 14·8 | 5·6 | 5·1 | 10·4 | 4·2 |

(Decimal points and loadings <0·20 are omitted)

only a minor role. This is true even for the Make-up Problems Test, which has one of the lowest loadings of the divergent thinking measures on the factor of divergent thinking. Although divergent thinking abilities might play a greater role in practical open-ended mathematical situations, we nevertheless hypothesise from these results that teaching procedures which encourage divergent modes of thinking will, for this range of ability at least, produce minimal effects on children's performance on tests of mathematical ability.

Table 10:9 presents means and standard deviations of the 30 variables for the three schools.

TABLE 10:9  *Mean scores for the three schools*

| | | Means (s.d. in parenthesis) | | |
|---|---|---|---|---|
| | | School A (N = 102) | School B (N = 71) | School C (N = 92) |
| 1 | Moray House VR81 | 101·46 (12·7) | 101·62 (12·6) | 104·14 (11·6) |
| 2 | Moray House VR82 | 105·34 (14·3) | 103·97 (14·3) | 107·46 (12·6) |
| 3 | NFER Inter. Maths (raw score) | 28·84 (10·2) | 26·35  (9·3) | 24·77  (9·3) |
| 4 | (standard score) | 104·30 (12·9) | 101·01 (10·8) | 99·46 (11·2) |
| 5 | NFER Arith. Progress C1 (mechanical) | 9·92  (7·6) | 9·28  (6·5) | 4·45  (3·1) |
| 6 | (problem) | 13·12  (7·0) | 13·28  (6·5) | 7·78  (4·7) |
| 7 | (standard score) | 106·81 (15·8) | 105·94 (13·2) | 94·74  (8·9) |
| 8 | Arithmetic Concept A (raw score) | 10·72  (3·4) | 11·93  (3·1) | 9·64  (3·4) |
| 9 | (standard score) | 103·96 (13·3) | 108·85 (12·5) | 99·59 (10·7) |
| 10 | (mensuration concept) | 3·85  (2·5) | 4·28  (2·9) | 3·51  (3·0) |
| 11 | Series Completion | 6·60  (2·8) | 6·83  (2·6) | 5·83  (2·8) |
| 12 | Filling Spaces | 6·06  (4·8) | 5·17  (4·7) | 5·16  (4·0) |
| 13 | Easy Problems | 8·93  (4·6) | 9·03  (3·4) | 9·29  (4·5) |
| 14 | Circles (fluency) | 19·27  (7·6) | 18·80  (7·1) | 26·24  (9·2) |
| 15 | (flexibility) | 14·02  (5·9) | 12·93  (5·3) | 18·09  (7·1) |
| 16 | (originality) | 6·88  (6·3) | 4·99  (6·3) | 11·74  (8·8) |
| 17 | Uses (fluency) | 23·86 (10·0) | 21·03  (5·1) | 21·64  (8·6) |
| 18 | (flexibility) | 19·82  (8·3) | 17·08  (4·6) | 18·03  (6·5) |
| 19 | (originality) | 23·80 (17·7) | 19·62 (11·8) | 20·08 (13·1) |
| 20 | Consequences (fluency) | 9·95  (4·2) | 9·03  (2·9) | 10·25  (4·3) |
| 21 | (originality) | 7·12  (4·5) | 6·61  (3·5) | 8·11  (5·1) |
| 22 | Pattern (fluency) | 16·64  (6·1) | 15·90  (5·5) | 15·82  (6·8) |
| 23 | Meanings (originality) | 14·73  (7·3) | 12·34  (5·3) | 13·28  (7·5) |
| 24 | Make-up Problems | 7·67  (4·8) | 6·20  (3·5) | 7·38  (3·7) |
| 25 | Attitudes (reading) | 5·20  (1·6) | 5·25  (1·5) | 4·70  (1·3) |
| 26 | (mathematics) | 4·25  (1·5) | 4·45  (1·9) | 4·01  (1·9) |
| 27 | (writing stories) | 4·79  (1·7) | 5·15  (1·5) | 5·10  (1·9) |
| 28 | (art) | 5·65  (1·7) | 6·01  (1·5) | 5·70  (1·9) |
| 29 | (p.e.) | 6·90  (1·3) | 6·42  (1·7) | 6·75  (1·3) |
| 30 | (summed score) | 26·84  (3·4) | 27·30  (3·3) | 26·25  (3·3) |

The conclusions that can be drawn from a small sample of schools must be treated with some caution, even though those schools have been carefully matched. However, it is apparent that mathematical attainments of children taught by discovery methods in this sample are significantly lower than those children taught either by traditional methods or by a combination of discovery and traditional methods. In mechanical and problem arithmetic (variable 5 and 6) both control schools are clearly superior to School C, though this is not entirely surprising in view of the greater attention they pay to mastery of routine skills and the fact that teaching in School C deliberately avoids problems involving computation in complicated mensuration systems which will disappear with metrication. The recently published NFER Intermediate Mathematics Test was thought initially to be the test most likely to do justice to School C as it is especially designed in a non-traditional form to stress understanding and avoid routine calculation. School C, however, has the lowest performance of the three schools, though only School A is significantly better, at the 1 per cent level.

The performance of School C on the Easy Problem Test, however, is equivalent to that of the other two schools. It will be remembered that this test was designed with reference to Wertheimer's (1961) work on productive thinking and it is possible that the inclusion of other, similar measures might do more justice to the effects of the discovery approach.

With respect to the tests of divergent thinking, only on the Circles Test was School C's performance significantly better than either of the other two schools, but it is noteworthy that Schools A and C tend to score consistently higher on these tests than School B, which used the most traditional mathematics teaching. There were no significant differences between the schools in liking for mathematics.

### CONCLUSIONS

The factor analysis reveals that performance on tests of mathematical ability is largely determined by a general ability factor, with the divergent thinking dimensions contributing to only certain of the mathematics tests and then to only a very small extent. It is suggested that teaching approaches which foster divergent thinking will, consequently, produce minimal beneficial effects on children's performance on tests of mathematical ability. The results supplied by a comparison of three schools taught by different methods support Biggs' (1967) finding that the use of activity methods in the junior school produces inferior mechanical and problem performance. However, the present study does offer some slight support for Biggs' suggestion that such methods might have positive effects on the productive and original aspects of children's thinking, but further studies in practical open-ended situations or exploring the type of problem described by Wertheimer (1961) are necessary to substantiate this hypothesis. The success of School A, which uses a combination of traditional and discovery methods, lends weight to Torrance's (1964) suggestion that we must determine which kinds of information are learned most economically by authority and which by creative means.

G

REFERENCES

BARTLETT, F. C. (1958) *Thinking: An Experimental and Social Study*. London : Allen and Unwin.

BIGGS, J. B. (1967) *Mathematics and the Conditions of Learning*. Slough : National Foundation for Educational Research.

BROWNELL, W. A. (1964) 'Arithmetical abstractions: the movement towards conceptual maturity under different systems of instruction.' *Co-op. Res. Proj. No. 1676*, U.S. Office of Education. Berkeley : Univ. of Calif. Press.

DAVIS, R. B. (1964) *Discovery in Mathematics*. Madison Project, Palo Alto : Addison-Wesley.

GETZELS, J. W. and JACKSON, P. W. (1962) *Creativity and Intelligence*. New York : Wiley.

GUILFORD, J. P. (1967) *The Nature of Human Intelligence*. New York : McGraw-Hill.

HADDON, F. A. and LYTTON, H. (1968) 'Teaching approach and the development of divergent thinking abilities in primary schools.' *Br. J. educ. Psychol.*, *38*, 171–80.

LUNZER, E. A. (1965) 'Problems of formal reasoning in test situations.' Monogr. Soc. Res. in *Child Dev.*, 100, Vol. 30, 2, 19–46.

NUFFIELD FOUNDATION (1964) *Mathematics Teaching Project*. Bulletin No. 1.

SHARPLES, D. (1969) 'Children's attitudes towards junior school activities.' *Br. J. educ. Psychol.*, *39*, 72–7.

TORRANCE, E. P. (1964) 'Education and creativity.' In C. W. TAYLOR (ed.) *Creativity: Progress and Potential*. New York : McGraw-Hill.

TORRANCE, E. P. (1965) *Rewarding Creative Behaviour*. Englewood Cliffs, N.J. : Prentice-Hall.

WALLACH, M. A., and KOGAN, N. (1966) *Modes of Thinking in Young Children*. New York : Holt, Rinehart and Winston.

WALLEN, N. E., and TRAVERS, R. M. W. (1963) 'Analysis and investigation of teaching methods.' In N. F. GAGE (ed.) *Handbook of Research on Teaching*. Chicago : Rand McNally.

WERTHEIMER, M. (1961) *Productive Thinking*. London : Tavistock.

# 11    Examinations and Marking

*Examination marks are of particular importance in educational research as academic attainment is a key variable in many studies. Attempts at improving the reliability and validity of assessments of academic performance are of concern to the research worker. But, of course, examinations are also of more general importance and recent criticisms of them has led both to experiments with new methods of examining and to attempts at improving the efficiency of old methods. Before introducing typical research studies in this chapter, it seems useful to start with a careful analysis of the function of examinations. This type of thinking is a necessary precursor of any research and is particularly important in a topic such as examinations, which tends to arouse uninformed or emotional reactions.*

## Examinations
## (A. E. G. Pilliner, 1968)[1]

### PURPOSES OF EXAMINATION PROCEDURE

Examination procedures serve a number of functions. To the student they are a stimulus and a goal. To the teacher they feed back information about the effectiveness of his teaching and hence serve as feedback. To society at large they furnish a guarantee of competence in those examined to perform the tasks demanded of them by the jobs or professions they take up (Oppenheim *et al.*, 1967). It cannot be assumed that the stimulus to the student is the most appropriate or that the feedback to the teacher is necessarily desirable. But it would be idle to deny the effectiveness of examination procedures in these respects. This point will be returned to later. Nor can it be assumed that the

[1] Extracted from a chapter in Butcher, H. J. and Pont, H. B., *Educational Research in Britain, Volume 1* (University of London Press), pages 167–72.

guarantee examinations offer to society is infallible. But whether right or wrong, decisions must be made on behalf of society which most of its members have to take on trust.

N. Morris (1961) classifies the purpose of examination procedures under four headings: (a) to maintain standards; (b) to act as an incentive to effort; (c) to serve as an administrative device; and (d) to provide a tool for social engineering. The first and second of these clearly include the stimulus and feedback functions and the guarantee of quality referred to above.

One example, by now historical, of the third (administrative) use of examination procedures was for determining school grants, the system of 'payment by results'. A second is the use of examination results to select children, at the end of the primary stage, for the most 'appropriate' type of secondary education. With the development of the comprehensive school, the 11-plus examination, as originally conceived, is becoming increasingly irrelevant. A third example is the use of 'A' level results to select university entrants—a use which, though still current, is giving rise to increasing disquiet.

An example of the use of an examination procedure as a tool for social engineering was the substitution in the twenties by Thomson (1921) of 'objective' tests for almost all children in Northumberland in place of the secondary school 'free-place' examination for which many schools in that area did not present candidates. This was the precursor of the 11-plus examination. It is ironical that a device which was intended by its originator to give (and which, indeed, did give) educational opportunity to children who would otherwise have been deprived of it should be seen in its later development as a chief obstacle to the democratization of education.

From a still different (though again related) point of view, examination procedures are 'backward-looking' in that they provide evidence of achievement to date, or 'forward looking' in that they predict what the examinee is likely to be able to do in the future. Much confusion has arisen through unclear specification of intention in these respects, and through the use of procedures primarily intended to be 'backward-looking' for essentially 'forward-looking' purposes.

### REQUIREMENTS OF A GOOD EXAMINATION PROCEDURE

Whatever the purpose of the examination procedure, ideally it should conform to the following requirements:

1 The content should consist of a representative sample of every aspect of the domain in which achievement or potential is to be assessed.

2    The procedure should be organized to impose as little stress on the candidate as possible so that each should 'do himself justice'.

3    The content and organization should make possible the consistent evaluation of the achievement or potential of each candidate.

4    The final outcome of the procedure should be the placing of candidates in a rank order, or in ordered categories, valid in respect of some acceptable criterion. Frequently the criterion is present achievement or potential success, or both, as defined explicitly, or accepted implicitly in a given culture.

5    The influence of the procedure on the work of pupils or students preparing for it, and on their teachers, should be educationally beneficial.

### DISCUSSION OF THESE REQUIREMENTS

These requirements are seldom, if ever, completely achieved.

1.    It is rarely possible to examine or test comprehensively every aspect of the domain concerned. Some kind of selection is necessary. The degree of arbitrariness, inevitable in the selection of material, can be reduced by the application of a good sampling procedure. This presupposes that the extent of the domain in question has been mapped and stated. The preparation of such a statement is a salutary exercise for the compiler of the examination in his capacity as educator.

2.    In any examination procedure some degree of stress is inevitable, and it is improbable that every candidate will 'do himself justice'. Pre-examination stress at the university level and its medical and psychological treatment have been discussed by Malleson (1957). Hallworth (1964) found a slight tendency for anxiety measurement and the performance of secondary school children to be negatively correlated. The effect of the 11-plus on children in primary schools has been summarized by P. E. Vernon *et al.* (1957). They report that despite a few authenticated cases of individuals for whom stress appeared directly linked to the examination, the anxiety for which this procedure was alleged to be responsible had been much exaggerated.

Well before the date of the examination, all candidates should know quite explicitly the form it will take, the number of questions they will be required to answer, and in particular the qualities the procedure aims to assess. By these means, not only will stress be reduced, but also whatever educational ends the procedure is capable of serving will be given fuller scope (Himmelweit, 1967).

Within the examination room, stress on the candidate should

be combated by making the occasion as informal as possible. More important still is absolute clarity in the paper itself, so that every candidate knows precisely and without ambiguity what he must do. A 'pilot' try-out would be the best way to detect and eliminate ambiguities, but it is frequently impracticable. This being so, considerable foresight and imagination, backed by experience of difficulties encountered by candidates in previous examinations, are required of those compiling the papers. Misprints in the paper itself often disconcert candidates, so that impeccable editing and proof-reading are essential.

Experiments in new procedural techniques, conducted so far mainly at the university level, might be extended to other educational levels. These experiments include : (a) procedures in which papers consist of a selection from a larger number of questions made available to the candidates well beforehand; (b) 'open-book' procedures in which the candidates can take texts into the examination room. These may or may not be prescribed (Cox, 1966); (c) procedures in which performance in course-work as well as the examination proper is taken into account.[1] Again, in addition to a possible reduction of stress, important educational ends might be served.

3 The problems involved in the consistent evaluation of each candidate's work are notorious and formidable. They will be more fully described later in this paper under the heading of 'Reliability'. Meanwhile, it is suggested that where the nature of the domain examined allows of it, 'objective' questions which require no evaluative judgment in their marking should be used. Where the nature of the domain calls for extended writing, the attendant difficulties of marking consistently have to be accepted.

4 Placing candidates in order of merit or in ordered categories perfectly valid in respect of some acceptable criterion must probably remain an aspiration. Difficulties arise when the criterion against which examination performance is to be validated is not made sufficiently explicit, or cannot be agreed on. Since the nature of the criterion delimits the content of the examination, no finality can be reached as to the content either. This is discussed further under the heading of 'Validity'.

Certainly, however, stress on the candidates and ambiguity in the questions reduce validity, a further reason for minimizing the first and eliminating the second.

5 The fifth requirement is at once the most important and the most difficult. There is a large measure of truth in the statement that those who control the examination dictate the work

[1] In recent years, the University of Edinburgh Education Department has awarded its Diploma in Education on the total of equally weighted course and examination marks. The correlation between them is about 0·6–0·7.

of the institutions preparing for it. The pejorative connotation of the expression 'back-wash effect' implies the conviction of those who use it that the influence of examinations cannot be for good. These critics argue that an external examination imposes on many schools a common syllabus which may stifle initiative and militate against the diversity among schools which they consider natural and right. They further argue that the examination, by its very nature, must depress the status of the aesthetic and creative aspects of education—which, they would maintain, are non-examinable—while exalting the status of memorizing and factual knowledge.

Few would deny the force of these arguments. Yet not all would share the critics' pessimism. The aim should be to improve rather than abolish examination procedures. Among teachers at all levels and in every official report from Robbins to Plowden, there is now a flow of discussion, probably unprecedented, of wide and important issues with implications for examination procedures. More specifically, this is a time of positive criticism of the procedures themselves, of research and experiment, of active modification, and the introduction of hitherto untried techniques. It is significant that universities, traditionally resistant to change, are now discovering researches into examination procedures conducted elsewhere and adding their own contributions (Jahoda, M., et al., 1967). It is significant, too, that the newest school examination, the Certificate of Secondary Education, is more flexible than its predecessors. The schools presenting candidates for the C.S.E. have three options available to them: external examinations on a syllabus provided by the local Regional Board; external examinations on a syllabus devised by a school or group of schools to take account of special local conditions; and examinations internally set and externally moderated. The schools are free to mix these options, if they choose, for different groups of candidates or different subjects. Another major difference between this and previous school examinations is the much greater degree of control of the C.S.E. by the teachers themselves.

REFERENCES

COX, R. (1966) Examinations and Higher Education: Survey of the Literature. London: Society for Research into Higher Education.

HALLWORTH, H. J. (1964) 'Personality ratings of adolescents: a study in a comprehensive school.' Brit. J. educ. Psychol., 34, 171–7.

HIMMELWEIT, H. T. (1967) 'Towards a rationalization of examination procedures.' *Universities Quarterly*, 21, 3.

JAHODA, M., *et al.*, (1967) 'Examining in universities.' *Universities Quarterly*, 21, 3.

MALLESON, N. (1957) 'Treatment of pre-examination strain.' *Brit. Med. J.*, 2, 551.

MONTGOMERY, J. (1965) *Examinations*. London : Longmans.

MORRIS, N. (1961) 'An historian's view of examinations.' In WISE-MAN, S. (ed.) *Examinations and English Education*. Manchester: Manchester University Press.

OPPENHEIM, A. N., JAHODA, M., and JAMES, R. L. (1967) 'Assumptions underlying the use of university examination.' *Universities Quarterly*, 21, 3.

THOMPSON, G. H. (1921) 'The Northumberland Mental Tests.' *Brit. J. educ. Psychol.*, 12, 201 ff.

VERNON, P. E. (ed.) (1957) *Secondary School Selection*. London : Methuen.

*Pilliner's clear exposition of the function of examinations also indicated that experimental procedures have been introduced. The extracts from research studies which follow illustrate different approaches to examining. Objective testing is still considered to be new and relatively untried—at least in this country. The first extract shows that the technique is far from being a recent development. P. B. Ballard reports the results of research carried out in 1921, in which essay marking was compared with objective testing. In the second reading B. Farrington reinterprets similar ideas within the modern context of a language laboratory. The final extract comes from a larger study on the multiple-marking of English compositions and serves as a reminder of the continued importance of this mode of assessment.*

### The New Examiner
### (P. B. Ballard, 1923)[1]

An important investigation into the value of the new technique was made at Columbia College, New York, in 1921, and a report, prepared by Mr Ben D. Wood, assistant to the Dean of the College, was published in the September issue of *Educational Administration and Supervision*. The subject selected for the experiment was 'Contemporary Civilisation'. Turning a deaf ear to the whisper of the cynic that the subject-matter does not exist,

[1] Extracts from the book of this title published by University of London Press, pages 79–86.

let us see what the report has to say. It claims that 'the Course in Contemporary Civilisation presents ideal conditions for a thoroughgoing trial of various kinds of measuring devices. This course, since it is required of all freshmen, includes a large number of students of varying ability, studying the same material as indicated in a very detailed syllabus, in the same time, by the same method of instruction and recitation, and under the direction of an unusually harmonious staff of instructors. In addition there was available a reliable objective mental classification of the students of the course, as well as other data indicative of what might be expected of them.' The term 'mental classification' refers to the findings of the Thorndike College Entrance Intelligence Examination, which all candidates for admission were required to take.

The experimental examination which was set at the end of the course was taken by 440 freshmen. It consisted of two parts: the first, which lasted an hour, representing the old examination; and the second, which lasted two hours, representing the new. The old examination required the answering in essay form of two questions out of four. I quote as an example one of the questions:

> Define the major groups or classes in England or in France in the early eighteenth century, and show in some details the conflicts of these groups and the changes wrought in them and their relative position by the political, economic, and social changes of the eighteenth and first half of the nineteenth centuries.

The new examination comprised three tests, the first of which was of the True–False type. It consisted of 139 statements, each of which had to be marked with a plus sign if the examinee thought it true, and by a minus sign if he thought it false. I will cite a few of the statements.

A.9   The civilisations of the Phoenicians, Greeks, and Romans centred about short river valleys.

12   Irrigation is carried on more extensively on the eastern than on the western slopes of the mountains of California.

B.16 Among animals under conditions of domestication instinctive behaviour tends largely to be displaced by habitual or acquired modes of behaviour.

18   The enclosing of the 'Commons' brought about a great increase in the number of small holdings.

51   By his conquests in Central Europe Napoleon retarded German unification by at least a hundred years.

The score for this test was the number right minus the number wrong.

The second test consisted of 14 paragraphs, in which certain missing words were to be supplied. This is technically known as a Completion Test. The eighth paragraph is here quoted:

> By the mercantilist policy the European Powers sought to increase their ... and to decrease their ... Especially the ... of raw materials and the ... of finished products was encouraged. A representative mercantilistic statesman was ...

The third and last test was a Recognition Test. Here 61 statements were presented to the candidate, who had to underline the one word or phrase which would make each statement true. It involved a choice of several possibilities. I quote three items:

> Most of the inhabitants of the British Isles belong to the race known as the—Alpine, British, Teutonic, Mediterranean, Basque, Celtic.

> Miserliness or kleptomania are abnormal exaggerations of the instinct of—Hunger, Love, Acquisitiveness, Fear.

> The passage of the Reform Bill of 1832 was a victory for the —Agricultural Landlords, Farm Labourers, Factory Workers, Well-to-do Middle Class.

Here we have a group of tests carrying altogether 250 points of credit, tests which satisfy all the essential conditions of the new examination. The items are small and numerous, they involve a minimum of writing, they are fool-proof, and they cover the whole course of study. The 'question paper' was not a paper but a booklet. The trouble of preparing such a booklet was compensated for by the ease of marking. The preparation however, was not very onerous, for the instructors in the course of Contemporary Civilisation (and there seems to have been at least a dozen of them) formed a committee, which divided the work amongst its members.

A cursory glance at this example of the new examination might give one the impression that it places too much emphasis on the memory of isolated facts; but a closer scrutiny shows it to be a severe test of judgment and of the power to organise the material studied.

Now comes the important point: how were the authorities to judge the value of the new examination? The obvious way was to compare its verdict with other criteria—other estimates of the same thing. The criteria actually used were threefold: the Thorndike Intelligence scores, the instructor's estimate of achievement (based on class work), and the result of the one-hour examination. There was in addition the evidence afforded by the distribution of marks. All the available data indicated that the real abilities and attainments of the students were distributed normally—that they roughly accorded with the probability curve—and it is significant that the scores of the new examination fitted this curve far more closely than did the scores of the essay examination. The initial presumption, based on statistics, pointed to the new examination as the better of the two.

The most cogent evidence, however, in favour of the new examination was furnished by the correlations between the various estimates referred to above. It has been found by extensive research that the more carefully and accurately school marks are accorded the more highly do they correlate with general intelligence, but only up to a certain limit—up to 0·5 or 0·6. Now the coefficient of correlation between the new examination and the Thorndike Intelligence scores was 0·513, and this was a higher index than that given by either the essay examination (which was 0·386) or the instructor's estimate of achievement (which was 0·358). This in itself proclaimed with much convincingness that of the three ways of measuring attainments—the tutor's opinion, the essay examination, and the new examination—the new examination was considerably the best.

The sceptic may urge that the new examination correlates highly with the intelligence examination simply because both test the same sort of thing. If that were so it would have lower correlations with the essay examination and with the tutor's estimate. In point of fact, they were not lower; they were higher; they were 0·654 with the essay and 0·620 with the tutor's estimate. The unavoidable inference is that the new examination really measures what it purports to measure—the students' attainments.

Now mark this new line of argument. It is reasonable to assume that where there are several guesses at a magnitude the average of the guesses is nearer the truth than any one of the separate guesses. The principle does not always hold good because of the occasional presence of a constant error—a drifting of all judgments in the same false direction; but in the main the principle is sound: the average of diverse estimates is the most likely to be the true estimate. In the investigation which we are considering there were two independent guesses—the instructor's estimate, and the scores of the essay examination—and there was no reason to suspect a constant error. The average of these two guesses are assumed to be nearer the truth than either of them taken by itself. And it was found that the new examination correlated more highly—tallied more closely—with the average of the guesses than with the individual guesses. And this was true not only of the new examination as a whole, but also of each of the three tests taken separately. The more trustworthy the standard with which the new examination was compared the better did it appear.

The same line of argument was applied again: to the essay examination exclusively this time. A number of the essay booklets (117 altogether) were chosen at random and marked afresh by different examiners. Thus were secured two independent appraisals of each of 117 booklets. After saying that the correlation between the two sets of marks was no higher than 0·663 I make no apology for calling the marks guesses. Here again then we have two guesses—the first marking of the essays and the second marking of the essays. The correlation of the new examination with the first guess was 0·599; with the second, 0·533; and with the average of the two, 0·623. Once more the new examination showed up better when the standard of comparison improved.

When it comes to the question of reliability, the new examination wins easily. By the reliability of an examination is meant the steadiness with which it measures. If it is given the second time to the same candidates and the results are nearly, if not quite, the same as those originally obtained, it is technically described as reliable. It would be unreasonable to expect identity in the results, for the thing measured has itself undergone a change; but the correlation between the two sets of results should be fairly high. It is often, however, inexpedient, and sometimes impossible, to give the same examination twice over. Fortunately we have another way of testing its reliability. If the questions are numerous enough we can pretend that there are two examinations instead of one; we can pretend that all the questions with even ordinals (second, fourth, sixth, etc.) constitute one examination and that all the questions with odd ordinals constitute another examination; and we can compare the two sets of marks. We can compare them informally by inspection, or, better still, we can compare them with mathematical precision by the method of correlation. If the two sets are alike, the reliability is high; if not, it is low. The new examination was treated by some such method as this, and the coefficient of reliability was found to be 0·905. This is exceptionally high; and although it was not possible to calculate the reliability of the essay examination in the same way, there was every reason to believe that the reliability was very much lower. If the correlations between two markings of the same set of essays was only 0·663, there was no ground for believing that it would have been higher if the essays themselves had been changed as well.

On the score of objectivity there was no comparison between the two examinations. While the objectivity of the new examination was perfect, and the correlation between the marks of two independent examiners of the same booklet was 1, the correlation between the two independent markings of the essays was no higher than 0·663; and this in spite of the fact that the essays in question were marked, as the report assures us, with much greater care than is usual at an examination.

Mr Wood's report ends with testimonies given by some of the instructors who sat in judgment on the new examination. They were at first sceptical as to its value, but the experiment converted them. Since the testimonies are all of the same tenor, I will quote from the first only, that of Mr Austin P. Evans, Assistant Professor of History. He says :

> All the evidence seems to point to the conclusion that it (the new examination) is much the most accurate method of testing student's knowledge of the subject that we have yet discovered. It does not, however, in my judgment, test sufficiently the student's powers of accurate and cogent expression, and his ability to organise his material. I should therefore feel that in an examination adequate time should be given for at least one or two questions of the essay type.

The others agree with Mr Evans in praising the new examination, and in pleading for the retention of the essay as part, but part only, of future examinations.

## A Computer-Aided Test of Aural Comprehension
## (B. Farrington, 1971)[1]

### COMPREHENSION AS A SKILL

There are three reasons in my view why aural comprehension is a skill that demands special attention. The first is a matter of plain practical convenience and efficiency. It is, as I hope the rest of this article will show, by far the easiest to test of the diverse skills that can be trained in a Language Laboratory. This is by no means a negligible or purely materialistic consideration. One of the principal problems facing those of us who would wish for a greater importance to be given in examinations in general to the handling of the spoken code, is the difficulty of testing it reliably. The cost of a thorough and systematic type of oral examination which would guarantee a higher standard of reliability and validity is very high. On the other hand testing comprehension of pieces of native spoken language by almost any procedure gives a guarantee of objectivity which is hard to obtain in individual interviews.

But this is obviously not the main reason for considering aural comprehension so important. The skill itself as has been

[1] Edited extracts from an article in *Audio-Visual Language Journal*, 9, 71–6.

pointed out (Dickinson, 1970) is a very valuable one to acquire, and its possession to a reasonable degree is essential to anyone who is called upon to communicate with native speakers. In fact informal tests suggest that at the level of linguistic attainment in question here, a speaker has less difficulty in expressing himself than he has in understanding what is said to him by a native speaker. It is certainly true of the more elementary levels, as anybody will testify who has used their Linguaphone-plus-phrase-book Spanish or Dutch to frame a very simple question and has been totally bewildered by the, probably equally simple, answer that it elicited.

My third reason for laying such an emphasis on aural com-prehension is that it is directly related to the use in the Labora-tory of a wide and interesting variety of linguistic material for listening. It is my view that the Language Laboratory should not be seen first and foremost as a teaching instrument, since this definition limits its functions excessively (Farrington, 1969). Rather, I would like to redefine its function as being that of in-creasing a learner's exposure to the foreign language, and this in as wide a range of language varieties as possible. Too little Lan-guage Laboratory material so far takes advantage of the oppor-tunities offered by the hardware of widening the learner's experi-ence, not just of the language, but of the culture of which it is a part. Exercises in intensive listening based on real-life recordings do this.

TRAINING COMPREHENSION

Two basic types of exercise suggest themselves for practising listening comprehension: one can require transcription of the text, or one may set questions upon it. Transcription has the ad-vantage of requiring a high degree of accuracy which makes the exercise a fairly difficult one, but it introduces what may be irrelevancies, namely the dictation skills, correct spelling and so on. It is of course very easy to prepare; all one needs to give the students is a tape recording and a blank sheet of paper. However, working in this way it takes an inordinately long time to get through a small quantity of text, and limitations of difficulty ex-clude much useful and interesting material. It is usually much better if one prepares material by handing out partial transcripts, in which the students have to complete missing parts. In this way irrelevant or uninteresting or too difficult patches can be bypassed. The second type of exercise is probably a better one. The student is given a recorded extract, which can be a speech, piece of conversation, song, extract from a lecture or a play, and at the same time a set of questions to find answers to. The questions are framed to cover varying types of difficulty, and varying levels of importance, dealing with the gist of largish sections of the text, or with the precise meaning of single phrases or expressions. The student finds the answers to them by playing and replaying sections of the recording. Since he has free control of his own machine there is no limit to the number of times he can listen to a given piece.

Finally a third type of exercise consists in letting the student listen to a recorded text once or maybe twice, and then giving a series of questions upon it to answer from memory. In my opinion this is the least useful type of practice, since it is as much an exercise in memory as it is in the actual comprehension of a running text, and it involves also the ability to summarise and organise concepts and content, which is only partly relevant to the business of understanding. Exercises of this sort need very careful grading, since if the passage is too difficult, once the listener has lost the thread of meaning in what he is listening to, most of the rest of the time he listens is largely wasted.

### THE TEST

The test described here was developed in conjunction with a course in which comprehension exercises (of the different types mentioned above) figured prominently. It was to be presented in a Language Laboratory and to consist of a recorded extract, from a radio programme or recorded conversation, lasting about ten minutes. Questions would be set then to see how well the candidates understood it. A Multiple Choice Question (MCQ) type examination seemed an obvious solution (Perren, 1968). There is nothing new of course about the use of Multiple Choice questions for testing listening comprehension. However most of the work that has been done in this area has been concerned with language at a more elementary grade and with learners whose total language ability is, I suspect, much more 'homogeneous'. The learners being catered for here, that is to say fairly typical post A-level students, are much more proficient in reading the language than they are in understanding its spoken form. What is described in this article therefore as aural comprehension, might be more accurately called the recognition of the spoken version of familiar linguistic forms. This makes it into a type of 'remedial' operation. This fact explains several features of the test procedures adopted. I shall not go into the question here of the relative values of MCQ type exams and more traditional types. However, in spite of the spectacular ease and speed with which this type of test may be marked, once the initial test has been constructed, this was not the main reason for adopting an objective test. The principal advantage of the MCQ in my opinion is that it is fairer, in other words that it is more efficient in discriminating between candidates, than any more traditional type of test.

There are several reasons for the greater efficiency of an MCQ. The principal one is the possibility that it offers of using the test as a whole to evaluate the efficiency of any of its constituent parts (Ingram, 1968). This means that it is easy to improve it every time it is applied, and to discard those elements which have shown themselves to be unsuitable or unsatisfactory, either because they were too hard, or because the wording of the questions was ambiguous or in some way confusing, so that they failed to discriminate between the most and least able candidates. However an analysis that will provide this information can be exceedingly laborious and time-consuming if it has to be done by hand, and in ordinary circumstances even in its simplest form is only worth while when the test can be applied to a sample set of candidates to prepare a satisfactory battery of questions for a full-scale exam involving very large numbers of candidates (Ingram, 1968). Without such an analysis, however, it is impossible to know for sure if the internal consistency of the test is such as to give a guarantee of reliability. In these circumstances the objective test is only really worth while if the services of a computer can be called upon. The whole process is then greatly simplified. It becomes possible not only to carry out a full item analysis but to use the test to test itself in the actual process of marking it, and calculate the final results from a selection of questions which excludes all those that have turned out to be unsatisfactory for whatever reason. What is more, it is possible to use the full power of the technique even when dealing with relatively small numbers of students.

## CONSTRUCTING THE TEST

The test can be constructed by simply listening to the recording and endeavouring to foresee the errors of understanding that are likely to occur. A faster and more efficient procedure is to give it to a sample class in the shape of a short-form or open-ended comprehension exercise. This can be incorporated in a course such as is described above. In fact some of the exercise material of one year can be used in constructing the tests of a later year by taking the answers given by a suitably varied group of students as a source of possible misunderstandings. Since the test has to fit into one hour in a Language Laboratory, there is a fairly strict limit on the number of questions and length of recording used. I have found that between nine and eleven minutes of recorded text for forty to fifty questions can be comfortably fitted into fifty-five minutes. This is only possible, however, if the questions are not difficult; it is important that this should not be a speed test. It is better therefore to err on the side of too few rather than too many questions, and for reasons to be explained later, they should be easy rather than difficult.

The questions are presented in the same order as the relevant matter occurs in the recording, and they are divided into sections corresponding to 'paragraphs' in the recording, changes of speakers or subject matter, in order that it may be easy to locate the part of the recording that they are referring to. Care should be taken to see that the questions are varied in difficulty. It is a good plan to start off with a number of distinctly easy questions, to give confidence. The questions should also be as varied as possible in type, testing comprehension of key-words, recognition of names, etc., and also gist-comprehension of whole sentences or paragraphs. As in the type of exercise described earlier the candidates are free to replay any section over as many times as they choose after the original transfer of the complete recording. They are discouraged from spending too long on any one item, since experience suggests that if they are going to get the right answer it is most likely to be almost immediately.

Because the candidates are free to replay any section of the text over freely, it was decided that the validity of the exam as a whole would be improved by including a certain number of questions that would measure general comprehension of the text as a whole, based on one hearing. Therefore the first six questions are presented separately and relate to the whole recording in a much more general way than the remainder of the test. In practice it was found simplest to put these questions on the tape itself, to be answered immediately, with a five-second interval between them. The answers to these six questions are collected before the candidates are given control of their own machines so that the answers cannot be altered when they come to listen to the recording more closely.

## MARKING

As stated above the marking of the test as well as all analysis of the results is done by the computer. Marking is not fully automatic. Procedures for automatic marking of objective tests of course exist, as is well known (Harris and Buckley-Sharp, 1968), and function to a very high degree of efficiency and accuracy. They have, however, the disadvantage of much greater complication for the student, since they require him either to punch a computer card himself, or to fill in spaces on specially prepared paper or cards with a mark-sensing pencil. In fact transferring the candidates' answers to punched cards is a simple if somewhat boring operation that takes only a few hours, negligible if compared to the labour of marking scripts.

A short preliminary program checks the punching for inaccuracies, for cards placed out of order, double punching and other anomalies. The actual marking in the main program[1] is done by presenting the first card punched with the correct responses to each item. The first operation of the program is then to compare each card with this, and to store a number for each candidate and each item. A later part of the program prints out a table showing totals, means, and the full distribution of marks for each candidate and for each separate item. This table will give a figure showing the difficulty-index of each item, which is equal to the percentage of candidates that got it right. Another table presents the most important part of the analysis of the different items, namely the discrimination index for each item. (These two indices allow decisions to be taken about the difficulty, discrimination or possible ambiguity of each item.)

If the examination itself is being tested by doing a dummy run on a sample class, then all those items which proved to be too hard, too easy or ambiguous must be replaced by new items, and this can be done also if the test is to be used on another occasion. But a satisfactory result can be obtained by simply listing those items which have proved satisfactory, instructing the computer to mark only these, and running the program a second time.

The final sections of the program print out the students' names, marks, means and standard deviations, also a list of students and marks arranged in descending order of magnitude and, for fixing to a noticeboard, a list not arranged in order of merit but alphabetically. On these final lists the actual marks are converted to standard scores and transformed scores, to a mean of 60 and standard deviation of 10. This gives a distribution ranging from about 20 to about 90 (which is more familiar to both students and colleagues alike).

REFERENCES

DICKINSON, L. (1970) 'The language laboratory and advanced teaching.' *English Language Teaching*, 25, 1, 32–42.
FARRINGTON, B. (1969) 'The place of the language laboratory in a University French department.' *Audio-Visual Language Journal*, 7, 1, 19–24.
HARRIS, F. T. C., and BUCKLEY-SHARP, M. (1968) 'Automation of

[1] The main program is adapted from one first developed in the Department of Physiology of Aberdeen University by Dr M. L. Diament.

multiple-choice marking.' *British Journal of Medical Education*, 2, 48–54.

INGRAM, E. (1968) 'Attainment and diagnostic testing.' In DAVIES, A., *Language Testing Symposium*. Oxford.

PERREN, G. E. (1968) 'Testing spoken language: some unsolved problems.' In DAVIES, A., *Language Testing Symposium*. Oxford.

*These last two extracts have made out a strong case for the use of objective tests. But the elegantly-written and persuasive arguments of Ballard were too one-sided. The issue is much more complex than his reasoning suggests. Objective items are, in fact, not particularly easy to write. It is not sufficient that these questions should cover the content of the course; they must also be in accord with its aims. This requirement is much more difficult to meet, as it is still far from clear precisely what skills different types of tests or examinations actually measure. This is a problem which could well be investigated by groups of teachers, as is being done already in the North-West region (Rudd, 1971). Research, to date, has been much more concerned with problems of accuracy and reliability, than with what has been measured. Cox (1967) quotes Getzels and Jackson as complaining that: 'The issue is not, as it is too often stated, short answers versus essay questions, objective versus subjective tests. Of course we want objective, that is consistently scored, tests. The issue is not one of method but of substance—not what kind of test but a test of what'. Until more is known about what these different assessments measure, examiners will continue to concentrate on traditional methods. The roots of the system of examining by essays can be traced back to medieval China; perhaps it is not surprising that the ideas of Ballard and his successors have taken some time in affecting accepted practice. Recent work by the Schools Council (Examinations Bulletin, numbers 3 and 4, 1964) and by various examining boards shows that the merits of objective testing are being explored further. But, for many purposes, it still appears that essays provide a useful method of assessment. It is important, however, that inconsistencies between markers should be minimised. The final extract comes from a large-scale project concerned with just this problem.*

### Multiple Marking of English Compositions
### (J. N. Britton, N. C. Martin and H. Rosen, 1966)[1]

#### GENERAL DESIGN OF THE ENQUIRY

The G.C.E. composition scripts of a representative sample of 500 boys and girls were marked by multiple marking methods and the results compared as described in (1) and (2) below with the official marking communicated to us by the G.C.E. Examining Board.

1   *Validity*        During the year leading up to the examination, candidates in the sample were given a monthly composition test in order to provide us with a broadly based criterion of their writing ability. The official marking and the experimental marking were compared in turn with this criterion to give an estimate of the validity of each marking.

2   *Reliability*        Arrangements were made for each of the marking procedures, the official and the experimental, to be carried out a second and a third time by independent markers or marking teams on a proportion of the scripts. The reliability of each marking method was estimated by directly comparing the three sets of results obtained in this way.

#### THE SAMPLE

The sample of 500 candidates finally used in this experiment was arrived at by the following procedure :

*a.   Participating schools*

The co-operation of the Examining Board enabled us to study their records of past examination results and select schools which would be highly likely, judging by the level and consistency of previous results, to give us the maximum spread of examination performance. Other criteria were then used in making a final selection of schools, namely :

   i.   a roughly equal number of boys and girls in the initial sample;

  ii.   single sex and mixed schools both represented;

 iii.   different types of school organisation represented;

 iv.   the types of area from which the schools drew their

[1] From J. N. Britton, N. C. Martin, and H. Rosen, *Multiple Marking of English Compositions* (H.M.S.O.), pages 13–25, substantially edited.

pupils were as varied as possible (within the limitations already imposed).

Seven schools were finally selected, were visited and agreed to co-operate.

### b.   The pupils

The schools submitted before the beginning of the academic year a list by forms and in alphabetical order of all their pupils who would be sitting the O-level English Language examination at the end of the year. The total number of pupils from all schools was 685 and, since the final sample aimed at was to be 500, it was reduced to 568 by cutting out complete classes from some of the schools, but in such a way that the spread of known ability was roughly maintained.

### c.   The final sample

On the day of the G.C.E. examination, the original sample of 568 was reduced to a final sample of 500 for the experimental marking by excluding

    i.   those who were not entered for G.C.E. or were absentees;
    ii.   those with three or more absences from the pooled assessment.

Boys and girls were equally represented, i.e. 250 each.

#### THE POOLED ASSESSMENT

In order to establish a criterion against which both the official marking and the experimental marking could be compared, an attempt was made to build up a measure of the candidates' writing ability derived from samples of their written work throughout the year. This was called the pooled assessment.

A set of composition subjects was sent to the participating schools at monthly intervals during the school year preceding the G.C.E.; there were in all ten sets each requiring the candidates to write on one of the subjects suggested. The scripts were arranged in our numerical order and sent out to markers in two halves, each containing some boys' and some girls' scripts. Each set of scripts was marked by a different pair of examiners, one man and one woman. Thus, the pooled assessment for any given pupil consisted of the sum of the marks given by twenty examiners to ten pieces of writing by that pupil.

## TEACHERS' ASSESSMENTS

About a month before the G.C.E. examination each school was asked to provide an assessment of the candidates' ability in writing as follows:

    i.   assessment on a five-point scale (A to E without plus or minus);

    ii.   to be as inclusive an assessment as possible of their ability to write English;

    iii.   not to be concerned with prediction of examination results but a straightforward assessment on the basis of the teacher's own judgement;

    iv.   not necessarily to use all five grades in any one class, or in any one school.

Inspection of these assessments showed such variation between classes and between schools that they could not serve, in their original form, as an additional criterion. Therefore, on the assumption that teachers' judgements would have an element of validity which we ought if possible to incorporate, we scaled their grades in accordance with the class by class distribution of marks in the pooled assessment. Where the distribution of grades in a teacher's assessment of a given class was out of step with the distribution of marks in the pooled assessment, his grades were brought roughly into line.

## THE EXAMINATION: G.C.E. 1964

*The composition paper*    The composition paper set by the Examining Board was subdivided into Papers A and B; in Paper A *one* subject out of nine had to be chosen and in Paper B, *two* subjects out of ten. Thus for some candidates our markers were dealing with one sample and for others with two. The existence of this alternative arrangement provided us with interesting data.

*The official marking*    The official marking followed the Board's customary practice. A detailed marking scheme is prepared and a number of scripts are photocopied. At a meeting of all examiners the marking scheme is discussed and amended or amplified and standards are as far as possible laid down by reference to the photo-copies. The scripts are then marked under the guidance of team leaders (who re-mark a proportion of the scripts and make recommendations for any necessary modifications in the marks of the assistants; and have in addition a set of scripts of their own to mark). A final moderation meeting is held at which the Chief Examiner is assisted by a number of team leaders.

Each examiner receives a confidential document some fourteen foolscap pages in length intended to aid him in his task. This consists of brief practical instructions (kind of pencil to be used, etc.), 'Notes on Marking', and discussion of the particular topics set on the paper. It is worth emphasising at this stage that this is a very elaborate document not merely prescribing for the examiners, but also discussing in detail the issues involved, and calling for close study by the examiners. It is in these respects very unlike the instructions to markers used in the experimental marking.

*The treatment of the experimental sample in the official marking*
It was the intention of this experiment that the scripts of those candidates selected as the final sample should go through the machinery of the examination in the normal way. However, in the event, the scripts were given independent marking by two examiners, in most cases team leaders. The effects of this on the results are discussed later in this report.

*Photo-copying the scripts*        By permission of the Examining Board it was arranged that the normal transfer of scripts from the schools to the examiners should be interrupted to allow us to photo-copy the scripts of the experimental sample. Accordingly the whole entry from these schools was personally collected by members of the research team on the day on which they were written. The following day was given up to the operation of separating out the sample scripts and making two photocopies of each. The originals were then put back in their examination order and checked, an official from the Examining Board sharing the supervision of this operation and despatching the scripts to the respective official examiners.

Two copies of each script had been made in order to hasten the process of marking teams. Each complete set of scripts was divided into two (A half and B half) in such a way that each roughly represented a reasonable spread of ability and a balance of boys and girls, and the half sets were sent out to markers with marking instructions, mark sheets and a copy of the paper. On completion of one half set, a marker was sent his second half, an interval of not more than three weeks between the two instalments being maintained throughout the operation.

*Reliability of the official marking*        As we have indicated above, in a large scale examination employing many markers, the critical index of reliability is that of the reliability of marking channels; that is to say, an estimate of the likelihood of a script being accorded the same mark by one marker (or marking team) as it is by another. In any examination proper, of course, each script goes through one channel only; for our scripts this is what we have labelled 'the official marking'. To obtain a direct estimate of its reliability we needed to duplicate its procedure. We were fortunate in obtaining the permission of the Examining Board to set up alternative marking channels as follows: two team leaders and two assistant examiners, all of whom had marked the composition paper in the current examination, were asked to carry out the same procedure on a hundred of our scripts (every fifth in the sample). Reliability was calculated by intercorrelating the three versions of the G.C.E. marking thus obtained.

*The experimental marking*     The system of multiple marking used in the experiment was the modification of Wiseman's method that had been tried out in the pilot experiment (Britton, 1963); that is to say, a candidate's mark consisted of the pooled marks (each out of a maximum of ten) given by four independent examiners, three of these being rapid impression marks and the fourth a mark for mechanical accuracy.

*The examiners*     In all, nine examiners (A to I) gave marks for rapid impression, one examiner ($M_1$) gave a mark for mechanical accuracy to all the scripts and two others ($M_2$ and $M_3$) did so for B half only, that is to 250 scripts. None of the experimental examiners had contributed to the pooled assessment. We recruited for the task men and women with teaching experience and, with one exception, experience as examiners in public examinations. The exception was Examiner G, who was chosen for her *inexperience*; she had four terms' teaching experience and had done no marking in a public examination. In contrast, Examiner I was chosen to represent G.C.E.

*Rapid impression marking*     The examiners were asked to read through a dozen or more scripts, taken at random, in order to establish a standard, and then to mark rapidly on their impression of the whole performance in each composition, using the full range of 0 to 10 marks. They were also asked to keep a detailed record of the time spent on the work. Since a mark out of ten was given to each of two essays in Paper B, all other marks (i.e., for Paper A and, in all cases, for mechanical accuracy) were doubled, giving a final maximum of 80 for the composite mark. No further instructions were given to examiners and there was no briefing and no revision or moderation of their marks. They did not meet each other until after the marking was completed.

Not less than eight weeks after the first marking they carried out a re-marking of a hundred scripts (every fifth of the sample), and after they had done so they wrote brief notes on the criteria upon which they had based their assessments.

*Marking for mechanical accuracy*    The use in our experimental marking of a separate assessment for mechanical accuracy introduced an analytic element into what is primarily a general impression procedure. It might be noted that the category thus separated out from general impression is one in which a relatively precise external standard is in existence.

The first three hundred words of each script were marked according to a detailed code of penalties, the resulting mark being out of a maximum of ten. Up to five marks could be lost for mis-spellings, at the rate of one mark for 'shocking' errors and half a mark for less serious ones; mis-spelling of ambitious and unusual words was not penalised. Many errors in punctuation were penalised on first occurrence only and, in particular, the penalties to be imposed on faulty punctuation of quoted speech were severely restricted. The code, though as specific as we could make it, did leave considerable room for subjective judgement by the markers; necessarily so since no final decision can be made about error except in the light of a particular context.

No marks were made on the scripts themselves, but as errors were observed the penalties were entered in a tabulated mark sheet.

*Multiple marking teams.*    When the first six impression markers had assessed the scripts they were randomly divided into two teams (Team I = A, B and C; Team II—D, E and F). In calculating validity (i.e. correlation with the pooled assessment) the mechanical mark given by $M_1$ was added to each team total in turn; in calculating the reliability of our marking, the second mechanical mark given by $M_2$ was added to Team II's marks for B half (250 scripts) and the totals correlated with the corresponding marks given by Team I plus $M_1$. Team III was not a random selection of examiners; it included the inexperienced examiner (G) and the examiner of long experience (I). $M_2$ was added to this team's totals to estimate validity and the third marking for 'M' ($M_3$) was added to their marks for B half to estimate reliability.

### RELIABILITY

If our justification for carrying out this enquiry had to be reduced to a single reason, we should not hesitate to state it as an attempt to find a marking procedure that was more reliable (and no less valid) than that in current usage. A crucial statistic is therefore a comparison of the reliability of the experimental marking with that of the method used by the Examining Board.

Marking reliability as we interpret it is the degree to which a candidate's work would be likely to be differently assessed according to the 'marking channel' it happens to pass through. In the official marking, a channel consisted of the assessment of a particular assistant examiner (one of some hundred or so) as moderated first by the team-leader and subsequently by the Chief Examiner and those who assisted him at the final stages. We are able, as has been explained, to set up two alternative 'channels' in our two assistant examiners each with a team-leader, but it must be pointed out that we were not able to complete the process by paralleling the final moderation that would normally have been provided by the Chief Examiner. It might therefore be argued that the two indices by which the special channels are correlated with the official marking constitute our nearest estimate of the marking reliability of the official assessment. These were in fact correlations of 0·51 (Special Marking 1) and 0·67 (Special Marking 2). It could, however, be argued, on the other hand, that since the official marking of the scripts differed from that accorded to the scripts in general (see above), the best estimate of the reliability of the procedure lay in the correlation between Special Marking 1 and Special Marking 2, i.e. a correlation of 0·52. (This is calculated on a sub sample of 100 scripts giving a standard error of ±0·08.)

Estimate of the reliability of the experimental marking is given by comparing the assessment of 250 scripts by the first random team (Markers A, B and C), together with the first marking for mechanical accuracy ($M_1$) with that of the second random team (Markers D, E and F), together with $M_2$. This gave a correlation of 0·82 (±0·02). Team III was not a randomly selected team. When $M_3$ was added to Team III's marks (250 scripts), it gave a correlation with Team I of 0·81, and with Team II of 0·78.

The figures clearly indicate that in this case marking by individual examiners with very careful briefing and elaborate arrangements for moderation was in fact significantly less reliable than a multiple mark consisting of three rapid impression marks and a mark for mechanical accuracy.

VALIDITY

Our criterion of validity was the pooled assessment derived from 20 markings—10 compositions each marked twice. We shall concern ourselves first with the nature of the criterion itself.

*The validity of the official and experimental markings*      The assumption is made that the most valid marking of the composition test will be that which most closely resembles the broadly based assessment of the candidates' writing ability constituted by our pooled assessment. Each marking was compared in turn with this criterion, using Pearson Product-moment correlations. Here are the results:

| (N = 500) | | Correlation with pooled assessment |
|---|---|---|
| Official marking | | 0·57 (±0·03) |
| Experimental marking, | Team I | 0·67 (±0·025) |
| | Team II | 0·66 (±0·025) |
| | Team III | 0·69 (±0·02) |

Since only one marking for mechanical accuracy covered the whole sample ($M_1$), this was added to each of the three experimental teams in turn for the purposes of the above calculations. Correlations of the teams of three markers without 'M' with the pooled assessment were as follows:

Team I: 0·65      Team II: 0·63      Team III: 0·68

The figures suggest that our multiple marking method has achieved higher reliability than normal marking methods without any loss of validity, indeed with some improvement in that respect also.

*Teachers' assessments*      We were interested in teachers' assessments as a possible means of setting up a criterion against which to measure the validity of examination marks: the existence of the pooled assessment gave us the opportunity of estimating their value as such a criterion. However, the correlation between the two forms of assessment proved to be low, 0·40, and it was clear from inspection that the trouble lay in the inconsistency of grades from teacher to teacher. We have already described how we therefore scaled the teachers' assessments crudely in accordance with the class by class distribution of marks in the pooled assessment. (The scaled version had a correlation of 0·65 with the pooled assessment.)

Correlations of the official and experimental markings with the scaled and unscaled teachers' assessments were as follows:

| | Correlations with the teachers' assessments | |
|---|---|---|
| | Scaled | Unscaled |
| Official marking | 0·48 | 0·31 |
| Team I   (without 'M') | 0·49 | 0·33 |
| Team II          „ | 0·46 | 0·27 |
| Team III         „ | 0·50 | 0·32 |

A regular examination procedure clearly could not incorporate a pooled assessment but it could make use of teachers' assessments and often has done so. Our figures suggest nothing beyond the fact that there is something here worth further investigation.

### REFERENCE

BRITTON, J. N. (1963) 'Experimental marking of English compositions written by fifteen-year-olds.' *Educational Review*, 16, 1, 17–23.

*Improving the accuracy of marking is important enough, but, returning to the original discussion of examinations by Pilliner:*

'*One final question remains. It is implicit in the following comment from Montgomery[1] (1965, page 12): "A considerable amount of research has been carried out ... into the actual mechanics of ... examinations, but perhaps less has been done to probe the fundamental reasons for having them." After reviewing the multitude of research reports, mainly of a technical nature, few would deny the existence of the imbalance Montgomery indicates. In the area of examinations, as in other areas, it is easier to answer—or to seek answers to—the question "How?" than the question "Why?"*

'*It is difficult to envisage a highly developed society without examinations of some sort. "Whether we like it or not," says Himmelweit, "society will continue to use the degree as a predictor device" (1967, page 364). If this is accepted, the "Why?" question changes its impact. It is to be answered by the development and specification of sound educational objectives. The present climate of inquiry gives reason to hope that in this highly important sense the balance will be redressed*' (pages 183–4).

[1] References in this section will be found at the end of Pilliner's main extract, pages 189–90.

# 12    Friendship Patterns

*The importance of academic attainment is still emphasised in most schools, but teachers are also concerned with broader aspects of education. Their pupils are being prepared for life in the wider society outside and school is often seen as a microcosm of that society. Besides their academic work, children have other interests—sometimes interests in conflict with the educational objectives of the school. The peer group has an important effect on the development of attitudes, but the converse is also true. Children may often choose their friends on the basis of shared values and interests, and these in turn are dependent, in part, on their home backgrounds. This chapter presents three extracts from studies using two contrasting approaches to measuring friendship patterns and social behaviour in school. The first extract describes the use of sociometric techniques to investigate the effect of social class on friendship choices in different types of secondary school. The two other extracts deal with participant observation as a method of inquiry in similar studies.*

### Making Friends at School
### (J. Ford, 1969)[1]

It has often been said that the school can be viewed as a society in miniature, both reflecting and affecting the wider society of which it is a part. Thus one might hypothesize that the peer social organization of the school would tend to incorporate the class stratification of the larger community. And, indeed, studies of American schoolchildren by Hollingshead, Neugarten and others lend support to this view by demonstrating that mutual friendship and popularity scores are related to social background. It has therefore come to be widely believed that the friendship

[1] Edited extracts from Chapter 5 of *Social Class and the Comprehensive School* (Routledge), pages 76–85, 87, 91 and 102–5.

choices of secondary school children are a reflection of their class backgrounds. However the results of two more recent studies suggest that, while class stratification does have an important impact on school peer group formation, this effect operates in a slightly more complex way than had formerly been assumed.

In this study of a number of London grammar schools, Oppenheim observed no clique formation along social class lines; the boys in his sample showed no preference for those from a similar background in their choice of friends. Now, when this finding is taken together with Turner's conclusion that there is more cleavage in friendship preference according to ambition than class background, an interpretation of the disparity between Oppenheim's results and those of the earlier American researchers suggests itself. It seems that the class structure of the world outside the school shapes the structure of informal relations within the school not only through the children's social class of *origin* but also through their class of *aspiration*. For the majority of children, of course, these will be the same, for, as we have seen in the preceding chapter, only a minority of children aspire to occupations in a different social class from those of their parents. Yet where children *are* anticipating social mobility it is probable that the social status they expect to achieve in adult life is a more important determinant of their interpersonal preferences than their class background. In their patterns of friendship these children trace the imprint of yesterday's class structure more faintly than that of tomorrow. Thus, as Turner says 'this future oriented cleavage may well contain the seeds of class consciousness which will emerge when the students leave school and establish their stable position as adults'. Most of Oppenheim's grammar schoolboys could look forward to a middle-class future. For many, of course, this would merely represent a continuation of the style of life and pattern of acquaintances they had always known. But among those who had come from a different world we would expect to find few who were looking over their shoulders.

Now liberal critics of the tripartite system of secondary education, unperturbed by reports of class-linked friendship patterns in American comprehensive schools, assume that comprehensive reorganization will go some way towards dissolving class cleavages in this country. They claim that tripartite selection leads to patterns of informal association among schoolchildren which not only *reflect* the separatism of class society but also *perpetuate* it. For children are literally segregated at an early age so that they are placed in schools and streams where most of their fellows resemble them fairly closely in class of origin and very closely in class of aspiration. Opportunities for interaction with children from different backgrounds or those who are destined for different occupational statuses are thus severely limited and the hostility (or at least distance) between social classes is thus perpetuated.

For such critics the idea of the comprehensive neighbourhood school 'with its cosy classless ring' is attractive. In these schools it is hoped that class barriers will be broken down, children will mix freely with the 'all sorts' that are supposed to make a world and thus learn the tolerance so essential in their education 'in and for democracy'. Or, as it is expressed in our main hypothesis, *'Comprehensive school children will show less tendency to mix only with children of their own social type than will tripartite schoolchildren.'*

Now behind this hypothesis are really two separate ideas. Firstly there is the notion that the organization of a comprehensive school does not, like that of the tripartite schools, encourage children to mix mainly with those of similar class origin and class destination because the basic units of the school are more heterogeneous than the class-linked streams of the tripartite school. Then there is the additional suggestion that within their administrative groupings comprehensive school children will show less tendency to prefer those from similar backgrounds and those bound for similar future statuses than do tripartite schoolchildren. In other words it is being hypothesized both that a greater *option* for heterogeneous interaction or 'social mixing' is created by comprehensive organization and that children subject to this form of school organization will tend to *take up* this option.

. . .

In Cherry Dale school, as in many other comprehensives, there is a deliberate attempt to undermine the influence of academic stratification by the introduction of a system of 'vertical' subdivisions or houses. On entering the school each child is assigned to one of the four houses and throughout his school life various activities are organized through the house system in order to increase the salience of house membership for the individual children. Thus sports competitions take place between houses and members of the same house can, for example, dine together in their house room. This vertical organization is elaborated by a system of horizontal divisions based on year groups, so that within each year group children are assigned to tutor groups on the basis of their houses not their ability. In the fourth year there are eight house tutor groups (two for each house) each with a tutor who goes 'up' each year with his tutees and is therefore expected to come to know them all intimately.

Officially the house tutor groups rather than the academic streams are regarded as the basic administrative units and it is in these groups that children meet for registration each morning and afternoon. The aim is to replace the form or class of the traditional school by a mixed ability group which moves up the school together and is expected to become a cohesive unit. Thus, while children spend the majority of their time at school in their socially homogeneous academic streams, one might argue that some opportunity for social mixing is presented by the organization of houses and house tutor groups.

However it is one thing to claim that children have some opportunity for heterogeneous social interaction in Cherry Dale school and quite another to suggest that they will take up this option. In order to find out whether traditional lines of stratification are indeed undermined by the house system, we need to know whether academic streams or house tutor groups have the greatest impact on friendship formation in the school. In an attempt to determine this, all the children were asked to imagine that they must choose one friend from all the people they knew, one 'real friend' in whom they felt they could confide and with whom, for example, they could envisage undertaking a long journey. Keeping this person in mind they were then asked to indicate whether he or she was in the same school, and, if so, in which academic stream. Cherry Dale children were then additionally required to indicate whether friends chosen from within the school were in the same house or a different house from themselves. The results are presented in Tables 12 : 1 and 12 : 2.

It is clear from Table 12 : 1 that children in all streams of all the schools are more likely to choose their 'one real friend' from their own form or stream or its equivalent than any other in the same school. In fact, when we consider only those children choosing an individual in their own school (64 per cent of the total), we find that in all schools more than two thirds choose someone from their own (or an equivalent) stream; in the grammar school 67 per cent do so, in the comprehensive 72 per cent and in the secondary modern 73 per cent, and these proportions are similar in all streams. This means that, of the children choosing their friends from their own school, the proportion choosing them from their own or equivalent streams is always more than twice as large as one would have expected by chance.

Table 12 : 2, on the other hand, indicates that among the Cherry Dale children confining their choices to other Cherry Dale children (65 per cent) there is no preference for friends in the same *house*. Since the numerical strength of the four houses in the fourth year is almost exactly equal then, purely by chance, we would expect one choice in four to be for an individual in the chooser's own house. And the percentages in the table never deviate by more than 5 per cent from this chance pattern, indicating that the relationship of friendship choice to house is no more than random.

TABLE 12:1  *All children: choice of 'one real friend' by stream of choosers and chosen*

| Characteristics of choosers | | Characteristics of chosen | | | | | |
|---|---|---|---|---|---|---|---|
| School | Stream | Same or equivalent stream % | Higher stream* % | Lower stream† % | Different school % | Left school % | N = (100%) |
| Grammar | 'A' | 40 | 17 | 3 | 33 | 7 | 30 |
| | 'B' | 32 | 12 | 12 | 28 | 16 | 25 |
| | 'C' | 37 | 11 | 7 | 22 | 22 | 27 |
| | 'D' | 33 | 7 | 13 | 7 | 40 | 15 |
| Comprehensive | 'A'1 & 'A'2 | 57 | 15 | 5 | 8 | 15 | 39 |
| | 'B'1 & 'B'2 | 39 | 4 | 13 | 26 | 17 | 46 |
| | 'C'1 & 'C'2 | 44 | 10 | 2 | 15 | 29 | 48 |
| | 'D' | 53 | 26 | 5 | 5 | 10 | 19 |
| Secondary Modern | 'A' | 62 | 7 | 7 | 14 | 10 | 29 |
| | 'B' | 33 | 11 | 11 | 28 | 17 | 18 |
| | 'C' | 46 | 4 | 17 | 12 | 21 | 24 |
| Total sample | | 41 | 11 | 8 | 18 | 18 | 320 |

* This includes those in a higher academic stream in the same year group *and* those higher up the school in the fifth and sixth forms.

† This includes those in a lower academic stream in the same year group plus children in the lower school (that is first to third forms).

H

Tables 12:1 and 12:2, then, offer little comfort for those who have put their faith in comprehensive reorganization as a means of destroying class barriers in interpersonal relations. For while one might argue that 'vertical' organization of the school into houses provides some opportunity for inter-class interaction, there is no evidence to show that this makes any difference to the actual processes of friendship choice within the comprehensive school. For, in contrast to Pape's finding for a sample of comprehensive school girls that 'they are just as likely to be found mixing with other members of their house who are in different forms', Cherry Dale children are more likely to choose their 'real friends' from their own class-homogeneous academic streams than their socially mixed houses.

TABLE 12:2   *Cherry Dale comprehensive pupils only: choice of 'one real friend' by stream of chooser and relative house of chosen*

|  | House of chosen relative to chooser | | |
|  | same | different | |
| Stream of chooser | % | % | N = (100%) |
|---|---|---|---|
| 'A' | 23 | 77 | 30 |
| 'B' | 27 | 73 | 26 |
| 'C' | 30 | 70 | 27 |
| 'D' | 25 | 75 | 16 |
| All | 26 | 74 | 99 |

Indeed I found little evidence that the houses meant much at all to the children and it was difficult to avoid the conclusion that house tutor groups were no more than nominal administrative aggregates rather than real social groups. For the children were frequently heard to refer to 'our form' (meaning academic stream not house tutor group) and, although I asked them to write their house tutor groups at the top of their completed questionnaires, most of them either added their academic stream number or gave only the latter. In fact a number of boys and girls claimed that they found it difficult to answer the question in which they were required to indicate the relative house of their chosen friend, as they did not *know* which houses their best friends were in!

We have seen that the 'real' social units of the schools, whether comprehensive or tripartite, are the academic streams or forms, for not only do these groups spend a considerable amount of time together *as* groups, but also their members show a preference for each other in their informal associations. We have also seen that these groups tend towards social homogeneity in terms of both class background and the future aspirations of their members. Yet this is obviously only a *tendency*, for while a majority of the children within one stream are usually socially similar the correlation is not perfect. In Cherry Dale school for example there are more middle-class children in the 'A' stream than in all the other streams put together; class background and stream are very strongly related. But, despite this fact, middle-class children make up less than one half of the total 'A' streamers, while in the 'B' and 'C' streams about one child in every seven is middle class. In other words, in spite of the strong class bias in streaming, the opportunity for children to mix with others from different class backgrounds within their streams, while greatly restricted, is not negligible.

There are therefore two more ways in which the main hypothesis can be examined. For the extent to which friendship preference *within* academic streams shows ingroup preference in respect of firstly social class of origin, and secondly social class of aspiration remains empirically problematic. It is just possible that some difference between the comprehensive and tripartite schools might show itself here, that comprehensive pupils might turn out to be less 'class conscious' on these criteria than tripartite school children.

In order to examine this possibility the children were asked:

Suppose you wanted to pick some people to be your *close friends*—people you would enjoy doing things with and like to have as close friends for a *long time*. Which three people *who are in this classroom right now* would you pick?

This, unlike the question reported above, is directed towards friendship *preference* rather than friendship *choice*. For the children, who were responding in the company only of the rest of their academic streams, would not necessarily normally choose their friends from within that universe, in fact we know from Table 12 : 1 that probably only about forty per cent would do so. Thus 'there is an important possibility that the individual may be forced to choose people he would not spontaneously select, with the result that the choices are arbitrary if not erroneous in character ... If, however, friendship is a relative matter, there is no reason why a subject should not be able to make choices as far down a continuum as desired. When we ask for hypothetical choices rather than existing friendships the problem is less severe. We need only assume that the students know others in the class well enough to be able to make some guesses as to who are most nearly the kinds of persons they would like to have as friends.'

Responses to this question can be analysed by the use of the traditional sociometric methods as developed by Moreno. The pattern of friendship preferences within each academic stream is described by a *sociogram*, a chart in which interpersonal preferences are represented by lines between individuals. Broken lines are used to represent unreciprocated choices, with arrows to denote the direction of choice, while solid lines represent mutual choices. The individuals themselves are graphically presented so that their sex and social class of origin are immediately identifiable, and in addition each is numbered to facilitate indentification of particular individuals. Thus the sociometric structure of each stream is described in the following charts.

The most cursory inspection of the two charts is sufficient to reveal immediately that responses to the request to name hypothetical friends are not random but do fall into patterns. In fact in most streams a number of separate groups or cliques of hypothetical friends are identifiable, the most tightly knit cliques being those linked by the greatest proportion of unbroken lines.

*(Figure 12:1 and 12:2 provide examples of sociograms and show the way in which friendship patterns may be identified. The impression from these two diagrams is that working class children are more effectively integrated within a grammar school than within a comprehensive. This impression was borne out by more detailed analyses of the data which are not reported here.)*

Returning to the major hypothesis that *'Comprehensive school children will show less tendency to mix with children of their own social type than will tripartite schoolchildren'*, there is no evidence whatever from this study of three schools that this is the case. In Cherry Dale as in most comprehensive schools, children are taught in doubly homogeneous social groups. They, like tripartite schoolchildren, mix during lesson time mainly with those from similar social background and those who are bound for similar eventual social status. The option for social mixing which is supposedly created in the comprehensive school by the house system is simply not taken up : children are more likely to choose their 'real friends' from their own academic streams than any others in the same school, and houses and house tutor groups have no impact on friendship formation. Within these homogeneous academic streams children apparently prefer to mix with those from similar social background. Indeed even in the 'A' stream there is, among the middle class, considerable in-group preference by class of origin. Since this is not so in the grammar school, one is tempted to consider the possibility that, for this academically successful group, 'the social effect of such schools is to reinforce rather than combat class consciousness'. Had they gone to a grammar school would these children have been less 'class conscious' at least as far as *class background* is concerned? Is it possible that in this group 'children tend to underline and emphasize class differences from the very fear that they will become blurred'?

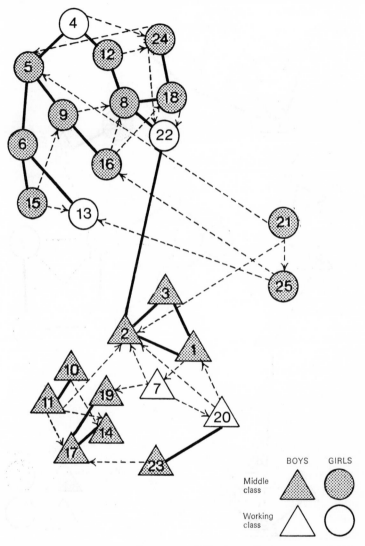

FIGURE 12:1  *Gammer Wiggins Grammar School Stream B*

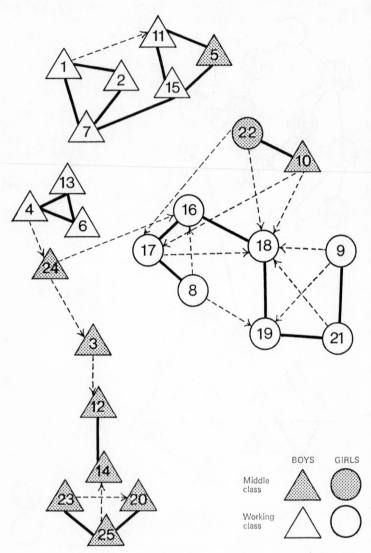

FIGURE 12:2 *Cherry Dale Comprehensive School: Stream A2*

*Ford used self-report measures in this investigation. The contrasting approach involves direct observation of behaviour. This can be done either by an observer who records behaviour against a rating scheme, as we shall see in the next chapter, or by participant observation, in which the research worker becomes recognised as part of the social scene in which he is interested.*

*A sociologist with experience in education will readily be accepted by pupils in the role of a teacher and may then observe social behaviour in a natural setting. There is an increasing concern among sociologists that the usual methods of measurement by test, questionnaire or interview may distort or misrepresent a social situation in ways which are difficult to detect. The very act of measurement may alter what we intend to measure, as has been found in atomic physics with the formulation of Heisenberg's 'Uncertainty Principle'. There has been an emphasis on non-reactive techniques which avoid changing the situation. Participant observation is commonly used for this purpose and it has produced interesting studies by Hargreaves and Lacey on social behaviour in a secondary modern school and in a grammar school.*

*The first extract is a comment by Hargreaves on the problems of being a participant observer in a school. The second extract illustrates the type of insights which can be obtained by using this method. Although participant observation can be accepted as being nearly non-reactive, it still lacks important ingredients of objectivity and comparability. The observer is left to interpret for himself the situation he encounters and selective perception may help to fit these into preconceived theoretical frameworks. All that can be said with safety is that Hargreaves and Lacey report an interesting alternative method of investigating social relationships in which the distortion of reality takes a different form from that found in psychometric or sociometric methods of measurement.*

## Social Relations in a Secondary Modern School
## (D. H. Hargreaves, 1967)[1]

### PARTICIPANT-OBSERVATION AND ROLE CONFLICT

Participant-observation, like any other research method, is subject to strains and limitations and if we are to evaluate the method, these must be made explicit. The validation of partici-

[1] Edited extracts from Appendix I of *Social Relations in a Secondary Modern School* (Routledge), pages 193–205.

pant-observation is in part a matter of determining wherever possible the reliability of the material obtained. The extent to which the participant-observer disturbs the situation he investigates, and the extent of the limitation imposed by accepting a role within that situation, lead not only to the uncovering of information which may be inaccessible by other methods, but also to deficiencies and difficulties which require elucidation.

The method of participant-observation leads the investigator to accept a role within the social situation he studies: he participates as a member of the group as well as observing it. In theory, this direct participation in the group life permits an easy entrance into the social situation by reducing the resistance of the group members; decreases the extent to which the investigator disturbs the 'natural' situation; and permits the investigator to experience and observe the group's norms, values, conflicts and pressures, which (over a long period) cannot be hidden from someone playing an in-group role. The fact that I had three years' experience of teaching and that I was to spend a third of my time in the school teaching classes allayed many of the fears teachers felt about my presence in the school. Within the first few days many of the teachers asked me about my previous experience as a teacher and my attitudes towards a number of educational problems—corporal punishment being a favourite test-question. This helped to remove the suspicion that I was some sort of 'spy' from the authorities. If I had been a teacher, the argument seemed to run, and I was going to do some teaching in the school, then surely I must be looking at the school from *their* point of view.

But not all the teachers remained unconcerned about my presence in the school. This was partly a result of the fact that the nature of my work was never adequately explained to the staff prior to my arrival. The question of my going to Lumley was discussed with the Chief Education Officer and the Headmaster. On this occasion the nature of my work was briefly explained and the headmaster consented to the study. However, when I arrived at the school two days later, I was told by the staff that the head had simply circulated a brief note to all the teachers, saying that a sociologist from the University would be coming to work in the school for a short period. The staff had no indication of the type of work I intended to do. Had I spoken formally to the staff for a few moments on my first day at the school, much of the misunderstanding and suspicion of which I was soon to become aware would have been avoided. As it was, too many fears and questions remained unexpressed and unanswered. Moreover, many of the staff came to wish me good-bye at the end of the summer term some three weeks later and were surprised to learn that my work had only just begun.

The problems of participant-observation in a school cannot be understood without a brief preliminary discussion of the teacher-role. We may define *role* as an aspect of the total behaviour of a particular actor occupying a particular *status* or position within a social system. The nature of the role is determined not only by the status of the actor but also by his orientation towards the *expectations* of other actors who hold complementary roles within the system. Since role is often used ambiguously by sociologists, we will, wherever necessary, distinguish between *role-performance* and *role-expectations*. Most roles are performed to different actors or groups of actors, who may have different role-expectations. It is this complement of role-relationships which R. K. Merton has termed the *role-set*. The content or definition of a role thus consists of the sum of the expectations of all members of the role-set, including the actor himself, and which aspects of the role are used in actual role-performance will depend upon the member(s) of the role-set to which the role-performance is directed.

The persons who form the constituents of the teacher's role-set are, amongst others, pupils, colleagues, the headteacher, parents, Her Majesty's Inspectors. It is, of course, the first two of these to whom the teacher principally directs his role-performance, since pupils and fellow-teachers are the groups with which the teacher is most frequently in face-to-face relationship. The headteacher, parents and Inspectors assume less significance because on only rare occasions need the role-performance be determined by their expectations. The teacher's situation is a highly autonomous one: most of the time he is 'his own boss' and not subject to the scrutiny of colleagues or superiors. In Merton's term, the role-set is highly 'insulated' from simultaneous observation by various members of the role-set.

*Role-conflict* is the exposure of an actor to conflicting expectations which cannot be simultaneously fulfilled. This may be due to one member of the role-set having conflicting role-expectations which require simultaneous fulfilment, or to two or more members of the role-set holding role-expectations which conflict with one another. Resolution of the conflict will often take the form of a compromise, involving the sacrifice of part of each conflicting expectation, or the complete abandonment of one expectation. For the teacher, resolution of role-conflict is often a comparatively simple matter, since he rarely has to perform his role simultaneously before different members of the role-set, whose expectations undoubtedly conflict. If a parent complains, the teacher may, if he wishes, present himself to the parent as a charming, friendly and gentle person whose behaviour has been entirely misunderstood by the child, and then return to the classroom as a harsh disciplinarian. The teacher may discuss the aims of education at length with his colleagues or the headteacher, but this does not mean that his views will necessarily be put into practice in the ensuing lessons.

When the barriers separating the various components of the role-set break down, a conflict will arise if the role-performance becomes simultaneously observed by two or more members of the role-set with different expectations. For the teacher, an Inspection may be such an event. Often the role-performance will change since now it is directed mainly to the Inspector rather than to the pupils; it is the Inspector's expectations which demand conformity if the teacher is to obtain formal approval as a teacher. If the teacher is a 'good' teacher, he can satisfy the Inspector *and* the pupils by his normal role-performance, but the presence of an Inspector often transforms the role-perform-ance. At the teacher's disposal are a number of devices by which he can mitigate the effects of the conflict and the danger it brings to his effective control of the situation. Thus he may inform the pupils that the Inspector has come to see *them* in order to reduce disciplinary infringements and increase artificially the enthusiasm of the pupils, both of which support a role-performance directed towards the expectations of the Inspector.

One aspect of my participant-observation in the school was to sit at the back of the form during an ordinary lesson. Whereas initially most of the teachers happily ascribed a teacher-role to me on the basis of my past experience and current teaching within the school, to observe them within the confines of their own classrooms involved a disruption of their usual autonomy and upset their ascription of a teacher-role to me. In exceptional circumstances teachers do see their colleagues at work but for most part the assessment any teacher may make of his colleagues' competency depends upon more indirect information, such as examination results, noise from the classroom, attitude of pupils outside the classroom and gossip. As soon as I became an observer of the classroom situation, I could no longer be regarded as a teacher. Instead my role became more that of the Inspector. The insulation of the teacher's role-set ceased. The conflicts between the teacher's self-image, the expectations of the pupils and the expectations of an observer became manifest.

The resolutions of this conflict took several forms. A few teachers reacted with some kind of withdrawal. (No teacher actually refused to allow me to observe his lessons, and in only one case was the lack of co-operation made open.) Whenever I went into a lesson conducted by Mr H., he made the boys work quietly out of textbooks, talked in a whisper to boys at his desk so that I could not hear from the back and declined to speak to the class as a whole unless this became unavoidable. On several occasions he was rather rude to me—although it is only fair to point out that his relations with many of the teachers were perfunctory. For some time I did not go into his lessons—and tried to find some common ground and a more personal relationship with him. This was entirely unsuccessful, but the problem was resolved for me when the teacher left at the end of the Autumn Term.

With other teachers, the changes my presence effected and their resolutions to the conflict took more subtle forms. Mr O. usually set the form some written work and then joined me at the back of the room, where he chatted with me or told me jokes. Some of his stories have been of considerable use to me, but hints to Mr O., that this was not the reason for my presence in the form were of no avail and later he took to inviting me into his room 'for a chat'. I did not see how I could prevent this occurrence without offending Mr O. Mr F. never refused to let me observe but if he could he decided to read a story to the form or directed a lesson in which the boys played a passive and silent role. Mr L. invariably sent boys to the back of the room with their books for me to examine and comment on, although when I had seen every book several times this practice declined.

Many of the teachers appeared to behave quite naturally and act as if I was not in the room at all, and it is difficult to check on the extent of the changes my presence produced. Sometimes the teachers would themselves indicate the effects of my presence. In the lower streams in particular the boys are caned comparatively frequently, if the conversations over lunch and in the common room are any measure of this. But is was notable how very rarely a teacher caned a boy when I was in the room. One day, as I was leaving the room, Mr G. said to me, 'They've got a bit noisy, haven't they? I think I'll cane a few when you've gone.'

A further check came from conversations with the boys, who revealed changes which might otherwise have not been at all obvious.

> When you're in he tries to act calmly as though he's a little angel and all that.

> Did you notice when you were in, Mr M's.— he called me by my first name? But when you're on the field (games) he calls you by your second name.

> They put on a show for you. They put the good act on, smiles and all that, and when you've gone out ...

> Like if Mr O.'s getting mad 'cos someone's ripped a book or something, but if you're in he seems to drop it. If you weren't there he'd get real mad.

Initially my presence also caused changes in the boys' behaviour though I am convinced these are of less importance, for once the boys became accustomed to me, they behaved normally.

> It depends on the teacher. With Mr A. and Mr O. we never muck about anyway. They're strict and we do what they say. But it's different with Mr L. Like when you came in the other day. (In the middle of an examination.) Before you came in they were all messing about and there was quite a few with cribs out. But they put 'em away as soon as you came in.

> We just forget you're there most of the time.

> I never know you're there when you're sitting at the back.

This lack of observability to the pupils is no doubt partially responsible for the small changes my presence made on the boys. But my presence at the back of the class was highly visible to the teacher and thus a constant reminder of the intrusion. It is boys from the lower streams who have commented most on the changes, and I suspect that this is because it is in these forms that disciplinary problems become more acute.

Sometimes the teachers went out of their way to tell me how they thought a class ought to be conducted and this came in direct conflict with their actual behaviour as reported to me from other sources. Mr M. gave me a long homily on the necessity of drawing information from the boys rather than pumping it into them, which, he said,

> would be like trying to pour a bucket of water into a sterilised milkbottle—a little would go in but most of it would end up on the floor.

He proved to be a strong advocate of some progressive methods of education, yet it is certain that Mr M. used the cane very frequently and on other occasions he expressed opinions which directly contradicted his lecture to me. Such attempts to deceive me resulted from the ascription to me of an Inspector-role. Yet my continued presence in the school, unlike the brief visit of an Inspector, made such attempts at deception detectable.

Through constant participation in the informal social activities of the staff and the consequent initiation and acceptance into the informal relations, cliques and private jokes and quarrels, I could to a large extent shed the Inspector-role. When matters concerning class discipline, for example, were raised in my presence, the teachers and I were able to obtain a degree of mutual indentification and I was able to renounce any expertise or authority that are part of the Inspector-role. An index of the increasing cordiality of my relations with the staff was the extent to which I was drawn into the informal activities: playing darts at lunch time, helping with the school concert, going on school holidays, attending staff parties at the end of term and over Christmas. Yet there were problems. Conversations with the staff over lunch or in the staff room were potential sources of conflict. When the conversation took a controversial turn—especially when the subject was education—I tried to keep silent, but my opinion was frequently sought and I was drawn into the conversation, and forced to take sides. On such occasions participation strongly overrides observation, and may well introduce frictions which could undermine the work. But I have come to the conclusion that if I had not participated naturally in the social life of the teachers—that is, be myself where possible—I could never have been integrated into the group and would have taken the risk of social exclusion. Inevitably I was constantly aware that I was working in the school with research aims, so that every event may be significant for the analysis. But I consider that unless I had behaved naturally my presence would have been more disruptive than ever.

Due to their lack of training in social science, many of the teachers did not realize that some of the casual remarks they made to me, or in my presence, presented me with a fuller picture of the social situation as a whole. In an article on participant-observation, Dr R. J. Frankenberg has written that:

> If the observer cannot participate with the knowledge and approval of the people to be studied he should not be there at all. The observer has a positive duty to be open that his intentions are to observe, to report and to publish an account of what he sees ...

The difficulty is that most of the people being studied could not appreciate that many of the apparently trivial things they said or the confidences they related *are* of social significance. When I behaved naturally to the teachers, they treated me as an individual person, be it as colleague or friend, and appeared to assume, at least for the moment, that I was not a social psychologist studying the school. Yet it was often at such times that the most significant things were said. Inevitably therefore, a certain amount of deception was involved. Dr Frankenberg's dictum, though highly commendable in theory, over-simplifies the practical situation. In light conversation with a teacher one cannot suddenly point out that what he has just stated is sociologically important, for this would seriously inhibit future relations. If the observer really does have 'a positive duty to be open in his intentions' then he must constantly remind the people he observes of this fact, whereas in reality they adjust to the researcher's presence and cease, in part, to treat him as such.

This mutual personal adjustment of observer and subjects revealed itself not only in improved personal relationships, but also in the gossip that was related to the observer. I am convinced that many of the stories recounted to me would not have been told at all had I reminded the teacher that I was observing the school. The personal relationship that I established with a teacher led him to say more than he perhaps originally intended and certainly more than he would consider fit for the ears of an observer, though it must be admitted that stories detrimental to the teachers' own colleagues might still be related, since motives for spreading gossip are complex.

The ethical issues raised by these problems are incapable of simple resolution. I do not think that the difficulties encountered make it necessary to rule out all forms of participant-observation as unethical. The moral question is one of the uses made of the material so obtained. Everything one learns in a participant-observer situation assists in the analysis, but the researcher has a duty to use only non-confidential evidence in a published report, and this may mean that there are some aspects of the situation which cannot be published at all because all the evidence must be regarded as confidential information. My information on teacher–teacher relations falls into this category.

By the end of the first term, the Inspector-role assigned to me originally was beginning to fade, and was replaced more fully by a teacher-role. This was partly due to my integration into the informal staff relations and partly due to my taking over some duties of a teacher who was suddenly taken ill.

There seem little doubt that, despite some difficulties, my assumption of a teacher-role whenever possible (and my conscious attempts to minimize the teachers' tendencies to ascribe other roles to me) proved an invaluable aid in consolidating my position amongst the staff of the school. Naturally, they never completely neglected to see me as a social psychologist, but I consider that my assumption of certain elements of the teacher-role reduced the disruptive effects of a more pure psychologist role. Over a period of six months I began to feel as much a part of the system as if I really were a member of the staff and the teachers, in their turn, treated me as a colleague. This betrayed itself in numerous small ways. For example, one morning when I arrived late at the School, a teacher asked me, quite seriously, if the headmaster had 'told me off'.

Yet the role-conflicts I experienced as a teacher-researcher existed along another dimension—my relationship with the boys. When I first arrived at the school the boys inevitably ascribed some form of teacher-role to me. Any adult (who is not dressed as a workman) appearing in the school must in their eyes have some strong connection with the teaching profession. Although the headmaster introduced me to them in assembly as 'a new member of staff', I did not undertake any teaching duties for several weeks, and even then for only a third of the normal teaching timetable. They were mostly aware of me as someone who sat at the back of the class and said little. For these reasons the boys seemed to think that I was either an Inspector or a student-teacher. Later, they discovered that I was teaching; I was seen walking around the school with piles of books; I ate separately with the staff at lunch time, and used the staff room. So the Inspector–student roles gave way to a teacher-role. The usual courtesy title of 'sir' was extended to me when the boys spoke to me or wished to attract my attention.

When I began to take lessons, I was faced with the normal problems of a teacher. Some of the classes I taught were junior forms, so discipline was an easy matter. But with the older boys, and especially the lower stream, I needed to control the class carefully if order was to prevail during the lesson. The first few lessons with a new form are always a period of testing for the boys: they use several techniques by which they check how strict a disciplinarian the teacher will be. During the first three weeks at the school I simply observed; and it became clear that the boys in the lower streams seemed to react negatively towards the teachers. For this reason I did not wish those boys to identify me too closely with the teachers. In my teaching duties I felt it was important not to invoke the usual teacher sanctions—the cane or sending the boy to the headmaster—for this would be to align myself very closely with the teachers, and thus create negative feelings towards me. But if my discipline was not reasonably strict then I would have chaos on my hands during each lesson and would lose the *respect* of the boys. In the event I tried to solve the problem by preparing interesting lessons which gave the boys little opportunity to 'play me up'. Unfortunately this attempt to avoid the necessity of using disciplinary sanctions lasted but a few weeks.

Simultaneously, I was trying to get to know the boys in an informal way. At Lumley this was particularly difficult to achieve. Many of the usual avenues of access to the boys were closed to me. During the short breaks in the middle of the morning and afternoon school, the boys were sent out into a small playground. Two teachers were on duty in case of trouble. Often, therefore, I was forced to spend as much time talking to the teachers as to the boys during these ten minute breaks. Moreover, the boys in the lower streams with whom I particularly wished to chat informally usually went to the far corner of the yard where they could smoke in a small alcove. From time to time several boys were caught and caned: but the alcove became their sanctum. I was unable to venture into the alcove, for if boys were smoking and another teacher appeared on the scene I would appear to be condoning the smoking. But if I expected the boys to put out the cigarettes on my arrival, I would be aligning myself with the teachers.

At lunch time the staff ate separately from the boys. After lunch only a few small boys remained in the playground for the rest of the lunch hour. The school had no formal societies, with the exception of a brass band, so I was unable to meet boys informally during such activities. There was no games field near the school: the boys travelled by bus to a field several miles away. But the boys used the bus as a changing room. Holidays, school trips and clubs outside the school provided the only means of making extended informal relationships with the pupils.

During the first term I felt that my relations with the higher streams developed well: but with the lower streams a rapid deterioration was evident. Whenever possible I explained the nature of my work to the boys who almost invariably showed interest and a willingness to co-operate. But a minority in the lower streams remained immovably suspicious. For this reason I took the radical step of giving up all my teaching periods except for two lessons a week with the B stream. This seemed to be the only way in which I could divest myself of the teacher-role. From that point my relations with the boys improved to a remarkable extent, who not unexpectedly passed through a period of ambivalence. The delinquent group, for example, began shouting out to me, 'Hello, sir,' in a rather cheeky way, which I would immediately have crushed as a teacher. Once again, they were putting me to the test, seeing how far they would go before I would try to punish them. When I failed to respond as they expected, these attempts at provocation ceased. My relations with Clint were always shallow: he simply did not trust me. But I was able to make considerable progress after an incident in the Spring Term. Clint was involved in a fight during the lunch hour with a boy from a neighbouring Further Education Centre. A woman who witnessed the fight rushed into school to complain to the headmaster. Fortunately, I saw her before she was able to inform any of the staff and hurried to the scene where I was able to warn Clint of the situation. He seemed very grateful and was less cold to me after this event. With other members of the delinquent group my relations were more cordial. Several times I was offered various pieces of stolen property. Two of these boys came to me to discuss their latest exploits—the theft of a motorcycle and robbery with assault—and seemed glad to talk about their misdemeanours with an adult who had no formal power over them and who would not judge them. Slowly the boys learned that they could trust me. In order to achieve this trust I often had to depend upon accidents. When they discovered I would not report them for offences against the school rules which I had observed, the teacher-role began to diminish, and was replaced by a new form of respect and trust. One day a boy told me how he had broken a school rule. Afterwards I assured him that I would not tell the teachers. 'I know that,' he said, censuring my statement of the obvious. On another occasion when a boy hid the teacher's cane I was admitted into the conspiracy with a wink. At times it was difficult to avoid entering into active collusion with the boys: a convenient attack of blindness or deafness proved to be invaluable in resolving such problems. Invitations to youth clubs, beat clubs and the billiard hall, which I gladly accepted, tended to cement my relations with the boys, though 'leaks' about such events caused some surprise to the staff.

Within organizations such as schools, factories, hospitals and prisons, a distinction can be made between the 'controllers' (teachers, managers, doctors and warders) and the 'controlled' (pupils, workers, patients, prisoners). Between these two levels yawns the gap of status distinctions, which a participant-observer cannot necessarily bridge. To participate and observe involves to some extent shedding the researcher-role, since participation means accepting in some degree a normal role within the social situation. But to accept such a role, whilst facilitating the process of absorption into the community, entails limitations on material obtained and bias in its interpretation.

As a social psychologist, I was inevitably something of an intruder in the school. It is difficult to define in detail the content of this role, but it is clear that it is a role which is *external* to the system and will thus create suspicions from the participants. By accepting a teacher-role, I was absorbed into the community of the teachers, but this integration was possible only after I had, through the informal personal relationships which developed over time, shed the Inspector-role which resulted from my observation of lessons. The researcher-role would tend to fade naturally because of its low visibility—in contrast to the high visibility of racial difference which might beset anthropological studies. Yet the gap between the teachers and the pupils could not be bridged. Whereas Whyte in *Street Corner Society* was able to participate as a member of the gang, I could never assume a pupil-role. In the nature of things, I could never stand completely on one side of the teacher/pupil division. When the study was planned it seemed that the assumption of a teacher-role would be the best way in which the participant-observation could be effected, but it was not foreseen that the assumption of a teacher-role, whilst facilitating my relations with the staff, would seriously inhibit my relations with the pupils. A choice had to be made, and I decided to abandon my carefully nurtured teacher-role to improve relationships with the boys. The conflicts with the staff which I expected to result did not arise: mainly, I suspect, because having once held a teacher-role I had become integrated into the community of teachers, and thus the assumption of a more pure researcher-role at a later stage did not arouse the suspicions which could have occurred if such a role had been assumed at the beginning of the study. To the boys, my place within the community was inevitably something of a mystery, but it was a mystery they seemed to accept uncritically. Part teacher, part psychologist, part friend and ally, they accepted me as an individual who suddenly became part of the system : but to achieve this, I had to abandon the teacher-role in so far as this was possible.

A social scientist is always a person with his own personality, idiosyncrasies and faults. One suspects that as a participant-observer he makes more impact on the people he studies as an individual person rather than as a researcher. Most scientists disturb what they observe to some degree, but in the case of the social psychologist or sociologist the extent of this distortion is relatively larger. A different researcher in the same social situation would make a different impact on the people and they would react to him in different ways. No doubt different discoveries would be made, different aspects emphasized, different interpretations elaborated, even though the central analysis might be the same. Yet more important than this is the extent to which the same single researcher can influence the situation by the roles he adopts. In my own case, the history is one of a conscious manipulation of roles to avoid and control conflicts at different levels in the situation at different stages. There is little doubt that a more consistent adoption of roles would have given me a somewhat different perspective of, and insight into, the social system of the school. As social scientists we assume that a common core of material and interpretation would result, especially if this is based on data collected by 'objective' methods which can be treated statistically. Yet the failure to make explicit the limitations and difficulties of participant-observation would be a failure to assess, however unquantitatively, the margin of error incurred by this method of social investigation.

*As an illustration of the insights which may be obtained by participant observation, the following extract is taken from a paper by Lacey. The main part of this study was concerned with the effects of streaming, but in this extract the emphasis is more on social relationships within one particular class.*

*Lacey contrasts the enthusiasm of the first-year pupils at 'Hightown Grammar' with the more passive, self-conscious or disruptive behaviour of older age-groups. He describes some of the processes which are involved, drawing particular emphasis to the informal social structures existing in classrooms.*

## Some Sociological Concomitants of Academic Streaming in Grammar School    (C. Lacey, 1966)[1]

### THE INFORMAL STRUCTURE—TWO CASE STUDIES

As soon as this highly selected first-year population meets at Hightown Grammar School and is allocated to the four first-year classes, a complex process of interaction begins. This process takes place through a variety of encounters. Boys talk and listen to each other, talk and listen to teachers, listen to conversations, notice details of accent, gesture, clothing, watch others at work and at play in various situations and in innumerable different permutations.

During the first few days much of this interaction appears to take place in a fairly random way influenced mainly by the physical and organizational arrangements. Soon, patterns of selection begin to emerge. Various initial interactions yield information and experience, which are retained by the individual and provide some basis for the interpretation and partial control of other interactions. This partial control is extremely important because it soon gives rise to a recognizable, although unstable and changing structure.

When I started observing the first-year classes in March 1963, the members of each class had only been together for about six months, but each class already had a definite structure of which the pupils clearly had detailed knowledge. When a master called a boy to read or answer a question, others could be seen giving each other significant looks which clearly indicated that they knew what to expect.

On one occasion, for example, a master asked three boys to stay behind after the lesson to help him with a task calling for a sense of responsibility and cooperation, the master called, 'Williams, Maun and Sherring.' The class burst into spontaneous laughter, and there were unbelieving cries of 'What, Sherring?' The master corrected himself. 'No, not Sherring, Shadwell.' From the context of the incident, it was clear that Sherring's reputation was already inconsistent with the qualities expected of a monitor. On another occasion, Priestley was asked to read and the whole class groaned and laughed. Priestley, a fat boy, had been kept down from the previous year because of ill health (catarrh and asthma) and poor work. He grinned apprehensively, wiped his face with a huge white handkerchief and started to read very nervously. For a few moments the class was absolutely

[1] The original article appeared in *British Journal of Sociology*, 17, 245–62.

quiet, then one boy tittered, Priestley made a silly mistake, partly because he was looking up to smile at the boy who was giggling, and the whole class burst into laughter. Priestley blew his nose loudly and smiled nervously at the class. The teacher quietened the class and Priestley continued to read. Three lines later a marked mispronunciation started the whole class laughing again. This performance continued with Priestley getting more and more nervous, mopping his brow and blowing his nose. Finally, the master with obvious annoyance snapped, 'All right, Priestley, that's enough!'

This short incident, one of several during the day, served to remind Priestley of his structural position within the class and to confirm the opinions and expectations of the class and the teacher towards him. Priestley's behaviour was consistent with his performance in the examinations at the end of the Autumn Term when he was ranked twenty-ninth out of thirty-three.

During this period of observation I also noticed the significance of the behaviour of another boy, Cready. Cready first attracted my attention because, although his form position was similar to Priestley's (twenty-sixth) he habitually associated with a strikingly different group. He behaved very differently in class, and had a markedly different reputation.

Cready was a member of the school choir and it so happened that the English master, whose classes I was observing, was also the music teacher and he had arranged the class so that the members of the school choir sat in the row next to the piano and his desk (row 4). To be a member of the choir one had to have a good voice and be willing to stay in school to practise during dinner time and at four o'clock, once or twice a week for certain periods of the year. In the next two rows were members of the first-form choir. To be in this a boy had only to be willing to sing. In the last row (row 1) were boys who could not or would not sing.

During the first three lessons I observed Cready answered four of the questions put to the class. On two of these occasions he had, before putting up his hand, discussed the answer with the boy next to him. If Cready got an answer wrong he was never laughed at. Priestley answered two questions in the same period. He got one of these wrong and was laughed at by the class. Also as I observed later, if Priestley attempted to discuss an answer with the boy next to him, he was reprimanded.

A sociogram for the class showed an apparent inconsistency. In class Priestley was frequently in the middle of a group of mischievous boys. If there was trouble Priestley was in it. I expected him to be fairly popular with some of the boys who led him into trouble, but none of them picked him as a friend. He chose five boys as his friends but the only boy to reciprocate was the other Jewish boy in the class.

The other boys used Priestley to create diversions and pass messages, and because he was so isolated he was only too pleased to oblige. He could never resist the temptation to act as if he was 'one of the boys'. However, when he was caught out they deserted him and laughed at him rather than with him. He was truly the butt of the class.

These incidents, seen in the context of the structure of the class, shows how Priestley had fallen foul of the system. He was not in control of his own situation, and anything he tried to do to improve his position only made it worse. His attempts to answer questions provoked laughter and ridicule from his classmates. His attempt to minimize the distress this caused, a nervous smile round the class, a shrug of the shoulders, pretending either that he had caused the disturbance on purpose or that he did not care, served to worsen his position with the teacher.

He compensated for his failure in class and lack of academic success by learning the stocks and shares table of the *Financial Times* every week. This enabled him to develop a reputation in a field outside the sphere in which the school was competent to judge. He would emphasize the *real* importance of this in his future career and thus minimize the effect of his scholastic failure. Even this did not improve his standing in the school, especially with the staff. It served only to explain his laziness, his bad behaviour and lack of concern with school work. 'Oh, Priestley, he is just biding his time with us, from what I hear his future is assured anyway.' 'He is just lazy,' said the English master.

It is interesting to note the family background of these two boys. Priestley is Jewish, second in a family of three and lives in an area of expensive detached houses. His father is a clearance stock buyer. Cready on the other hand lives on a council estate, is fourth out of six in the family and his father is a quality inspector in an abrasives factory.

Cready and Priestley do not, therefore, conform with the established correlation between academic achievement and social class. Cready, a working-class boy from a large family on a council estate, is making good, while Priestley, an upper-middle-class boy from a smaller family, is failing academically. However, this negative case highlights the point I want to make; there was a measure of autonomy in the system of social relations of the classroom. The positions of Cready and Priestley are only explicable in the light of an analysis of the system of social relations *inside* the classroom. This system is open to manipulation by those who are sensitive to its details. Hence Cready, who had all the major external factors stacked against him, was able to use the system of social relations to sustain and buoy himself up, while Priestley, despite all the advantages that he brought to the situation, had fallen foul of the system and was not only failing but also speedily losing any motivation to succeed in the sphere in which the school was competent to judge him.

I reiterate that this is not an attempt to disprove the general established trend but to highlight the fact that there are detailed social mechanisms and processes responsible for bringing it about, which are not completely determined by external factors. By studying these mechanisms it will be possible to add a dimension to our understanding of the general processes of education in our schools.

## DIFFERENTIATION AND POLARIZATION

It is important to discuss these processes in a more general way and set up a model which describes the passage of pupils through the grammar school. To do this, I will need to introduce two terms—'differentiation' and 'polarization'.

By differentiation is meant the process of separation and ranking of students according to a multiple set of criteria which makes up the normative academically orientated, value system of the grammar school. This process is regarded here as being largely carried out by teachers in the course of their normal duties.

Polarization on the other hand is regarded as a process taking place within the student body, partly as a result of differentiation but influenced by external factors and with an autonomy of its own. It is a process of sub-culture formation in which the school-dominated normative culture is opposed by an alternative culture which I will refer to as the anti-group culture. The content of the anti-group culture will, of course, be very much influenced by the school and its social setting. It may range from a folk music, C.N.D. group in a minor public school to a delinquent sub-culture in a secondary modern school in an old urban area. In Hightown Grammar School it fell between these extremes and was influenced by the large working-class and Jewish communities of Hightown.

There are a number of scales on which a master habitually rates a boy. For the purposes of the analysis I will consider two.
a.   Academic Scale.
b.   Behaviour Scale. This would include considerations as varied as general classroom behaviour and attitudes, politeness, attention, helpfulness, time spent in school societies and sports.
The two are not independent. Behaviour affects academic standards not only because good behaviour involves listening and attending but because a master becomes favourably disposed to-

wards a boy who is well-behaved and trying hard. The teacher, therefore, tends to help him and even to mark him up. I have found in my own marking of books that when I know the form (i.e. good and bad pupils) I mark much more quickly. For example, I might partly read the essay and recognize the writing. 'Oh, Brown. Let's see, he tries hard, good neat work, missed one or two ideas—7/10', or, 'This is a bit scruffy, no margin, not underlined, seems to have got the hang of it though. Who is it? Oh, Jones, that nuisance—5/10!'

There is another reason why good behaviour is correlated with academic achievement. A boy who does well and wishes to do well academically is predisposed to accepting the system of values of the grammar school, that is he behaves well. This is because the system gives him high prestige and it is therefore in his interest to support it; the membership of the choir illustrates this point. He is thereby supporting his position of prestige. On the other hand a boy who does badly academically is predisposed to criticize, reject or even sabotage the system, where he can, since it places him in an inferior position.

A boy showing the extreme development of this phenomenon may subscribe to values which are actually the inverted values of the school. For example, he obtains prestige from cheeking a teacher, playing truant, not doing homework, smoking, drinking and even stealing. As it develops, the anti-group produces its own impetus. A boy who takes refuge in such a group because his work is poor finds that the group commits him to a behaviour pattern which means that his work will stay poor and in fact often gets progressively worse.

The following extracts from an essay entitled 'Abuse' and written by a first-form boy for his housemaster, illustrates a development of anti-group values of an extreme nature for a first-year pupil.

> I am writing this essay about abuse in the toilets ... What they (the prefects) call abuse and what I call abuse are two different things altogether.
>
> All the people where I live say I am growing up to be a 'Ted' so I try to please them by acting as much like one as I possibly can. I go around kicking a ball against the wall that is nearest to their house and making as much noise as I can and I intend to carry on doing this until they can leave me alone ... It seems to me the Grammar School knows nothing about abuse for *I would much rather be a hooligan and get some fun out of life than be a snob always being the dear little nice boy doing what he is told.*

Earlier on we saw that at the beginning of the first year, the pupils constitute a relatively homogeneous and undifferentiated group. They are uniformly enthusiastic and eager to please, both through their performance of work and in their behaviour. The pupils who are noticed first are the good pupils and the bad pupils. Even by the Spring term some masters are still unsure of the names of quiet pupils in the undifferentiated middle of the classes they teach.

It is fairly rare for an anti-group to develop in the first year. Although one or two individuals may develop marked anti-group values, they are likely to remain isolates. In the 1962 first year, I was able to recognize only one, Badman, quoted earlier. He wished to be transferred to a secondary modern.

The more usual course of events associated with a marked degree of (relative) failure in the first year is for the child to display symptoms of emotional upheaval and nervous disorder and for a conflict of standards to take place. Symptoms that occurred in the first year intake of 1962 included the following:

> Bursting into tears, when reprimanded by a teacher.
> Refusal to go to school or to go to particular lessons, accompanied by hysterical crying and screaming.
> Sleeplessness.
> Bedwetting.
> Truanting from certain lessons or truanting from school.
> Constantly feeling sick before certain lessons.
> One boy rushed to stage in assembly clutching his throat and screaming that he could not breathe.
> Consistent failure to do homework.
> High absence record.
> Aggravation of mild epilepsy.

The 15 cases recorded probably represent all the cases of major disturbance but a large number of the cases of minor disturbance probably never became known to the school.

The individual significance of these cases cannot be discussed here but their general significance is important to the model under discussion. We have seen that the 11 + selects the 'best pupils' from the top forms of the junior schools. These forms have been highly differentiated in preparation for the 11 + examination. The pupils have, in many cases, been 'best pupils' for some time and have internalized many of the expectations inherent in the position of 'best pupils'. Their transfer to the grammar school not only means a new environment, with all that such a change entails—for example, new class-mates, new teachers and new sets of rules—but also for many of them a violation of their expectations as best pupils. It is when this violation of expectations coincides with 'unsatisfactory' home backgrounds that the worst cases of emotional disturbance occur.

In the second year the process of differentiation continues. If streaming takes place between the first and second years as it did in the year group I am studying it helps speed the process and a new crop of cases of emotional disturbance occur. In the 1963 second year most of these cases were associated with boys who were failing to make the grade in the top stream and boys who were in the bottom half of the bottom stream. After six months in the second year this bottom stream was already regarded as a difficult form to teach because, to quote two teachers:

   i.  'They are unacademic, they can't cope with the work.'
   ii.  'Give them half a chance and they will give you the run around.'

The true anti-group starts to emerge in the second year, and it develops markedly in the third and fourth year. It is in the third and fourth years that strenuous efforts are made to get rid of anti-group pupils. Considerable pressure is put on the Headmaster by the teachers that take the boys and the Head in turn transmits this to the Board of Governors. In most cases application to leave will also be made by the boy and his parents. However, the Board of Governors are often loath to give permission for a boy to leave or transfer for two reasons. (i) The governors are also the governors for the secondary modern schools in the area and cannot readily agree to passing on discipline problems from the grammar school to the secondary modern. (ii) They are generally very suspicious of grammar school teachers and feel reluctant to risk injustice to a pupil who is often a working-class boy.

However, there are some requests that cannot easily be refused, for example cases of ill health, family hardship or consistent truanting. There are also a number of cases of unofficial leaving. In these cases the boy has actually left school and taken a job but is still being marked as absent in the register. It is difficult to estimate accurately the extent of the total loss but in two years somewhere between 10 and 15 pupils left or were transferred from each year before taking O-level or reaching the age of 16.

A similar process can be observed in the sixth form and results in a crop of leavers in the first-year sixth. The extent to which differentiation develops and is internalized in the sixth is illustrated by the following remark made to the Economics master. He had just rebuked a boy in the Upper Sixth Modern and told him that unless he worked harder he would not pass Economics A-level: 'Well, the way I look at it is this: If some of the boys in the General form can get it and they usually do, then I should be all right.'

*This extract illustrates the use of participant observation in understanding classroom behaviour, without doing justice to the theoretical model which is subsequently developed. The full report of this study has been published under the title of* Hightown Grammar *(Lacey, 1970), and shows how such observations can be incorporated within a more theoretical perspective.*

# 13 The Teacher's Day

In the previous chapter the method of participant observation was described. The essential subjectivity of that method is both its main strength and an important weakness. By participating the observer tries to avoid any artificial influences on the situation, but involvement carries with it the danger of bias and inaccuracy in the interpretation. Moreover, as the research report is essentially anecdotal, the evidence from which deductions are made cannot be presented as part of the findings. Used on its own, participant observation is of dubious validity in educational research; used in conjunction with more objective approaches, its wealth of speculative insights is harnessed and can lead to a clearer understanding of social behaviour.

The method high-lighted in this chapter is the systematic observation and analysis of teacher–pupil interaction, an important and growing area of research. The observer using this method does not participate: he stays as an onlooker who systematically records and categorizes the behaviour he observes. The relative isolation of the teacher in the classroom has meant that little is known in any detail about the way in which teachers and pupils interact, and yet such information is the raw material without which accurate theories of teaching are impossible. Initially the problem for the research worker is to decide which of a multiplicity of occurrences in a classroom are significant and should be recorded. The next problem is to decide on a category system which adequately describes these significant events. Finally these records have to be analysed in such a way as to allow interpretation and explanation, rather than simple description, of what happens in the process of classroom instruction and learning.

Most of the extracts in this chapter have used detailed behaviour schedules, but the first is rather different. By moving only one step away from participation, the teacher can learn a great deal simply by using a tape-recorder. Subsequent analysis of the use of language can be instructive in itself and by pre-

*serving a record of these events, the observer has moved a step away from total subjectivity of interpretation. In* Language, the Learner and the School, *Barnes argues that vocabulary is a key element in instruction.*

> 'Much of the language encountered in school looks at pupils across a chasm. Some fluent children ... adopt the jargon and parrot whole sketches of lingo. Personal intellectual struggle is made irrelevant and the personal view never asked for. Language and experience are torn asunder. Worse still, many children find impersonal language mere noise. It is alien in its posture, conventions and strategies ... These are extremes. Many children have areas of confidence and understanding but frequently have to resort to desperate mimicry to see them through' (quoted by Barnes, p. 12, from an unpublished document by H. Rosen).

Barnes used only a tape-recorder and made transcripts of what was said in the course of the lessons he observed. (Those who wish to copy this procedure should be warned that there are serious technical difficulties in recording. Unless special attention is given to acoustics, much of a recording in a classroom will be indecipherable. Some research workers have overcome acoustic problems by using microphones and micro-transmitters carried by the teacher or by each pupil only to run into the problem of licensing for the use of radio-transmitters.)

### Language, the Learner and the School
### (D. Barnes, 1969)[1]

My original conception was of a 'Study of the linguistic expectations set up in first-year lessons in secondary schools'. I expected that generalizations drawn from a few secondary lessons could be put beside others drawn from primary schools, and light thrown on some difficulties of adjustment faced by new entries to secondary schools. I was able to attempt the first part of this when, in October 1966, I undertook a series of seminars in 'Language and education' with teachers studying for a Diploma in Curricular Studies at the University of Leeds Institute of Education. As they were also attending my lectures on this subject I determined that the seminars should be devoted to practical study; they tape-recorded first-year lessons taught by friends, transcribed them, and analysed them according to a scheme I

[1] Edited extracts from Part I of *Language, the Learner and the School* (Penguin), pages 12, 27–9, 31, 43–4.

supplied. The teachers participating found this an enlightening and disturbing task. The study provided information on far more matters than I had expected, and did so in a way which challenged the group to inspect their own assumptions about teaching. It undoubtedly provided an excellent method for the study of teaching. The results were not, however, of a kind to encourage me to move on to the language of the primary school.

This led to a redefinition of the task. I now saw it as a preliminary investigation of the interaction between the linguistic expectations (drawn from home and primary school experience) brought by pupils to their secondary schools, and the linguistic demands set up (implicitly or explicitly) by the teachers in the classrooms. It seemed likely that extraneous barriers were introduced into children's learning (a) by linguistic forms whose function was social rather than intrinsic to the material and processes being learnt, and (b) by unfamiliar socio-linguistic demands and constraints arising in the control systems of the secondary classroom. It was in terms such as these that I embarked on the descriptive study of lessons experienced by eleven-year-old children during their first half-term in a secondary school.

Seven lessons were recorded and transcribed (one with a second-year class) and the following year, another seven lessons (all from one class) were recorded, though only five of these were analysed. The procedures for analysing the transcripts of these twelve lessons are described in the book, and subsequently a number of extracts are quoted and analysed. The first example is taken from a lesson in chemistry, in which the teacher is explaining that milk is an example of the suspension of solids in a liquid:

| | |
|---|---|
| T | You get the white ... what we call casein ... that's ... er ... protein ... which is good for you ... it'll help to build bones ... and the white is mainly the casein and so it's not actually a solution ... it's a suspension of very fine particles together with water and various other things which are dissolved in water ... |
| P.1 | Sir, at my old school I shook my bottle of milk up and when I looked at it again all the side was covered with ... er ... like particles and ... er ... could they be the white particles in the milk ...? |
| P.2 | Yes, and gradually they would sediment out, wouldn't they, to the bottom ...? |
| P.3 | When milk goes sour though it smells like cheese, doesn't it? |
| P.4 | Well, it is cheese, isn't it, if you leave it long enough? |
| T | Anyway can we get on ... We'll leave a few questions for later. |

What is happening here? The teacher talks about milk, using his specialist language to help him perceive it as an exemplar of the category 'suspension', and to free him from all other contexts and categories it might appear in. But for his pupils 'milk' collocates not with 'suspension' but with 'cheese', 'school', 'shook', 'bottle'; they perceive it in that context and his use of 'casein' and 'fine particles' signals to only two of them that some different response is expected. Pupil 1 recognizes 'particles' and, searching his experience, comes up with lumps of curd. Trying to conform to the teacher's expectation, he manages 'the side was covered with ... like particles', his uncertainty finding its expression in the deprecatory 'like'. Pupil 2 follows this line of thought and, associating the idea of sedimentation with suspended particles, tries 'they would sediment out'. These two pupils are beginning to use the language of science to make the specifically scientific abstraction from the experience. But pupils 3 and 4, although they are *attentive to what the teacher appears to be saying* are unable to make this abstraction; the words the teacher has used do not signal to them which aspects of the 'milk' experience should be abstracted. Far from helping them to bridge the gulf between his frame of reference and theirs, the teacher's language acts as a barrier, of which he seems quite unaware. They are left with their own first-hand experience—'it smells like cheese'. The state of the other less articulate members of the class can only be guessed at. The teacher, frightened by his sudden glimpse of the gulf between them, hastily continues with the lesson he has planned.

This teacher teaches within his frame of reference; the pupils learn in theirs, taking in his words, which 'mean' something different to them, and struggling to incorporate this meaning into their own frames of reference. The language which is an essential instrument to him is a barrier to them. How can the teacher help his pupils to use this language as he does? Certainly not by turning away from the problem.

Besides this we may place a sequence from Lesson K (1967; history) in which the teacher, aware of the gulf between what the word 'language' means to him and to his pupils, attempts to bridge it.

T      Now what do we mean by language?
P.1    The alphabet.
T      That's part of it ... what else?
P.2    How to speak.
T      How to speak ... yes ... what else? ... What else do you do with a language apart from speaking it?
P.3    Pronounce it.
T      Well that's part of speaking ... What else?

P.4   Learn how to say it.
T     Still the same thing ... yes?
P     Sir, you can tell the countries by the language they speak.
T     Yes, but what else can we use a language for? We don't always speak a language ... I don't always speak a language when I want to get something over to someone who is not in the same room ... probably a long way away ... I can't shout or use the telephone ... What do I do?
P     Write.
T     I write ... right, therefore it's the written word as well as the spoken word.

Without the initial question the teacher is unlikely to have known how hard the pupils found it to conceive of language as a whole. He pursued the matter with some determination, but even at the end one does not know how far his reference to the 'written word' and the 'spoken word' could mean anything to his pupils. He has, however, enabled a few pupils to take an active part in testing how far their meanings match with his.

Information about the 'gulf' can only come when the teacher either asks an open question (such as 'What do we mean by language?') or when he requires pupils to use what they have been taught, as in writing. The disadvantage of writing as a means of making knowledge their own is that the reply to it may be both delayed and restricted to a general comment or assessment. It is in the give and take of reciprocal discussion that the pupil can best try out the new concepts and modify them in response to the teacher's replies.

Recording of a physics lesson provided other examples to illustrate this point: The teacher had put in front of the class a mechanism illustrating the working of an aneroid barometer. After a lengthy demonstration with explanations, the teacher asked about the function of part of the apparatus. A pupil replied:

Well the silver knob is to turn that pointer.... If you turn that to say twenty or whatever the other hand says ... when the other hand moves you can see the difference in pressure.

This clearly illustrates some of the linguistic–conceptional apparatus that the pupil lacks, and which he will need if he is ever to be complete master of the process. He lacks a general term such as 'the position of' for the phrase 'say twenty or whatever the other hand says'. More important, he needs to be able to name an intermediate conceptual stage between setting the pointer and reading off the difference in pressure. This would produce something like: 'from *the angle between* the two pointers, you can see ...'. Nor has the pupil realized that 'when the hand moves' does not make the time scale explicit enough, though he seems to understand what he means. These kinds of mental and verbal inadequacy cannot easily be dealt with by direct instruction because they are so difficult to predict. It is only in relatively 'open' discussion that they become apparent.

Not all the recordings were used to criticize inadequacies in the language of instruction. A geography lesson is quoted as an example of a sensitive awareness of vocabulary. The class were looking at a photograph of sand dunes.

T    Sand dunes. They're usually in an unusual ... a specific shape ... a special shape.... Does anybody know what shape they are? Not in straight lines ...

P    They're like hills.

T    Yes, they're like low hills.

P    They're all humpy up and down.

T    Yes, they're all humpy up and down.

P    They're like waves.

T    Good, they're like waves.

P    They're like ...

T    They're a special shape.

P    They're like boulders .. sort of go up and down getting higher and higher.

T    I don't know about getting higher and higher.

P    Something like pyramids.

T    Mm ... wouldn't call them pyramids, no.

P    They're in a semicircle.

T    Ah, that's getting a bit nearer. They're often in a semi-circle and nearly always ... we call them ... well, it's part of a semicircle.... What do we call part of a semi-circle? You think of the moon ... perhaps you'll get the shape.

P    Water.

T    No, not shaped like water.... Yes?

P    An arc.

T    An arc ... oh we're getting ever so much nearer.

P    Crescent.

T    A crescent shape. Have you heard that expression ... a crescent shape? I wonder if anybody could draw me a crescent shape on the board. Yes, they're nearly all that shape....

Although the teacher seems from the first to have been look-ing for the verbal label, 'crescent', in the course of searching for it language was used in quite other ways than in merely offering a series of labels for rejection or acceptance. At first the girls, who had a picture (and probably some personal experience) to start from, took the question as an invitation *to make this experience explicit.* Thus we have 'like hills', 'like waves', 'sort of go up and down getting higher and higher', and the strikingly evocative 'all humpy up and down'. They are not taking the shared experience of shape as given and finding a name for it they are exploring *what meaning any agreed name should have.* But 'like pyramids' turns the class towards the labelling function of language, so that 'in a semicircle', having earned the teacher's approval, directs the class towards 'arc' and 'crescent'.

Would the class have gained as much if the name 'crescent' had come as an immediate answer to the first question? What did they gain? Why is this the only case in twelve lessons when the personal meaning of a word was explored? Does this represent a significant lack in the learning experience of younger secondary pupils, or is this merely a chance bias of the small sample? What function has language like 'all humpy up and down' for the child who used it? Is it the vestige of something to be outgrown, or the unformed promise of something to come? This single example can raise these questions but not answer them.

*The tape-recording certainly preserves a record for subsequent detailed analysis. Being able to play over important pieces of dialogue facilitates understanding of how language is used. But the recording also preserves an enormous amount of redundancy and irrelevance. Significant events are often easier to detect within the classroom, with all its visual cues, than on the audio-recording. Recent research has concentrated on categorising classroom events in terms of a variety of classroom behaviour schedules. Two of the studies used to illustrate sampling procedures in Chapter 2 were concerned with teacher–pupil interaction. The N.F.E.R. study of The Teacher's Day provided many useful insights into the work of the teacher. A similar study in Scotland has been chosen for description here. The sampling basis of the* Primary School Survey *conducted by J. H. Duthie has already been described in Chapter 3. Techniques of categorising the observations and methods of analysing and interpreting the data are illustrated by summarising Chapter 9 of Duthie's report[1] and by presenting edited extracts.*

From the range of instruments which have been developed to record classroom behaviour, Duthie chose Form 4V of the OScAR series (Observation Schedule and Record). This schedule allows the observer to classify different verbal statements and 'interchanges' (question and answer) in the classroom. Form 4V comprises a number of 'boxes'. Those on the left-hand side of the record sheet are used to record the teacher's statements and the

[1] *Primary School Survey: a Study of the Teacher's Day* (H.M.S.O., Edinburgh), pages 57–61.

I

interchanges which are initiated by the teacher; those on the right of the form record the pupil's statements and the pupil-initiated interchanges. The actual words are not recorded: each statement is classified under one of a number of headings and the form is used to record the frequency of the different categories of statement or interchange.

The teacher's statements are classified under six headings:

RBK = *Rebuking*
DRC = *Directing*
INF = *Informing*
CNS = *Considering*
DSC = *Describing*
PRB = *Problem structuring*

Each of these is defined in the OScAR manual (Medley, Impelletteri and Smith, 1966): for example, a Describing statement is one which merely tells what the class, the teacher, or a pupil has done, is doing, or will do, without pressuring students to behave in a certain way. Problem-structuring statements pose issues, questions or problems about substantive content without giving solutions to them.

Teacher-initiated interchanges are classified under three headings:

DVG = *Divergent*
ELB = *Elaborating*
CVG = *Convergent*

Divergent interchanges relate to questions by the teacher which are 'open-ended'—i.e. there is no one correct answer. In a Convergent interchange only one answer is acceptable. Elaborating interchanges show the extent to which the lesson 'hangs together'. Here '... the question the teacher asks refers directly to a pupil response immediately preceding it, asking the pupils to discuss, correct or enlarge upon it'. Each of these categories of interchange is subdivided to show how the teacher reacted to the pupil's reply to her question or statement: by Supporting it (SP), Approving it (AP), Acknowledging (AC), Not Evaluating it (NE), Neutrally Rejecting it (NR) or by Critically Rejecting it (CR). These represent a six-point scale of type of response, from a strongly positive response (SP) to a strongly negative (CR). Using this form to categorise the statements and interchanges in a classroom lesson (or in sample five-minute periods of the lesson), the observer builds up an objectively recorded picture of the classroom discourse.

It will be recalled that, during their visits to schools, the Team observed in pairs. One member of each pair collected information for the technological study whilst the other collected information for the theoretical study. Since the theoretical study was purely exploratory we decided to utilize the opportunity of observing a random sample of Scottish primary classes by employing also an established instrument for classroom observation. For this purpose we used what was probably the best available technique —OScAR 4V (Medley, Impelletteri and Smith, 1966). The member of the pair who was collecting information for the theoretical study accordingly employed the OScAR technique on two occasions during the observation day : for a five-minute period in the morning and for a further five-minute period in the afternoon.

Some caution should be exercised in interpreting the results. Norms have not yet been established for this purpose. On the other hand, since these results are themselves based on a representative sample of Scottish primary school classrooms, they may be used as preliminary norms for this country. At the same time it is possible to interpret the results in terms of the numbers of given occurrences during a specified period and this we have done below. These interpretations give some idea of the patterning of activities in classrooms. Comparisons among Infants, Junior and Senior in many case indicate trends which we were intuitively aware of as observers and the general impression of the Team is that these figures provide, in objective form, reasonably accurate measures of the patterns of teacher and pupil verbal behaviour in the classes observed.

A summary of results from the Scottish survey is given in Table 13 : 1 (adapted from page 59 of the report) :

TABLE 13:1  *Mean frequencies for statements and interchanges in two observation periods totalling 10 minutes, in a national stratified random sample of 117 classrooms*

|  | Mean frequency | | | |
|---|---|---|---|---|
|  | Infants | Junior | Senior | Infants, Junior and Senior |
| Statements: | | | | |
| RBK (Rebuking) | 3·3 | 6·1 | 3·3 | 4·0 |
| DRC (Directing) | 7·7 | 8·6 | 5·2 | 7·2 |
| INF (Informing) | 2·3 | 3·7 | 4·4 | 3·3 |
| CNS (Considering) | 2·6 | 2·0 | 1·0 | 2·0 |
| DSC (Describing) | 5·6 | 4·0 | 5·0 | 5·0 |
| PRB (Problem structuring) | 3·8 | 5·5 | 4·4 | 4·4 |
| PPL (Pupil statements) | 0·4 | 0·0 | 0·0 | 0·2 |
| Interchanges: | | | | |
| DVG (Divergent) | 1·6 | 1·3 | 1·7 | 1·6 |
| ELB (Elaborating) | 0·7 | 1·0 | 0·6 | 0·8 |
| CVG (Convergent) | 7·6 | 8·0 | 6·4 | 7·3 |
| SPI (Substantive—pupil initiated interchange) | 2·7 | 2·9 | 2·9 | 2·8 |

Table 13 : 1 gives the total number of entries for each of the boxes and capsules. Thus there were on the average, 3·8 instances of problem structuring by the teacher in ten minutes of obser-

vation in Infants classes, 5·5 such instances in Junior classes and
4·4 in Senior classes.

Categories in Table 13:1 for which there appears to be a
trend are as follows: *Rebuking* approximately twice as frequent
in Junior as in Infants and Senior classes; *Directing* (orders or
commands) falls off for Senior pupils; *Informing* (facts, principles
and ideas) increases linearly with age of class; *Considering* ('Statements reflecting affection or concern for pupils or their needs,
desires, feelings …') falls off with age. (There is no clear trend
for *Describing* although teachers do a lot of it (5 instances in 10
minutes on the average).) *Pupil statements* (pupils addressing
each other as an integral part of the lesson) should be compared
with the remainder of the statements, since the others are all
made by the teacher.

The first three interchanges are teacher-initiated. There is no
clear trend with age of pupil. A comparison of the three categories however shows that Convergent questions are much more
common than the others.

A breakdown of these interchanges in terms of the way in
which the teacher dealt with the pupil's response to her questions is given in Table 13:2. Most responses are Acknowledged.
The extreme positive end of the continuum (Supported) is used
more frequently than the extreme negative end (Critically
Rejected).

TABLE 13:2   *Breakdown of interchanges (final column of Table 13:1, last
four items) by type of entry and type of exit*

| Entry | Exit: SP | AP | AC | NE | NR | CR |
|---|---|---|---|---|---|---|
| Divergent | 0·1 | 0·3 | 0·6 | 0·2 | 0·2 | 0·0 |
| Elaborating | 0·0 | 0·2 | 0·4 | 0·1 | 0·1 | 0·0 |
| Convergent | 0·4 | 1·8 | 3·5 | 0·4 | 0·7 | 0·1 |
| Pupil initiated | 0·3 | 0·8 | 1·0 | 0·3 | 0·3 | 0·1 |

*In Duthie's study the interpretation of these results is sim-
plified by the use of formulae to combine 'scores' in the various
categories, which provide a more general impression of different
classroom 'climates', or different teachers' strategies', in the form
of a classification by 'type of entry' and 'type of exit'. Thus,
among the 'types of entry', Pupil Initiative is measured by the following formula: number of pupil-initiated interchanges minus
one-third of the number of teacher-initiated interchanges. (Although these headings are now of a more descriptive or evaluative
kind, it is important to remember that they are based on objective
recording, and different observers will come to the same conclusion in thus categorising the classroom discourse which has
been subjected to this analysis. The method allows comparisons
to be made between classrooms or between teachers.) The following categories are used in the report:*

*e.g. Types of entry:*   Pupil initiative
                          Cohesion
                          Divergence
*Types of exit:*          Feedback
                          Valence
                          Enthusiasm

Pupil Initiative *is described above; the others are defined as follows.* Cohesion: *'The teacher who scores high on Cohesion tends to ask interrelated questions: his discussions hang together more than do those of the average teacher.'* Divergence: *'. . . The teacher scoring high tends to prefer open-ended questions to closed, factual ones.'* Feedback: *'Scores on this key will indicate how likely a teacher is to give his pupils feedback'* (information about the appropriateness of their response) *'about what they say about content.'* Valence: *'Where Valence is high, pupils are more likely to be right than wrong when they talk about content.'* Enthusiasm: *'The enthusiastic teacher praises a (pupil) for being right and also criticises him for being wrong more often than the average teacher does.' Each of these categories is constructed from various combinations and weighting of the observations described on page 250. Tables 13:3 and 13:4 give the average 'scores' on these categories: negative values indicate lack of the characteristic in question.*

**TABLE 13:3**   *Scales based on contrasting types of entry*

| Scale | Infants | Junior | Senior |
|---|---|---|---|
| Pupil initiative | −0·6 | −0·6 | 0·0 |
| Cohesion | −3·9 | −3·6 | −3·4 |
| Divergence | −5·9 | −6·7 | −4·6 |

**TABLE 13:4**   *Scales based on contrasting types of exit*

| Scale | Infants | Junior | Senior |
|---|---|---|---|
| Feedback | −2·5 | −4·1 | −3·0 |
| Valence | 2·2 | 0·9 | 2·4 |
| Enthusiasm | −2·9 | −2·8 | −2·6 |

*A simpler procedure, using the Flanders System of Interaction Analysis, is described in an article by E. C. Wragg, which also reviews the early research in this area and describes its application in the training of student teachers.*

*Interaction Analysis as a Feedback System For*
*Student Teachers*    (E. C. Wragg, 1970)[1]

## INTRODUCTION

'It is a serious indictment of the profession, however, to hear so many education instructors say that their students will appreciate what they are learning *after* they have had some practical teaching experience. What hurts is the obvious hypocrisy of making this statement and then giving a lecture on the importance of presenting material in such a way that the immediate needs and interests of the pupils are taken into consideration. Such instances reveal a misunderstanding of theory and practice. To be understood, concepts in education must be verified by personal field experiences; in turn, field experience must be efficiently conceptualised to gain insight. With most present practices, the gorge between theory and practice grows deeper and wider, excavated by the very individuals who are pledged to fill it.' (Flanders, 1963).

Professor Ned Flanders' indictment of teacher training procedures in the United States would equally well apply in this country. During the period of teaching practice, the 'personal field experiences' to which Flanders refers, students are largely left on their own in the classroom. Feedback about their behaviour usually comes in the form of comment from other observers, visiting tutors, experienced teachers, fellow students, or the children they teach. Such feedback is often unsystematic, highly personalised, and has little chance of affecting the behaviour of the student teacher, unless he himself accepts the insights as relevant and meaningful.

What this means is that students on teaching practice are constantly losing opportunities to understand and control their own teaching behaviour at the most formative stage of their career. There is now considerable American evidence (Wallen and Travers, 1963) that most experienced teachers have fairly constant patterns of teaching which are not likely to change very much even after in-service training. In addition there is quite a lot of research evidence on the acquisition of classroom behaviour patterns by teacher trainees. Joyce and Harootunian (1964) found that methods were intuitively arrived at and not consciously chosen from alternatives. Furthermore the format of most lessons was a reflection of current practices in the school and an imitation of co-operating teachers. That student teachers imitate the practice of the schools in which they find themselves must have

[1] This article originally appeared in *Education for Teaching*, *81*, 38–47.

been verified by every tutor who has ever visited students. My own favourite teacher greets new students with, 'You can forget all that rubbish they told you up there. I'll show you how to teach.' He does too.

If, then, most teachers have a fixed teaching pattern, and if student teachers are likely to imitate the patterns of the teachers around them, it is clear that current practices, however good or bad, are likely to be propagated indefinitely with only minimal changes. Furthermore there is some evidence (Wragg, 1967) that student teachers, whilst consciously *rejecting* certain aspects of the teaching they themselves received at school, and of the teaching they see during teaching practice, and *wishing* to change their behaviour accordingly, often find themselves unable to do so when actually standing in a classroom confronted by a group of children. The pressure to conform to current practices is enormous, whereas the ability of the student teacher consciously to control his own classroom behaviour is comparatively small.

Is it possible, then, to equip students with some means of gaining insights into their own teaching, of conceptualising what they see, and subsequently of changing their behaviour if they think fit?

The most hopeful development towards some kind of solution to this problem is probably to be found amongst the large volume of research on teacher-pupil interaction in the United States, and, more recently, in Britain, Scandinavia, India and even places like Ghana.

### EARLY RESEARCH ON CLASSROOM CLIMATE

The earliest attempt to analyse and describe in a systematic way the spontaneous interaction between a teacher and the children in his class was probably the work of Anderson, Brewer and Reed (1939, 1946), who, from as early as 1939, observed for a number of years the sort of 'contacts' between children in nursery and elementary school classes, and related these to the behaviour of the teacher towards the children. They regularly found that the teacher who was 'dominative' would have more dominative contacts between the children in the class, i.e., snatching toys, striking playmates, giving commands to others, whereas the 'integrative' teacher would find more integrative acts in his classroom, such as sharing toys, offering help and playing harmoniously.

Soon after Anderson's early work Lippitt and later White (1940, 1943) working with Kurt Lewin from 1940 onwards, carried out their well-known, and often quoted and misquoted pieces of research into the effects of adult leaders' behaviour on groups of five boys engaged in various activities. Despite the shortcomings of this pioneer research, including its partial irrelevance to school classes of much larger size, the concept of children's dependence on the leader shown by Anderson clearly came through. The leaders, who played authoritarian, democratic and laissez-faire roles, produced different patterns of behaviour from the boys according to whether they were present or absent. The absence of the authoritarian-type leader, for example, led to acts of aggression by the group, whereas the democratic leader's group functioned in what Anderson would have called an integrative way, whether the leader was there or not.

Withall (1949) was amongst the first to develop a category system. His classification of the teacher's verbal statements into seven categories showed a pattern of teacher *verbal* behaviour similar to that produced by Anderson's categorisation of *general* behaviour.

From these early studies it was becoming clear that since it was not possible to record every detail of what happened in a class, it was best to concentrate on some aspect. More and more research was devoted to teacher *talk*. Flanders (1965) developed a ten category system for categorising talk by both teacher and children. After many hours of live classroom observation he formulated his 'rule of two-thirds'. Of all the lessons he observed roughly two-thirds consisted of talk. Two-thirds of this talk was by the teacher, and two-thirds of the teacher's talk was devoted to giving information. Since it had already been shown that talk was highly correlated with behaviour, it seemed logical to subject spontaneous verbal interaction between teachers and children to systematic analysis and see what emerged.

### THE FLANDERS SYSTEM OF INTERACTION ANALYSIS

The Flanders System of Interaction Analysis divides verbal activity into ten categories each of which has a number. There is no scale implied by the numbers.

#### The Ten Categories

1 Accepts feeling: accepts and clarifies the feeling tone of the students in a non-threatening manner. Feelings may be positive or negative. Predicting and recalling feelings are included.

2 Praises or encourages: praises or encourages student action or behaviour.

| | | |
|---|---|---|
| **Teacher Talk** | Indirect influence | Jokes that release tension not at the expense of another individual, nodding head or saying 'uh huh?' or 'go on' are included. |
| | | 3 Accepts or uses ideas of students: clarifying, building or developing ideas or suggestions by a student. As teacher brings more of his own ideas into play, shift to category five. |
| | | 4 Asks questions: asking a question about content or procedure with the intent that a student answer. |
| | Direct influence | 5 Lectures: giving facts or opinions about content or procedure; expressing his own idea; asking rhetorical questions. |
| | | 6 Gives directions: directions, commands, or orders with which a student is expected to comply. |
| | | 7 Criticizes or justifies authority: statements, intended to change student behaviour from non-acceptable to acceptable pattern; bawling someone out; stating why the teacher is doing what he is doing, extreme self-reference. |
| | Student talk | 8 Student talk-response: talk by students in response to teacher. Teacher initiates the contact or solicits student statement. |
| | | 9 Student talk-initiation: talk by students, which they initiate. If 'calling on' student is only to indicate who may talk next, the observer must decide whether student wanted to talk. If he did, use this category. |
| | | 10 Silence or confusion: pauses, short periods of silence, and periods of confusion in which communication cannot be understood by the observer. |

Categories 1 to 4 which Flanders calls 'Indirect Influence' correspond roughly, though by no means exactly, to Anderson's 'Integrative' concept, and categories 5, 6 and 7, where to some extent the teacher is limiting the verbal activity of the class, correspond approximately to his 'dominative' concept.

The procedures for using the Flanders system are quite straightforward (Amidon and Flanders, 1963). An observer watches a teacher during a lesson and every three seconds he writes down the category number of the interaction he has just observed. He records these numbers in sequence in a column, writing approximately 20 numbers per minute, so that after, say, 25 minutes, he will have a sequence of approximately 500 numbers. The observer has first been trained for several hours from tapes, videotapes and live situations if possible, until he shows considerable agreement with other trained observers. Inter-observer agreement can be calculated by a formula suggested by Scott and it takes only 10 or 12 hours of training to produce inter-observer agreements of 0·8 or above. (At Exeter 35 students were trained for 12 hours before teaching practice, and all except four achieved inter-observer agreements with an experienced observer of 0·8 or above). If, of course, the activity is not appropriate, i.e. a film being shown, everyone working in silence, or if the observer cannot hear, then he stops tallying.

## COLLECTING AND RECORDING DATA

Suppose, for example, a teacher comes into the class and says 'Open your books at the map on page 60', then the observer writes 6, signifying a command. If he then goes on to ask 'What is the country coloured green?', the observer writes a 4. If silence follows the question he writes a 10, and when someone replies 'I think it's Finland, but I'm not sure', he writes 8. Now the sequence of command, question, silence, answer is shown by the observer's set of four numbers 6–4–10–8.

When the observer has collected several hundred such tallies he needs to be able to present these to the teacher in an understandable form. One way obviously is to give the totals of each category as a percentage of the whole so that a teacher can see how much praise he uses, how much spontaneous talk by the children occurs, or how much use of questioning he makes. But more interesting is an analysis of the actual sequence of the events. For example questions may always be followed by silence, or sequences such as 4–8–4–8–4–8–4–8 will show rapid question and answer, almost like drill.

A particularly interesting way of showing the data is to put it on to a 10 × 10 matrix as shown below. To do this the numbers are taken in pairs and put into the appropriate cell.

Take the sequences given above, 6–4–10–8, the first pair of

numbers is 6–4, i.e. command followed by question, so the tally goes into the 6–4 cell, (counting *down* 6, *across* 4) as shown in Figure 13 : 1. The next pair is 4–10 (each number is the second of the previous pair and the first of the next pair), the third pair 10–8 and so on.

|    | 1 | 2 | 3 | 4 | 5 | 6 | 7 | 8 | 9 | 10 |
|----|---|---|---|---|---|---|---|---|---|----|
| 1  |   |   |   |   |   |   |   |   |   |    |
| 2  |   |   |   |   |   |   |   |   |   |    |
| 3  |   |   |   |   |   |   |   |   |   |    |
| 4  |   |   |   |   |   |   |   |   |   | 1  |
| 5  |   |   |   |   |   |   |   |   |   |    |
| 6  |   |   |   | 1 |   |   |   |   |   |    |
| 7  |   |   |   |   |   |   |   |   |   |    |
| 8  |   |   |   |   |   |   |   |   |   |    |
| 9  |   |   |   |   |   |   |   |   |   |    |
| 10 |   |   |   |   |   |   |   | 1 |   |    |

FIGURE 13 : 1    *10 × 10 matrix showing sequence 6–4–10–8 tallied in three cells*

Now it is possible to gain all sorts of insights about one's lessons from the data collected. Figure 13 : 2 shows a completed matrix of 542 tallies representing approximately 27 minutes of a lesson.

Analysis of Figure 13 : 2 which was a 3rd form chemistry lesson given by a student teacher in the eighth week of a one-term teaching practice in a girls' grammar school shows that well over 90 per cent was talk, most of it by the teacher. Most of the time the teacher gave information (category 5). The 43 tallies in the 4–8 cell (question followed by answer) show that question-answer technique was used, and the 35 tallies in the 8–3 cell (answer followed by teacher accepting answer, suggests that usually the answers were accepted by the teacher). Absence of any tallies in the 8–7 cell (answer followed by criticism), suggests that on this occasion the teacher did not criticise answers.

Obviously there are many things one can deduce from the data, and even more if one had seen the lesson as well.

### INTERACTION ANALYSIS FOR STUDENTS

It is quite easy to train students to use the Flanders system of interaction analysis and indeed it is a useful tool for those engaged in teacher-training to have at their disposal. Tutors tend to disagree with each other as well as with their own students in their perceptions of lessons as can easily be demonstrated by using a videotape of a lesson to initiate discussion. A more objective tool can be a useful adjunct to one's subjective impressions and give both students and observing tutors additional insights.

| | 1 | 2 | 3 | 4 | 5 | 6 | 7 | 8 | 9 | 10 | Total |
|---|---|---|---|---|---|---|---|---|---|---|---|
| 1 | | | | | 1 | | | | | | 1 |
| 2 | | | 1 | 3 | 1 | | | | | | 5 |
| 3 | | 2 | 1 | 7 | 26 | | | 1 | | | 37 |
| 4 | | | | 27 | 9 | | 1 | 43 | | 10 | 90 |
| 5 | 1 | 1 | | 39 | 280 | 1 | 3 | 2 | | 2 | 329 |
| 6 | | | | | 1 | | | | | | 1 |
| 7 | | | | 1 | 2 | 1 | 1 | | | | 5 |
| 8 | | 2 | 35 | 8 | 5 | | | 9 | | 1 | 60 |
| 9 | | | | | | | | | | | 0 |
| 10 | | | | 5 | 4 | | | 4 | | 1 | 14 |
| | | | | | | | | | | Total | 542 |

FIGURE 13:2     *Completed matrix of student teacher's third form chemistry lesson*

At Exeter I needed 12 hours to train a group of 35 students to a stage where they could first of all reach a good level of agreement with an experienced observer (Scott coefficient of 0·8 or above), secondly transpose the data collected on to a matrix, and thirdly interpret the information provided by various areas of a completed 10 × 10 matrix.

The students were all postgraduate students in the Exeter University Department of Education, and were about to embark on a one term teaching practice in a variety of schools. They were from a wide range of degree subject backgrounds. Only one or two found training at all difficult. One woman student confessed to a complete blockage to numbers of any kind going back to all kinds of traumatic mathematical experiences at school. She was one of the eight who subsequently failed to use the technique during teaching practice. The sequence of events was as follows :

*Stage* 1.    December 1968. Volunteers were invited to learn Interaction Analysis after a lecture/discussion on teacher-pupil interaction. 35 volunteers were then trained on five separate occasions for 12 hours in all. Sound tapes and live classroom situations were used. Final reliability checks were taken to see what level of agreement there was between observers. This was found to be high with very few exceptions.

*Stage* 2.    January–March 1969. Students observed other students on teaching practice at fortnightly intervals, always with the same class on the same day of the week. Some students worked in pairs. Both had been trained in the technique, so they could observe each other. Written reminders and a general letter of instruction were sent to all students about three days before they were due to make each of the fortnightly observations.

*Stage* 3.    April 1969. All data was returned to be analysed. Some students had dropped out, some had been prevented by examinations, sports days, etc., from carrying out all the observations. Finally data was available from nearly 100 lessons given by 31 students producing nearly 50,000 tallies.

*Stage* 4.    May–June 1969. Some students went out to a variety of schools and collected data from experienced teachers in order to gain further insights.

### RESULTS

The results, even though to some extent predictable, were nevertheless surprising. There was an almost unbelievably stable pattern. Table 13:5 shows a breakdown by categories of the first 35,000 tallies analysed.

TABLE 13:5   *Distribution of 35,000 tallies from 23 students' lessons*

| Category | 1 | 2 | 3 | 4 | 5 | 6 | 7 | 8 | 9 | 10 | Total |
|---|---|---|---|---|---|---|---|---|---|---|---|
| % of talk | 0·7 | 1·6 | 2·4 | 10·7 | 36·7 | 4·5 | 1·5 | 12·6 | 5·5 | 23·8 | 100% |

What was remarkable was not only that the distribution was more or less the same whether one looked at all the lessons in the early part of term or all the lessons in the latter part of term, but that almost any lessons by any student with any class at any stage of the term would vary only slightly from the pattern shown in Table 13:5. Some students, of course, did vary quite remarkably. Those pairs of students who were both trained in the technique were to some extent able to control their distribution by the end of term, and some teachers, as Flanders himself had found, just had a varied pattern in any case. But most did not.

After teaching practice some students argued that it was almost inevitable the teacher would talk over 70 per cent of the time. We then despatched them into primary schools, E.S.N. schools, approved schools, schools for severely subnormal children to look for some answers. We were not able to build up enough data on each school to suggest even crude norms, but suffice it to say that different patterns did emerge. Yet even these patterns, which were often different from the pattern seen in secondary schools, were often similar to each other within the same school. In one primary school the teachers observed always talked for around 50 per cent of the time. There were also clear patterns in the use of praise and question and answer in the E.S.N. and S.S.N. schools.

A further follow-up was to compare student's matrices with those of experienced teachers. For example a student teaching history in a grammar school tended to lecture for much of the time, occasionally putting in bursts of question and answer. This pattern of presenting information would often be something like the following, using categories 4 (question), 5 (lecture) and 8 (child answers).

5–5–5–5–5–5–4–8–4–8–4–8–5–5–5–5

This shows mainly lecture, a short burst of questioning with answers rarely taking more than three seconds, and more lecture. Another student might ask questions which were too difficult and were followed by silence (10) or criticism (7)

5–5–5–5–5–4–4–10–10–7–7–4–10–7–7–5–5–5

This sequence does not even get a response from the class.

An experienced teacher of history, however, was shown to have a technique whereby he 'seeded' his questions with information (4–5–5–4), got longer answers from children (8–8–8), praised or clarified these answers (2 or 3) and then added a little more supplementary information (5). So that his sequence would be more like—

5–5–4–5–5–4–8–8–8–2–3–3–5–5–4–4–5–8–8–8–2

One caveat about using Interaction Analysis with students. First of all it is imperative to understand the technique thoroughly before even beginning, and Amidon and Hough's admirable book *Interaction Analysis: Theory, Research and Application* (1967) will provide most of the basic information. Secondly students tend to expect there is some 'good teacher pattern' which they can learn. Interaction Analysis can certainly attempt to analyse the teaching patterns of those teachers regarded as good by anyone or everyone, but Flanders found no single 'good teacher pattern' emerged. It is for the student to look at his own data, and, in consultation with other students or his tutor discuss how he might adapt his teaching. Ultimately he has to decide for himself; the analysis technique is merely a useful tool to enable him to conceptualise more easily.

## ADAPTATIONS OF THE TECHNIQUE

Amidon and Hough (1967) mention 20 different category systems being used in the United States in 1965. Today there are well over 100, many of which are adaptations of the Flanders system. The Flanders system has been adapted for use in foreign language lessons (Wragg, 1970a), it has been extended to 20 categories by Amidon and Hunter (1966), it has been used for training student teachers (Hough, 1966) and experienced teachers (Storlie, 1961).

Some users object that because it does not identify individual children who respond and because modern primary schools are so informal the techniques cannot be applied in primary schools. It is true that it is harder to categorise verbal behaviour when a teacher is not addressing the class, but if the teacher is talking and one can hear him, then one can try to categorise. I have developed a technique for selecting two children only, calling them A and B, and concentrating on those two children, labelling any category number which includes them A or B, so that 4A means teacher asks child A a question), 8B mean child B answers something, 7A means teacher criticises child A and so on (Wragg, 1970b). This produces a lot of information about teachers' interactions with individuals in an informal setting.

## CONCLUSION

Student teachers appear to be caught up in a giant web of forces acting on their behaviour, their former school, the teaching practice school, the college or university department course, the teachers who help them during practice, their visiting tutor. Ultimately they must control their own behaviour. Interaction Analysis provides a tool which helps them gain insights into their own teaching soon after they have finished the actual lesson. Students trained in the technique can work in pairs. Tutors armed with the technique can share concepts which students will understand too. Flanders has provided strong evidence that students trained in Interaction Analysis are better able to control their own behaviour than untrained students.

Teaching utimately is behaviour in the classroom. Lectures, discussions, reading will all influence behaviour to a small extent, but it seems most probable that behaviour is more likely to change if it is analysed and manipulated in the field.

Some students never praise, never criticise, never clarify children's ideas, never get spontaneous responses from children. Some students just saturate children in information and hope they will learn. The great weakness of teacher training as Flanders points out is the gulf between theory and practice. Already some experimental teacher training courses in the United States use conditioned groups, where rules are introduced, such as 'You must clarify the previous idea before introducing your own', or 'you must simplify your questions if they don't produce a response', or 'you must limit your own contribution to 30 per cent of the time.' This way teacher trainees are enabled to try out patterns of behaviour they might never discover by chance. They don't have to accept a single philosophy or a single stereotype of good teacher, but at least they get the opportunity both under laboratory conditions and in the field to try out different patterns of interaction and see how they work.

## REFERENCES

AMIDON, E. J., and FLANDERS, N. A. (1963) *The Role of the Teacher in the Classroom*. Minneapolis : P. S. Amidon.

AMIDON, E. J., and HOUGH, J. B. (1967) *Interaction Analysis: Theory, Research and Application*. Reading, Mass.: Addison-Wesley.

AMIDON, E. J., and HUNTER, E. (1966) *Improving Teaching: Analysing Verbal Interaction in the Classroom*. New York: Holt, Rinehart and Winston.

ANDERSON, H. H. (1939) 'The measurement of domination and of socially integrative behaviour in teachers' contacts with children.' *Child Development, 10*, 73–89.

ANDERSON, H. H., *et al.* (1946) *Studies of Teachers' Classroom Personalities*. Stanford: University Press.

FLANDERS, N. A. (1963) 'Intent, action and feedback: a preparation for teaching.' *J. of Teacher Education, 14*, 251–60.

FLANDERS, N. A. (1965) *Teacher Influence, Pupil Attitudes and Achievement*. Washington, D.C.: Co-operative Research Monograph No. 12.

HOUGH, J. B. (1966) 'Interaction analysis in a general methods course.' *Classroom Interaction Newsletter*, May 1966, *1*, 2, 7–10.

JOYCE, B. R., and HAROOTUNIAN, B. (1964) 'Teaching as problem-solving.' *J. of Teacher Education, 15*.

LIPPITT, R. (1940) *An Analysis of Group Reaction to Three Types of Experimentally Created Social Climates*. Unpublished doctoral dissertation, University of Iowa.

LIPPITT, R., and WHITE, R. K. (1943) 'The social climate of children's groups.' In BARKER, R. G., KOUNIN, J. S., and WRIGHT, H. F. (eds.) *Child Behaviour and Development.* New York: McGraw-Hill.

STORLIE, T. R. (1961) *Selected Characteristics of Teachers whose Verbal Behaviour is influenced by an In-service Course in Interaction Analysis.* Unpublished doctoral dissertation, University of Minnesota.

WALLEN, N. E., and TRAVERS, R. M. W. (1962) 'Analysis and investigation of teaching methods.' In GAGE, N. L. (ed.) *Handbook of Research on Teaching.* Chicago: Rand McNally.

WITHALL, J. (1949) 'The development of a technique for the measurement of social-emotional climate in classrooms.' *J. of Experimental Education, 17,* 347–61.

WRAGG, E. C. (1967) *Some Attitudes, Anxieties and Aspirations of Students following the Post-graduate Certificate in Education.* Unpublished M.Ed. thesis, University of Leicester.

WRAGG, E. C. (1970a) 'Collecting interaction data in the foreign language classroom.' In SIMON, A., and BOYER, E. G. (eds.) *Anthology of Observation Instruments,* Vol. 13, Section 70, 1–7. Philadelphia.

WRAGG, E. C. (1970b) 'Identifying individual responses during classroom interaction.' *Classroom Interaction Newsletter, 5,* 2, 11–14.

# 14    Curriculum Development and Evaluation

*The growth of curriculum development in recent years reflects a significant change of emphasis in educational research. In the past, the main research effort has been put into psychological and sociological studies. While such investigations continue to be important, there is now a greater concern with classroom events, as shown in the preceding chapter, and with the curriculum. Curriculum development is not simply a matter of devising new syllabuses. The study of the content of the curriculum is linked to the study of methods, and both are considered in the context of defined objectives. (See, for example, Hooper, 1971.) Also, experimental work is involved, in that new material and methods are tested in pilot schools and these development stages are (or should be) followed by systematic evaluation, to assess how effectively the objectives have been achieved by the content and methods which have been adopted.*

*To illustrate this process, the first extract is a description of one project, Science 5/13, which began as a Nuffield Foundation Project but was later taken over and developed by the Schools Council. The extract illustrates the defining of objectives, the procedures for developing materials and methods, the involvement of teachers in the work of the project, the arrangements for diffusion of the products and the provision for evaluation.*

### The 'Science 5/13' Project
(J. D. Nisbet, 1972)[1]

The Nuffield Junior Science Teaching Project started in 1964 with a team of eight workers seconded from schools and colleges. In 1965 trials of their materials began in schools drawn from twelve

[1] Extract from a description of the work of the Schools Council in *Case Studies of Central Institutions in Educational Change* (Paris, O.E.C.D., in press).

pilot areas set up by the Schools Council. Interest was so great that in 1966, forty other areas were added. The project ended in 1966; but from 1967, the Schools Council, in collaboration with the Nuffield Foundation and the Scottish Education Department, sponsored a five-year continuation project, with the title Science 5/13. The principal aim of this project was not just to continue the previous development work, but to relate topics or areas of science to 'a framework of concepts appropriate to the ages of the pupils,' in order to cater for children of different abilities and from different backgrounds, and to provide help for primary school teachers and the colleges of education which train these teachers.

In April 1967, Len Ennever, the project director, left the Inspectorate to set up the new project; and in the course of the next two years, a team of six full-time staff and three office staff was formed, including Wynne Harlen appointed as evaluator. Their first task was to decide what they wanted the project to achieve; and working groups of teachers were formed to discuss objectives. The evaluator was involved in the discussion even at this initial stage. A check list of objectives was produced, intended to be used as a guide to be kept in mind and not as a limiting restriction on development: hence the title, *With Objectives in Mind*. In this statement, the team used Piaget's stages as a framework for specifying objectives—

STAGE 1:  transition from intuitive thinking to thinking with the aid of concrete operations;

STAGE 2:  when thinking with concrete aids is powerfully applied;

STAGE 3:  when this kind of thinking is being supplemented by hypotheses, and thinking is related to abstract ideas.

Objectives were formulated within this framework, in order to help teachers see the curriculum as a steady progression, and to help prepare children in the later primary years for the transition to secondary school.

Materials were prepared as 'units'—specific subject-areas within the children's experience: Trees, Metals, Time, Structures and Forces, Minibeasts (invertebrates), Coloured Things, and so on. Ideas for these were obtained with the help of teachers, and of their pupils. For example, in 'Coloured Things', a rough outline of the proposed unit was given to groups of teachers, and (to quote) 'within a month, the teachers returned with armfuls of materials from their pupils'. Many changes, of course, were needed subsequently, when the materials were tested in the trial schools. Additional supporting material was gathered as background information for teachers, and this was published separately. A set of materials of a different kind is being planned—for the use of teachers and tutors in colleges—to explain the project and the use of its products: it is likely to consist of work cards, recorded tape, 8-mm. film-loops showing children at work on the materials, case studies, and a guide and notes. A series of *Newsletters* was begun, and these are circulated to all the participating schools: 40,000 copies of *Newsletter 2* have been printed. Nineteen local education authority areas (involving 430 schools) are pilot areas in which the materials are evaluated, but the materials are in fact being used in 141 areas (out of 146 in England and Wales).

Evaluation of the units has gone on throughout the process of development. *Newsletter 2* contains a diagram (see below) which summarises the evaluation procedures. The tests for children included both cognitive and affective items, and were based on film loops (to reduce the influence of differences in reading

*Evaluation Procedure in Science 5/13*

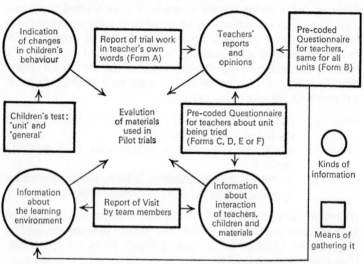

ability) for group testing. In each local authority area, pairs of schools had been designated by random allocation as trial and control schools. The evaluation of the material by teachers was done by filling in a booklet of questions: it is evidence of teachers' goodwill that out of 80 trial schools in a recent evaluation check, only three failed to cooperate fully (and one of these was due to a postal failure). The scale of this evaluation can be indicated by the number of children's booklets used—24,000 in one set of testing. Sophisticated techniques, including computer analysis, have been used, and have identified patterns of teaching and conditions of work which are associated with growth of interest in science. This strategy of concurrent or on-going evaluation has the advantage that units are evaluated while there is still time to alter them. On this view, the evaluator is most effective if he is neither too closely involved with the team nor separated from them by too wide a gulf.

In addition to the actual publication of the materials, their diffusion is helped by information on strategy and progress, given in the *Newsletters* which have been mentioned, and by courses for teachers, in all parts of the country, by designated persons on a regional basis. One member of the central team has a special responsibility for contacts with teachers' centres.

The task, as the project team see it, is not just to provide good materials for science teaching. By emphasising objectives, and placing these in a framework of development stages, by working through teachers' centres, and especially by involving teachers in the development work at all stages of the process, the intention is to develop ideas and methods of approach and to encourage teachers to think critically about their teaching.

*The report which follows describes the North West Regional Curriculum Development Project, which provides an interesting contrast with the Science 5/13 Project. The account begins with a criticism of the Schools Council approach to curriculum development.*

## Curriculum Model Building
(W. G. A. Rudd, 1970)[1]

The following paragraph, dealing with discovery methods and drawn from the Plowden Report, typifies contemporary English reaction to the confused state of curriculum theory.

'Free and sometimes indiscriminate use of words such as discovery has led some critics to the view that English primary education needs to be more firmly based on closely argued educational theory. Nevertheless great advances appear to have been made without such theory, and research has still a long way to go before it can make a marked contribution. At many points even so fruitful an approach as that of Piaget needs further verification. What is immediately needed is that teachers should bring to bear on their day to day problems astringent intellectual scrutiny. Yet all good teachers must work intuitively and be sensitive to the emotive

[1] Extracted from a chapter in Butcher, H. J., and Pont, H. B., *Educational Research in Britain*, Volume 2 (University of London Press), pages 121–34.

and imaginative needs of their children. Teaching is an art and, as long as that with all its implications is firmly grasped, it will not be harmed by intellectual stiffening' (DES, 1967).

This philosophy appears to underlie the Schools Council's main approach to curriculum development, typified by heavy reliance upon small national teams, each working to a tight budget and time schedule and each engaged in a single-shot exercise. Publication of each team's product is intended to be followed by induction courses (held in local development centres and elsewhere) for teachers who are to adapt and use the materials. It is true that a substantial number (though a minute proportion) of schools co-operate in developing the materials : but the partnership between central team and practising teachers leans heavily against the latter, whose essential contributions lie in carrying out field trials and subsequently commenting on how a pilot programme functioned and how it might be improved at particular points.

In this approach much obviously depends upon the Council's skill in backing winners when selecting leaders for national projects. To the extent that the Council is successful at this point its programme can yield courses which function well in action. As Peters (1969) has demonstrated, a danger in this approach is that popular educational theory is too often based on panaceas stemming from important half-truths, and at least fifteen years of sustained effort will be needed before any convincing evidence begins to accumulate that a curriculum developed in this way is functioning adequately in the majority of the classrooms for which it was designed.

In part, this is due to the tenuous nature of the link between the central development team and the mass of teachers who are to use the programme. Whilst it may be comparatively easy for the latter to learn the basic ideas underlying new course content, it may well prove more difficult for them to master the preferred teaching methods, and even more difficult for them to grasp the subtleties of the programme's underlying educational theory.

However, even this is not the whole story, for there are often very good reasons why the curriculum as taught in particular classrooms *should* differ markedly from that envisaged by its proposers. As will be shown, teachers add to the specific objectives of any course other objectives for which the course serves merely as a vehicle. Very often these are concerned with social and cultural learning, i.e. with changing motivation, controlling emotional patterns, raising levels of aspiration and accepting discipline. Such objectives all have important emotional components, which for the pupil (and hence for the teacher) take precedence over the more academic objectives in the classroom. Accordingly, it would be unwise (in this author's view) to concentrate curriculum evaluation on the general features of pupil performance, as Williams (1968) suggests, if by that term is meant pupil progress towards a fairly narrowly defined set of common goals. Such an evaluation would be open to many of the same criticisms as have been levelled so vehemently against external examinations.

An alternative approach has been proposed by Taba (1962), who argued that those responsible for generating theories of curriculum development omit the very important step of creating models for ways of translating theoretical ideas into functioning curricula and testing these ideas in classroom experiments. She therefore proposed that innovation start at the teaching level, with the planning of specific teaching–learning units. This proposal strongly appealed to the organizers of the North West Regional Curriculum Development Project who saw in it both the prospect of having by 1972–3 (when the school-leaving age is due to be raised) some practical *and tested* study units, and also that the results of such experiment might offer some basis for the creation of a general design for curriculum development during later phases of the total process. Arrangements were therefore set in motion for study units to be prepared in local development centres (i.e. as near as possible to the classrooms concerned), for the developers to be teachers who were to implement the programmes and for development activity to be cyclical, including study of objectives, evaluation and feedback, as well as the writing of new study courses.

## THE STUDY OF OBJECTIVES

The North West Regional Curriculum Development Project is a consortium of fifteen local development centres, established and maintained by thirteen LEAs, whose work is co-ordinated through the University of Manchester School of Education and controlled by a steering committee having a majority of practising teachers. The project was launched in 1967 and is partially supported until 1970 by a Schools Council grant.

Since few of the local centres were in existence when the project was launched, much of its early work was organizational in nature. However, in September 1967, regional groups were set up to prepare handbooks on objectives in ten curriculum areas for early-leaving pupils: English, mathematics, science, religious and moral education, social studies, boys' crafts, girls' crafts, music, art and studio subjects and physical education. Groups comprised one teacher-representative from each local area, were chaired by one or other of the curriculum development leaders and enjoyed the support from certain distinguished teachers in the region, from H.M. and local inspectorates and from university and college of education lecturers. In the spring term, 1968, the ideas set out in the handbooks were studied in each local centre, under the leadership of those teachers who had represented the centre in the regional discussions.

These handbooks were regarded as working papers and have not been published. However, the scope of the work at this stage can be exemplified from the report of the girls' craft panel. This panel listed five major aims: to encourage an awareness of the importance of developing harmonious relationships, and to foster a capacity to feel sensitively about others; to develop a sense of responsibility both towards work and towards other people; to develop the capacity for judgement (forming an opinion) and discrimination (exercising a choice) at an appropriate level of understanding; to foster the ability to adapt to a changing pattern of life; to encourage a wide capacity for enjoyment (education for leisure and pleasure). Each major aim encompassed some five subsidiary aims, all of which were stated, and in the report each list of aims (one major and its subsidiaries) was followed by a detailed description of a sample learning situation indicating how that list of aims might be pursued.

For example, the five subsidiary aims linked to the first major aim were (in a slightly condensed form): to foster in the pupils an awareness of how they and other people feel; to encourage a real and practical interest in young children by a responsible study of their needs: to develop understanding of simple psychology from birth to maturity; to promote recognition of the importance of justice, respect, affection and willingness to commit oneself when working with others; to develop a tolerant attitude towards the contrary opinions held by others. The sample learning situation given described the organizing and running (by the pupils) of a play group for young children, set up partly to give mothers an opportunity to maintain or develop interests outside the family. Before beginning their planning the pupils were to visit local infant schools and day nurseries; and in preparation for the play group toys were to be made and activity materials gathered, refreshments were to be planned and prepared and stories and other quiet time activities were to be selected. During the play-group pupils were to note as much as possible of the conversation and reactions of the one or two children for whom they had special responsibility; but pupils were also to take turns in acting as non-participant observers. The fruits of all this activity were to serve as study material for the course envisaged.

It may well be that one's first reaction to such a list of aims is to wonder whether any curriculum in domestic studies would be capable of rendering the manifold services now demanded of it (Musgrove, 1968). Certainly in this formulation the subject has moved far from its earlier aims of teaching the techniques of cookery, laundry work, housewifery and needlework.

Beyond this, perhaps the most striking point is the clear recognition shown in this statement of the need for a curriculum based on a sequence of learning experiences, each of which is aimed at the pursuit of multiple objectives. Some of these are specific, in the sense of being attainable only through a course in domestic studies. However, many are overarching, and need to be pursued simultaneously in all parts of the school curriculum. It is pleasing to record that all our reports showed eagerness to include school-wide objectives. The corollary, of course, is that all concerned should know where and when fruitful links between one part and another of a school's curriculum can be established. In the North West project we hope to provide for this as part of our backroom review of all pilot programmes, to which reference is made.

This panel's report, like others, gave clear indication of teachers' recognition that all objectives are developmental, roads to travel rather than terminal points to reach. Equally encouraging was the emphasis given to the generation and extension of emotions, attitudes and values—in particular the recognition that these need to be discovered rather than taught (e.g. 'to develop the realization that the discipline imposed by a task differs from that imposed by a teacher').

One possible criticism is that these aims offer insufficient guidance to a teacher as to the detailed knowledge and skills at which a domestic studies course should aim. Another is that the statements include umbrella-terms like 'understanding', 'judgement' and 'creativity', each a complex of several kinds of behaviour and in need of separation before effective teaching programmes can be developed.

Such criticisms invite further consideration of the function of educational objectives. In this project objectives provide a general orientation for development work by indicating appropriate emphases in course content, by guiding evaluators seeking evidence as to the programme's effectiveness and by serving as reference points when all experience gained is being fed back to provide starting points for further study. This means that objectives become increasingly clearly defined as the programme is written, taught and evaluated, and also that they can be changed when a new cycle of operations is being planned.

## INITIATION OF DEVELOPMENT SCHEMES

In the spring of 1968 teachers in all secondary schools in the region were invited to submit details of any new teaching programmes they wished to develop for early-leaving pupils. Over one hundred replies were received, on which seven regional and numerous other local schemes were based. One of the regional teams is concerning itself with experimental methods of teaching and school organization. The remainder are preparing teaching programmes for early leavers in English, moral education, technology, domestic studies, social (including health) education and creativity in the arts. The remainder of this paper deals only with the regional schemes.

Each development team was built up to about twenty-five teacher-members, and was supported from the same quarters as were our earlier group studies. Development work was begun in September 1968 and, apart from week-end conferences held at the beginning of each term, was carried on in one or other of the local development centres. Teacher-members were seconded from their normal school duties for one half day each week for this work.

It was thought necessary to set a definite target for 1970, the year in which the Schools Council grant runs out, when the project is due for review. Accordingly, the academic year 1968–9 was spent in programme writing, and the year 1969–70 is allocated for first field trials of the new courses. Approximately half of these trials are being carried out by teacher-members of the development teams in their own schools, the remainder being undertaken by volunteers from other schools in the region. Since all these teachers will also gather the data needed for evaluation, programme revision and second field trials should be possible before 1972–3.

However, this time-table imposed great pressure during 1968–9, when development teams needed to re-establish group identity (most of the development teams are inter-disciplinary), master the skills needed to translate objectives into planned teaching-learning experiences, write, review and print the programmes on which the trials are based. Inevitably, this meant that little time was available for exploring the potentialities of relatively unfamiliar resources, and our first trial programmes therefore reflect quite closely existing circumstances in schools in the region. For example, the domestic studies panel favours the use of the Velcro board rather than other forms of visual presentation, in the belief that many of the teachers to be concerned will lack technical skill in manipulating projectors and that many of the classrooms lack adequate black-out facilities.

Another consequence of this pressure is that arrangements

for evaluation had to be made before programme writing was complete; but this circumstance was turned to good account. Each development team appointed two of its teacher members to a regional assessment panel which met every other week. These members were encouraged to press the programme writers during intervening weeks for information, given in behavioural terms, about features of the programme which relate to particular objectives. In this way it was hoped to avoid the basic weakness of many teaching programmes, that of equating the curriculum with course content rather than with learning experiences. This linkage should also help to ensure consistency of viewpoint between programme writers and evaluators.

Since very few fifth-year early leavers are currently attending secondary schools in North West England the domestic studies team, in common with other panels, decided to prepare for 1970 a one-year programme for fourth-year early leavers, one requiring two half-days of teaching time per week. It was suggested that approximately half of this time be spent on cookery, needlework and other practical activities, and that the teaching be shared either by needlework and domestic science specialists or by one needlework/domestic science teacher and one other teacher.

By the time this programme had been written its specific objectives had been formulated in the following terms: to develop an understanding of the major stages of growth between birth and adolescence; to help young people to analyse, evaluate and develop their own emotional and physical characteristics; to develop an understanding of the needs and characteristics of others; to develop the capacity for judgement (forming considered opinions) and discrimination (exercising a choice); to foster skill in working co-operatively with a peer group rather than competitively to encourage pupils to develop an efficient system of organization.

The scheme is based on three major topics (the pupil herself, the family and the family within the home), each of which is intended to occupy one term's work. The first aims to increase the girls' understanding of her own physical and emotional development, to be achieved by making use of her interest in improving her appearance and by stimulating her sense of social awareness. The key episode is the planning, preparation and carrying through of a Christmas party for some section of the community. However, the term's work also features choice of clothes and making of gifts, a dress show and studies of diet, personal hygiene, hair styling and make-up, and a study of physical and emotional changes in adolescence.

The scheme subdivides into units, each covering the work of half a day; but this should not be taken to mean that during this period the pupil is expected to gain all the insights at which the unit aims. The major ideas are all to be studied many times during the scheme, in the contexts in which they arise. With this proviso the unit on emotional aspects of adolescence can be used to illustrate the degree of detail with which the scheme is presented.

The teachers' notes open with a general rubric listing the major insights of the unit, namely that though all pass through the stages of adolescence each does so in his own way and at his own rate, that early and late developers may worry about their differences from their contemporaries, that one of the tasks of adults is to help adolescents to fit into society (and therefore to conform) and that adolescents must also develop their own identity and autonomy. Next comes a statement of the knowledge content of the unit, followed by details of materials needed, of practical organization and of the lesson plan. In this case the pupils were asked first to list ways in which they had changed during the previous four years in appearance, behaviour, preferences and attitudes. Next, the pupils were to illustrate these changes in any appropriate way, and a list of emerging ideas for which the teacher should watch was given (e.g. that adolescents sometimes experience loneliness and depression, that it is sometimes difficult for parents to be less protective to adolescents than they were when the adolescents were children, that the onset of adolescence for the daughter may coincide with onset of the menopause for the mother). Next, the girls were to develop in role play their own interpretations of situations outlined on cards prepared by the development team. This would lead to discussion of questions arising from these improvizations and also of others previously written (anonymously) by the girls themselves and dropped into a question box. The unit also made provision for optional extensions to the work, should these be thought necessary.

Once a programme has been developed to this degree of definition it becomes possible both to examine critically its provision for pursuing the specific objectives on which it is based and to study those objectives in relation to the more general aims which would serve as an orientation for an extended programme in domestic studies. Together these two studies constitute the backroom review which, with the classroom review (the study of effects upon pupils of exposure to the programme) comprise the formative or intermediate evaluation. In other words formative evaluation of a curriculum attempts to answer the question 'How good is this course?' rather than merely the question 'How well does this course achieve its objectives?'

## GATHERING EVALUATIVE DATA

It will be clear that data gathered from our classroom review must be consistent with objectives, i.e. based on the same ideas of what is significant behaviour. Because of the multiplicity of our objectives this will entail testing pupils' knowledge, cognitive and affective powers, creativity and skills, a programme which can be realized (if at all) only through close co-operation with those who are teaching the trial programmes.

The North West project has adopted Tyler's (1967) approach to curriculum evaluation. This involves a comparison of each pupil's demonstrated abilities and attributes before and after the trial programme is given. This is not the basis normally used either in standardized achievement tests or in school examinations where results are recorded in terms of relative status. In criterion tests, however, emphasis is on the proportion of pupils who have mastered certain knowledge or skill.

This procedure can be illustrated from the assessment programme for the domestic studies panel. The panel's first objective was to develop an understanding of the major stages of growth between birth and adolescence, and it devised a four-part test to assess progress in this dimension. The first part dealt with the ages at which young children can be fed from a spoon, walk, scribble with a crayon, etc. The second part referred to the most important needs (from given lists) of babies, five-year-olds, eight-year-olds and eleven-year-olds. The third and fourth sections presented true–false statements about adolescence and adulthood respectively, e.g. it is impossible for a girl of thirteen to have a baby, during a period it is best for a girl to carry on normal activities, all women undergo physical changes in middle age, it is easy for adults to remember the changes they went through themselves in adolescence.

Once a test of this nature is available many new matters are opened up for discussion. Are all the questions asked worth including in this test and are any of the important areas of knowledge concerned with this objective left untested? Are the answers for which credit is given the most correct ones? Were the pupils handicapped in responding to the test by failure to understand its form (though they knew some at least of the answers for which it called? Is the mark scheme properly weighted, so that pupils awarded high scores may fairly be assumed to know more (or to have more important) knowledge than those who have been awarded lower scores? Does the test paper as a whole represent a valid sample of the knowledge we wish our pupils to acquire under this objective from the new programme? What total score is to be accepted as the threshold for adequate pupil performance? Is knowledge such as that called for in this test to be equated with 'understanding'? If not, what elements are missing, in which situations could their existence be detected and how might these be assessed? If all objectives are roads to travel, how might the level of achievement reached here be improved upon in the succeeding year's programme?

This approach to data-gathering has been adopted in respect of all six of this panel's objectives (as well as in other panels), but restrictions of space limit discussion here to one more example of the panel's procedures. Objective 6 was concerned with the development of an efficient system or organization. The instructions made it clear that this objective concerned efficiency of individual rather than of group organization, and teachers were asked to rate their pupils on three separate occasions—when making a dress or presents, when entertaining family groups and when planning assignments and meals for particular family circumstances. A twenty-point scale was constructed, as follows:

17–20 Pupil plans and carries out a complex piece of organization, unaided and with good results. Pupil shows the ability to construct a plan and keeps to it or to adapt it where necessary. In making her plan the girl takes into consideration all relevant factors, e.g. the time and space available.

13–16 Able to pre-plan but has difficulty in adapting where necessary.

9–12 Shows some ability to pre-plan, but sometimes goes beyond her capabilities or does not plan enough work to occupy her time.

5–8 Able to carry out work but needs help with planning.

1–4 Able to carry out work only with constant help in organization and planning.

0 Unable to carry out work in an organized way.

Again, once these proposals for gathering data are formulated an array of questions for discussion is opened up. Is the grading scale uni-dimensional? Are the selected work situations typical of those covered by the objective? Does the behaviour demonstrable within these situations cover the full range of behaviour implied in the objective? How could one build upon achievement at this level in a later programme, etc.?

FORMATIVE EVALUATION AND FEEDBACK

Since evaluation is to be based on a comparison between pre-trial and post-trial performances decisions in three areas will be needed before data processing can begin. First, wherever progress is seen in terms of exceeding a critical level of performance it will be necessary to decide what that level is to be. Once this is done results can be summarized in the following form :

At the end of this course we found that, of our sample of fifteen-year-old early leavers drawn from a wide range of areas in North West England :

75 per cent (38 per cent) knew details of the physical, emotional and social stages of development through which all human beings pass from birth to adolescence;
57 per cent (41 per cent) could work efficiently in individual practical tasks in domestic studies, etc.

In this report the percentages in brackets would refer to results recorded for the same pupils before the experimental programme was taught.

Another interpretation of progress is based on improvement made during the course, irrespective of the end-of-course level of achievement. Thus a second area for decision might focus on an attempt to classify as successful all pupils whose post-trial awards exceeded their pre-trial awards by, say, five points on a twenty-point scale. Whilst this procedure might add considerably to the information available about the outcomes of a trial it suffers from the handicap of assuming an equality which may not exist among the intervals comprising a scale.

Analytic assessments of the types outlined above are frequently criticized as being 'atomistic', i.e. as assuming that human behaviour is composed of isolated reactions each of which can be understood, explained and assessed as a separate entity. It is necessary, therefore, to affirm our recognition that, since organic unity is the essential characteristic of human behaviour, no single type of growth can be fully achieved without progress also in others, and no single aspect of pupil behaviour can be fully understood without reference to the total behaviour pattern. We therefore intend to supplement our data on the number of pupils who progress in each dimension with data on the number of dimensions in which each pupil progresses. This will involve a third area for decision on critical levels of performance, to permit separation of those pupils who have from those who have not made general progress.

In an attempt to save time backroom review of our experimental programmes is being begun during 1969–70, whilst the first field trials are taking place. This review of all programmes will be in the hands of a single study group, thus enabling linkages to be arranged between different programmes at appropriate points.

The essential problem in curriculum construction (and hence in curriculum evaluation) is one of reconciling its logical and its psychological requirements. The scope of our review may perhaps best be appreciated by listing a series of questions we intend asking about each of our trial programmes.

First, we must consider the content, the ideas round which the course is built. Does our teaching accord with contemporary knowledge in the field or are we including discredited ideas? Furthermore, does our programme include *all* the basic ideas concerned or are we wasting valuable time on insignificant detail? Beyond this we need to decide whether the course is consistent with social reality, in the sense of providing the most useful orientation to the world in which these pupils live.

Another range of questions focusses on the balance between breadth (coverage) and depth in study. Does our programme provide an adequate but not excessive range of opportunities for pupils to grasp the basic insights we aim to teach? Does the range of experiences offered encourage cognitive mastery of basic ideas, growth of increased sensitivity and study of appropriate values?

Many questions focus on the sequence in which learning activities are scheduled. What provision is made for reinforcing at appropriate intervals understandings accumulated earlier? Is the programme appropriately focussed (i.e. can a term's work towards the stated objectives adequately be concentrated on the planning, preparation for and carrying through of a play group for young children)? Does the programme provide adequately for a variety of ways of learning—reading, writing, observing, organizing, analysing, discussing, tabulating, cooking, constructing, dramatizing, etc.—so that all pupils have the opportunity to gain fundamental insights from those types of activity in which they can gain these most easily, and also that these insights are eventually more firmly rooted through being tied to a number of different kinds of experience? What provision is made for acquiring the needed 'service' skills (e.g. of library research) before these skills are needed? What provision is made for cumulative learning when the course is extended?

Finally, a range of questions focusses on the adaptability of the programme. What provision does it make for supplementary (remedial or extension) work to cater for individual differences among the pupils? Above all, perhaps, how adaptable is the programme to unanticipated experience or insight on the part of the pupils?

We expect to find from our first trials that the experimental programmes are comparatively crude and in need of substantial refinement before there is any hope of achieving much success with them. We may also have to reconsider after this trial the content and form of some data-gathering devices. The results of all such evaluation will be fed back into the programme before second trials begin. However, we do not expect at this stage any substantial changes in the range of our objectives, though they may then be reformulated rather more precisely.

Present arrangements are that the year 1970–1 will be given over to evaluation of first field trials and revision of trial programmes. Second field trials are due in 1971–2 and, if our earlier work has been adequate, may be expected to function relatively smoothly. This will make it possible to concentrate attention in our second formative evaluation on the range of development patterns exhibited by pupils successfully following this programme. What these patterns will be it is difficult to forecast at present with any degree of accuracy, for reasons indicated at the beginning of this paper. However, they may be attributed to the programme's offering a suitable combination of coherence, support and flexibility to the pupils concerned in their attempts to master the ideas, skills, sensitivities, attitudes and values underlying the programme. Thus the feedback from the second evaluation will take the form of capitalizing on the programme's demonstrated strengths and eradicating its evident weaknesses, so as to increase its effectiveness for pupils of the types concerned and, hopefully, to increase the range of its effectiveness, for other pupils. During this feedback it may be decided to amend or to drop some of the objectives originally postulated, and/or to add others to the programme.

At this point in the project study of the common characteristics of different programmes can be begun, and from this we may identify some dimensions of a model teaching-learning unit for pupils in this age and ability range. If these can be identified one method will have been demonstrated for translating theoretical ideas into functioning curricula and testing these in classroom experiments. From such beginnings a new approach to the formulation of a more adequate theory of curriculum could perhaps be attempted in due course.

### REFERENCES

DEPARTMENT OF EDUCATION AND SCIENCE (1967) *Children and Their Primary Schools*. London: H.M. Stationery Office, para. 350.

MUSGROVE, F. (1968) 'Curriculum objectives.' *J. Curr. Studies*, *1*, 5–18.

PETERS, R. S. (ed.) (1969) *Perspectives on Plowden*. London: Routledge and Kegan Paul.

TABA, H. (1962) *Curriculum Development: Theory and Practice*. New York: Harcourt Brace, ch. 20.

K

TYLER, R. W. *et al.* (1967) *Perspectives of Curriculum Evaluation.*
Chicago : Rand McNally.

WILLIAMS, J. (1968) 'The Curriculum : Some Patterns of Develop-
ment and Design for Evaluation.' In BUTCHER, H. J. (ed.)
*Educational Research in Britain 1.* London : University of
London Press.

*Curriculum development is essentially a task for a team of
workers and is usually planned and carried out on a national, or
at least a regional scale. The important task of evaluation—
basically a large-scale national matter also—may be supplemented by local studies, and the article which follows provides
an example of an evaluation study on the scale which can be
tackled by a small local group.*

## A Local Evaluation of Primary School French
(J. D. Nisbet and J. Welsh, 1972)[1]

### INTRODUCTION

With the introduction of French in nearly all primary schools
in Aberdeen, the secondary school intake of 1969 offered a last
opportunity of comparing the subsequent performance in French
of those who had, and those who had not, studied French in
primary school. The evaluation was planned to use available
school records as far as possible, and though it extended over
two years of secondary education, it involved only two short
extra assignments for the pupils—a 20-minute oral test and a
five-minute rating scale administered twice in one school.

### PROCEDURE AND SAMPLES

The sample was initially defined by the application of NFER
Listening Comprehension Test (LCA), a test of spoken French
recorded on tape, administered by one of the writers to pupils in
secondary schools in Aberdeen in December 1969 at the end of
their first term of the first year. In all, 1,947 pupils' scores were
recorded; and at the same time the pupils stated whether or not
they had been taught French in their last year at primary school
or previously in primary school, and named the teacher who had
taught them French. The teacher's name was included as a

---

[1] This article appeared in the *Journal of Curriculum Studies, 4,* 1972.

check on the pupils' replies and also to allow the influence of teachers' experience and qualifications to be examined.

The pupils were allocated to one of three groups for the analysis of the data :

GROUP  F :    964 pupils who had been taught French in the last year of primary school (and possibly also before that) by a teacher on the education authority's list of teachers of French.

GROUP FX :    116 pupils who reported that they had been taught French, but not in the last year of primary school, or not in Aberdeen, or by a teacher not on the 'official' list.

GROUP NF :    867 pupils who had not been taught French in primary school.

All these pupils had sat a verbal reasoning test, Moray House VR 81, in the second last year of primary school, and another parallel test, MH VR 85, in the last year of primary school. Also, headteachers of the primary schools had made a general assessment of the pupils' attainment on a nine-point scale (1 high, 9 low). When the mean scores on these three assessments were calculated for Groups F, FX and NF, Group F was shown to be slightly superior to the other groups (see Table 14:1). Two matched groups were therefore constructed from Group F and NF, equating the frequency distribution of each group on VR 81, with random selection until numbers were equivalent in each frequency grouping: from Group F, 388 boys and 347 girls; from Group NF, 388 boys and 347 girls also. Performance in French of these two matched groups provided a more precise measure of comparison (see Table 14:2).

At the end of the first year of secondary school, marks in school examinations in French were recorded for 731 of the pupils in Group F, and 610 of the pupils in Group NF. There were 76 pupils from Group FX also involved in these examinations, but they were omitted from the analysis of results. A number of other pupils were omitted because of absence, and because two of the schools did not reply to our request for access to marks. Each school set its own examinations, and some set separate examinations for different class groupings. It was not possible to combine the marks on these different examinations. Each examination was therefore considered separately. Two cut-off levels were determined in each set of marks, separating the top third, the middle third and the bottom third. In each third, the number of pupils from Group F and the number from Group NF were noted. The hypothesis tested by this procedure was that, if primary school French did not give Group F pupils any advantage, the proportions of Group F and NF in each third would not differ from chance distribution. If primary school French did confer an advantage, one would expect a larger proportion of Group F to be in the top third. (The slight superiority of Group F mentioned above introduced a bias in their favour; but if the null hypothesis were confirmed and no differences in proportion were observed, the result could then be accepted all the more confidently.)

At the end of the second year of secondary school, this procedure was repeated in six schools, involving 687 pupils, 379 from Group F and 308 from Group NF.

A different form of criterion was applied to a group of 535 pupils, 271 from Group F and 264 from Group NF, from three secondary schools where pupils made a decision to continue or drop French at the beginning of the third year. This decision was taken as an indication of attitude as well as of attainment.

A direct measure of attitude was obtained in one secondary school, where 162 pupils (76 from Group F, 86 from Group NF) ranked six school subjects (English, French, history, geography, maths, science) in order of liking at the end of first year, and again at the end of second year.

Other aspects which were considered included :

*i.* the attitudes of headteachers and primary school teachers of French, as assesed by ten items of the NFER scale of attitude to French in primary school, and the relation of these attitudes to the performance of pupils from the primary schools in which these teachers worked;

*ii.* the qualifications of the teachers of French, assessed in three categories (university degree in French; Higher French in Scottish Certificate of Education and in-service training; SCE French without in-service training), in relation to their pupils' performance;

*iii.* other school and teacher variables, including age and experience of teacher, time spent on French, whether the classes were mixed or streamed, and whether the teacher was a visiting teacher or was working with her own class;

*iv.* the performance in French of pupils whose verbal reasoning quotient was below 100.

RESULTS

Mean scores in the NFER Listening Comprehension Test (LCA) at the end of the first term in secondary school, are given in Table 14:1 for the whole group, and in Table 14:2 for the matched groups equated for verbal reasoning score. Mean scores for the other primary school assessments are also shown in these tables. The results show clearly that those who had been taught

French in primary school scored higher on average in this test of oral comprehension of French vocabulary. The mean score for girls is significantly superior to that of boys in both the F and NF groups.

TABLE 14:1  *Mean scores on first-term oral test (and primary school assessments)*

| Test | Group F | FX | NF |
|------|---------|-----|-----|
| NFER LCA | 24·82 | 20·50 | 18·94 |
| MH VR 81 | 104·05 | 99·90 | 99·70 |
| MH VR 85 | 103·10 | 99·65 | 100·05 |
| School rating | 4·49 | 4·80 | 5·03 |
| (1 high, 9 low) | | | |
| N | 964 | 116 | 867 |

TABLE 14:2  *Mean scores on first-term oral test: matched groups (standard deviations in brackets)*

| | Boys | | Girls | |
|------|---------|-----|-----|-----|
| Test | Group F | NF | F | NF |
| NFER LCA | 22·74 | 18·66 | 24·82 | 20·10 |
| | (7·20) | (6·40) | (7·92) | (7·16) |
| MH VR 81 | 101·75 | 101·75 | 101·25 | 101·25 |
| | (13·55) | (13·55) | (13·25) | (13·25) |
| MH VR 85 | 100·65 | 101·75 | 101·20 | 101·60 |
| | (13·60) | (13·45) | (12·90) | (13·10) |
| School rating | 4·81 | 4·90 | 4·75 | 4·75 |
| | (1·82) | (1·71) | (1·68) | (1·65) |
| N | 388 | 388 | 347 | 347 |

By the end of the first year of secondary school, however, it appeared that this advantage had diminished or even disappeared. The division of each set of school examination marks into top third, middle third and bottom third, showed only a slight tendency for Group F pupils to appear more often in the top third of the examination order of merit; but this trend was not significant on chi-square tests applied to the total of 1341 pupils, nor to the boys or girls separately (Table 14:3). The girls' performance was still significantly superior to that of the boys.

TABLE 14:3  *Numbers of pupils from Groups F and NF in the top, middle and bottom thirds in school examinations in French at the end of first year*

| | Boys | | Girls | | All | | |
|------|-----|-----|-----|-----|-----|-----|--------|
| | F | NF | F | NF | F | FN | Totals |
| Top third | 103 | 82 | 150 | 102 | 253 | 184 | 437 |
| Middle third | 113 | 126 | 145 | 94 | 258 | 220 | 478 |
| Bottom third | 129 | 138 | 91 | 68 | 220 | 206 | 426 |
| Totals | 345 | 346 | 386 | 264 | 731 | 610 | 1341 |

(76 pupils from Group NF excluded)

As a check on the validity of this procedure of grouping into thirds, results for each school, and for each examination within schools, were analysed separately. In only two of the twelve

secondary schools involved, was there a significant difference in
the proportions of Group F pupils and Group NF pupils in the top
and bottom thirds. In these two schools, more F pupils were in
the top third; and this finding was confirmed by a significant
difference between the mean examination scores of F and NF
pupils, in favour of the F pupils. In spite of further inquiry, no
obvious reason emerged why these two schools should show a
different pattern of results from the others. Both schools, however, were distinctive in the extent to which they used audio–
visual aids, television and language laboratory. Also in both
schools, the French teachers expressed favourable attitudes to the
teaching of French in primary school, and spoke enthusiastically
about the competence of the teachers of French in the feeder
primary schools.

By the end of the second year, the slight and non-significant
superiority of Group F pupils had disappeared completely. Marks
in French were obtained from seven of the largest secondary
schools; and the division into the top, middle and bottom thirds
yielded no significant results in any school, or in the seven schools
combined Table (14:4).

TABLE 14:4    *Numbers of pupils from Groups F and NF in the top, middle
and bottom thirds in school examinations in French at the end of second
year*

|  | Group F | NF | Total |
|---|---|---|---|
| Top third | 117 | 102 | 219 |
| Middle third | 135 | 104 | 239 |
| Bottom third | 127 | 102 | 229 |
| Total | 379 | 308 | 687 |

In the three secondary schools which were able to supply
information on the numbers of pupils continuing French into the
third year of secondary school, a significant difference did emerge,
with proportionately more Group F pupils continuing the study
of French and fewer dropping the subject (Table 14:5).

TABLE 14:5    *Numbers of pupils continuing French in third year of secondary
school*

|  | Group F | NF | Total |
|---|---|---|---|
| Continuing French | 96 | 62 | 158 |
| Dropping French | 175 | 202 | 377 |
| Total | 271 | 264 | 535 |

These results are consistent with the earlier assessments of
attitudes to French. Only one school was involved in this exercise, but from the limited evidence it appeared that learning
French in primary school had removed some of the initial interest
in the subject. At the end of first year, only 30 per cent of Group
F pupils rated French among the three most liked subjects, against

42 per cent of Group NF pupils (Table 14:6). Since the F pupils were repeating ground already covered, this result is not surprising. At the end of the second year, however, the position had changed: now 50 per cent of Group F pupils rated French in the top three, and only 36 per cent of Group NF pupils.

TABLE 14:6 *Numbers of pupils rating French among the three most liked subjects, in first year and in second year*

| Rating of French | First year | | Second year | |
| --- | --- | --- | --- | --- |
| | F | NF | F | NF |
| In top three | 24 | 36 | 38 | 31 |
| In last three | 52 | 50 | 38 | 55 |
| Total | 76 | 86 | 76 | 86 |

In both first and second years, more girls than boys rated French among the three best liked subjects: first year, 48 per cent of girls, 25 per cent of boys; second year, 57 per cent of girls, 26 per cent of boys.

The remaining aspects of the evaluation can be summarised briefly. The scores of primary school headteachers and of primary school teachers of French on the NFER scale of attitude to French in primary school showed a non-linear relationship, significant on a chi-square test, with the performance of their pupils on the LCA test in first year of secondary school. Where heads and teachers had either very favourable or unfavourable attitudes, pupils tended to have fewer high scores on LCA. However, this result was probably attributable to differences between schools in the general level of pupils' ability. The teachers' qualifications in French showed no significant relationship with pupils' LCA score; but this finding may also be specific to the Aberdeen situation, as the teachers had been specially selected. There were no significant relationships with any of the other school and teacher variables, such as age and experience of teacher, time spent on French, and whether the classes were mixed or streamed.

The performance of pupils who had low scores on the verbal reasoning test at age 12, was examined separately to explore the hypothesis that primary school French might reveal oral skills among pupils customarily regarded as below average. In the total group of 1,947 pupils, there were 626 who scored 94 or less on Verbal Reasoning Test 85; and of these 72 (41 boys, 31 girls) scored above 20 (out of a maximum of 40) on the oral test LCA. In the total group, 1080 scored above 20 on LCA. Of the 72, all except eight scored between 21 and 28 on LCA. Individual examination of the eight high-scoring cases gave no indication of any reason for this level of achievement other than possible test unreliability. In this sample, therefore, there is little support for the view that primary school French reveals talent hidden by conventional teaching.

CONCLUSION AND DISCUSSION

The results from this follow up to the beginning of the third year of secondary school suggests that primary school French confers some initial advantage, but this advantage diminishes and disappears during the first two secondary years. This is perhaps to be expected, as no provision was made for continuity of teaching from primary to secondary school. Presented with mixed classes, some having studied French previously and some not, secondary school teachers started again from the beginning with all pupils. In the current session (1971–72), a few secondary schools have been able to group together first-year pupils who show achievement in French. When numbers are sufficient to allow a separate study of the performance of these pupils, the results of the present inquiry will provide an interesting basis for comparison.

The effect of primary school French in this study appears to have been on attitude rather than on attainment, and possibly this is in keeping with the objectives of those who advocate the teaching of French in primary school. In the first year of secondary school, since all pupils started French afresh, the stimulus of novelty was lost for those who already knew some French, and its popularity suffered. But subsequently the subject re-established a favourable position with those who had been introduced to it in primary school.

Girls had consistently more favourable attitudes to French, and better performance in it, than boys.

The interest of this study—and also its limitation—is that it is a local study based on the special circumstances of the session when it was initiated. Clearly, some of the findings have only local application—for example, that the qualifications of the primary school teachers of French were unrelated to the attainment of their pupils. If generalisation is permissible from this limited study, the conclusion would appear to be that one should not expect primary school French to confer a lasting advantage, but that justification for the inclusion of French should be within the context of the primary school curriculum in terms of its contribution to the enlargement of interests and understanding and the development of general language skill, rather than its effectiveness as a preparation for secondary school work. An evaluative follow-up of the kind described here is of value if it highlights problems such as the fluctuations in pupils' attitudes and the need for continuity in teaching.

*If the articles and questions selected for this chapter appear to emphasise evaluation rather than curriculum reform, this is a bias which would be approved by many of those who are engaged in curriculum development. Until quite recently, there was a ten-*

*dency to neglect evaluation, as Wiseman noted in the lecture
from which the following extract is taken.*

## Curriculum Development and Curriculum
## Evaluation    (S. Wiseman, 1969)[1]

Evaluation is an essential part of the process of curriculum
development: if it is ignored, then the new syllabuses, produced
with hope and optimism, will become entrenched as firmly as
those they replace, and the end results will merely be the substitution of a new set of chains for the imprisonment of the
teachers and their pupils. The present wave of curriculum reform
has occurred—somewhat belatedly—in response to the demands
of a rapidly changing social environment. Such change will undoubtedly continue, and our new curricula must be capable of
adaptation to continuing change. In any case, we are all neo-
phytes in the difficult process of curriculum planning: our first
efforts are bound to be deficient and inexpert in many respects.
It is necessary, therefore, to validate our new products and to
test our expertise, and this can only be done by building-in to the
process, right from the start, an adequate system of evaluation.

I would be the last person to denigrate the previous efforts in
curriculum change such as the Nuffield Science projects, but it is
clear that the necessity for evaluation was not fully recognised
when such projects were planned. And I seem to discern a similar
lack in those Schools Council projects already under way. If this
is indeed so, then it is a crucial weakness that must be remedied
with all speed, since evaluation must form an integral part of
curriculum change right from the start: we ignore it at our peril.

*Evaluation is the part of curriculum development which
draws most heavily on the techniques and procedures of research
described in previous chapters. It is customary to distinguish
research and development, as two interacting phases of the
process of change. Research aims to give new insights; development is the working out of these new ideas within the context
of what is practicable. But the boundary between research and
development is not a sharp one, as Wrigley (1970) explains.*

> 'Most of us in the Schools Council do not believe that there
> is a very clear division between curriculum development and
> research. Obviously there is some difference, but it is not a
> clear-cut one. My colleagues in the Research Team are
> certainly interested in curriculum development, and curricu-

[1] Extracted from an article in *Research in Education*, *1*, 1–8.

*lum developers are often engaged in research activities. Perhaps an obvious difference is that in a development project, materials, either for teachers or pupils, are usually produced in the form of books, work cards, throw-away temporary packages, structural and scientific apparatus, film loops, tape recordings, etc. It is worth noting that, at the time of writing, only one set of materials has been published as a result of Schools Council projects, though, of course, materials have emerged from the Nuffield work. When more Schools Council materials do emerge, the impact of the Council and its influence will be seen to be rather different from what it is at present when its publications are still mainly in the form of research reports and working papers of a general nature' (pages 24–5).*

Even where research has provided evidence of the value of a new syllabus, implementation in the development phase may still create difficulties. Some of these problems are considered in the final article in this chapter: though this article refers to the Schools Council Humanities Project, the points made have a wider application.

## Curriculum Research and Development Projects: Barriers to Success
(B. Macdonald and J. Rudduck, 1971)[1]

### INTRODUCTION

This article is based on our experience of one curriculum project which, following three years of research and development, is now on offer in the educational market place. Given that proposals for curriculum reform differ in their concerns and in their levels of aspiration, we recognise that much of our experience may be idiosyncratic and that all of it has been limited. It may be helpful to suggest that our experience is particularly relevant to curriculum interventions which have the following characteristics :

    *a.* They make heavy demands upon the people and institutions engaged in the enterprise.
    *b.* They embody value positions which are sufficiently innovatory to mobilise forces of resistance.
    *c.* They are so unfamiliar in their design that they pose serious problems of understanding.

[1] This article appeared originally in *British Journal of Educational Psychology*, 41, 148–54.

Given that the focus of this article is upon barriers to curriculum experiment, we believe that these constitute crucial features of the Humanities Project. This is a national curriculum development project which is very exacting of resources and skills, and is not readily assimilated to existing practice. Its exploratory stage in a limited number of schools enabled the central team to estimate the demands of the programme on the schools in terms of management, resources, roles and relationships. In the diffusion stage, these demands extend outside the school in terms of personnel and resources for training and support programmes.

Despite the title of this article, we are concerned less with conceptions of success than with identifying certain obstacles to experimentation and implementation. We want to look at the anatomy of innovation from the point of view of the pathologist.

There may be a suspicion that the weak points that give rise to failure in curriculum development must lie within the system. But the system is 'given' and it is for a development team to find out how the system works in order to cope effectively with its characteristics. Curriculum development teams, particularly in America, evince a preference for a pattern of development and diffusion in which a finished programme, by virtue of the prestige and authority of its originators, is carried intact through the diffusion chain to the classroom. This article explores the problems of opting for an alternative plan which is sensitive to the diversity of educational settings and recognises the autonomy of decision makers at different levels of the system.

The Humanities Curriculum Project is an example of this alternative approach. The central assumption of the Project's design is that there can be no effective far-reaching curriculum development without teacher development. It has, therefore, attempted to share both its research and its development role with participating system personnel. Our experience of the problems encountered in this kind of exercise underlines the need for development teams to pay greater attention to the following:

1   Studying the range of environments in which the programme will eventually be located. In a decentralised system in which individual schools enjoy a great deal of autonomy, this means more than the observation of classrooms. It encompasses the study of institutions and of areas.

2   Communicating effectively the nature of the enterprise. Dilution and distortion of a programme can frequently be traced to the persistence of mistaken assumptions.

What these propositions add up to is a need for an understanding of the school situation. 'A new look at teaching, if there is to be one, seems to require us to move up closer to the phenomenon of the teacher's world' (Jackson, 1968, page 150).

The teacher's world is complex, and it is a heavy responsibility for a development team to set out to recognise (or anticipate) and to work within such complexity, particularly when elements in the compound might be institutional apathy and a generally cautious conservatism. A major point of failure for this paper would be an over-simplification of the reasons why curriculum development fails to have impact.

### PROBLEMS OF UNDERSTANDING

Ultimately one must have teachers who participate in the management of their own development. But there is a tendency in curriculum development programmes which are centrally organised for teachers to invest the development team with the kind of authority which can atrophy independence of judgement in individual school settings. Probably some degree of authority or charisma from a body external to the school is necessary to stimulate re-thinking of curriculum activity. Once the development project is under way, however, the authority becomes dysfunctional and can create either a cult or a rebellion; teachers look to the development team for answers, and this reliance on authority implies that there is little independent self-criticism in the innovatory approach. On the other hand, the development team's concern to impart an understanding of procedure as it relates to theory can release the professional judgment and imagination of teachers : 'Failure to grasp underlying principles leads to unintelligent rule-of-thumb application of rules and the inability to make exceptions on relevant grounds and to bewilderment in novel situations' (Peters, 1967, page 6).

Allied to the idea of 'corrosive effects of dependency' is the concept of individuality. Whereas some teachers hesitate at the prospect of self-direction, others are anxious about effacement of personal style through mandatory and narrowly interpreted specifications of method. Curriculum development will not be effective in the long term unless it is seen to be capable of being tailored to the circumstances and temper of particular schools and individual teachers.

There is often an assumption that the values of a curriculum development programme are intrinsically good and that it is therefore the task of the school to make the programme succeed. Where the development team is relying, during the preliminary trial period, on feedback from teachers, the reports can be biased in that teachers interpret difficulty as a reflection on their own competence, or alternatively on the competence of the project, and not as a possible cue to modifying one of the experimental variables. The burden of report forms necessary for feedback can add to unfounded feelings of anxiety and guilt. In experiment, it would seem to be important for people involved to understand that the curriculum developers are the learners and that the school is the teacher.

The head, or principal, of the school is such a key figure that effective curriculum development requires of him not merely goodwill but also understanding. From a reasonably full knowledge of the curriculum development he will be able to make appropriate choices in terms of staff, material resources and organisation, to be sensitive to the tensions that invariably arise in the process of innovation, and to provide for the innovating teachers a background of support without dominance.

It is for the development group to anticipate the importance of the nature and quality of the project's early communication with the head or principal of the school. For instance, the head will be concerned about the presentation of the curriculum development exercise within his school, and he may need to be alerted to possible effects of different strategies of organisation and communication. Where the innovating group involves only a small proportion of the total staff, and where it draws status members, the system will clearly have given recognition to the development exercise and open communication with the system can take place—but at a cost; the norms and pressures of the system are likely to modify the innovation. Where a number of teachers outside the nucleus of innovating teachers can be initially informed and even peripherally involved in the curriculum development, effects of the experiment which transfer into other areas of the curriculum are likely to be more favourably regarded. Alternatively, from his knowledge of the climate of opinion within his school, a head may decide to protect the experiment from general scrutiny until it has developed some degree of autonomy and resistance. It is for the central development team to bring to the notice of the head or principal what appear to be crucial points for decision so that he can act autonomously. They must make clear, in those early stages, the need for support from the head for innovating teachers, and possibly also from meetings with colleagues involved in similar curriculum projects in other schools; it is also the responsibility of the central team to set up ways of helping teachers to interpret and make judgments about the feedback from their own new practices. The capacity for constructive self-criticism is central to the concept of teacher development through curriculum development.

## TAKING ACCOUNT OF THE SYSTEM

People who have to make decisions about organisation may do so on the basis of insufficient understanding of the nature of the curriculum development project. It is for the central development team to provide as much information as possible at the stage of diffusion about organisational preconditions and the likely effects of particular patterns of organisation. The following statements are speculative, but would seem, in our experience, to focus on critical areas for decision-making. Our experience suggests that there are two settings which may not be conducive to curriculum development exercise. Heads, recognising these settings in their schools, may need to give particular consideration to the desirability of involvement in the development project:

*i.* It seems that an experiment settles well in a school where teachers are confronting a problem and contemplating action. The experiment should extend the range of their strategies for dealing with the problem. However, where an internally conceived programme is already well advanced, involvement in a national curiculum development project either produces bewilderment or results in a exploitation of elements of the national programme with no generalisable experimental data.

*ii.* It is sometimes suggested that experiment is more likely to succeed against a background of stability rather than of flux. This may be so; it needs to be looked at carefully. Many schools in England are in process of re-organisation (this generally implies that a secondary school is becoming comprehensive). The new system which emerges may retain or even reinforce the existing values, but it may represent a change of values. Where the hierarchy is likely to be re-shaped through reorganisation, and where teachers are anxious about their future, the tendency may be to demonstrate solidarity with the *status quo* and not to undertake the risks of innovation—unless the values of that innovation are ones towards which the school is seen to be moving.

A development team which at its exploratory stage stays close to the working context of its operations will encounter a range of institutional phenomena and become aware of the range of concerns which influence curricular action. The unfolding form of the project in particular settings may reveal powerful motivations which are not made explicit.

For instance, it seems that there may be a phenomenon which could be described as innovation without change. A head or principal may be beguiled by the cachet of innovation and become involved in a development project without its being esteemed by the power nucleus of the school. The school may try to protect itself from real change by immuring the curriculum development within a small area of the timetable, by involving only one or a few low-status teachers and by providing little opportunity for communication with the rest of the school. Such a phenomenon is consistent with the growing concern of schools —and particularly English secondary modern schools—to improve their 'brand image' through external appearances such as school uniform. On this analogy, innovation without change involves merely a modification in the packaging of the curriculum and does not necessarily involve the school in any concern with modification of content.

In assessing the change potential of the project, the developers need to understand what are the major concerns of teachers. For instance, the question of social control is often a dominant feature of teacher sub-culture and will probably be a concealed criterion in a school's examination of the aims and effects of the curriculum development. Where curriculum development works towards changing student/teacher relationships, it can be important that the difficulty of the task facing the school be estimated from an approximate identification of the school's position on a custodial humanistic-continuum of attitudes towards pupil control.

> 'A custodial pupil ideology stresses the maintenance of order, distrust of students, and a punitive, moralistic approach to pupil control. A humanistic ideology emphasises an accepting, trustful view of pupils and optimism concerning their ability to be self-disciplining and responsible' (Willower, 1958).

Many schools have not clearly articulated their own ideological stand, and part of the problem is to help a head to analyse the situation in such a way that he can predict the unique effects which a curriculum development exercise, clearly described, is likely to have within his school.

If the curriculum development experiment demands an unlearning of teaching habits, then it can initially breed diffidence. Habits are 'comfortable, predictable and anxiety-free'. In the early stages of experiment there will be periods when progress is becalmed. It takes time to learn to handle a new tool and it will appear less effective than the one it replaces until the practitioner comes to know its potential and to feel confident in the new style. This is probably even true of the introduction of a new textbook. Rubin (1969) of the University of California, Santa Barbara, has described this initial decrease in effectiveness as an inverse Hawthorne effect.

Pressures on the individual teacher and on the school as a whole may be great. It may be that the school which can best cope with experiment is one where there is some slack in the system. In practice, teachers generally are so concerned with system maintenance that their energy is spent in running to keep up with the *status quo*. Innovation needs time : time for teachers to familiarise themselves with any new teaching materials; time to reflect individually and with colleagues on new experiences. Louis Rubin argues that any school can, if it values curriculum development, make time for the professional growth of its staff; but it is not unknown in this country for teachers involved in experiment to lose free time as the price of enthusiasm. It is in their managerial role that heads may need assistance.

In organisation backing, it is the little things, such as plugs for tape-recorders, and shelving for materials which can mean a lot. Lack of foresight here can have absurdly far-reaching effects, and it is for the central development team to ensure, through adequate communication, that decision-makers have foresight rather than merely hindsight.

Enthusiasm is no substitute for adequate resource support. If the organisation specification has been made known to heads, it is their responsibility to see that the pattern of implementation and support is adequate. There is a misconception of curriculum heroism that boasts : 'The experiment demands small classes of pupils, but we are game enough to try even with our large groups.' Equally out of tune with the nature and conduct of experiment is the head who believes in the Spartan test of experiment proving itself in the very worst conditions : 'If it works here, it will work anywhere.' But the first task in the preliminary trial period is to see what is possible in normal conditions. Only then can the programme's tolerance to different kinds of organisational disadvantage be productively studied.

Care with the selection of rooms and resources will release teachers from peripheral anxieties and unnecessary fatigue which, in an intellectually demanding exercise, can quickly lower morale.

A NOTE ON CONTINUITY TRAINING

If the lessons of experience are learned, they will influence the structure and emphasis of diffusion patterns. This final section focuses on precautions against the dilution of the project as it is widely introduced and as responsibility for communication is invested in points increasingly more remote from the centre.

a. *Communications*

The development team needs to give thought to the language of communication. A central team working closely together and with its experimental teachers will inevitably build up an in-group set of words and phrases which function as a relief map to the project's thinking. In time, as novel insights are more confidently identified, language hardens into an efficient in-group shorthand. Familiarity diminishes the expectation of misinterpretation, and either new phrases and new uses of old words will have to be carefully defined against present understandings, or simple long-hand equivalents will need to be traced out. The inbred language of the early stages of experiment will not meet the needs of the diffusion of curriculum development.

If Jackson's propositions are sound, the problem of language is still more complex. His observations in schools led him to conclude that the teacher subculture discourse tends to be relatively free of technical terms: 'The absence of technical terms is related to another aspect of teachers' talk: its conceptual simplicity. Not only do teachers avoid elaborate words, they also seem to shun elaborate ideas ... Four aspects of the conceptual simplicity revealed in teachers' language are worthy of comment. These are:

1  an uncomplicated view of causality;
2  an intuitive rather than rational approach to classroom events;
3  an opinionated as opposed to an open-minded stance when confronted with alternative technique practice;
4  a narrowness in the working definitions assigned to abstract terms' (Jackson, 1968, page 144).

This has implications for a curriculum project which aims at development through teacher understanding and which does not give careful thought to the uses and effects of its language of communication.

Communication presents hazards at all stages of a curriculum enterprise, for there is no standardised method of describing curriculum projects for people (heads, local authorities) who have to make decisions about them. Moreover, no relevant typology of schools has received wide enough currency for it to be used in conjunction with descriptions of curriculum projects in order to anticipate the goodness of fit.

## b.  Training

Where there is, in the structure or ethos of the system, no precedent for quality control—where materials are not withdrawn from schools which are judged not to be meeting the specifications of the development team, and where certificates of proficiency are not awarded or withheld at the close of a training course, there can be a fairly rapid distortion of the development project. The hazard throws a heavy burden on training courses and the after-care service.

The central development team will probably have a limited

life span. Major responsibility for continuity may be invested in a newly-formed national centre, in institutions concerned with teacher training, or in local areas through *ad hoc* groups based on teachers' centres. The decision points for the development team will include these :

1   What are the criteria for the selection of trainers? Do teachers working in participating schools make the best trainers or teachers?

2   In what respects should a programme to train trainers differ from a programme to train teachers?

3   What are the comparative advantages of

  *a.*   a system with one trained teacher or 'facilitator' in each school who will be responsible for training and giving support to other teachers in that school;
  *b.*   a system whereby a nucleus of trainers inducts interested teachers, on an area basis, at locally organised sessions?

4   Under what circumstances are intensive training courses more effective than an extended course of regular short sessions?

5   What rewards are desirable and feasible for teachers acting as trainers?

6   Do heads and local authorities fully recognise the need for participating teachers to have time for professional growth; time for individual study and reflection; time for in-school discussion with experimental colleagues; time for occasional meetings with experimental teams from other schools in the area?

The development team should also ask whether the tendency to ascribe authority to them (with subsequent reduction of teacher initiative) is likely to be replicated at local level and, if so, how this effect can be combated through the presentation of the experiment at the training courses.

Where emphasis is placed on the development of teachers, training may be an appropriate word. It is a truism that training limits the options open while education extends them. As Peters suggests :

> 'The Spartans for instance, were military and morally trained. They knew how to fight; they knew what was right and wrong; they were possessed of a certain kind of lore, which stood them in good stead in stock situations. They were thus able to comb their hair with aplomb when the Persians were approaching at Thermopylae. But we could not say that they had received a military or a moral education; for they had never been able to understand the principles underlying their code. They had mastered the content of forms of thought and behaviour without ever grasping or being able to operate

with the principles that would enable them to manage on their own' (Peters, 1967, page 6).

In an article which lays emphasis on teacher development, it is perhaps appropriate to leave the last word with Professor Peters.

REFERENCES

JACKSON, P. W. (1968) *Life in Classrooms*. New York: Holt, Rinehart and Winston.

PETERS, R. S. (1967) 'What is an educational process?' In PETERS, R. S. (ed.) *The Concept of Education*. London: Routledge and Kegan Paul.

RUBIN, L. (1969) *A Study of Teacher Retraining*. Santa Barbara: University of California, Center for Co-ordinated Education.

WILLOWER, D. J. (1958) Paper published in *Samplings*, *11*, *3*, 45–60.

*In* Educational Research Methods *the chapter on curriculum development emphasised the necessity to develop curricula from precisely defined objectives. Within the readings presented in this parallel chapter just two years later, the emphasis has shifted. There is still a recognition of the importance of evaluation, but there is growing uncertainty about the use of behavioural objectives specified in advance. Allied to a movement away from precise objectives is a recognition that evaluation should be broadly based. Many innovatory curricula are aimed as much at improving children's attitudes, as at increasing their knowledge. Sometimes there are no suitable objective measures of the outcomes of a particular curriculum. As Rudd explained, teacher consensus linked with criterion-based assessments of pupils and tests of attitudes can build up a picture of what the course has achieved. For some curriculum theorists this is the time to decide on objectives, or rather to examine which of the 'learning outcomes' have been most beneficial.*

*The danger in defining objectives in advance is that broader aims and unexpected outcomes may be ruled out by designing the curriculum to fit preconceived and narrow ideas. But leaving the obectives until afterwards may lead to programmes which are not carefully thought through at the planning stage. Whichever process is preferred, there is the advantage of a systematic and conscious examination of the content of the curricula and a continuing evaluation of the effectiveness of teaching.*

*This work on curriculum justifies the term 'research' only where there is a systematic attempt at evaluation. When this happens the research worker may have to draw on the whole range of measurement techniques which have been illustrated in previous chapters and then research skills become important. But there is still a need to develop evaluation techniques which match the imagination shown in some of the new curricula. It will also be important, as MacDonald and Rudduck argued, not to stop curriculum development work too soon. Teachers must be shown how to work with the new materials and how to utilise new ideas in their own schemes of work. Communication of reports about educational innovations has not been effective in the past. Chapter 15 takes up some aspects of this communication 'gap' in relation to difficulties in interpreting research findings.*

# PART THREE
## Implications and Speculations

# 15 Interpretation and Communication

*Each of the chapters in Part Two took a particular area of research with its characteristic techniques and methods of measurement. In this penultimate chapter we return to the stages of research described in Chapter 2: the final stage of any project involves the task of interpreting the findings and writing a report. The first of these activities is particularly difficult. It requires a thorough grounding in the social sciences, an intuitive understanding of classrooms and teaching, and an imaginative application of both of these to alternative explanations of the results. The most obvious conclusion may be quite wrong.*

*These skills can be developed by reading and reviewing research carried out by others—or by trying to formulate a research design for a hypothetical future project. In both these exercises it is helpful to go through each stage of the research and to ask pertinent questions. Not all the questions will be appropriate to every study, and many research reports will leave important questions unanswered. However, a check-list of points to consider highlights many of the problems which research workers encounter in interpreting their findings and communicating the implications for teachers and administrators. It may be instructive to apply the checklist to some of the studies reported in earlier chapters.*

### EVALUATING RESEARCH STUDIES

| | |
|---|---|
| 1 | *The problem* |
| 1.1 | Is the problem chosen worthy of investigation? |
| 1.2 | Does it have practical or theoretical relevance? |
| 1.3 | What impact are the findings likely to have on teachers or other researchers? |
| 1.4 | Has the importance of the general topic or problem been carefully outlined? |
| 1.5 | Has the general topic been effectively narrowed down? |

1.6   Has the rationale of this 'focussing' been explained?

1.7   Have the concepts been translated into measureable entities?

1.8   Has this process of 'operationalization' been achieved without losing the essence of the original concepts?

1.9   Is the choice of 'experiment' or 'survey' appropriate?

2     *Review of the literature*

2.1   Does the review of the literature cover all aspects of the investigation?

2.2   Are primary sources (original research reports) used wherever possible?

2.3   Is the review logically ordered and concise?

2.4   Are the methodology and conclusions of previous studies constructively criticised?

2.5   Is there evidence that the theoretical background of the relevant concepts is understood?

2.6   Does the review appear to have any bias in the selection of studies or in the summarizing of findings?

2.7   Are the results of previous studies used to generate hypotheses or to narrow down the questions to be posed?

2.8   Are the hypotheses, if used, stated in terms of the measures to be applied?

2.9   Are the references presented in full somewhere in the report?

3     *Methods of measurement*

3.1   Have all necessary variables been included?

3.2   Has the research worker avoided the 'jingle fallacy' of assuming that the name of the test is an accurate indication of what the test actually measures?

3.3   Is the evidence or reliability and validity of the published tests indicated by reference to the manuals?

3.4   If tests have been developed especially for this study, is evidence of reliability and validity reported?

3.5   Is the content of the tests at the appropriate level for the age and ability of the participants?

3.6   Will the language used in the tests be fully understood?

3.7   Are any of the items likely to be specific to a particular sub-culture (or to a different country, if the test is foreign)?

3.8   Are many of the questions asked likely to be seen as contentious, offensive, ambiguous, trivial, or pointless?

3.9   Have any of the responses to questions been coded in such a way that the results will be uninterpretable?

3.10  Has sufficient attention been given to accurate measurement of key variables?

3.11   Is a variety of methods of measurement used?

4      *Sampling*

4.1    Is the population from which the sample is to be drawn carefully defined?

4.2    Are the methods of sampling fully described?

4.3    Is the sample size large enough for the purposes of the investigation?

4.4    Is there any possibility of bias in the method of sampling adopted?

4.5    If the sample is non-random, is the likely effect discussed?

4.6    If the sample is chosen for convenience or has been affected by external constraints, has evidence been collected about possible bias thus created?

4.7    If population statistics or test 'norms' are available, are the characteristics of the sample compared with those of the population?

4.8    If an experimental design was used, have the control and experimental groups been properly matched?

4.9    In an experiment or follow-up study, is the sample with *complete* data still representative of the population?

5      *Data collection*

5.1    Are full details of the data collection provided?

5.2    Was a pilot study used to try out the measurement instruments?

5.3    Was the purpose of the enquiry carefully explained to the participants, but in such a way as to avoid affecting the results subsequently obtained?

5.4    Was the collection of data carefully planned in advance and organised to ensure no undue inconvenience to schools or colleges?

5.5    Were arrangements for testing designed to ensure that the participants were subject to no unnecessary inconvenience?

5.6    Was the period of testing too long?

5.7    Were the conditions for testing appropriate (for example, spaced-out desks)?

5.8    What steps were taken to ensure that conditions were standardized between sessions?

5.9    If the sample included young children, were effective steps taken to ensure that all procedures and items were fully understood?

5.10   Was the time allowed for each test appropriate?

5.11   Was the balance between time spent in measuring the various variables in keeping with the importance of those variables in the research design?

5.12  Were excessive demands made on incidental participants, such as teachers?

5.13  Were important items or tests omitted because of non-cooperation?

5.14  If an experimental design was used, have the variables which were not measured been effectively controlled?

5.15  In such an experiment, were the 'treatment' differences sufficiently clear-cut to create differences in the dependent variables?

5.16  If observations have been made, were adequate precautions taken against subjective bias?

6     *Statistical analysis*

6.1   Does the statistical analysis allow the initial hypotheses to be adequately tested?

6.2   Is the analysis suitable for the type of scale used (nominal, ordinal, or interval)?

6.3   Are the assumptions of the statistics used checked against the data (e.g. normal distribution)?

6.4   Are appropriate tests of statistical significance used?

6.5   Are alternative methods of analysis reported?

7     *Interpretation of findings*

7.1   Are the findings related to the outcomes of previous research?

7.2   Have sampling deficiences been overlooked in generalizing the results to the population?

7.3   Have weaknesses in measurement instruments been ignored?

7.4   In arguing from the measurements to the underlying concepts are the dangers of this extrapolation made explicit?

7.5   Are relationships between variables made inevitable by similarities in the methods of measurement?

7.6   Is there any circularity in the reasoning?

7.7   Are the explanations based on *ex post facto* reasoning without prior expectations?

7.8   Is causality in relationships unjustifiably assumed, where only concomitant variation has been established?

7.9   Is there any evidence of the 'Hawthorne effect' distorting the results?

7.10  Are alternative explanations of the results evaluated?

7.11  Is statistical significance confused with educational significance?

7.12  Is the borderline between evidence and speculation made clear?

7.13  Are educational implications spelled out clearly, but fairly?

7.14 Are any value judgements in the implications made explicit?

7.15 Does the report use any emotive language showing emotional involvement in the outcome?

7.16 Are there any other indications of bias in the way the results have been described?

*The reasons for asking most of these questions are probably clear enough, but, put together, the questions add up to a formidable list of requirements—and this should help to explain why few educational research studies seem to be flawless. The practical constraints, mentioned in Chapters 4 and 5, crop up again in several of these questions. If there are technical weaknesses in a research project or faulty reasoning in the interpretation of the results, the whole labour may prove useless in the end, because of the difficulty in moving from results to implications.*

*Many of the problems brought out by the questions have already been discussed in our earlier textbook. While it would be impossible to develop all the remaining points in full, there are several general difficulties which are worth elaborating here. For more detailed discussions of specific problems, the reader is referred to the following texts.*

BORG, W. R. (1963) *Educational Research: an Introduction.* London: Longmans.

BURROUGHS, G. E. R. (1971) *Design and Analysis in Educational Research.* University of Birmingham, School of Education.

COOK, D. R. (1965) *A Guide to Educational Research.* Boston: Allyn and Bacon.

FOX, D. J. (1969) *The Research Process in Education.* New York: Holt, Rinehart and Winston.

LOVELL, K., and LAWSON, K. S. (1970) *Understanding Research in Education.* London: University of London Press.

TRAVERS, R. M. W. (1969) *An Introduction to Educational Research.* New York: Macmillan.

VAN DALEN, D. B. (1966) *Understanding Educational Research.* New York: McGraw–Hill.

## LIES, DAMNED LIES AND STATISTICS

*Probably the greatest difficulty in communicating research results to teachers is the necessity, at some stage, to present evidence in the form of statistical tables. The figures in themselves are meaningless, and interpretation depends on some knowledge of the statistics used and of their underlying assumptions. Essentially the educational research worker is trying to simplify* the description of complex social situations by looking for recurring patterns of regularity. His main technique is comparison, either of groups which differ in some controlled way, or of two or more variables. The whole range of statistical methods can be seen as attempts, at different levels of complexity, to make comparisons which will bring out the anticipated regularities in the data. Such patterns of regularity can then be used to set up simplified models through which to understand the complex reality of the educational process.

Where the data are in the form of categories, the idea of comparison comes out clearly. For example in Table 1:3, on page 7, percentages are used to compare the responses of children from different housing areas about their anticipated careers. The regularity in the responses indicates a relationship. A similar pattern is clear in Table 6:2, on page 82, in which the level of adjustment of two intakes to secondary school is compared. From this comparison, inferences are made on the basis of a test of statistical significance. In this case the appropriate statistic was 'chi-square' and the value of 'P' (probability) indicated only one chance in a hundred of such a pattern of results occurring by chance ($P < 0.01$), if there was in fact no relationship between the two variables.

Without statistical significance it is difficult to draw any general inference from the research. The observed pattern of results is likely to be a chance event specific to the particular sample chosen and to have no general value. But statistical significance is not a sure guide to educational significance. Tests of significance depend on the size of the sample used; if large enough samples are used, trivial differences between groups or faint correlations between tests become statistically significant. If the sample is small, quite substantial differences may fail to reach significant level. (And it does not follow that because two groups are not statistically different, we can treat them as if they were alike: see Educational Research Methods, page 158.) In interpreting the analyses it is thus crucial to examine the size of differences and the strength of relationships, as well as the probability levels, before arguing towards practical relevance.

Another statistic commonly used in educational research is the 'product-moment' correlation coefficient. It is easy enough to point out the relationship between two variables on a scale running from $-1.0$ to $+1.0$, representing the range between disagreement and total agreement. But what does a correlation of $+0.5$ mean? Is this a high value or a low one, even if it is statistically significant? As a correlation coefficient is affected by test unreliability and sample homogeneity, the meaning depends on the context. So $+0.5$ may be a high correlation if, say, one of the measures is unreliable and the sample is homogeneous with *respect to the other variable. The low correlation in universities between academic performance and A-level grades is often taken as an example of this effect. Moreover low correlations may also indicate that fundamental assumptions have been disregarded. For the correlation coefficient to give an accurate indication of a relationship, the scores on both variables must approximate to 'normal' distributions and the relationship itself should be linear —regular increases in the value of one variable should be paralleled by equivalent increases in the value of the other variable. Any serious departure from the assumptions underlying any statistic can invalidate subsequent interpretations. Some knowledge of statistics, at least at a simple conceptual level, is thus crucial before attempting to interpret research results. But even if the appropriateness of statistical techniques has to be accepted on trust by most teachers, many of the other issues are less esoteric. Practical experience can be of considerable importance in making sense of other aspects of research findings, particularly problems of measurement.*

## MEASUREMENT OF SCHOOL ATTAINMENT

*If there is any single key variable in educational research, it must surely be academic attainment. Several of the studies mentioned in earlier chapters attempted to explain attainment in terms of say, home background (Plowden), school organisation (Barker Lunn), academic motivation (Entwistle), or divergent thinking (Richards and Bolton). In all these investigations school attainment is the keystone: if there is any lack of care at this point, the whole edifice of the subsequent work crumbles. In assessing attainment, content and construct validity are crucial. The test must cover the whole syllabus and measure all aspects of attainment within the school curriculum. This, at least, is the ideal to be sought after, but it is particularly difficult to achieve.*

*Research studies are generally carried out in several different schools, whose curricula and syllabuses are unlikely to be identical. And yet, if there is to be comparability in the findings, the criterion of attainment must be the same for all the pupils in the sample. There is no simple solution to this dilemma. It is possible, in theory, to administer standardised attainment tests which cover all areas of the curriculum—but such a range of tests does not exist in reality. At secondary level there are standardised tests in important areas of the curriculum, such as English and mathematics, although many of these tests are based on out-of-date syllabuses. Verbal reasoning or even non-verbal reasoning tests have also been used to measure attainment. While these tests are certainly related to attainment, they are hardly valid* measures of *attainment in anything other than reasoning. In many studies these tests have been used to explain attainment: it is confusing to find them also being used as an index of school performance. But even if there are appropriate attainment tests of English, mathematics or reading, are we justified in equating scores on these tests with academic success? Clearly these are, at best, indicators of performance in only part of the school curriculum.*

In the Plowden Social Survey (Chapter 7) the aim was to isolate a small number of variables which, taken together, would 'explain' school attainment as effectively as possible. The criterion chosen in this important study was a comparatively short reading test. The ensuing complex step-regression analysis is thus explaining performance in a reading test, rather than 'primary school attainment'. It is tempting to suggest that school variables might have been more important and parental attitudes less important had a broader-based criterion been adopted. Of all parts of the primary school curriculum, reading is probably the most likely to show high correlation with social variables. The explanations of attainment in writing or arithmetic, not to mention project work, mathematical set theory or imaginative story-writing, might well have been rather different.

Again, even if appropriate standardised tests are available, each test would not be equally suitable for every school. Assessment should presumably be related to the objectives of each teacher. The only way to approach this ideal is by asking teachers to provide rank-orders of pupils. Presumably these estimates will reflect both the teacher's objectives and the relative extent to which each pupil has achieved these objectives. The estimates can then be scaled against a standardised test of scholastic aptitude, designed to have the highest possible correlation with overall school attainment. In this way the standard of each class can be fixed against national norms, while the teacher decides each child's relative position within the class.

This method has been a common solution to this difficult problem, but it is still far from being fully satisfactory. The teachers' estimates contain elements of subjectivity; they measure 'perceived attainment', not 'absolute' attainment. The different educational perspectives adopted by the teachers in making their assessments also create problems. We can no longer be sure that children in different schools are being assessed on the same dimensions of attainment. Under these circumstances different correlates of attainment between schools would be inevitable; they would also be inexplicable in terms of the measurements made. In fact some teachers, particularly those in 'progressive' primary schools, strongly resist making the judgements necessary to create a rank-order of attainment. In schools *where competition is not encouraged, the pupil's achievement is related to his own previous work, and not to norms for the age-group or for the class.*

## THE STRATEGY OF A 'MIXED ECONOMY'

*If we recognise the weaknesses in alternative approaches to the measurement of a particular variable, like school attainment, the obvious solution is to use more than one type of measure. It is then possible to investigate differences between the alternative instruments, or to use a sum of the various measures, or to derive a factor score which extracts the elements common to all the measures. The advantages of such a 'mixed economy' are important. Relationships with the composite score are much less likely to be contaminated by the design of the instrument than are relationships with scores from one test. (This principle was applied in the research on marking English compositions in Chapter 11.) Where a single test on its own represents an important dimension, doubts about its reliability or validity will put the whole research study at risk. A 'belt and braces' strategy has much to commend it.*

*The philosophy underlying this approach goes far beyond the use of several comparable tests. In terms of research design it suggests that we should not necessarily think in terms of choosing between experiment and survey, between case study and large-scale survey, between interview and questionnaire, between psychological and sociological concepts, or between individualistic and nomothetic explanations. Increasingly several approaches are being used within a single investigation. In Chapter 8, for example, the research projects made use of both case studies with interviews and also surveys with questionnaires. And the whole point of Chapter 6 was to illustrate both the multi-disciplinary approach and the way in which evidence was drawn from different sources—headteachers, teachers and pupils—in various ways. Many persistent disagreements in educational research would be resolved were the problems to be attacked within the same study using, for example, both psychological and sociological perspectives. The difference in approach can range from a current sociological trend—ethnomethodology—which emphasises the essential singularity of experience, to the traditional psychometric outlook which sees a test under standardised conditions as presenting an identical stimulus to all the participants. It is quite reasonable to look at man as an idiosyncratic person, whose behaviour is influenced by his previous experience, by the particular social setting he is in and by the particular role he decides to adopt in those circumstances. It is similarly valid to* describe traits which people have in common and to look for stability in behaviour over widely different social settings. Both strategies provide partial explanations of behaviour, but it is often difficult to see these descriptions as being complementary. It is almost as if the two groups of research workers were observing people's behaviour with the aid of mirrors with opposite curvature. One image is magnified to show minute psychological detail of the individual, while the other is diminished to bring into view a large number of people interacting in social groups. It is thus difficult to recognise their descriptions of these images as originating in the same world of experience. Educational research has borrowed both these 'traditions' of methodology without resolving their contradictory descriptions. A similar lack of match can be found between the concepts used by social scientists from either camp and the language of the teacher.

## MEASUREMENT SPACE AND CLASSROOM REALITY

Plato compared man's perception of his surroundings to the flickering, distorted shadows of reality projected on to the walls of a cave. The findings of the research worker in education can be seen in a similar light. He is interested in educational reality, but his attempts to measure what he sees in classrooms lead him into the unreal world of measurement space. The initial problem may well be expressed in everyday language. Do mature children fit in more readily to secondary school than do immature children? The key variable is 'maturity'; but what sort of maturity? The teachers probably mean social maturity. How can this be measured? Well, socially mature pupils will show different patterns of interests and attitudes from immature pupils; so give attitude tests to fifteen-year-olds and to children in primary school. Having identified 'mature' and 'immature' attitudes, the scale is administered to children entering secondary school and their subsequent 'adjustment' is assessed. The research results show, perhaps, that children who tick off a large number of 'mature' items on the inventory have few problems in adjusting to secondary school. But the teacher wants to know whether mature children adjust easily to life in secondary school. The research worker is caught in his web of operationalised unreality and runs the risk of being misunderstood if he states his conclusions in everyday language. On the other hand if he refrains from such extrapolation from research findings to practical relevance, there can be no communication at all. The teacher has little interest in test scores; he is concerned mainly with how children actually behave. The research worker thus presents his results cautiously, in terms of the underlying concepts, wrapped around with qualifications about inaccuracy of measurement and sampling error. The resulting package may still infuriate the enthusiastic teacher, who sees this scientific caution as an attempt to avoid giving an answer to a simple question.

The problems in interpreting research findings explain many of the misunderstandings between teachers and research workers. The language of statistics combined with problems of measurement and the jargon of social science have together effectively destroyed the possibility of easy communication between these two groups of people. And yet one of the basic aims of educational research is surely to improve the efficiency of the educational process. To do this a continuous dialogue between research worker and teacher is of paramount importance. In Chapter 8 Cane and Schroeder demonstrated the existence of a communication gap, but suggested that, on the whole, teachers were interested in research and wanted to be involved. It is perhaps in such involvement that the future of educational research lies.

# 16 The Future of Educational Research

*To what extent has educational research improved the efficiency of the educational process? Just how much effect can we expect research to have in the future? Would effective communication of results lead directly to changes in educational practice? These questions indicate the theme of this final chapter. In the first extract, the Vice-Chancellor of Lancaster University indicates what he sees as the future priorities in research.*

### Research into Higher Education
### (C. F. Carter, 1972)[1]

The purpose of research in higher education, for most of us, is a practical one. We do not want merely to describe the quaint or awful things which are going on : we want to make things better. How far are we succeeding? In what sense can it be claimed that higher education is better now than in 1961? To what extent can any improvement be ascribed to the researchers?

You will probably be disposed to take, at this point, the classic evading movement or Researcher's Dodge : the time, you will say, is not yet ripe. The task of the last decade has been to accumulate the facts and develop the insight from which practical results may one day flow. We belong, you will assert, to the ancient and respectable craft of Foundation Layers; the somewhat less respectable trade of Superstructure Builders will follow after. This two-part contract, however, is not really a sensible mode of building, for it can readily lead to a misallocation of resources. In any case, the evasion or dodge is suspect, since many researchers during the past decade have *claimed* to have a practical or applied purpose. What success have they had?

The success has, I think, been disappointingly small. One

[1] Presidential address to the Annual Conference of the Society for Research into Higher Education, December, 1971.

can instance, for example, the rather limited proved contribution of the educational technologists, at least outside the Open University. The results here have been so disappointing as to put in doubt, in the university sector, the willingness of the University Grants Committee to find more money for development. Or consider the lack of relation between research results on the efficacy of teaching in classes of different sizes and the actual practice in higher education. Or, to take another example, the great majority of our examination systems operate in a way which cannot possibly be justified by our knowledge of the examination process—for instance, putting great weight on differences of marks which are statistically insignificant, or combining together sets of marks which are unstandardised.

In these circumstances, I believe that the aim, over the next ten years, should be to produce some real but rather simple changes. I stress simplicity because we are hardly likely to convince our colleagues about the correctness of erudite and complex solutions if we do not appear to be talking sense about simple things. Now it is a temptation, in all research, to suppose that the simple and the obvious, the things which can be done on the back of an envelope, have a lower importance and status than those things which are complex, obscure, or require a lot of hardware to bring them about. It is sometimes very difficult to persuade research workers to notice that a very simple question needs answering before they rush round to the computer.

So I hope that, in planning research, you will stand back a little from the problems; refrain from chasing along familiar paths and surrounding what you find with a spurious appearance of erudition; and see if your colleagues can be helped with some of the simple and obvious faults which have persisted in higher education far too long.

*Enthusiastic schoolteachers also look to educational research to provide solutions to pressing problems. They are often deeply disappointed by the tentative statements made by research workers. But there are fundamental limitations to what research can achieve in either schools or universities. It can provide evidence from which solutions to practical problems may emerge: it cannot provide the solutions themselves. The shift from research results to implications often involves value judgements as to what is desirable in education, and it is this step which many social scientists prefer to avoid. It is safer to present statistical analyses and to speculate about theoretical issues, than to suggest what practical steps might follow from the research. If the research worker puts aside his cautious objectivity, he may well be criticised for the values which then creep into his conclusions. The risk in stopping short of the implications is to lose the sympathy of the teacher altogether and hence to prevent any meaningful communication.*

*This dilemma is also reflected in different views about the basic function of research in education (see, for example, Cronbach and Suppes, 1969). Should research contribute actively to the process of decision-making or should its role be more passive, influencing attitudes and producing evidence which may or may not be of use to administrators? In Britain educational research has tended to be cast in the passive role. By contrast in Sweden educational research has been geared towards providing the evidence required by administrators. The two extracts in this chapter illustrate these approaches which, though differing in tradition, do show attitudes in common. The first is from an article by W. D. Wall who was the Director of the National Foundation for Educational Research until 1968; the second is part of a paper read by T. Husen of Stockholm.*

## The Future of Educational Research
(W. D. Wall, 1968)[1]

Educational research workers are frequently criticized for the 'irrelevance' or merely marginal relevance of their work. It is said that the problems they tackle are not those of the class teacher, nor have they solved central and burning questions on what makes children learn or the best ways of organizing a school. What is more, it is alleged, the findings of elaborate inquiries are either confirmations of 'common-sense' or manifestly absurd—that is, they merely prove what we think we know, or failing to confirm our prejudices, must be rejected.

In remarks of this and similar kinds there is a grain of truth, and sometimes more. Much of what is listed as research in education and in the sciences basic to education has been conducted principally for the purpose of gaining a higher degree. University regulations and the natural tendency to play safe have led students rather to choose the intensive, usually statistical, study of a small area than to attempt the solution of highly complex problems. The language of research reporting—especially in a thesis—is hedged about with qualifications which fail to satisfy the practitioner's thirst for striking and certain generalizations. A few leaders in the field have managed to direct and co-ordinate thesis work of their postgraduate students over a very long period and have emerged with a coherent study of a considerable series of related problems. Godfrey Thomson in Edinburgh in the field of

[1] Extracted from an article which appeared originally in *Educational Research*, 10, 163–9.

psychometrics; Burt in London in the study of delinquency, back-
wardness and the theory of ability; Valentine in Birmingham pursuing the psychology of early childhood, and at the same time,
fostering an extensive series of studies of adolescence; and Schonell, over a lifetime, studying the teaching of arithmetic, reading,
spelling and written English and embodying the results in a
widely used series of text books—these and others are the giants
of the dawn of the educational sciences in this country. Neither
must we forget the immense American, French, Swiss and,
recently, Swedish contributions—and particularly the work of
men such as Thorndike, Stanley Hall, Terman, Piaget, Vallon and
Binet.

Of course they have not provided all the answers to all the
questions posed by teachers; they have not done more than lay
the foundations of theory in some parts of the field. We could
hardly expect more since the experimental study of education is
barely seventy years old. But since the turn of the century we
have gained at least as much knowledge of the educational process as was won about disease from the time Harvey expounded
his theory of the circulation of the blood (1616) to the rise of
notions about environmental sanitation in the nineteenth century.

In fact, one can reasonably claim that the contributions of
research to the development of education cannot be passed off
as slight or marginal—they are certainly far in excess of what
might have been expected from the insignificant financial resources devoted to it. We know more about education, about
children, about the social psychology of the school, about learning and its hindrances, about how to measure the educational
product, and such like matters, than we as yet apply in practice. And such knowledge as we have has been at least as central
to the educational revolution which has taken place since 1918
as have driving impulses of economic or political and social kinds.

The fact that the general body of teachers has to be reminded
of these and similar facts is significant. It suggests that teacher
training has been somewhat at fault if the profession is not
critically aware of the scientific bases of much of what it does.
One paradoxical result of this is that now, in a climate suddenly
favourable to technology and scientific advance, many professional educators are hard put to it to distinguish between reasonably firmly-based theories from which good educational experiment may be derived, and bodies of doctrine which may be
called pseudo-scientific since they owe as much to particular
social or political philosophies as they do to objectively ascer-
tained fact.

Research in education, emerging rapidly from the 'tintack and
glue' era, is now confronted with immense opportunities. The

last four years have seen a proportionately huge increase in the money available for educational research and an even greater increase in the funds directed towards curriculum development. In 1958, the total expenditure on educational research was of the order of £150,000 annually, representing no more than 0·01 per cent of the total expenditure on education. The figure for the current year certainly exceeds £500,000—still a fraction of one per cent of the total educational expenditure, but nonetheless a massive advance. In addition, private foundations have given funds for curriculum development and the Schools Council has been set up for much the same purpose. We may expect too, that the Social Science Research Council, and particularly its Educational Research Committee, will stimulate considerable research activity in the sciences basic to education and in specifically educational research.

Money, and the public interest which it represents, is of vital importance, but it is not everything, and may present considerable dangers. Because of the comparative neglect of education as a research field, there are few organizations in this country at present capable of sustaining major programmes over the minimum period of years necessary to gain worthwhile results. Men and women with the basic scientific qualifications as well as educational experience—particularly first-hand experience of the classroom—are few in number and hard to come by. In spite of the general advances in psychology, child development, psychometrics, social psychology, statistical methods and sociology in the past decade, we have little but partial theories directly relevant to education. Finally, there is a noticeable (and understandable) tendency on the part of some teachers and administrators to consider the process of research to be too slow and to wish to plunge on their hunches without too much in the way of objective checks on their value. With education and educational decision-making moving more and more into the centre of political controversy, voices are not wanting to play upon this, to promise quicker results from hastily-mounted impressionistic studies and to urge particular reforms as if they were already justified by research evidence and merely needed implementation.

Such strains and tensions are inherent in rapid growth, but they may prejudice the sound development of research in education—which is after all the biggest and probably the most fundamental field of applied social science—and of education itself. In the future, then, we must get our ideas straight, and sort out the relations between the sciences basic to education and direct educational research activity, and between research and curriculum or other development and general decision-making in education.

It is perhaps easiest to work backwards in thinking about this. Let us imagine a primary school teacher in the relatively common, apparently simple situation of wishing to choose between teaching arithmetic of a traditional kind by traditional means and teaching the so-called 'new' mathematics. How can research aid him? He would probably like to know how far either form of mathematics conformed to the general structure and development of children's thought—and here, such basic theory of child development as exists and bears upon this problem would help, in so far as he was able to interpret and apply it to individual children. He would also like to know—since both approaches might be equally possible—in what ways the outcomes, both short and long term, differ from each other and from one kind of child to another. He would also probably wish to know how far the goals achieved by either method were compatible with others he wanted to achieve in the education of his pupils. Thus, the teacher will be using his professional knowledge and skills to interpret and use information and basic theory from the social sciences and from the technology of his craft. He will attempt as a result to set up some viable hypotheses. He will also quickly realize, if he approaches his work in a critical objective spirit, that these hypotheses should be tested (and the outcomes of the work measured) in real day to day situations—that is, he or someone else on his behalf, will have to undertake some action research. When all this is finished, he will arrive at a conclusion such as the following: that method or curriculum A appears to achieve effectively results C, D and E, while method B produces results X, Y and Z, and that result M is common to both. His previous study of theory and his more or less elaborate action research will not have solved his problem for him in any absolute way. But they will have defined the possibilities of his alternative curricula, suggested refinements of technique, sharpened up and made clear the choice to be made. The choice itself between attainable goals, the value judgements about the aims of what he does, he will have to make on moral, philosophic, social or perhaps even political grounds.

A similar situation arises in deciding on matters of policy at the national or local level—to stream or not to stream; whether transition from primary to secondary schooling should take place at eleven, twelve or thirteen; whether to teach a foreign language to young children. There is no objective way of making the final *value* judgement. Research can define the limits within which choice is possible and avoid the confusion between the desirable and the practicable which befogs so much educational controversy. It can also provide the means of seeing whether the aims proposed by the innovator or policy-maker are achieved. In short, while it cannot tell us, for example, if it is *good* to set up comprehensive schools, it can throw light on whether the proposed aims (or others) are achieved, which forms of organization are more or less efficient than others in achieving them, how far the gains under one system are greater than, different from or simply incompatible with, those of another.

These examples throw light upon the relations between the growth of knowledge in the basic sciences (psychology, sociology, child development, and social-psychology) and the applied, essentially multi-disciplinary, science of educational research, and between both of these and what is called 'development'. Research in education is essentially concerned with the problems of learning as they confront the teacher, the administrator and the policy maker in all the complexity and untidiness of the real day to day situation. It is an applied science—or rather an array of investigatory techniques—derived from the social sciences. It is therefore dependent upon theoretical and experimental developments in the various contributory fields, both for its hypothetical structures and its research instrumentation. It is, too, the bridge between the 'purity' of academic research in, say, child development, learning theory or even animal behaviour and the teacher in front of his class. Just as the academic research worker supports by his work the technology of educational research, it is from the practitioner that the educational research worker derives his problems, and through him that he checks his hypotheses.

As our armoury of hypotheses and of investigatory techniques improves, and as trained workers and money become more readily available, we can hope to get the best of both worlds in what might be called 'action research'. In this approach, changes based upon an amalgam of theory and practice are deliberately introduced, and are varied systematically and in fairly massive ways. In the curriculum and method field, the current long-term study of the introduction of French in primary schools is one example (*see Chapter 14*). The work on teaching methods and materials for primary school mathematics is another (*Chapter 10*). Rather narrower and more precise in scope is the work on the initial teaching alphabet (*Chapter 5*). The Swedish researches on comprehensive education (which are mentioned in the next reading) illustrate the kind of action study which enables organizational reform or change to proceed with reasonable caution and objectivity in understanding, modifying and evaluating what is done.

Probably a large part of the future of what is specifically *educational* research lies in the development and refinement of action studies of all kinds—in the field of curriculum, in specifically pedagogical methods, in differing ways of deploying teaching and other staff in schools, for organizational changes and similar matters. Even so, many educational decisions, whether in the classroom or on a national scale, will, for a long time yet, have to be taken in the absence of firm knowledge derived from research. Nor perhaps will it be possible or desirable to wait for the results of long-term action studies before implementing decisions on a wide scale. Many curricular changes are like this at present and will probably always be so; so may be such decisions as whether to raise the school leaving age. In such cases, however, two forms of research inquiry are valuable—limited feasibility studies to explore and anticipate the snags and likely difficulties of an innovation; and in-built evaluation to check—in time to influence or even radically change development—whether the proposed aims are in fact being realized.

What has been discussed so far represents an immediate intensification of more or less traditional forms of research activity in education; it is in fact the first stage in the transition from the partial examination of partial problems—for which research workers have been so often (and by and large so unjustly) criticized. Many of the most important problems of education are such that the methods and concepts so far described are not the best means of attack. Nor can these problems be even approximately studied by simple applications of methods of any of the basic social sciences, important as their contributions may be. We can only hope to move towards an understanding of the complex central core of the educational process, when resources allow us to develop and maintain considerable multi-disciplinary teams applying themselves to studies of real classrooms over considerable periods of time. We must examine the varieties of teaching task, the tissue of interactions between pupil and teacher, the factors which influence school and classroom climates and, through them, the motivations of pupils to learn or to resist learning. We must also explore the school as a plastic, transitional community, set between the family and society. If we can carry out a reasonably well-specified job analysis of teaching in its many facets we shall have some certain basis for teacher training—at present little more than an apprenticeship with educational overtones.

Such an increase in the relevance and power of educational research cannot come about simply through the activities of research workers themselves. It involves some fundamental re-thinking of the concepts of research by which we work, and of the relation between practice and research activity. Basically it is true to say that, while very many teachers and educationists are aware that there is or should be an educational technology, most regard this as peripheral. On the other hand, many research workers in the social sciences fail to distinguish between particular scientific methods—those hallowed by success in the natural sciences—and scientific method as a way of analysing experience. They tend to fall victim to the prestige of the natural sciences and strive to prove themselves respectable by approximating as closely as possible to their procedures. Even if one could do so, the attempt (in, say, an experiment in teaching poetry) systematically to isolate and vary one factor after another—social class, cultural background, sex, ability, teacher competence, prior experience, etc.—would be a failure on two counts: that of defining and separating the factors to be varied; and that —which most teachers know in their bones—of failing to see that in the educational process the whole is qualitatively different from the sum of its parts. The crucial characteristics of good scientific method are an attempt to diminish (and to estimate and allow for) the bias of the observer, with known degrees of error, and a careful objectivity in recording and reporting which allows rigorous comparison with experiments of a similar kind conducted by others.

If we are really to approach such questions as what makes children learn, how they are motivated, what their aspirations are, and how true equality of opportunity may be provided for pupils of differing kinds from differing environments, our laboratory is the school. This implies two other things. The research team itself must have within it practising teachers; and it must collaborate with teachers actually engaged in the classroom. For practical as well as scientific reasons, it is probably best to base the initial research work on a number of experimental and laboratory schools closely associated with research institutions and constituting the equivalent of the physicists' or chemists' laboratory. Such schools and classes would provide the facilities for the close study of real educational situations, for action research and development work in their initial stages. Once some clear insight or theory is gained, or a new development has shown a reasonable prospect of success in these manifestly favourable circumstances, then should come field trials on a larger scale in a sample of ordinary schools, with adequate evaluation to explore whether generalization to the entire system is possible and under what conditions.

This concept has implications for the role and training of teachers and of educational research workers. There must be a basis of common respect and common experience—all or most of the research workers should have had teacher training and real experience, all or most teachers should have at least a minimum knowledge of research. Just as agricultural research and medical research are heavily tributary to the natural and biological sciences, so educational research will depend upon scientists outside the educational field and will need to employ some in its terms. Just, too, as many of the more important research problems in medicine or agriculture have arisen from the work and experiment of the busy but inquiring doctor or farmer, so we may hope that teachers, part of whose training has turned their attention to the scientific study of education, will identify problems, spearhead their study, and in many cases move over themselves to full-time research. Indeed the great hope of real advance lies in making the present barriers between professional practice and professional research really permeable, so that it becomes normal for a career in teaching to include a period of full-time research.

There will probably always be aspects of education where the teacher's intuition and insight are more valuable as guides than scientific knowledge. Education too is not static; it is in fact highly responsive to changes in society, particularly to changes in the beliefs and values held almost below the threshold of consciousness by parents and teachers or implied by the way the world confronts the young. Because of this, the established facts of one generation of research workers tend to seem to be the fallacies to be attacked by the next. We shall be nearer the truth if we say that advances in knowledge in as changing a field as education, will be of the nature of successive approximations rather than securely established platforms from which to launch the next probe. However—even if we regard education as unequivocally an art rather than a science—there is an advancing technology which can subtend even the greatest artist and make his work easier and more effective. Most of us are not great artists in education; and the major value of the technological advance which we can hope for from research is that we can considerably improve, by taking thought, what it is that we do. At least we can define the possible, count and measure the cost of alternatives, challenge superstition with facts, and define the area within which value-loaded choices have to be made. If this is done well, it will increase the central responsibility of the teacher for choosing that which he believes to be *good*; but it will also make it more possible for him to carry out his decision hopefully.

### Educational Research and the State
(T. Husen, 1968)[1]

We are now witnessing how the social and behavioural scientists in country after country, are called upon to help in solving or dealing more effectively with problems pertaining to school

[1] Abstracted from a chapter in *Educational Research and Policy Making* (N.F.E.R.).

structure, curriculum content, and methods of instruction. In some quarters they are apparently regarded as useful, but in what respects? Let me spell out my own conception of their useful-ness.

Firstly, the researcher can be helpful in tidying up problems as they are first conceived by the policy-maker ... The problems which are submitted to us are not only too broadly stated and, therefore, in need of being broken down but, in most cases, they also need thorough reformulation if they are to be solved by research methods. Thus, for instance, in studying the relation between age and language teaching, the cardinal problem is not age but methods of instruction. In 1941, the professors of educa-tion replied that the age of eleven would seem most appropriate, thus tacitly assuming that the traditional grammar approach should be used. Since then in Sweden we have started to teach all children English at the age of ten and even at nine, a decision which two decades ago would have been regarded as a pedagogi-cal sacrilege. The comparisons between the comprehensive and the selective school structure in Sweden during most of the 1950s were naively carried out in terms of the conventional end-products. Thus, the 'grammar school' students in both structures were compared without consideration of the fact that, at least partly, they pursued different objectives and that they differed considerably in terms of grade-repeaters and dropouts. They were compared, in fact, without reference to differences in the price paid for the end-products. Therefore, it seems to me to be of great importance to establish at least occasional contact be-tween researchers and policy-makers. The dialogue between them should help to create more articulate conceptions of the problems and their implications.

You have probably heard how we tried to take advantage of a unique situation in the city of Stockholm in 1954. The City Council decided to introduce the nine-year comprehensive sys-tem on a pilot basis in the southern half of the city. The dual or parallel system was kept in the northern part for a transitory period. This provided researchers with an opportunity to follow an age cohort over a five-year period and to carry out continuous evaluations of the two systems, keeping social background and initial scholastic ability under control. This study was sponsored by the 1957 Royal Committee which dealt with the structure and curriculum of the comprehensive school. As the results from the evaluation emerged at the successive grade levels, they were reported to the Committee, with the Minister of Education in the chair and representatives of political parties among members. We met several times with the Committee and discussed at some length the possible interpretations of the findings we had submitted. These deliberations often touched upon thorny and highly technical methodological problems.

Secondly, more closely at hand and certainly more obvious than the tidying-up task, is the 'know-how' or technical craftsmanship that researchers are expected to bring to bear on problems which the administrator and/or policy-maker with (or as a rule, without) the help of the researcher, is trying to formulate. The researcher is called upon to do the fact-finding, to carry out the surveys which clarify the descriptive picture of a certain educational phenomenon. One fully appreciates the technique the researcher is applying when, for instance, he carries out sample surveys. The various Royal Commissions in England, such as the Robbins and the Plowden Committees, are cases in point.

Some years ago one of my former co-workers, Dr Sixten Marklund, carried out a study on the relationship between class size and homogeneity and the outcome of instruction. National survey data were used, and, for the first time, size and homogeneity were studied simultaneously : the effect of size was analysed, keeping homogeneity under control, and vice versa. The monograph which reported the study happened to be submitted a few weeks before the Budget Committee of our Parliament was reviewing an amendment to the Education Bill made by some of its members and proposing a successive reduction of class size, which, by the way, in Sweden is one of the lowest in the world. The argument for the motion was that a reduction of size would improve the outcome of instruction, a rationale which clearly was refuted by the study within the class-size interval considered in this particular case, i.e. between twenty and thirty pupils.

Thirdly, the researcher can be called upon to assist in interpreting more adequately data which have already been collected. As part of the routine administrative procedures within all ministries of education, hosts of statistical information are collected. These data are particularly useful in improving planning within the ministry. The researcher can assist not only in interpreting data already gathered but also in advising what might be collected, so that more relevant aspects of the educational reality are covered by the statistics.

In recent years the planning function has grown rapidly to such an extent that research has become part and parcel of planning. I am not thinking primarily of fancy mathematical models which seem to shun encounters with empirical reality but rather of the basic surveys that are needed.

It would be useful to distinguish between two types of educational research which, by their very nature, call for a different relationship between researchers and policy-makers. I am not thinking of research *versus* development or of 'pure' research *versus* 'applied' research, but rather of the actual problems tackled.

The first type of problem concerns school structure. At what age should children enter the regular compulsory school? At what age is it appropriate to differentiate with regard to variation in ability and performance? What is the total 'yield' of a retentive system compared with a selective one? These problems are particularly pertinent in countries where decisions are taken by the Parliaments' top-ranking policy-makers, such as the many European countries which, during the last twenty years, have been debating the relative merits and drawbacks of the comprehensive or retentive schools and the dualistic or selective system.

The structure of the school system of a country is not only a reflection of pious and abstract political principles; it also mirrors rather closely the social class composition and the economic structure of the society it is supposed to serve. By no means does the school operate in a social vacuum, even if the opposite impression is sometimes conveyed by the conception certain educators express of its proper role.

The second type of problem is, in a wide sense, related to classroom practices, such as methods of instruction, the use of teaching aids, and guidance of pupils. I am fully aware that problems arising from *what* should be taught, particularly in terms of what subjects should be taught, at what level, when, and with what objectives, occupy an intermediate position between the structural and instructional. On the whole I think the division I have made is applicable. For instance, in Sweden it is up to Parliament to determine the overall objectives of the school system and to decide upon the timetable which defines the subjects and their respective number of periods, since it then makes the relevant appropriations. But, by and large, within the set framework, it is left almost entirely to educators to decide what will happen to the pupils in the classroom. Let me now point out differences in the approach of the academic man and the policy-maker. The researcher makes the undogmatic approach to problems a virtue. Faced with hardcore facts, his approach is not 'What can I do?' but 'How can they be explained?' His is the meditative and inquiring life. The policy maker, by definition, is a pragmatist and an active man. Facts are for him material for decision and, sometimes, immediate action. He would not be a real policy-maker if most of his problems did not require rather rapid action. All the caveats, 'ifs', and 'it depends' of the academic man imply postponement of action. The mere encounter of these two modes of life carries some germs of conflict. A colleague of mine, who served as an adviser to the Ministry of Education in a developing country a couple of years ago, was asked to conduct a survey which implied a follow-up of certain pupils over at least one academic year. The Minister impatiently started to bargain and ask whether it would be possible to make it in half a year, because he was under heavy pressure to do something about that particular problem!

I shall now turn to a discussion of how the nature of the research problem affects the relationship between the researcher and the policy-maker, thereby distinguishing between problems of school structure and classroom practices. Problems pertaining to school structure are, in this part of the world, issues which easily can cause political temperatures to rise and governments to be overthrown. This brings considerable pressure to bear upon the researcher. The directive given to him might be confined to the study of certain aspects of a problem, depending upon the terms of reference of the research. The temptation to spread a certain type of 'gospel', whether he deeply believes in it or not, is particularly strong if the researcher (or the institution to which he belongs) is more or less entirely dependent on the financial support of the agency that commissioned the project. Instead of confining his role to research, and studying the problem with the aim of increasing understanding, he can easily become an evangelist who tours the country selling ideas. To function appropriately, the researcher has to be 'the eternal skeptic'; the one to whom the slogan of the day or the policy statement is an hypothesis, which, as best, lends itself to scientific inquiry.

It has repeatedly been stated that education as a discipline (if a discipline can be defined by its problems and not by its methodology) tends to be located at the bottom of the academic pecking order, particularly in the United States, but also in some places in Europe. One important reason for this sad state of affairs lies in the isolation of education in some quarters from other fields of inquiry, and particularly from the behavioural sciences. Solid training in the behavioural sciences is therefore a necessary prerequisite for fruitful research endeavours in education.

Thus, if education as an academic discipline has suffered from provincial isolation, until recently this applied even more to its role on the international scene. School structure, historic and socio-economic roots, and classroom practices vary from country to country. If we want to conduct research which meets the principal criterion of good inquiry, which is better understanding, we must advance better concepts and theoretical models, and establish, at an international level, the same cross-disciplinary research in education that is now emerging at the national level. This could then create the kind of international community of educational researchers which has long existed in the natural sciences.

Educational Research in Action

In conclusion, I see the future of research at three different levels and for three different purposes :

1   The universities should pursue their genuine and unique function, which is basic research. This does not imply a complete withdrawal into an ivory tower, but simply that their researchers should be given sufficient time and resources to develop the new concepts and models without which further research, particularly short-range and expensive developmental work, cannot be productive. It is not the role of the university scholar to develop instructional systems or introduce new classroom practices. His role is properly fulfilled if he stays aloof and indulges in the 'irresponsible' thinking that precedes developmental work.

2   Large-scale surveys evaluating new organizational set-ups introduced by central or local authorities, or projects producing instructional systems which are expected to guide classroom practice, ought to be carried on outside the universities. Since quite a lot of this research deals with the evaluation of new structures or curricula, it is obviously important that the evaluation should be carried out by independent research bodies, such as the National Foundation for Educational Research in England and Wales. Apart from the fact that ethically, a governmental or quasi-governmental agency ought not to evaluate its own operations, research within a bureaucratic setting can easily become a nightmare to the researcher. His work is by definition anti-bureaucratic, informal, innovative, not limited by time-tables.

3   Obviously, certain administrative functions within the central or regional educational agencies cannot be successfully performed unless special research techniques are used to secure data. I am thinking primarily of the planning function which has to be guided by the collection of information on pupils, teachers, schools and finance. In some instances, regular sample surveys have to be conducted. In recent years, research in some countries has focused on massive attempts to improve curricula and instructional methods. The tremendous increase of funds which the federal government of the United States is investing in improving school practices is well-known to all of us. In countries where a central ministry of education more decisively influences the curriculum—I am not thinking particularly of England—one has begun to realize the possibilities of changing practices by preparing teacher aids or instructional systems. The mere size of such an enterprise and its financial implications make it a task for a ministry.

We can draw up a continuum which is located between two poles : on the one side, complete aloofness in the ivory tower, and, on the other, total immersion in the noise of actions and discussion of issues in the educational market-place. The problem is that of striking a proper balance : of establishing good liaison with the policy-makers without becoming evangelists and without scaring the other partner into withdrawing his support.

I am perfectly aware that the educational researcher today cannot avoid being brought into the process of action—I am myself a living example. But if healthy criticism, the principal driving force behind change and innovation, is to be kept alive, the researcher must at all costs retain his aloofness and his integrity.

*The message from both these extracts is clear enough. Educational research is of positive benefit to both teacher and administrator, and should play an increasing role in the development of educational policies and the improvement of teaching strategies. Research findings can be used as an 'agent' of change, acting in a variety of ways. Social psychologists have drawn attention to three models for introducing change into organisations (Bennis, Benne and Chin, 1969).*

*Power–coercive—    change is introduced by regulation or by force, through administrative decision or through exercising economic or political power (using, for example, control of finance, recruitment and promotion, or strikes, sit-ins and demonstrations).*

*Empirical–rational—    change is introduced through persuasion, on the basis of evidence and logical reasoning. The assumption here is that people are rational and hence, when factual evidence is convincing, the need for change will be accepted.*

*Normative–re-educative—    change is brought about by altering people's attitudes and hence mobilising the forces of the whole social system towards change. The assumption of this model is that people are only partly rational and that they will resist change, unless reforms appear to originate from their own ideas. The technique adopted is to alter the context in which the problem is presented; in this way stereotyped attitudes are less effective in blocking the desired change.*

*The distinction between empirical–rational and power-coercive describes, in part, the contrast between the use made of educational research in Britain and in Sweden. The empirical–rational approach has a powerful hold in British education: central control is resisted. Indeed this way of treating issues has become an accepted part of our whole civilisation. Persuasion is expected to depend on rational argument and factual evidence. But in an educational system, major changes take too long to implement in this manner. Many decisions in education involve highly specialised knowledge, and must take into account a mass of detailed information. For example, the question of the supply*

of teacher-training places involves an analysis of interactions between a wide variety of factors—population growth, class sizes,
school building provision, 'wastage' of teachers out of the profession, married women 'returners', and the balance between graduate and non-graduate entrants. Statistical information has to be
gathered on all these facets of the problem and policy decisions
taken. Certainly interested bodies, such as teachers' unions, are
consulted, but probably only in the Department of Education and
Science can the significance of the sometimes contradictory implications be fully appreciated. Eventually a decision has to be
taken, and change follows almost immediately in this 'power–
coercive' mode by imposing a regulation.

Where national or local policy is not involved, effective educational changes can rarely be brought about simply by coercion,
and on past experience, the 'empirical–rational' approach acts
slowly, if at all. It is certainly possible for an authoritarian headteacher to change teaching methods in his school 'at a stroke', but
the ultimate effectiveness of any such drastic change is doubtful.
As Barker Lunn demonstrated in her study on streaming (Chapter
8), teachers in non-streamed classes may still hold attitudes and
continue with techniques which would be more suitable in a
streamed school. Only if the teachers believe in the change is it
likely to have any real effect.

The implication of this reasoning is that both research workers, headteachers or administrators who wish to produce effective changes within schools will have to adopt a 'normative–re-
educative' strategy. Certainly research evidence or other information should be presented, but not with any 'take it and like it'
undercurrent. In this normative–re-educative mode increased involvement in either research or decision-making is of great importance. In the earlier readings Wall and Husen were both
looking towards closer co-operation between teachers and professional research workers, as a means of improving both the
quality of research and the impact which its findings would
have on classroom practice. There are many 'growth points' in
educational research, such as classroom observation or curriculum evaluation, in which teachers could actively take part.
And by becoming participants in research, teachers would be
more likely to appreciate both the strengths and the limitations
of the research findings. Moreover, involvement in research can
affect more generally ways of thinking about education. It can
foster an enquiring but critical attitude and a concern for objective proof. Even if the research findings from small-scale studies
by teachers prove inconclusive or emphemeral, the habits of
thinking have a more permanent influence. The main purpose of
research is still to provide impartial, factual evidence, but a beneficial side-effect is, as Waismann (1968) said about philosophy,

'the piercing of that dead crust of tradition and convention which bind us to inherited preconceptions, so as to attain a new and broader way of looking at things ... (and) an attempt to unfreeze habits of thinking, to replace them by less stiff and restricting ones' (pages 32, 34).

Advantages of this kind might well accrue from co-operation between teachers and research workers. 'Involvement' is a popular notion, and accords well with ideas about 'democracy' and 'grass roots' participation. But it would be over-optimistic to assume that involvement alone could solve anything.

'No committee ever has, or ever will, form an idea. It can only adopt one. Ideas are formed by individuals from the depths of their personalities.'[1]

Even to know which questions to ask, we need something more than the involvement of as many participants as possible, for experience suggests that most people approach problems within the accepted framework of their assumptions—and these may lead backwards, rather than forwards. For example, one of the continuing weaknesses in educational research, and in education at large, is the obsession with general solutions—we look for the best method of organisation or the right approach to teaching. Less often do we ask the more subtle—but possibly more appropriate—question: Under what conditions, for which type of children and with which teachers will this method be most effective? C. F. Carter demanded simplicity in the pursuit of research into higher education. Certainly there seems to have been a lack of concern with many apparently simple practical problems, but one of the reasons may well be that the search for simple answers has so often led nowhere.

When we look further, towards the organisation of research in Britain, there is no obvious solution to the present lack of coherence in the efforts being made by a variety of institutions and individuals. Perhaps a neat administrative structure would be counter-productive in the end. In Chapter 15 we made the point that a research project should not be planned along a single line of investigation, but should adopt a variety of approaches. A similar argument may apply to the more general problem of the future of educational research. We must anticipate not one single line of development, but several. We should not look to one agency for research or even one type of agency, but to different people and different institutions taking part in varied activities.

The final extract suggests what type of activities might be carried out by teachers and by university researchers, and summarises neatly many of the arguments made earlier in the chapter. It finishes, however, with another series of questions. There

[1] D. Morrell, former Joint Secretary of the Schools Council, in an address to the Association of First Division Civil Servants, May 1969.

*is some agreement that research can make important contributions to education, but uncertainty about the way in which this can best be done.*

## Educational Research and Development[1]

The public associates the phrase 'research and development' with science and technology. This is natural because much greater sums are expended in activities that belong in these fields than on projects within the social sciences or the humanities. The need for, and the consequences of medical research are self-evident; research and development expenditure for educational ends is by no means as widely acceptable. Most of those employed in education seem to regard sums of money devoted to research and development as a justifiable call on national resources, but inside the profession there are some who don't and outside it there may be many. One might speculate on the reasons for this, and almost certainly reach the conclusion that an analogy between the research process as applied to education and as applied to science or technology is misleading and the cause of much misunderstanding.

Development of course takes place within the structure of the educational system and within the scope and practice of teaching. On the surface few of the significant developments seem to have been, in any obvious way, related to research. A massive development involving substantial new investment occurred when the unexpected decision to raise the school leaving age was taken in 1947 but behind it lay the forces of history rather than the forces of science. It could perhaps be argued that subsequent developments in secondary education were derived from the scientific evaluation of what happened in schools after the age was raised. Eventually there were more teachers, more equipment, more pupils entered for external examinations. Research studies clearly contributed to the comparatively solid structure which now replaces the nebulous concept of secondary education for all.

If empirical research is applied to some specific piece of teaching—to teach one's own child to sail a boat, to teach a selected group to pass Latin at O-level—operational control by objectives is a perfectly reasonable approach. A judicious teacher will proceed from the achievement of one objective to the next until the entire operation is satisfactorily completed. Close application to a taxonomy of educational objectives would always be advisable

[1] Extracted from an anonymous contribution to *Trends in Education* (D.E.S. and H.M.S.O.) April 1972, pages 2–3.

if the job were teaching someone to become a high-class slave for top people. But if the desired end-product is a free man or a liberated woman—that would be more difficult. We may disagree on whether Concorde is worth having but we all know what it's for. On the other hand, as parents, we almost all feel that our children are worth having, but there is endless disagreement amongst us as to what they are for. We may unite in wanting them to be happy and good, but such a customer prescription is not of much help to the designers of educational programmes.

Education is not a product like penicillin or the jet engine. There is no process within education comparable to that by which a research team makes a discovery, and this is followed by investment on development, which leads eventually to large-scale manufacture and an ultimate 'pay-off'. Why then does anyone suppose that benefits will accrue from research and development in the educational field?

The answer may lie in the general awareness that education serves a social purpose and consumes public money. It is as much necessary to try to collect information about its efficiency and its cost as with any other charge on the resources of the community. Research may thus contribute to the necessary control mechanisms and indeed also to the marshalling of arguments on which policy decisions will be based. It has done so in the past and it would seem certain that any large-scale enquiry into a contemporary educational issue would examine relevant research findings and probably initiate new research. If this is the procedure which a central authority for education would follow, it would appear reasonable for a local authority, or indeed a single educational institution, to adopt the same approach. Up to this point those who support research activity are doing little more than the teacher who addresses to a struggling pupil the time honoured injunction—'Now think carefully about what you are doing.'

Research in fact implies not merely enquiry and the collection of information but controlled experiment. Both implications often involve elaborate and sophisticated techniques if any reliance is to be placed on the findings. The word development associated with research has the further implication of constructing, testing and evaluating a prototype. In this way project teams have been set up by the Schools Council and others and indeed by groups of teachers to develop new methods, new materials, new processes of assessment. Not all research takes place within an institutional framework designed to promote scientific studies of the educational scene, but much of it does and it is therefore on the adequacy of this framework that much depends. Before that can be tested the ends to be served by educational research have to be established. Obviously these are various—can they be expressed in terms of the institutional arrangements at present in operation?

It seems clear that there is one set of enquiries and experiments in which most educational institutions are involved and with which it is essential that practising teachers should be concerned. These are the activities designed to influence the work of the teacher, his power of communication, his choice of method and material. Work of this kind is widespread and the contribution it can make has been recognised in the establishment of the Schools Council. In further and higher education the absence of similar institutional foundation for work of this kind is already being felt. There seems to have been no doubt, however, in the minds of those responsible for the Open University that this was a type of work for which provision had to be made.

Another set of considerations affecting research arises from the exigencies of educational planning, and the need to take policy decisions. In most activities of government it is regarded as important that enquiries and experiments should take place with these ends in mind. Research may sometimes influence policy decisions with dramatic directness. More often it serves to clarify the issues, to identify more plainly the alternative choices and, in so far as prediction is possible, what their results might be. Our own, and most other governments, promote an institutional framework for educational research of this type. Up to now they have considered that it is on the whole best entrusted to scholars working in an atmosphere of scholarship. Whatever other agencies may be established the universities are bound here to play a prominent part, but there is a third kind of research which is hardly likely in the modern age to be carried out anywhere else. This is the work of individuals or groups and teams in the field or in libraries and laboratories who are making it their purpose to mark out new territories for investigation. Their work at its best will have the effect of increasing the sensitivity and critical awareness of all whom it influences.

In our own case there is now much questioning of the adequacy and effectiveness of these arrangements and indeed of the educational research results produced. Is the institutional framework up to its task—that of organising, co-ordinating and in the end spreading the results of research and development projects? How far are we prepared to allow for freedom of judgement over the factors in the educational process which are to be investigated or tested? How are teachers and others to become better informed about the nature of research and its outcome? Do we today evaluate with accuracy the actual or potential significance of research and development in education?

# References

The following references relate to the linking passages and give full details of the readings. References given within each extract will be found at the end of that extract.

BALLARD, P. B. (1923) *The New Examiner*. London: University of London Press.

BARNES, D. (1960) *Language, the Learner and the School*. Harmondsworth: Penguin Books.

BENNIS, W. G., BENNE, K. D., and CHIN, R. (1969) *The Planning of Change*. New York: Holt, Rinehart and Winston.

BORG, W. R. (1963) *Educational Research: An Introduction*. London: Longmans.

BRITTON, J. N., MARTIN, N. C., and ROSEN, H. (1966) *Multiple Marking of English Compositions*. London: Schools Council and H.M.S.O.

BURROUGHS, G. E. R. (1971) *Design and Analysis in Educational Research* (Educational Monograph Number 8) Birmingham: University of Birmingham, School of Education.

BUTCHER, H. J. (1966) *Sampling in Educational Research*. Manchester: Manchester University Press.

BUTCHER, H. J., and LOMAX, D. E. (1972) *Readings in Human Intelligence*. London: Methuen.

CANE, B. S., and SCHROEDER, C. (1970) *The Teacher and Research*. Slough: National Foundation for Educational Research.

CARTER, C. F. (1972) Presidential Address to Society for Research into Higher Education, December, 1971. In FLOOD-PAGE, C., and GREENAWAY, H. *Innovation in Higher Education*. London: S.R.H.E.

CASHDAN, A., and WHITEHEAD, J. (1971) *Personality Growth and Learning*. London: Longman and Open University Press.

COX, R. (1967) 'Examinations and higher education.' *Universities Quarterly*, 21, 292–340.

CRONBACH, L. J., and SUPPES, P. (eds.) (1969) *Research for Tomorrow's Schools*. New York: Macmillan.

DEPARTMENT OF EDUCATION AND SCIENCE (1967) *Children and their Primary Schools (Plowden Report)*. 2 volumes. London: H.M.S.O.

DEPARTMENT OF EDUCATION AND SCIENCE (1966) *Progress in Reading, 1948–1964*. London: H.M.S.O.

DOUGLAS, J. W. B. (1964) *The Home and the School*. London: MacGibbon and Kee.

DOUGLAS, J. W. B., ROSS, J. H., and SIMPSON, H. R. (1968) *All Our Future*. London: Peter Davies.

DOWNING, J. A., and JONES, B. (1966) 'Some problems of evaluating i.t.a.: a second experiment.' *Educ. Res.*, 8, 100–14.

DUTHIE, J. H. (1970) *Primary School Survey: a Study of the Teacher's Day*. Edinburgh: H.M.S.O.

ENTWISTLE, N. J. (1968) 'Academic motivation and school attainment.' *Brit. J. educ. Psychol.*, 38, 181–8.

ENTWISTLE, N. J. (1972) 'Personality and academic attainment.' *Brit. J. educ. Psychol.*, 42, 137–51.

ENTWISTLE, N. J. (1972) 'Students and their academic performance in different types of institution.' In BUTCHER, H. J., and RUDD, E. *Contemporary Problems in Higher Education*. London: McGraw-Hill.

ENTWISTLE, N. J., PERCY, K. A., and NISBET, J. B. (1971) *Educational Objectives and Academic Performance in Higher Education*. Unpublished report, Department of Educational Research, University of Lancaster.

EVANS, K. M. (1968) *Planning Small-scale Research in Education*. Slough: National Foundation for Education Research.

EYSENCK, H. J., and COOKSON, D. (1969) 'Personality in primary school children: 1—Ability and achievement.' *Brit. J. educ. Psychol.*, 39, 109–22.

FARRINGTON, B. (1971) 'A computer-aided test of aural comprehension.' *Audio-Visual Language Journal*, 9, 71–6.

FORD, J. (1969) *Social Class and the Comprehensive School*. London: Routledge and Kegan Paul.

FOX, D. J. (1969) *The Research Process in Education*, New York: Holt, Rinehart and Winston.

FOX, R. S., and LIPPITT, R. (1964) 'The innovation of classroom mental health practices.' In MILES, M. B. *Innovation in Education*. Columbia: Teachers' College Bureau of Publications.

FRASER, E. D. (1959) *Home Environment and the School*. Scottish Council for Research in Education Publication 43. London: University of London Press.

GETZELS, J. W., and JACKSON, P. W. (1962) *Creativity and Intelligence*. New York: Wiley.

HARGREAVES, D. H. (1967) *Social Relations in a Secondary School*. London: Routledge and Kegan Paul.

HASAN, P., and BUTCHER, H. J. (1966) 'Creativity and intelligence: a partial replication with Scottish children of Getzels' and Jackson's study.' *Brit. J. Psychol.*, 57, 129–35.

HIGSON, C. W. J. (1968) 'Finding out about educational research.' *Educ. Res.*, 11, 31–7.

HILSUM, S., and CANE. B. S. (1971) *The Teacher's Day*. Slough: National Foundation for Educational Research.

HOOPER, R. (ed.) (1971) *The Curriculum: Context, Design and Development*. Edinburgh: Oliver and Boyd with Open University Press.

HUSEN, T. (1968) 'Educational research and the state.' In *Educational Research and Policy Making*. Slough: National Foundation for Educational Research.

LACEY, C. (1966) 'Some sociological concomitants of academic streaming.' *Brit. J. Sociol.*, 17, 245–62.

LACEY, C. (1970) *Hightown Grammar: the School as a Social System*. Manchester: Manchester University Press.

LUNN, J. C. BARKER (1970) *Streaming in the Primary School*. Slough: National Foundation for Educational Research.

MACDONALD, B., and RUDDUCK, J. (1971) 'Curriculum research and development projects.' *Brit. J. educ. Psychol.*, 41, 148–54.

MEDLEY, D. M., IMPELLETTERI, J. T., and SMITH, L. H. (1966) *Coding Teacher Behaviour in the Classroom: A Manual for users of OScAR 4V*. New York: Division of Teacher Education in the City University of New York.

MEDLEY, D. E., and MITZEL, D. W. (1963) 'Measuring classroom behaviour by systematic observation.' In GAGE, N., *Handbook of Research on Teaching*. Chicago: Rand McNally.

MINISTRY OF EDUCATION (1954) *Early Leaving*. London: H.M.S.O.

MINISTRY OF EDUCATION (1957) *Standards of Reading, 1948–1956*. London: H.M.S.O.

NISBET, J. D. (1972) 'The Schools Council.' In *Case Studies of Central Institutions in Educational Change*. Paris: O.E.C.D.

NISBET, J. D., and ENTWISTLE, N. J. (1966) *The Age of Transfer to Secondary Education*. Scottish Council for Research in Education Publication 53. London: University of London Press.

NISBET, J. D., and ENTWISTLE, N. J. (1969) *The Transition to Secondary Education*. Scottish Council for Research in Education Publication 59. London: University of London Press.

NISBET, J. D., and ENTWISTLE, N. J. (1970a) *Educational Research Methods*. London: University of London Press.

NISBET, J. D., and ENTWISTLE, N. J. (1970b) 'Transfer from Primary to Secondary Education.' In BUTCHER, H. J., and PONT, H. B. *Educational Research in Britain, Volume 2*. London: University of London Press.

NISBET, J. D., and WELSH, J. (1972) 'A local evaluation of primary school French.' *J. Curric. Studies*, November 1972 (in press).

OPPENHEIM, A. (1966) *Questionnaire Design and Attitude Measurement.* London : Heinemann.

PEAKER, G. F. (1971) *The Plowden Children Four Years Later.* Slough : National Foundation for Educational Research.

PILLINER, A. E. G. (1968) 'Examinations.' In BUTCHER, H. J. *Educational Research in Britain, Volume 1.* London : University of London Press.

RICHARDS, P. N., and BOLTON, N. (1971) 'Type of mathematics teaching, mathematical ability and divergent thinking in junior school children.' *Brit. J. educ. Psychol., 41, 32–7.*

RUDD, W. G. A. (1970) 'Curriculum model building.' In BUTCHER, H. J., and PONT, H. B. *Educational Research in Britain, Volume 2.* London : University of London Press.

RUDD, W. G. A. (ed.) (1971) *C.S.E.: a Group Study Approach to Research and Development.* London : Schools Council and Evans/Methuen Educational.

SCHOOLS COUNCIL (1968) *Young School Leavers (Enquiry 1).* London : H.M.S.O.

SCOTTISH COUNCIL FOR RESEARCH IN EDUCATION (1968) *Rising Standards in Scottish Primary Schools.* S.C.R.E. Publication 56. London : University of London Press.

SIMON, J. L. (1969) *Basic Research Methods in the Social Sciences.* New York : Random House.

THOULESS, R. H. (1969) *Map of Educational Research.* Slough : National Foundation for Educational Research.

TRAVERS, R. M. W. (1969) *An Introduction to Educational Research.* New York : Macmillan.

VAN DALEN, D. B. (1966) *Understanding Educational Research.* New York : McGraw-Hill.

VERNON, P. E. (1971) 'Effects of administration and scoring on divergent thinking tests.' *Brit. J. educ. Psychol., 41, 245–57.*

WAISMANN, F. (1968) *How I see Philosophy.* London : Macmillan.

WALL, W. D. (1968) 'The future of educational research.' *Educ. Res., 10, 163–9.*

WALLACH, M. A., and KOGAN, N. (1965) *Modes of Thinking in Young Children.* New York : Holt, Rinehart and Winston.

WISEMAN, S. (1969) 'Curriculum development and curriculum evaluation.' *Res. in Educ., 1, 1–8.*

WRAGG, E. C. (1970) 'Interaction analysis as a feedback system for student teachers.' *Education for Teaching, 81, 38–47.*

# Index

*(Numbers in italics indicate quoted material)*